Geoffrey Wheatcroft is a journalist and historian. A former literary editor of the *Spectator* and 'Londoner's Diary' editor of the *Evening Standard*, he is the author of several acclaimed books including *The Controversy of Zion*, which won an American National Jewish Book Award, *The Strange Death of Tory England*, which was short-listed for the Channel 4 Political Book Award, and, most recently, *Yo Blair!*. He has always been fascinated by the Tour de France, and covered it several times in preparation for writing this highly original book, which was short-listed for the NEC Sports Book Award. He lives near Bath with his wife, the fashion designer and painter Sally Muir, and their two children.

LE TOUR

A HISTORY OF THE TOUR DE FRANCE

Geoffrey Wheatcroft

POCKET
BOOKS

LONDON • SYDNEY • NEW YORK • TORONTO

In memory of
Polly Muir 1925–2004

First published in Great Britain by Simon & Schuster UK Ltd, 2003
This edition published in 2007 by Pocket Books,
An imprint of Simon & Schuster UK Ltd
A CBS COMPANY

1 3 5 7 9 10 8 6 4 2

Simon & Schuster UK Ltd
Africa House
64–78 Kingsway
London WC2B 6AH

www.simonsays.co.uk

Simon & Schuster Australia
Sydney

A CIP catalogue for this book is available
from the British Library.

ISBN 13: 978-1-84739-086-8
ISBN 10: 1-84739-086-2

Typeset in Baskerville by M Rules
Printed and bound in Great Britain by
Cox & Wyman Ltd, Reading, Berks

Contents

Preface		vii
Maps		xvi
Prologue	Paris, 1903	1
1	**Sowing the Seed** 1903–1908	15
2	**To the Mountains** 1909–1914	31
	Repos: PICARDY	50
3	***Braves Belges*** 1919–1924	61
4	**Convicts of the Road** 1925–1929	76
	Repos: GASCONY	90
5	**French Renaissance** 1930–1934	101
6	**'Raisons Politiques'** 1935–1939	116
	Repos: NORMANDY	132
7	**Italian Duel** 1947–1951	140
8	**Bobet Divides France** 1952–1957	156

Repos: BURGUNDY   172

9   **Anquetil's Apotheosis**   1958–1962   180

10   **'Put Me Back on My Bike'**   1963–1967   189

Repos: PROVENCE   201

11   **Merckx Devours the Field**   1968–1973   211

12   **Heart and Nerve and Sinew**   1974–1980   225

Repos: BRITTANY   238

13   **The Yanks Are Coming**   1981–1987   249

14   **Induráin in Excelsis**   1988–1994   264

Repos: SAVOY   276

15   *L'affaire Festina*   1995–1998   286

16   **The American Enemy**   1999–2002   298

17   **A Big Injustice**   2003–2006   309

Epilogue   329

Some Tour Words   340

Some Tour Books   346

Some Tour Facts   351

Index   384

Preface

Even on a blindingly cloudless day in July, it is never really hot at the Col du Galibier. The pass is more than 2500 metres or 8205 feet above sea level; in a postcard home, I ask my young son if he knows how much higher that is than the highest peak in the British Isles (it's more than 1000 metres, or nearly 4000 feet, taller than Ben Nevis). After driving up to the pass – second gear all the way, except when occasionally changing down to first – I make my way breathlessly on foot to my vantage point, and an astonishing sight. This is one of the greatest natural amphitheatres on earth. Perched a little precariously on a mixture of tussock and rock, I look several miles down the road which ascends through a long series of hairpins, and train my field glasses at the furthest point, where they're coming round the mountain when they come.

After a long wait, a distant speck of colour appears, then grows a little larger before taking shape as a man on a bike, agonizingly making his way uphill, accompanied by a crescendo of cheering from the crowds lining the road and followed by a steady, strung-out line of riders racing and pacing each other – not the big bunch which speeds through villages from Brittany to Provence, but in its way more impressive – before the first riders crest the summit and one by one descend the other side at scary speed. In more senses than one, that was for me the high point of the 2002 Tour de France: an unforgettable, even exultant moment. That day on the Galibier, more even than in the Pyrenees or on Mont Ventoux, I was seized of the sheer awesome magnitude and grandeur of this most extraordinary of all sporting contests. And I realized there and then what a privilege as well as a pleasure it was to be on the road, and working on a history of the Tour.

How did I come to be writing it? a reader may ask. A 'general-purposes journalist' (as I was once all too accurately described in the *Journals* of the novelist Anthony Powell), I had quite often written about sport, but no book on a sporting subject, until Andrew Gordon of Simon & Schuster in London told Gill Coleridge, my agent and spiritual counsellor, to both of whom I am much indebted, that he wanted a history of the Tour de France for its centenary in July 2003. It might not seem to have much in common with my previous books on the South African mine-owners and the story of Zionism (although, as it happens, the entry 'Dreyfus Affair' appears in the index of all three books), but it was an enthralling subject.

Doing justice to the Tour presented me with some difficulties, and my attempts to resolve them have made this book both degressive and digressive. My first task has been to give some account of the ninety runnings of a bike race, but if I had devoted equal space to them all the book would have become unmanageably long and unmistakably tedious. It's far from the case that one Tour is much like another. Some have been frankly dull, bloodless victories decided in the first week, while others have been unbearably exciting. There are episodes of high drama which need to be related in full, from Christophe's heroic recovery after breaking down to Coppi's great escape over the mountains, from the *coude à coude* duel between Anquetil and Poulidor up the Puy de Dôme to LeMond snatching an eight-second victory from Fignon. The only thing to be done was to let each race tell its story at appropriate length or brevity.

And the book is also digressive: narrative chapters are broken up by interludes called 'Repos' (the name of a rest day in the

Tour), in which I have strolled around the provinces of France, touching on their various aspects, topographical, literary and not least culinary, taking in *un peu d'histoire*, giving a little advice to other travellers about what to see and where to eat – as it were from Michelet to Michelin, two of my own guides – and then dilating on themes which caught my fancy, from the waning of dialect to popular song, while trying to set the Tour in its national and cultural contexts.

Although an ardent lifelong sports enthusiast (nowadays a notably inactive one, offering no competition to those admirable writers who have themselves pedalled up the Izoard or the Aubisque), I came a little late to the Tour. When I was a young schoolboy in the late 1950s, my heroes were Graveney and Benaud, Sharp and Kyle, Wright and Puskas, Hawthorn and Fangio, and I didn't as yet share some of my friends' fanatical absorption in cycling. But I knew who Anquetil and Bahamontes were, and I had some inkling of the fascination of the race, which grew on me over the years.

Even then, if I had followed the Tour, in the English sense of the phrase, I had never *suivi le Tour* until 2002 when I was asked to cover the race for the *Daily Mail*. I am most grateful to Colin Gibson, who was then that paper's sports editor, for this won- derful assignment, and to his assistant Helen Bonner for all her help, as well as to Tim Jotischky, Colin's successor, for whom I covered the Tour in 2004 and 2005. I describe later the placards being held aloft on Mont Ventoux in July 2002, one of which read 'Phil Liggett I want your job'. I don't myself, in fact, but by way of covering the race somewhat as an amateur I have come greatly to admire the authority of the professionals, notably Liggett in the *Daily Telegraph* and on television, William Fotheringham in the *Guardian* and *Observer*, and Samuel Abt in the *International Herald Tribune*, not to say everyone at *Cycling Weekly*, the *Figaro* and *Equipe*. Just why the standard of sports journalism and not least cycling journalism is so high is an interesting question. Is it because in those pages, more than in the political or financial pages of a newspaper, a writer can assume the reader's complete attention, and treat him as an equal?

Having said that, I should add that, among other useful advice, men more learned than I warned me to be careful what sources I used, since many books on cycling were unreliable, and certain writers (who shall here be nameless) were notoriously inaccurate. As it happened, I had already made this discovery myself the hard way; I discuss in 'Some Tour Books' (p. 346) the problems of compiling an accurate account when even official documents, let alone popular books, are erroneous or contradictory. All this is by way of anticipatory apology. What Philip Larkin observed in another context – 'They fill you with the faults they had / And add some extra, just for you' – seems to be true of writing about the Tour, and I dare say that includes me. I can only plead that I have done my best, and add that I shall be most grateful for any corrections to errors I have repeated, or made up all on my own.

In my first paragraph above, heights were given in feet, for the last time. For the sake of brevity and simplicity the metric form only is used, kilometres for stages and metres for mountain climbs, which is bound to make anyone of my generation feel his age. On the other hand, and in defiance of a concerted pedantic movement to use local versions, I have kept the traditional English forms of place names. This is evidently regarded as polit- ically incorrect or fogeyish, although there is no reason why people in Rheims, Lyons or Marseilles should be any more offended by those names than we are by the French saying 'Londres' and 'Edimbourg'; and anyway, in any battle between tradition and didacticism, I know which side I'm on.

My personal debts of gratitude are numerous. In Dublin, my colleague and friend Eamon Dunphy put me in touch with his countryman David Walsh of the *Sunday Times*, an old Tour hand who marked my card and gave me good advice, apart from rightly telling me that the Tour was not only one of the greatest sporting occasions anywhere, but the best organized of them all, and I must also thank the Tour's excellent press office. More help was provided by other friends and colleagues. Stan Hey and Bob Low lent books and Graeme Fife lent the delightful CD *Le Vélo en Chansons*, as well as the transcript of his Radio 3 talk on music and cycling, while subsequently correcting a number of errors; Rick MacArthur in New York and my father in Lot-et-Garonne sent newspaper cuttings; and two of my Oxford tutors from long ago, Sir Raymond Carr and Eric Christiansen, respectively helped me with Spanish sporting history, and commented on part of the script with customary lucidity and acidity. Two very old friends, Dr Jeffrey Tobias and Dr Elisabeth Whipp, gave me the benefit of their oncological learning to explain how a man in remission from advanced cancer could win a great bicycle race five times running, while also talking me through other medical aspects of cycling. I am grateful to John English for his attentive and thoughtful copy-editing, to Patricia Hymans for preparing the index, to Alison Rushgrove for typing out 'Some Tour Facts', and to Edwina Barstow for her help with the picture research. And I owe a special debt to my *bon copain* Robert Harris. He encouraged me to write the book, he cheered me up with sardonic e-mails about the passing scene, and although he was hard at work on his own splendid novel, *Pompeii*, he found time to act as my *soigneur* on many a day's *défaillance* (see 'Some Tour Words', p. 340) with much-needed reviving lunches at the George and Dragon in Rowde.

My dear late mother-in-law Polly Muir took only a modest interest in cycling, but she was half French, and was constantly helpful while I was writing this book, explaining obscure phrases in her maternal language and finding obscure books. Not least, she lent me her flat in Corsica, where I wrote a substantial portion of the book, and my thanks are due also to Jo-Jo Martini and my other friends in the Pasturella bar in Monticello. This book was originally dedicated to Polly; I now sadly rededicate it to her memory.

It's always tempting to quote 'without whose never-failing sympathy and encouragement this book would have been finished in half the time', a joke P. G. Wodehouse should have copyrighted; let me say instead that, if it hadn't been for my wife and children, Sally, Abigail and Gabriel, this book might have perhaps been written a little sooner, but I would have gone mad much faster.

Perhaps I might be permitted what may seem a sweeping or sentimental generalization, from the perspective of a political and literary journalist who is also a member of the MCC, a recovering Arsenal fan, and a somewhat tepid supporter of Bath rugby club. Political reporting may not be as ruthlessly competitive as some think, nor literary London quite the snakepit George Orwell believed, but it would be fair to say that one does not always encounter helping hands on every side. That has been true also when I have dipped into other sporting subjects. Almost my first publication in a grown-up paper was an article for the *New Statesman* nearly thirty years ago about the financial structure of cricket. I recall ringing an editor of *Wisden* and shyly asking for some advice, only to be told that he indeed knew all the information I sought, but could think of no reason to share it with me.

By striking contrast, while I have been working on this book I have met with nothing but friendliness and helpfulness. Whenever I rang the offices of *Cycling Weekly*, who had no idea who I was, or when I first contacted Richard Allchin, who had then never heard of me but has since given me invaluable advice, I was offered ungrudging assistance. And so it goes throughout the sport, which has a comradely ethos all of its own, just possibly because cycling remains a true sport of the people, untouched by what Proust called the *lâcheté des gens du monde*.

That is not, of course and alas, the whole story. *Le Tour* was originally written to mark the centennial Tour de France of 2003, and this new edition is being published to mark the 2007 'Tour de Londres', which begins around and about Buckingham Palace, and which ought to be a cause for celebration. And yet there is too much else which no one could possibly celebrate, too many unlucky deeds to relate, nothing extenuating nor setting down aught in malice.

Since I began writing this book five years ago we have seen Lance Armstrong complete his unprecedented and perhaps unrepeatable seven Tour victories, while devoting almost as much energy to legal battles in order to protect his reputation amid a miasma of innuendo, which culminated in a direct accusation (vehemently denied) that he had used drugs while winning his first Tour in 1999. We have seen the winner of the Tour before that one die of a cocaine overdose. We have seen the man who won the Tour before that in turn, along with other leading riders, slung out of last year's race on suspicion of blood-doping. And we have seen, after the 2006 Tour ended, a Tour winner disqualified (*de facto* if not quite yet *de jure*) after testing positive for drugs, a dismal first occurrence for the great race.

It would be not so much silly as quite absurd to ignore all this, or to minimise its seriousness, and I deal with these sorry stories candidly in the new final chapters of this edition. Anyone who loves cycle sport and the Tour has had his affection tested to breaking point, and must sometimes wonder whether bike racing can survive much more shame and scandal. Apart from the gravity of the offence itself, and with all the repetitious, irrefutable evidence that has emerged over the years, the sport has been for far too long in denial about doping and the extent to which it has penetrated. Not long ago, the French sports minister Jean-François Lamour said that the doping culture was so deeply embedded in cycling that it would take a generation before it is uprooted, and he might be right.

When I first wrote this book, I ended this Preface on a high or even exalted note, saluting the amiability and decency of so many cyclists, which I do again, and expressing my love of France, which I do again and again. I have had the amusing experience of being denounced by name in a *Wall Street Journal* editorial, which was disappointed by someone it had thought a 'Eurosceptic'. If that word means misgivings about what the European Union sometimes does in practice, then it fits many of us. If it means an innate antipathy towards what Donald Rumsfeld sneered at as 'Old Europe', then I am the least sceptical of Old Europeans. Covering the Tour for several years now has only increased my love of France: its ravishing landscapes, its splendid cities, its charming villages, its wonderful roads and railways, its glorious restaurants and vineyards and, actually, its rather likeable populace. To repeat those words gives me an opportunity for what is not (I pray) merely fond or foolish hope for the future of the Tour. Before now France herself has been on her knees and has risen again. Maybe bike racing needs its de Gaulle to redeem the hour. And I still hope that my grandchildren in old age may be able to follow the great race when it reaches its bicentenary.

GEOFFREY WHEATCROFT
Bath
March 2007

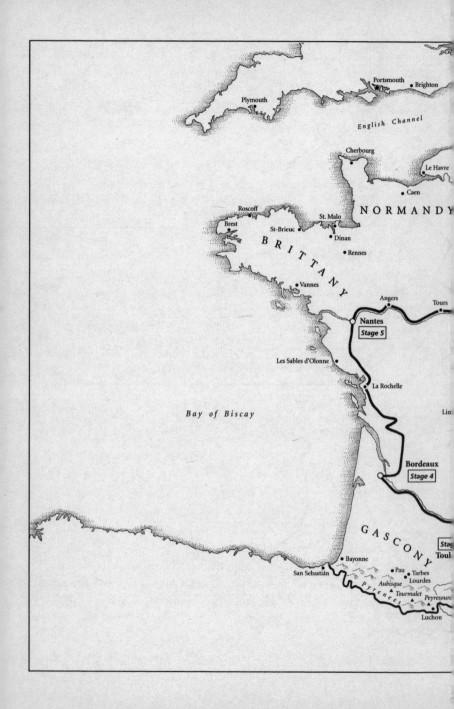

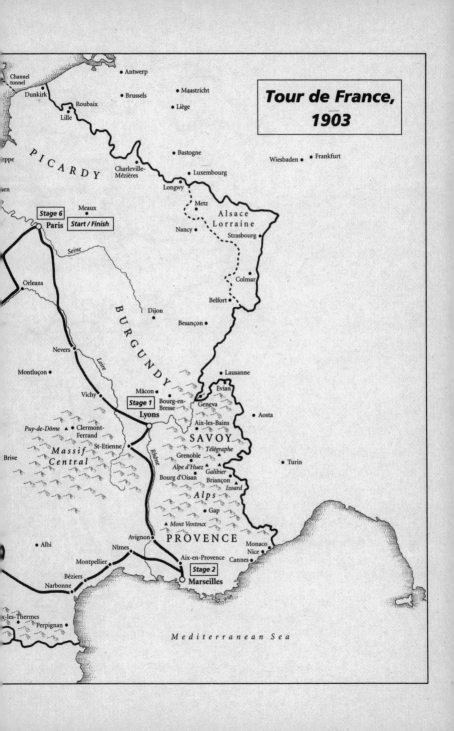

Tour de France, 1903

Channel tunnel

Antwerp

Dunkirk

Brussels

Maastricht

Roubaix

Liège

Lille

eppe

PICARDY

Bastogne

Wiesbaden • Frankfurt

Charleville-Méziéres

Luxembourg

en

Longwy

Metz

Stage 6

Meaux

Alsace

Paris

Start / Finish

Lorraine

Nancy

Strasbourg

Seine

Colmar

Orleans

Belfort

BURGUNDY

Dijon

Besançon

Nevers

Lausanne

Montluçon

Loire

Evian

Vichy

Mâcon

Bourg-en-Bresse

Geneva

Stage 1

Lyons

Aix-les-Bains

Aosta

Puy-de-Dôme ▲ • Clermont-Ferrand

SAVOY

St-Etienne

Télégraphe ▲

Brive

Massif Central

Grenoble

Alpe d'Huez ▲ *Galibier* ▲

Turin

Bourg d'Oisan

Briançon

Izoard ▲

Alps

▲ *Mont Ventoux*

Gap

Avignon

PROVENCE

Albi

Nîmes

Monaco

Montpellier

Aix-en-Provence

Nice

Stage 2

Cannes

Béziers

Marseilles

Narbonne

-les-Thermes

Perpignan

Mediterranean Sea

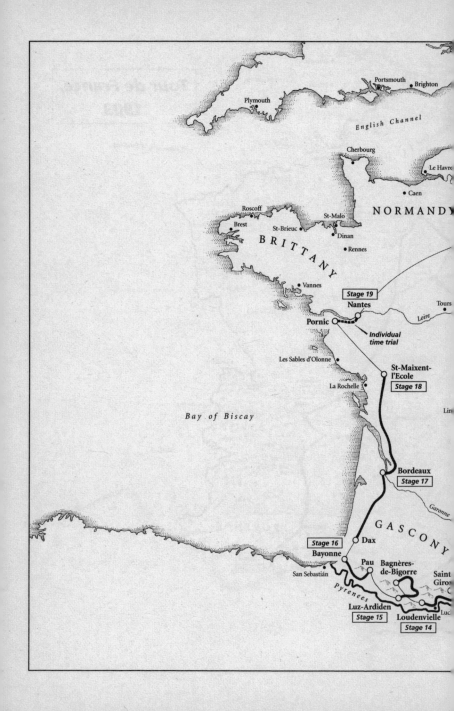

Prologue

Paris, 1903

During his sad last years of exile, Oscar Wilde was staying in Paris when he dined with the symbolist writer Maurice Maeterlinck and 'his wonderful mistress', Georgette Leblanc. The author of *Pelléas et Mélisande*, somewhat implausibly dubbed 'the Belgian Shakespeare' by Octave Mirbeau, lived with Leblanc, the great soprano of the Opéra Comique and creator of several of Massenet's roles, at their 'lovely little house' near the Bois de Boulogne, and had abandoned writing, or so Wilde told a friend. 'He only thinks of making life sane and healthy, and freeing the soul from the trammels of culture. Art seems to him now a malady . . . He rests his hope of humanity on the Bicycle.'

Whatever touch of irony there may have been on Wilde's part, or Maeterlinck's, this would not have been the most foolish of hopes in July 1898. In the past few years the machine and the phenomenon called the bicycle had begun a social revolution that would do far more for humanity than many other more exalted inventions. It was also the fulfilment of a centuries-old dream. Although the bicycle's origins are not quite lost in the mists of time, they go back much further than the nineteenth century. From the moment the simple fulcrum was discovered, men knew that energy could be transmuted, by magic as it must seem to any tribesman encountering a wheel for the first time. Earlier in that century, one extraordinary breakthrough had seen steam power harnessed to iron vehicles mounted on rails, but long before that the ingenious had dreamed of some mechanical substitute for the horse, a mechanism that could allow a man to travel faster and further with no more – or even with less – expenditure of energy than in walking.

Although the drawing of something looking like a bicycle attributed to Leonardo da Vinci is almost certainly an ingenious fake, more or less serious experiments continued over the following centuries. In London in 1769, as Boswell records, the astronomer and 'self-taught philosopher' James Ferguson told Dr Johnson of his 'new-invented machine which went without horses'. Then in Paris in 1790, at a time when the city was an asparagus-bed of strange notions and projects, a M. de Sivrac rode out in a wooden horse mounted on four wheels. It became known as the *célérifère*, and then the *vélocifère*, and it was used for races of a sort round the Champs-Élysées, adumbrating the great final sprint now seen there every July. *Vélocifère* became velocipede, or 'fast foot', in 1818, when Baron Karl von Drais of Karlsruhe unveiled in Paris his improved version that could be steered round bends. This 'Draisienne' soon spread to London, as Keats reported: 'The nothing of the day is a machine called the Velocipede. It is a wheel-carriage to ride cock horse upon, sitting astride and pushing it along with the toes . . . They will go seven miles an hour'; but alas, 'a handsome gelding will come to eight guineas', an impossible price for such a toy. Many years later, in 1987, the riders in the greatest of all bicycle races would ride out of Karlsruhe in tribute to the baron.

Despite its cost, the new toy crossed the Atlantic: Oliver Wendell Holmes recalled how, well before the Civil War, 'Some of the Harvard College students who boarded in my neighbour-hood had these machines they called velocipedes, on which they used to waddle along like so many ducks.' In the 1840s Kirkpatrick Macmillan, a blacksmith, staked arguably a better claim to be the grandfather of the bicycle when he produced a form of hobby horse with pedals that for the first time took the rider's feet clear of the ground and were linked by rods to the back wheel. And at the Great Exhibition of 1851 there were three velocipedes on show, one designed by William Sawyer. He made a later model to present to the Prince of Wales (it is not known whether Sawyer's machine was ever actually ridden by the prince, a man designed neither by physique nor temperament for doing so), which was then put on sale in 1860 for the enormous sum of £17 2s. 6d., many months' pay for a labourer.

In France meantime, at their workshop near the Champs-Élysées, Pierre Michaux and his sons had adapted the old Draisienne with a crank to power the front wheel. This was introduced in turn at the Paris Exposition of 1867, one of the great events of the Second Empire in what proved to be its last years. And the 'bicircle' or 'veloce' was soon the rage, Michaux producing 400 a year, despite its expense, its impracticability, and its considerable discomfort. A year after the Exposition a revue opened called *Paris-Vélocipède*, Daumier drew a cartoon light-heartedly showing the figure of Death astride the new contraption and, in Vienna, Josef Strauss wrote a 'Velocipede Polka'. One, albeit unutilitarian, use was shown by the great stunt-man Blondin when he rode a velocipede on a high wire across Niagara. Although his agility and balance were unusual, for most people it was still difficult to ride one of these machines over any distance, with its pedals mounted on the hub of the front wheel. The nickname 'boneshaker' spoke for itself, and not everyone was enamoured of the novelty. One French paper, the *Gaulois*, thought that 'velocipedists are imbeciles on wheels'. In return, a velocipedic magazine pointed out that the two-wheeler compared favourably with the horse, as it 'does not cart loads of hay, and does not wax fat and kick. It is easy to handle. It never rears up. It won't bite.'

And yet even enthusiasts ruefully admitted that riding the machines of the period was exhausting and often painful, and that 'a railway bridge or a very slight rise in the ground brought us to a standstill'. The *English Mechanic* thought that it was a sport only for those 'possessed of legs of iron and thighs of brass', and warned that riding 'to any great extent, results in depression, in exhaustion and in wear and tear'. Another false turn in the search for a less depressing or exhausting machine came with the 'ordinary', or penny-farthing, which had a front wheel several times larger than the rear and, although surprisingly fast, was extremely ungainly and perilous, and one more came with the safer but slower tricycle.

Both boneshaker and ordinary could at any rate be raced. The social history of the nineteenth century saw few more important developments than the advent of competitive sports, or more accurately 'games'. The word 'sport' had always meant in England – which was very much where this change originated – country pursuits, hunting, shooting, fishing, coursing, archery; games meant teams competing on a field of play with a ball. Cricket had emerged from rural chaos and corruption in the eighteenth century, football had been played immemorially in English villages, in some towns at Shrovetide, and at public schools following their own arcane codes (still played today at Winchester, Harrow, and – in two versions – Eton), which made a common national game difficult. One school gave its name to the game from which two different forms of Rugby football as well as American football all now descend. And on an historic day in 1863, at a pub in London, sportsmen from Oxford and Cambridge, and from different schools, met to lay down a common code for Association Football, sometimes known by the dire Oxonian diminutive 'soccer' but most often and in most countries simply as 'football' or some version of that name. As A. J. P. Taylor truly said, this 'game of eleven men against eleven' first codified there that day was one of his country's greatest gifts to mankind: 'By it the mark of England may well remain in the world when the rest of her influence has vanished.'

Five years later just outside Paris came a scarcely less historic moment, when competitive cycling began. On 31 May 1868, a 1200-metre race was run from the fountains to the entrance of the park of St-Cloud. It was won by an 18-year-old English expatriate called James Moore, who confirmed this victory on 7 November by winning the first road race in France, from Paris to Rouen over 135 kilometres against a large local field; sadly, not an augury of much future English success on the roads of France. The 10 hours 25 minutes it took Moore included a good deal of time spent walking his bicycle up the steeper hills. Since none of them is particularly steep in that part of France, it was clear that racing over real mountains was some way in the future. Indeed, although French roads may well have been the best in Europe, Moore's average speed of less than 13 k.p.h. spoke for itself about the conditions for road racing there, let alone in other countries, and also about the quality of the machine he was riding, still some way short of technical excellence. Although the Pickwick Bicycling Club was founded in London in 1870, the first such in England, followed by seven more within another four years, and although the Hon. Mr Keith-Falconer beat a professional at Cambridge over a two-mile race in June 1882, it wasn't surprising that bicycle racing in this incunabular period was mostly confined to tracks.

Certainly that was so in the United States. The first bike race there seems to have been in Boston on 24 May 1878, which is to say two years after professional baseball had begun and thirteen years before basketball was invented. Almost all early American racing was on tracks, and largely took the form of paced races, with some riders setting a fast early speed and then dropping away. By the 1890s there were about 100 dirt, cement, or wooden tracks around the country, mainly in big cities. More than 600 professionals travelled on this national circuit, which ranged from Boston to San Francisco, with competitions in such cities as St Louis, Salt Lake City, Denver and Los Angeles. The sport received an enormous boost on 30 June 1899, when one of these riders, Charles M. Murphy, rode on a wooden track behind a Long Island Rail Road train and covered a mile in 57.8 seconds, to become inevitably Mile-a-Minute Murphy.

Meantime another race was on, to find a vehicle that really worked. James Starley's improved Coventry Gentleman's Bicycle appeared in 1875. Although it still cost a huge £16, it earned him the title of 'father of the bicycle' and a monument in Coventry. But the consummation came in 1885, when James's nephew John Kemp Starley introduced his Rover Safety bicycle. It was safe, that is, by comparison with all previous models; and by comparison with all of those, it was a work of genius. At last the bike had found its true shape, the diamond or lozenge frame whose perfection is attested by the fact that it has remained essentially unchanged for almost 120 years. There were two horizontal parallel bars, one from the handlebars back to the base beneath the saddle, another from pedals back to the hub of the rear wheel hub. Another two more or less parallel bars sloped backwards, the forward one from handlebars to pedals, the rear from saddle to back axle. And in young Starley's other masterstroke, those two points on the lower bar were also connected by a chain, linking one cogged wheel next to the pedals with another attached to that hub, a principle which has been modified or improved since, but not basically changed. The bicycle thus designed was at once much stronger and much lighter than previous mechanisms: tricycles had weighed 40 or even 60 kilos and earlier bicycles some 20 kilos. The first Rover racer weighed 16 kilos.

One more technological breakthrough was still to seek. When the Rover Safety first appeared, its wheels had solid rubber tyres, an improvement on earlier metal or wooden wheels but still no great shakes, or rather many great shakes for the rider. In 1888 the Scot John Boyd Dunlop patented the pneumatic tyre, which he developed more fully between 1889 and 1891, while the Frenchmen André and Edouard Michelin perfected the detachable inner tube. With all these, both recreational and competitive cycling began to enjoy an explosive success. Social life was transformed: in Jane Austen's time and for nearly a century later, the extreme limit for a day's visit in the English country was about fifteen miles, though more normally the extent was about six; both distances were doubled by the bicycle. And speed was dramatically improved also. A new record was established on the Rover, 100 miles in 7h5'16", or 12 m.p.h., half as fast again as Moore's ride to Rouen.

Cycling for pleasure was still a pastime of the rich, or at any rate the better off. Even when the price of a Rover had fallen to £10, that was many weeks' wages for a miner or a mill hand. In France likewise, a bike might cost 500 francs in the early 1890s, which was three months' pay for a schoolteacher. But a great breakthrough was in the offing. More than 800,000 bikes were manufactured in England in 1895, and even though France lagged a little behind, there were at the same time reckoned by H. de Graffigney (in his *Manuel pratique du constructeur et du conducteur de cycles et d'automobiles*) to be 300,000 bicycles in the country. And as output increased, prices fell. By the late 1890s a bike could be bought for between 100 and 150 francs, and the schoolteacher could now afford one. If in 1893 a French factory worker had needed to work an unimaginable 1655 hours to earn the price of a bike, by 1911 falling prices and rising wages meant that a bike cost the equivalent of only 357 hours, and the bicycle was before long within reach of many working men as well as clerks and teachers.

One such teacher in Normandy acquired his first bike in 1898, and exulted that 'henceforth I was king of the road, since I was faster than a horse'. This wasn't literally true of the fastest horses: except in the peculiar circumstances of short, artificially paced sprints, cyclists can barely match the 65 k.p.h. or 40 m.p.h. that a thoroughbred racehorse touches over five furlongs (American 'quarter-horses' are faster), or even the steady 55 k.p.h. or 35 m.p.h. of a staying horse in the twenty-furlong Ascot Gold Cup. The speed was exhilarating all the same. More than a hundred years on, it's possible to feel something of the excitement this revolution brought, and to feel still that it was wholly admirable: 'that most beneficent of all the period's machines, whose contribution to human emancipation was immediately recognized,' as E. J. Hobsbawm calls 'the modest bicycle', had so many virtues, marred by no vices. Is there any other invention of modern times of which the same can be said? With every other innovation, costs as well as benefits don't need dwelling on. The internal combustion engine almost defines 'blessing and curse': it has hugely enhanced the lives of millions, in the United States first of all and then elsewhere; and, in the course of the twentieth century, five times more Americans were killed in automobile accidents than died in war. So it went with powered flight, and nuclear fission. The bicycle was and is unsullied. As one of Iris Murdoch's characters says, 'Other forms of transport grow daily more nightmarish. The bicycle alone remains pure at heart.'

Not everyone was immediately convinced of this. Although one French enthusiast, Baudry de Saunier, could think of only two reasons 'to refuse to taste velocipedic delights: poverty and piles', medical science amplified that last anxiety. The Nantes Medical Society wondered in 1893 whether the new machine might be not only undignified but dangerous for the spinal column, a question that was, it is to be supposed, quietly forgotten ten years later when the inaugural Tour de France visited Nantes, the first of many times the Breton capital would be a *ville-étape*. In 1894 the Congress of the French Association for the Advancement of Science took up the matter again, with the improbably named Dr Ludovic O'Followell warning against the dangers of riding a bike too soon after sexual intercourse (fore-shadowing in his way an anxiety that would one day trouble team managers in many sports, including cycling); and, while denying that riding a bike must inevitably lead women to the same hysteria and 'nymphomania' into which, it was agreed, seamstresses were led by the use of sewing machines, he was concerned that it could nevertheless 'procure genital satisfactions, voluptuous sensations' or even 'sportive masturbations'.

If not necessarily for that reason, the fashion grew apace. Cycling clubs multiplied in France, and became more popular in the full sense of more plebeian. Clubs defined by occupation in the late 1880s had been distinctly mercantile or professional, for businessmen, civil servants, professors. The following decade saw a dramatic expansion and 'declassing', as clubs were formed for clerks, artisans and NCOs. The Société des Cyclistes Coiffeurs-Parfumiers and the Union Cyclistes des Postes et Télégraphes began in 1896 and 1897 respectively, while the socially exclusive Club Vélocipédique de Bordeaux prompted in response the founding of the petit-bourgeois Cyclistes Girondins in 1897; and Eugen Weber notes that before long 'dignified labels like Club Vélocipédique and Véloce Club are outnumbered by light-heart-edly vulgar ones: Société des Cyclistes Rigolards Argentonnais, La Bécane d'Ecueillé, or Le Rasoir Sportif Montpellerain': the Larking-About Lads from Argenton, the Risky Bike, the Sporting Razor of Montpellier, all names redolent of hearty Victorian facetiousness.

As the nineteenth century closed, sportsmen were rarely as yet the public idols they later became, not least because the 'mass media', which is to say in the first place the popular press, had barely emerged; but they were beginning to be well known. Dr W. G. Grace, the Gloucestershire and England cricketer, became a national figure, but he was at least technically a 'Gentleman', or amateur, and there were unmistakable class tensions that held back the emergence of professional sportsmen as heroes. In England the pattern had been for the educated classes to take away games from the populace and make them their own, so that the Football Association Cup was dominated in its early years by patrician clubs like Corinthian Casuals and Old Etonians, before the masses gratifyingly reclaimed their inheritance. French racing cyclists weren't necessarily 'varsity men', but the first generation of French cycling heroes were bourgeois boys. Two of them in the 1880s, Frederic Charron and Paul Ruinart, were heirs to prosperous business concerns, grocery and wine merchant respectively.

When in 1892 a cycling stadium was built on the site in Paris of Buffalo Bill's Circus and called the Vélodrome Buffalo to commemorate its origins, it was run by another bon bourgeois, Tristan Bernard. That was soon joined by several more velodromes in Paris alone, the Clignancourt, the Parc des Princes and the Vel de l'Est, with the most famous of all, the 'Vel d'Hiv' – winter stadium, Vélodrome d'Hiver – to come in the new century. Even now there was an element of the craze about cycling; and it was still a craze of the superior classes. 'BCBG', Parisians say, and bicycles were *bon chic* for the *bon genre*. The famous dandy Robert de Montesquiou – certainly the model for Des Esseintes in Huysmans's novel *À Rebours*, and possibly for Proust's Charlus also – was photographed with a bicycle, and one of the Comte de Vogue's sons was riding in a race watched from Madame de Rochetaillée's box by the young Pauline de Broglie, who thought that, despite those aristos in the saddle, the sport was 'brutal, smelly and barbarous'.

If track racing was exciting, there was a different kind of excitement to come with road races. From early on these had a close economic link with the new manufacturing interests: the Paris–Brest race in 1891 was run on Michelin tyres, and the next year Michelin promoted a Paris–Clermont race specifically to demonstrate the superiority of its tyres to Dunlop's. At the same

time a new kind of popular journalism was emerging, epito-
mized in England by the *Daily Mail*, the first 'halfpenny paper'.
This burgeoning press included an array of sporting papers.
Some had long been devoted to horse racing and sometimes to
boxing, but in France especially publishers now began to see
commercial possibilities in *cyclisme*.

As the new century approached, several factors thus con-
verged. There was the wonderful new bicycle; there was the
new passion for competitive sport; there was another highly
characteristic trend of the late nineteenth century, publicity
and advertising; there was a vogue for tourism and travel, not
least by that other innovation, the motor car, to encourage
which Michelin began to publish its famous Guides in 1900.
And there was politics. Although Wilde did not live to see the
birth of the Tour de France, he had by coincidence met one of
its indirect begetters only months before he heard Maeterlinck
make his startling pronouncement about humanity and the
Bicycle. He had been 'dragged out' one night in Paris, Wilde
told another friend, 'to meet Esterhazy at dinner!' during which
this 'astonishing' man had of course talked 'of nothing but
Dreyfus *et Cie*'.

This dinner companion was one of the central figures in the
drama by which, in the late 1890s, France was riveted and riven
as by nothing else during the near seventy years that the Third
Republic lasted. More exactly, Commandant Marie-Charles
Walsin-Esterhazy was the villain of the piece, the traitor in place
of whom the Jewish officer Captain Alfred Dreyfus had been
falsely convicted of treason in January 1895, to howls of glee
from the mob and the reactionary anti-Semitic Right, and sent to
Devil's Island. When Zola and Clemenceau, with the heroic assistance of Colonel Georges Picquart, recognized that Dreyfus had
been framed, they began a campaign to right the wrong, and also
conveniently enough to pummel their clerical and monarchist
foes.

For years, *l'Affaire* – Dreyfus's name didn't need to be added – set France in a frenzy, dividing friend from friend, brother from brother, the Dreyfusard Monet from the anti-Dreyfusard Cézanne, the Prince de Guermantes from the Duc de Guermantes – and Albert, Comte de Dion from the *Vélo*. This was an early cycling paper founded in 1891 and taking as its name the colloquial word the French had adopted for the bike (although some frowned on this vulgar abbreviation of *vélocipède*, Samuel Beckett later apostrophizing his 'Chère bicyclette, je ne t'appellerai pas vélo'). It was an instant success, claiming within three years to sell a remarkable 80,000 daily. The paper's original backer was Dion, an enthusiast who sponsored such eccentricities as a steam-driven tricycle as well as early motor cars, founding the Automobile Club de France in 1895. The membership of this club was aristocratic, reactionary and anti-Semitic, like Dion himself. He was one of the group of anti-Dreyfusards who, at the height of the Affair in June 1899, were arrested at Auteuil race-course for attacking President Emile Loubet. The *Vélo* was edited by Pierre Giffard, a Dreyfusard who also wrote for the *Petit Journal*, where he dared to criticize Dion for this episode. Dion was enraged, withdrew his patronage from the *Vélo* and, with a group of nationalist friends who included Michelin, began a new paper.

As its name suggested, the *Auto* was intended for motorists, but it took a keen interest in other fields as well. Its masthead read 'Automobile – Cyclisme' and then listed almost encyclopaedically athletics, yachting, fencing, weightlifting, horse racing, gymnastics and alpinism as the sports with which it concerned itself. Its editor was Henri Desgrange. Born in 1865, he had been an ardent cyclist on both bikes and tricycles, who had ridden races and had broken the one-hour record with 35 kilometres at Neuilly in 1893. He was neither a politically enlightened nor a very lovable man, as one episode showed. When he was running the Parc des Princes, a track event was organized pitting the French champion Edmond Jacquelin against Major Taylor, the first notable black cyclist (not that there have been many since). Taylor duly won, and Desgrange was so angered by this affront to the white race that he insulted the winner in turn by paying his large prize in 10-centime coins, so that Taylor had to take the money away in a wheelbarrow. Desgrange was bigoted, he was gifted, imperious and irascible, he was at times an obnoxious or even intolerable personage; all the same, he was one of the great Frenchmen of the twentieth century.

What the new paper needed was a *truc*, some publicity coup to boost its fortunes. Other papers in other countries were dreaming up their own such stunts. In New York the *World* sponsored a new baseball championship between the winners of the National and American Leagues, and although the paper later folded, it left behind what might have seemed (for a sport barely played outside America) the somewhat grandiose name of the World Series.

That was in 1903, the same year that the *Auto* gave birth to its great new race. The paper had already revived the Paris–Brest race; now it would sponsor something truly spectacular, a race all round France, 'from Paris to the blue waves of the Mediterranean'. The idea of the 'Tour de France' was a very old one, at one time linked with apprentices' initiation, recently popularized by more than one historian and travel writer, and the *Tour de France par Deux Enfants*, in which two intrepid boys called André and Julien made their way round the *hexagone*, had become one of the classic schoolbooks of the age, 'le petit livre rouge de la République' that consciously united the corners of France. Now intrepid cyclists would do the same.

1

Sowing the Seed

1903–1908

Not only romantic hindsight makes the *époque* into which the new race was born look *belle*, nor the century between 1815 and 1914 seem a golden age, but retrospect certainly adds to its attractions. Those years of peace would be gazed back at with yearning by a Europe which, in the subsequent decades, did its best to tear itself to pieces. And Paris in 1903 was not merely the *ville lumière* or city of earthly delights beloved of visitors, and deplored by stern moralists (one of whom found it 'very significant that when well-to-do Victorians gave way to vice they commonly went to Paris to indulge it'), but the place that the Impressionists had made their (not always welcoming) home and that was about to see another artistic explosion: Matisse, Derain and de Vlaminck exhibited at the Salon des Indépendants that March. Paris remained the world's undisputed capital of civilization.

Already there were portents that the golden age which it adorned was nearing its end. Elsewhere in Europe that year, there were savage pogroms against the Jews in Russia and massacres by the Turks in Bulgaria. An unlikely new movement called Zionism was considering whether to accept an unlikelier proposal to found a Jewish homeland in east Africa, fierce clashes between Germans and Czechs in Bohemia had flared up again, and in Switzerland the police were watching an obscure extreme left-wing agitator from Italy called Mussolini. France itself was far from placid, as the Dreyfus Affair finally reached a sour outcome. In 1899 Dreyfus had reluctantly accepted a pardon rather than complete vindication, but in April 1903, shortly before the great race that was an indirect consequence of *l'Affaire* had begun, startling new evidence transpired of the forgeries which had been used to convict him. Underlying the affair had anyway been a much deeper *Kulturkampf* ; far from fading away, this battle between Left and Right, aggressive laicism and the Catholic Church, radical republicanism and its unreconciled foes, was now more bitter than ever. This was the very year that the government (under President Emile Combes, himself ironically a 'spoilt priest' or sometime seminarian) abolished religious instruction in schools, and troops were sent in to remove the monks from the Chartreuse monastery as part of what would be a larger expulsion of religious orders from France. With all of that upheaval, a bicycle race could only be a welcome distraction.

From the beginning Henri Desgrange treated the Tour as his private property. The *Auto* was sponsor and 'journal organisateur', and it provided Géo Lefèvre, the course director, time-keeper and judge, as well as Desgrange himself as Directeur Général, not to say lord high publicist, who followed Beaverbrook's principle that if you don't blow your own trumpet, no one else will. On 1 July 1903 Desgrange marked the birth of his brainchild with no false modesty in an editorial headed 'La Semence' (The Seed): 'With the grand and powerful gesture that Zola gave his working man in *La Terre*, the *Auto*, newspaper of ideas and action, will from today send across France those unconscious and hardy sowers of energy, the professional road racers.'

Grandiloquent as his words might have been – and they certainly set the tone in which *le patron* would write about the race for almost four decades – 'inconscients et rudes' was a fair description of the cyclists as they set off on what by later – or any objective – standards was a terrifying three weeks. It was an individual event with no teams; riders paid no more than 10 francs to enter (with bread costing 40 centimes a kilo, this may be reckoned about 87.5 euros or £57 in 2003 values), competing for a first prize of 3000 francs (26,500 euros or £17,000) out of a pool of 20,000 francs. The race covered 2428 kilometres and lasted almost three weeks, with three lengthy periods of rest. But what made it such an ordeal to later or indeed contemporary eyes was that, although those *répos* interspersed no more than six *étapes* or stages, these stages were all enormously long, lasting more than twenty-four hours at a stretch, by night as well as day, punctuated only by pauses to grab food and effect repairs. Even the starting times of these stages were at notably unsocial hours: 2.30 a.m. in Lyons, 11.30 p.m. in Marseilles, 11 p.m. in Bordeaux.

The men who were prepared to race in these conditions were no longer good bourgeois like Charron and Ruinart, still less sprigs of fashion like the Comte de Vogue's boy. Staring out of the first photographs of the Tour, the riders seem less like well-fed and well-trained modern athletes than the rough artisans they in fact were. From the beginning, one of the Tour's deleterious traditions was the riders' nicknames bestowed by the press, babyish or facetious or whimsical, with great sportsmen like Raymond Poulidor or Bernard Hinault reduced to 'Pou-Pou' or 'Le Blaireau'. When Maurice Garin was called 'Le Petit Ramoneur' in 1903 it may have been tiresome, but it wasn't whimsy: he was in fact *petit*, no more than 5 foot 3 inches (1.60 metres) tall and 64 kg (140 lb, or 10 stone), and he had in fact been a *ramoneur* or chimney sweep by trade. Other racers were bakers' apprentices like Constant Huret and Edmond Jacquelin, butchers' boys like Louis Pothier, errand boys or labourers. A few years earlier the

British governing classes had been dismayed when large-scale enlistment for the Boer War had revealed the appalling physical condition of the industrial poor, whose social status could be deduced when they were naked from the state of their limbs and teeth. These first Tour men were far from physical wrecks, but they have the unmistakable proletarian appearance of their time, gnarled and knotty.

As Georges Abran, the eccentric martinet who had been appointed official starter, sent them off at 3.15 p.m. from the inappropriately named Reveil-Matin café at Montgeron, they faced an extraordinary challenge. The longest stage of this new race was the first, 467 kilometres from Paris to Lyons. Twelve hours after they had departed, at 3 a.m. on a moonlit night, officials caught up with the cyclists, 'riding like sleepwalkers' and strung out in groups of two or three. Ahead of most of the riders were Léon Georget and the German Josef Fischer, but the two leaders were only identified when an official descried two more figures looming in the dark and shouted, 'Who are you?' They proved to be Garin, and Emile Pagie from Tourcoing.

At 8.45 a.m., after 27 hours 47 minutes in the saddle, Garin crossed the line ending the first *étape* of the first Tour. He was followed a minute later by Pagie, exhausted almost to the point of collapse, and then after thirty-five minutes by Georget. The race had already taken its toll: Hippolyte Aucouturier had abandoned at La Palisse suffering from stomach cramps despite – or not necessarily despite – fortifying himself with bumpers of heavy red wine on the road, setting a pattern of dangerous artificial stimulation for the riders that would last a hundred years. He made his way to Lyons by train, and announced his intention of riding in the next stage to Marseilles, after three days' rest. Although the regulations then permitted this, it posed a problem for Desgrange when Aucouturier won that second stage but couldn't be placed in the *classification générale*, the general classification (GC) that determined who was the overall leader at any moment and thus who, come the last stage, had won the race. Aucouturier's victory distorted the placings for Georget and Garin, and so Desgrange for the first but very far from the last time made up the rules of the Tour as he went along, and found the ingenious if unsatisfactory compromise of declaring that the next stage would be started in two groups, one merely 'Marseilles–Toulouse', the other the Tour de France proper.

And so, at 10.30 a.m. on 8 July, a starting pistol sent off the thirty-two remaining Tour competitors, followed an hour later by the others. This ingenuity was almost frustrated by 'le terrible Aucouturier': riding with a will, he gradually caught up with the Tour group and then, from afternoon to night, ticked off one worn-out rider after another. But he couldn't catch the leaders, and reached Toulouse twenty-eight minutes after a group of four, Eugène Brange, Samson (the nom de guerre of Julien Lootens), Garin and Pothier.

On the next, 250-kilometre, stage from Toulouse to Bordeaux, the field split into bunches, and then the second group crashed. For bike racers, crashes remain an ever-present dread, which interrupt many stages of the Tour to this day. The worst crashes of all are on descents, when the riders have breasted the top of a climb and are careering downhill at high speed with an exhilarating sense of release that sometimes leads to lapses of concentration. Only one rider needs to lose his wheel's grip on the road to bring down all those behind him who can't take evasive action in time. Next worst, and all too common, are crashes in bunch finishes sprinting to the line. But a tight group of riders can all be brought down together at any time, even on a flat road at quite modest cruising speed.

That day in the Garonne valley the culprit was a dog sauntering across the road, which brought down fifteen riders, Aucouturier among them. He picked himself up, cursing roundly and glaring at his blood-covered legs. Declaring that he had finally had enough, he took the train to Paris. By this point Garin had established an unassailable three-hour lead, and although he lost a little time, he won the final stage from Nantes and reached the finish 2h49′45″ minutes ahead of Pothier in second place, a record margin to this day. He had completed the Tour at an average speed of 25.68 k.p.h. (15.96 m.p.h.), almost walking pace by later standards. Magne would break 30 k.p.h. for the Tour in 1934, Walkowiak 35 k.p.h. in 1956, and Lance Armstrong 40 k.p.h., or 25 m.p.h., in 1999. In all, seventy-eight riders had entered for the 1903 race, sixty had actually taken part, and twenty-one had finished: twenty-first was Millocheau, holding the place that would become sardonically known as *lanterne rouge*, red lamp for the last place.

The first winner of the Tour was a wiry little 32-year-old of Italian parents, but the true winner may have been Desgrange. His race had succeeded far beyond his or Dion's expectations, with great numbers turning out to watch, even when their enthusiasm had been tested by the absurdity of a race passing through their town or village in the small hours. When the twenty-one riders who completed the race reached Ville d'Avray south-west of Paris, a crowd of 100,000 greeted them, with another 20,000 at the Parc des Princes for the *Arrivée*.

In several senses the Tour was rudimentary, in this first year, and for some years to come, with few of the features that would later seem inescapably part of the race. With only half a dozen albeit enormous stages, large parts of France couldn't be visited; there was no real distinction between sprinting and plain road racing; and no serious hills were climbed. All the same, if not yet fully formed, the Tour de France was born. But it very nearly didn't survive infancy.

In only the second year of its existence the Tour did its best to illustrate Marx's saying that history repeats itself as farce, with a race marred by every kind of irregularity and skulduggery. Desgrange had tried to tighten up the regulations, insisting that no one could compete in just one or two stages: it was all or nothing. In a field that had grown to eighty-eight riders, Garin and Aucouturier started as warm favourites, but Aucouturier came a cropper at the start and never recovered from his fall, finishing the first Paris–Lyons stage two and a half hours behind Garin.

On the next stage, after a tedious five-day rest, violence erupted. Garin was chased and harassed by a car whose occupants shouted that he would get no further than St-Étienne before he was 'dealt with'. And although nothing had happened by the control station at St-Étienne, Garin was menaced as the field was leaving the town by a mob waving cudgels, apparently supporters of the *stephanois* rider Alfred Faure, and badly beaten. When the caravan of official cars belatedly arrived on the scene, the mob vanished into the night. Faure duly won the stage, though not much honour. Trouble was far from over. Ferdinand Payan had been disqualified for hanging on to cars, to the rage of his supporters, and on the next stage from Lyons to Bordeaux there was more violence in Nîmes, where barricades were put up to stop the race and Aucouturier had to fight his way through using his bike as a shield.

When the field managed to escape the town it was under a fusillade of bottles and stones, the road between Bellegarde and Lunel was covered with broken bottles and nails, and those following in cars could only make their way through another mob by flourishing pistols. Aucouturier won the stage, though Garin still led the GC, observing that, 'If I'm not murdered before Paris, I'll win the race again.' The culprits appeared at first to be a claque supporting Payan, but the broader trouble was ferocious local patriotism, hooliganism of a kind that later in the century would all too often be associated with football.

On 24 July a weary and nerve-racked twenty-seven surviving riders reached the Père Auto restaurant at Ville-d'Avray, the official finish, before processing to the Parc des Princes, where Garin, still alive after all, was acclaimed as the winner. And still the

dramas hadn't ended. A storm of protests now erupted. Garin
and Pothier among other riders, it was alleged, had received
illicit feeding from their *soigneurs* (a *soigneur* is literally a 'carer': in
a factory, a machine-minder, in a boxing ring, a second, in bike
racing, a trainer cum physio cum masseur), and, on more than
one occasion after puncturing, Aucouturier had returned to the
head of the peloton – the bunch – with suspicious speed. The
lengthy rap sheet was examined for several months, before the
devastating announcement came: the first four riders, Garin,
Pothier, Maurice's brother César Garin, and Aucouturier were all
disqualified. A new final classification was announced, with the
original fifth, Henri Cornet, now the winner, followed by
Dortignacq and Catteau. Pothier was disqualified for life, Garin
for two years. He retired from the saddle, returning in 1911 at the
age of forty when he managed a creditable tenth in the
Paris–Brest–Paris race, and also rode once more in the Tour.
Golden lads and girls all must, as chimney sweepers, come to
dust, and 'the little chimney sweep', truly a golden lad after the
first Tour, spent the rest of his long life running a garage at Lens
and complaining at the injustice of the 1904 disqualification,
until his death in 1957 aged eighty-six.

To say the least, none of the original first four was happy at
this outcome, but no one was unhappier than Desgrange. 'The
Tour de France is finished,' he wrote in his characteristically irate
tones, 'and its second running will be, I am sure, also its last.' But
it wasn't. Desgrange changed his mind, decided that he would
lead 'a grand crusade' to restore cycling, appointing the journalist Victor Breyer as *commissaire général* to clean it up. In truth
Desgrange was doing very well out of the Tour, even after the
scandal: the circulation of the *Auto* was going up, while the *Vélo*
folded, and Giffard went bankrupt, to be magnanimously (or
patronizingly) given a job by Desgrange.

The third Tour was longer, at 2994 kilometres, and increased
to eleven stages. Much more significantly for the future, it essayed

serious climbs for the first time. A new points system was introduced, ostensibly to make cheating harder, and trainers or pacers were permitted on the first and last stages. Despite Garin's absence, the field of sixty was a strong one, with Aucouturier, Cornet, Louis Trousselier, René Pottier, Lucien Petit-Breton, and the previous year's *révélation* – then and ever after a beloved word of the Tour journalists – young Jean-Baptiste Dortignacq. And bikes were divided for the first time by type, those for 'speed riders', and *machines poinçonées* or standard models (*poinçonées* for 'punched' or stamped, as a document is authorized). If Desgrange thought that increased regulation would expunge last year's disgraces and absurdities, he was soon disabused.

After leaving Noisy-le-Grand just to the east of Paris early in the morning of 9 July, the field rode to Nancy. Before they left the riders had all been offered a new invention by an enterprising tradesman from Toulouse, M. Calvade's nail-puller: 'With my gadget it's impossible to puncture.' Some riders may have taken up the offer, but Calvade's device could not prevent the disaster that awaited. Between Chalons and St-Dizier the road had been strewn with nails, and one bike after another punctured. The 'cracks' were able to borrow their trainers' bikes, but the *culs-de-plomb*, the lead-arsed lesser cyclists riding on their own account, had to effect their own repairs. Only fifteen out of sixty finished the stage, led by Trousselier ahead of Dortignacq. With rare humility Desgrange begged everyone to rescue his race.

And so they did. The second stage reached the mountains, and, as a reporter put it, 'for the first time in cycling history a supposedly unpassable peak was attempted', in the form of the Ballon d'Alsace. At 1247 metres it was only half the height above sea level of the greatest Alpine cols that would later be climbed, but forbidding enough at the time. Maybe there was some political *arrière pensée* in this choice. The Ballon then lay on the border of the French Republic and the German Empire that had taken Alsace (or, as it might be thought, reclaimed Elsass) and much of

Lorraine as prizes of war in 1871. Even though Alsace (or Elsass) is historically, geographically, linguistically and culturally German, French nationalists saw in this an irredenta and a bitter grievance, and for almost half a century they drank revanchist toasts 'A l'Est'.

To the east rode Pottier, shaking off Trousselier and Cornet as he climbed the pass. This wonderful moment went sour when nails appeared on the road again between Lunéville and Epinal. When Pottier punctured, he had no more spare tyres, but Aucouturier generously lent him one as he passed; chivalry was rewarded when Aucouturier won the stage. Pottier was still leading the GC, but abandoned at Lyons, after tearing a muscle in a bad fall. Two more climbs faced the riders, the Col de Laffrey and Col Bayard, respectively 900 and 1246 metres, won by Aucouturier and Julien Maitron. Aucouturier reached Toulon alone, twenty-four minutes ahead of Trousselier and Dortignacq, after riding this tough stage at what then seemed an incredible average speed of 26 k.p.h. (16 m.p.h.). But, just as in 1903 on the first Tour, he was undone on the next stage by stomach cramp after he had drunk too much heavy red wine, and finished eighteenth. The race was now Trousselier's for the taking. Aucouturier revived enough to win the Bordeaux–La Rochelle stage, and Dortignacq took the last two stages, but Trousselier, 'le Fleuriste', florist's assistant and part-time cyclist, rode in his disciplined and determined way to hold the overall lead at the finish. As to the sabotage, the Paris police learned that 125 kilos of nails of the type found on the roads had been bought at a Paris ironmongers the day before the Tour began, by two men whose identity was never discovered.

A complex system of classification by points continued for eight years in all, frequently modified, so that from 1905 to 1912 there are no *écarts* or distances by time separating the winner from second or second from third. This didn't mean that those results were spurious. As far as can be judged, Trousselier was a worthy winner in 1905 and Pottier still more so in 1906: more so, that is, because it was a much harder race. In the space of the three years 1904–6, the Tour's distance increased dramatically, in fact almost doubled, from 2428 to 2994 to 4637 kilometres. In 1906 the race crossed the French frontier for the first time, into 'occupied Alsace-Lorraine' at Metz, Italy at Ventimiglia, and Spain at Irun. For the first time a *flamme rouge* marked the last kilometre of a stage and, for the first time also, there was a departure from a different place from the previous arrival, so that the race had to be transferred lock, stock and barrel – or riders, bikes and team cars – from Lille where the first stage ended to Douai where the second began. Today this is the rule rather than the exception: in the 2003 Tour, only four towns see both one stage finish and another begin the next day. The change did not bring good fortune. After Emile Georget, Léon's brother, had won the first stage, the riders found nail-strewn roads yet again, and on that Douai–Nancy stage every single rider punctured except Petit-Breton. On the next stage to Dijon there was a different kind of villainy: Maurice Carrère, Henry Gauban and Gaston Tuvache were ejected when it was discovered that they had taken the train.

But the story of the race was the domination of Pottier. He won five out of thirteen stages, including four consecutive stages, Douai–Nancy–Dijon–Grenoble–Nice, making several long, brave escapes to break away from the other riders, and confirming in the most striking way the unofficial title 'King of the Mountains' informally awarded after his conquest of the Ballon d'Alsace the year before. On that same climb this year he again toyed with his rivals, winning the stage by forty-eight minutes, before continuing to crush them over the Col de Laffrey and the Col Bayard. He was beaten into Marseilles by Georges Passerieu, just turned pro, after the two had fought wheel to wheel over the Turbie and Esterél. Aucouturier abandoned on the next stage with stomach cramps, Trousselier was declassified for an irregular change of bike after beating the local hero Jean-Baptiste Dortignacq to Bayonne but won the next three stages also, to Bordeaux, Nantes and Brest, and one reporter described his performance in a vivid phrase: 'il pétait le feu' – he was farting fire. But Pottier took the last stage into Paris by a wheel from Passerieu, and beat him into second in the final classification, winning the Tour narrowly on points. A total of ninety-six riders had entered, all French apart from three Belgians, two Germans and an Italian; only fourteen completed, all of them French; and one marque as well as one country dominated the race, with Peugeot riders taking the first four places. Trousselier was philosophical in defeat – or defiant: 'It's a pity there weren't another dozen stages. I'd have beaten the lot!'

A famous victory was followed by the saddest story ever told about the Tour de France. René Pottier might have been a very great champion, maybe winning the race several times. But 'le Boucher' – the sobriquet again from his occupation rather than any reflection on his character – was a melancholiac, notorious for never smiling. He sank into deeper depression, and on 25 January 1907 a mechanic from Peugeot found him hanged from the hook where his bike usually hung. His brother André said that René was unhappy in love, or suffering from a 'sentimental disappointment', but the full reason for his suicide was never established. He left a widow and orphan.

Six months later, Pottier's death still cast a pall over the 1907 race. The race itself was much like the one that Pottier had won, though with some further developments: fourteen stages with a rest day after each, a stage into occupied territory at Metz again, a visit to Switzerland for the first time, passing through Geneva on the way from Lyons to Grenoble, more mountains to climb, the Col de Porte and Col du Sappey in the Massif de la Chartreuse. By that point a duel had developed between Faber and Emile Georget, with Georget winning a succession of stages.

He had won the Roubaix–Metz stage from Trousselier 'by a tyre', as the race now nicely called what in horse-racing is known as a short head (or in French racing as *un nez*), though Desgrange and the commissioners, after a form of stewards' inquiry, decided to treat it as a dead heat and the two were awarded the stage 'ex aequo'. Then Georget increased his lead over the Luxembourger François Faber across the Col de la Porte, a technical as well as a personal victory since Georget was riding a bike with a free wheel.

In this year's Tour, eighty-two out of ninety-three riders used standard *poinçonées* machines, which could be repaired but not use fresh parts, but the cracks stuck to the old model. All bikes were inspected and guarded by armed gendarmes at night to ensure that a rider finished the race on the machine he had begun on. No one had won on a *poinçonée* bike for the first two years they were used, and very likely no one would have done in 1907 but for the events of the Toulouse–Bayonne stage. It was won by Petit-Breton with a long breakaway. But Georget had punctured, borrowed a bike from Privat, another rider, and taken another again at the control, only to find that it hadn't been authorized and sealed by the officials, whereat he changed yet again to another. After all this ado, he was relegated to last place and fined 550 francs.

Some riders complained that the punishment was insufficient, and several, led by Trousselier, left the race in protest at Bordeaux, handing final victory in Paris to a distinctly fortunate Lucien Petit-Breton – or rather to Lucien Mazan. That was the name under which he was born in 1883 in Plessé, in Loire-Inférieure, but he had gone as a boy with his family to Buenos Aires where he became familiarly and inevitably the 'little Breton'. His family disapproved the idea of professional cycling, and when he began riding he used his nickname as a *nom de guerre*, though his Tour nickname was just as inevitably also geographical: 'L'Argentin'.

Plenty of carpers took a dim view of his victory, but he silenced them the following year by becoming the first man to win the Tour twice. He did it methodically rather than excitingly, riding an intelligent and careful race, taking five stages of the 1908 race to the four won by the eventual second, Faber. There was a deeply poignant moment at the Ballon d'Alsace, where a monument had been placed to René Pottier. When his brother André reached the spot he was overcome and broke down in tears, though he was gently coaxed into continuing, and eventually finished the Tour in seventeenth place. More drama came on the Belfort–Lyons stage when Faber emerged on his own out of an unseasonal blizzard to win, but the hero of the stage was Gustave Garrigou, who had a six-minute lead on one climb, crashed badly descending, watched the field pass him, but then recovered remarkably to finish in third. From Nice to Toulouse the stages were shared by Petit-Breton and Faber, as one rider after another suffered some or other *défaillance*, with Trousselier, the brothers Hippolyte and François Aucouturier, Dortignacq, Georget and Maurice Brocco among the many who abandoned.

Both words are crucial to the Tour: *défaillance* is literally a lapse, decay, weakness or dereliction, and for a rider it means any form of breakdown of body or sometimes morale – the spirit may be willing when the flesh is weak, though sometimes the spirit is none too willing either – which forces him to abandon. If he broke down on the road he would be swept up by the *car balai*, the broom wagon decorated with a witch's broomstick, and would then be formally removed from the race, his numbers taken from his bike and from the back of his jersey: not quite the horror suffered by Dreyfus when he was degraded from the army, his badges of rank torn from his uniform and his sword broken, but a ritual with overtones of public humbling.

By the last stage Petit-Breton's lead was unassailable but there was a fierce battle for second between Faber, Passerieu and

Garrigou, fought with the help of pacing cars in the last stage from Caen, with Garrigou fading and Faber crossing the line in the Parc des Princes only two lengths of a bike behind Petit-Breton. Those absent riders weren't the only ones to experience breakdown: Desgrange's car packed up, and he reached the finish in a horse-drawn conveyance.

Petit-Breton collected the first prize of 4000 francs, while Faber picked up a handsome consolation of 3500 francs offered by the tyre manufacturers Wolber for the first rider to finish using its tubular *démontable* tyre; that is, the replaceable inner tube, which all sorts and conditions of cyclists would ever after come to know and love as they learned to remove and repair it with rubber solution and patches, or more simply replace it. Of the 114 riders who began in 1908, 36 were using Wolber's product. And for another fifty years or more, one of the Tour's most familiar images would be the cyclist riding with a spare tyre or two looped around his shoulders.

There were five Belgian riders in the 1908 Tour, an inkling of what would one day be a part played in the race out of proportion to the size of Belgium. By sombre coincidence this was the very year that the Brussels government bought the Congo Free State from King Leopold, whose personal fief it had been, and who had already made a vast fortune using atrocious methods to extract 'red gold' from the peoples of the country and satisfy the great new appetite for rubber, not least in the form of bicycle tyres.

That snowstorm from which Faber had emerged was not only unseasonal but untypical of this summer, whose weather was for the most part fine. And the French made the most of it, in town and village. After six years the Tour was now an established feature of national life, 'a big event and front-page news', as one chronicler recorded. People increasingly took the opportunity for a day out when the race passed by, with family picnics by the roadside, and excursions laid on to take spectators up hills where they could watch the climbing stages. The potential for local patriotism, and for commercial exploitation, was grasped by mayors and by businessmen, with hotels and restaurants booming as the Tour came to town, and with banquets laid on for the riders, which were then milked thoroughly for publicity value. And it was the great publicist himself who had best reason to be pleased: Desgrange had seen the circulation of the *Auto* nearly double, from 140,000 to 250,000.

Not that France could otherwise be called a country at ease with itself. There was continuing social upheaval, with a population still predominantly rural but slowly becoming more urban, there was harsh industrial unrest, there was sharp political conflict. A few weeks before the 1908 race had begun, a distant echo of its political origins was heard when, at a ceremony honouring Zola, a journalist tried to shoot Major Alfred Dreyfus. And across Europe there were signs of coming conflict this year. The Young Turk revolution in the Ottoman Empire meant, as few immediately recognized, that 'the sick man of Europe' would once again become a formidable military power. Kaiser Wilhelm II gave an extraordinary interview to the *Daily Telegraph* in which he spoke almost light-heartedly about the strength of anti-British feeling in Germany. In London national pride was puffed up by the many British successes in the Olympics held there, after the stadium at the White City had already been opened by the Prince of Wales for the Franco-British Exhibition, with an anthem composed by Sir Charles Stanford to the words, 'Jolly Britons advance – here's a health to old France. Welcome! Welcome! Welcome!' Here was a public display of the recent entente between the countries, which might yet take very practical military form: one of too many intimations that the end of that golden age of peace was in sight.

2

To the Mountains

1909–1914

Speaking to reporters in the Parc des Princes on 9 August 1908, Petit-Breton had said tersely, 'Faber will win next year,' and so he most convincingly did. It was a summer of more upheavals, with strange portents almost hinting at greater violence to come in Europe. Six months before the 1909 Tour, 200,000 Sicilians died when a terrible earthquake destroyed Messina, and less than three weeks before the race began at the Pont de la Jatte, a smaller earthquake – though still the strongest ever known in France – had left forty dead near Aix-en-Provence. While the Tour wasn't directly affected by these shakings of the planet's surface, there may have been a meteorological connection between them and – in sharp contrast to the previous July – the wintry weather in which the race was run.

An enormous field was entered for the Tour, 150 in all, 112 of them racing as *isolés* or individuals, but the first 38 in numbered order for the first time divided or *groupés* into teams under the name of bike manufacturers: Nil-Supra, Biguet-Dunlop, Le Globe, Atala, Legnano, Felsina, and Alcyon who were the great coming force. For the past four years the Tour had been won by cyclists riding Peugeot machines, but Alcyon would win the next four.

After the first stage from Paris to Roubaix was taken by Cyriel van Houwaert, 'the Lion of Flanders' and the first Belgian to win a stage, Faber assumed complete command, winning five consecutive stages from Roubaix to Nice, despite everything the heavens could throw at him. In England, if it rains on St Swithin's Day it's meant to rain for forty days and nights; according to French peasant lore, when 'Saint-Médard is angry' it rains fiercely and icily for days on end. He was angry this summer, and conditions in the mountains were frightful. Quite undaunted, Faber made a long escape.

As the pattern of racing took shape, two more words entered its vocabulary. Riders on the road tended to form into a "peloton" – a cluster if it's insects, a ball if it's wool, a squad if it's soldiers, or simply a bunch, as of cyclists – and often into more than one. From this bunch one or more riders would attack to make an *échappée*, escaping or breaking away from the peloton into the distance. As this became a recognized feature of the race, escapes were recorded and measured, both by distance and by time: that is, the number of kilometres from when the escape began to when the field caught up with the escaper, or to the end of the stage if he held his lead to the line; and the average interval the escaper put between him and his pursuers. Figures are unreliable in the early days, but the record *échappée solitaire* since the race resumed after the Second World War in 1947 was in that very year's race, Albert Boulon's 253-kilometre escape at an average of 16′30″ on the Carcassonne–Luchon stage, which he held successfully to the end when he finished still 16′20″ in the lead.

In this earlier case, Faber's escape was also successful, and he reached Metz thirty-three minutes ahead of the field. He was first over the Ballon d'Alsace, first over the Col de Porte, first over the Col Bayard, followed at a distance by Gustave Garrigou, Eugène

Christophe, Constant Ménager and the young riders Jean Alavoine and Paul Duboc from Rouen. Another professional debutant was Octave Lapize, aged twenty, who rode well until a bad knee forced him to abandon at Nancy.

One man challenged Faber's dominance, his own half-brother Ernest Paul, who won the Nice–Nîmes stage. The next stage to Toulouse was taken by Jean Alavoine, the French 100-kilometre champion, but Faber struck back to take the stage into Bordeaux by seven minutes from Duboc. The peloton did what it could to check him, holding him back for a while, but he still ended in the Parc des Princes comfortably ahead of Garrigou and Jean Alavoine, to win for Alcyon and break Peugeot's domination of the past four years. The hero of that day was Jean's brother Henri Alavoine who, having cycled for almost 240 kilometres, covered the last ten kilometres on foot carrying his bike after it had been wrecked in a crash. Ernest Paul was sixth, but took the newly inaugurated prize for *isolés* of whom there had been 112 among the record 150 starters, with the other 38 in teams. And thirty-second out of fifty-five finishers was the Italian Gaetano Belloni, at seventeen the youngest rider ever to take part in the Tour let alone finish.

If Faber was the first non-French rider to win the Tour, France had another national hero to compensate. Six days before the race finished, Louis Bleriot landed his little aircraft near Dover Castle, forty-three minutes after taking off from Sangatte outside Calais, to claim the *Daily Mail*'s £1000 prize as the first man to cross the Channel by air: a happy day and an ominous one. Bleriot's mission was peaceable, but in little more than five years' time, anyone attempting to follow the 1909 Roubaix–Metz stage would look up to see airmen killing each other in the skies above.

During the course of the 1910 Tour, Desgrange was taken ill and handed over his authority to Victor Breyer at Luchon. He thus missed witnessing the great new climbs in the Pyrenees, now essayed for the first time. A serious stage through the mountain range which divides France from Spain had been suggested to Desgrange by his friend Alphonses Steinès, and Desgrange had said, 'Fine. Go and scout them for me.' Steinès duly did so, and drove most of the way up the great Tourmalet. But within a few miles of the 2115-metre summit he abandoned his car in heavy snow and crossed the pass on foot to reach the gendarme post at Bareges and telegraph Desgrange that the road was passable.

Even apart from his own experience, this wasn't entirely candid. It is not the historian's province to describe and explain these mountains, Michelet says, but you need to go there 'to comprehend the fantastic beauty of the Pyrenees – their strange, incompatible sites, brought together as though by some freak of fairy hands'. They are for the large part more beautiful than the Alps, without the awe-inspiring and often simply terrifying scale of the greater range, but also gentler, greener and lusher in summer: romantic richness against the classical grandeur of the Alps. And the Pyrenean passes ridden in the Tour are also less ferocious than the Alpine: even now, the highest, the Port d'Envalira, which wasn't climbed until 1964, is 2407 metres to the Galibier's 2556, and the riders don't look forward to the Pyrenees with quite the same sense of dread that they feel for the Alps.

And yet, in the early years of the twentieth century, the Pyrenees were if anything more backward than the Alps. Roads in the south-west were very primitive, and the riders who embarked on the Portet d'Aspet between Perpignan and Luchon on 19 July 1910, and then the Peyresourde, Aspin, Tourmalet and Aubisque two days later, were cycling over rough gravel and dirt. These 'roads' were for the large part little more than mule tracks, and the race here was often more like modern cyclo-cross or mountain biking, an adventure where finishing a climb at all is quite enough of a feat. It's a tribute to their machines and tyres that they didn't break down and puncture more often than they did.

From its early stages the 1910 race was largely a contest among riders from what were once called the Low Countries and now less attractively 'Benelux': a sign that Belgium, the Netherlands and Luxembourg were destined to play a part in the history of the Tour out of all proportion to their size or population. The Belgian Charles Crupelandt took the first stage into Roubaix, close to where he lived, and the next stage was taken by Faber, riding in a fierce storm, who also took the fourth to Lyons. But Lapize won Lyons–Grenoble, and the race was to develop into a duel between the two, helped by the tally of victims. Faber was badly hurt after colliding with yet another dog in Nice, but there was a much graver tragedy during the rest day at Nice. Adolphe Hélière, an *isolé*, went down to the sea to swim and drowned, perhaps after some kind of stroke. Although he is not usually included on the sombre roll-call of those who have died riding in the Tour, his was the first death during the course of the race.

On the next stage to Nîmes, Petit-Breton abandoned after a couple of accidents had rendered his bike unrideable. He continued in the car of a sporting paper, to hold forth on the race rather than compete in it, and inaugurate a pattern that would be followed by many others. After they had crossed Provence and the Midi, Faber reached the Pyrenees fifteen points ahead of Lapize, but it was the new Pyrenean climbs that proved the decisive phase of the race, following a strange incident on the Nîmes–Perpignan stage. Gustave Garrigou had taken his bike – an Alcyon, for whom he was riding like Lapize – up to his room at Nîmes. Riders were allowed to do this, to tend to their bikes, and also to keep an eye on them in case miscreants should be on the prowl. As Garrigou told Jean Bobet of *Sport et Vie* forty years later, 'I forgot to lock my door, and I paid dearly for the mistake.' Cycling through Lunel at 3 a.m. the next morning, his front wheel came apart, 'ball bearings everywhere. Someone had done a good job of unscrewing the hub, and I hadn't noticed a thing.'

He had to search for a mechanic, no easy thing at that hour, and lost about ninety minutes, when he had been within seconds of Faber. 'But don't misunderstand me – it wasn't Faber who sabotaged my machine, definitely not,' though he didn't say who he thought the culprit had been. Over the Portet d'Aspet and the Col des Ares, Lapize dominated the field, reaching Pau eighteen minutes ahead of the crack climber Emile Georget. Then came a gruelling series of climbs, Peyresourde, Aspin, Tourmalet, Aubisque: a test that Jean Robic, the 1947 Tour winner, would many years later call 'the circle of death'.

After a large crowd had gathered on the Col d'Aubisque, they waited so long that a rumour spread of some calamity befalling the field, until a complete outsider appeared, the *touriste-routier* Lafourcade. Another fifteen minutes later, Lapize came into view, pushing his bike, as he and other riders often did on steep climbs: a prime, or special prize, of 100 francs was on offer at the Tourmalet for any rider who could reach the summit without putting foot to ground, won by Garrigou who arrived in second place. The ordeal enraged Lapize. When he saw a group of officials, he shouted 'Murderers!' at them. Back on his bike, he made a fast descent to pass Lafourcade, who had collapsed. The whole field was strung out for many miles behind, and some riders reached Bayonne hours behind Lapize: although Faber still held the lead, Lapize's victories in the two huge mountain stages meant that he had the race lead in his sights. As they reached Nantes on a long stage from Bordeaux, it was Trousselier who outsprinted van Houwaert, and Garrigou who won the next stage to Brest.

The penultimate stage was an enormous 424-kilometre trek to Caen. As they left Brest in darkness – this year's stages began anywhere between 11.45 p.m. and 6.30 a.m. – Faber attacked early and drew away, but he punctured, once, and then again, which enabled Lapize and Garrigou to pass him. On the last stage to Paris it was Lapize's turn to puncture, so that Faber took the lead, only to puncture yet again. The stage was taken by Ernest Paul, but Lapize managed to keep within two points of Faber on that last day, and the race was duly won by 'Le Frisé', as the press called Lapize from his curly hair, although it was one more bogus nickname: he was 'Tatave' to his friends.

Since the Tour began, relations between the race organizers and the business interests that controlled the bicycle industry had been tense and often strained. Plainly they needed each other – there could be no Tour de France without bikes, while the race had been immensely lucrative for the bike-makers – but they didn't love each other, something far from concealed by Desgrange's habitually vituperative daily column in the *Auto*. Just before the 1911 Tour he denounced the manufacturers once again for their unscrupulous determination to stop at nothing to win the Tour.

If Desgrange's polemic was meant to restore order to his great race, it was not an immediate success, but the Tour itself was unmistakably successful, expanding by several measures. Within nine years the race had more than doubled in length, from 2428 to the 5343 kilometres the riders had in front of them when they left the Pont de la Jatte at 4.00 a.m. on 2 July 1911, to ride through Dunkirk, Longwy and Nancy towards Alsace. They comprised sixty-eight *isolés* on top of thirty-seven *groupés*, despite Desgrange's remonstrances, in four teams, La Française, Alcyon, Le Globe and Automoto.

It was a tough race from the beginning: fourteen riders fell by the wayside on the first day, one of them Petit-Breton. In Boulogne a rider ahead of him swerved to avoid a collision, not with a dog this time but with a drunken sailor, and the resulting crash put Petit-Breton in hospital. As a result, he never had the opportunity to test in the mountains a new type of gear he was using, but others in the race did so. A designer called Panel had already been experimenting with new gearings, and in the Pyrenees Brocco and Garrigou tried a 22×11 ratio.

Bike gears were then in their technical infancy, with only one ratio available on a bike, more than a quarter-century before the advent of the derailleur, which could offer a rider a choice of five, then ten, then more gears to choose from. Even now the subject of gear ratios is one which more than any other distinguishes what the Italians call the *tifoso*, the ardent cycling fan, from the non-specialist. The true Tour fan can discuss the merits of 55×14 against 48×12 with the passion of any golfer arguing about whether a player should use an 8-iron or a sand wedge. Since this is not meant to be a technical account, it will leave those arguments to the zealots, but it's perhaps worth explaining the basic point that the former figure in a ratio is the number of teeth on the chain set of the chain and the latter that of the sprocket, and that a 22×11 gear means quite simply that each turn of the pedals will turn the rear wheel twice. At any rate, Brocco's and Garrigou's innovation prompted Steinès to write in the *Auto* what might have seemed a science-fiction prediction: 'We do not despair of seeing multiple-geared bikes one day or another. The world must evolve. No one can avoid that rule.'

Several other stars followed Petit-Breton out of the race: Lapize took a purler into a ditch coming down the Ballon, and Faber departed late after a succession of incidents. He made a solo escape of 206 kilometres to win the stage into Nancy, crossed the Ballon d'Alsace alone to reach Belfort seventeen minutes ahead of Marcel Godivier and Garrigou, and another 260-kilometre fugue or breakaway to win Grenoble–Nice over a new pass, the Col d'Allos. He was still in the race when it reached Quimper, but was finally obliged to retire by the severe boils which were, along with piles and sores, among the problems perennially afflicting riders' hind quarters.

After one near disaster – tumbling into a ravine while swerving to avoid a German car – Emile Georget had finished one stage on foot carrying his battered bike on his shoulders, before winning the stage from Chamonix to Grenoble. This was some feat. For the first time the Tour was crossing another of the two greatest Alpine passes, the Col du Galibier, whose height has varied (not according to nature but to the construction of the pass road) between 2556 and 2645 metres, and the Col de Télégraphe at 1566 metres.

Never shy of the grandiose phrase, Desgrange had announced the Galibier climb in a leader headed 'Acte d'Adoration': 'O, col Bayard, O, Tourmalet . . . a côté du Galibier vous êtes de la pâle et vulgaire bibine.' To call the Tourmalet small beer, common or garden, was a little hard, but it was no exaggeration to say that the Galibier has an awesome grandeur of its own, which has to be witnessed while the riders ascend towards the summit to be fully understood.

In the Pyrenees a duel developed between Georget and Duboc, the little man from Rouen. After leading into Perpignan, Duboc attacked over the Aspin and Tourmalet to win again into Luchon and close on the leaders – before one of the Tour's great scandals erupted, on the Luchon–Bayonne stage. After escaping from the field, Duboc was near the top of a climb when he keeled over and lay vomiting in obvious pain and distress until a doctor reached him. After treatment he returned to the race, having lost some ninety minutes, to finish the stage, won by Brocco. On closer medical examination it was clear that Duboc had been poisoned. But just how – by a rival, or through inadvertent food poisoning – was never properly established.

The other scandal in the south-west concerned Maurice Brocco. He won the stage into Bayonne by thirty-four minutes, but did so while he was appealing against disqualification by an angry Desgrange, who had accused him of selling his services as a pacer to other riders. The disqualification was upheld, Brocco was ejected, and Desgrange gave a new word to the vocabulary of the Tour, when he wrote that Brocco was good for nothing and unworthy to ride in the Tour. 'C'est un domestique' – he's no more than a household servant. It was one of those curious expressions like 'Quaker' or 'Old Contemptibles', a casual insult destined to become an everyday word and even a badge of honour: as the team structure of Tour racing developed, the *domestiques* would be the loyal team players who had neither hope nor intention of reaching the podium but would serve their leaders devotedly, though also self-interestedly 'all for one and one for all'.

By La Rochelle Duboc had made a remarkable recovery, and was in second place behind Gustave Garrigou. Duboc was spurred on by his own determination and by a groundswell of public support. Mutterings about the poisoning had hinted that the culprit was Garrigou – or even Desgrange, whose favourite Garrigou was held to be, while abusive letters poured into the office of the *Auto*. After Garrigou had won the Brest–Cherbourg stage, the race approached Rouen, Duboc's home town, and for all his bluster Desgrange was alarmed enough to suggest unusual measures of discretion: Garrigou shaved off his conspicuous moustache, changed his jersey, took the number off his bike, and was guarded by cars fore and aft. Duboc won that stage to Le Havre, and then he, Godivier and Georget made an escape on the final stage to Paris. Duboc and Georget both punctured, while the unlucky Godivier broke his handlebars only a few miles from the Parc des Princes and finished on foot, to take a plucky sixth place out of only twenty-eight riders who finished.

Despite his courage, Duboc was still twenty points behind Garrigou at the finish. As it proved, a French rider wouldn't win the Tour for another ten years, but Garrigou went out on a high note for his country, and 1911 was all in all a good sporting year for France: the 17-year-old boxer Georges Carpentier burst on the scene to win the European championship, and the French rugby team won its first ever international match, beating Scotland 16–15.

In the shadow of the Duboc and Brocco affairs Desgrange decided before the 1912 Tour to cede some of his authority over the race, which was both dictatorial and suspect: he was held to have favoured some riders, and to have been susceptible to pressure from the teams, his publicly expressed dislike for which was as great as ever but whose money was essential for his race. And so some disciplinary powers passed to an independent judge, the number of riders in a trade team was fixed at ten, the use of trainers was more stringently controlled, and pacemakers from outside teams forbidden. At the same time, yielding to the inevitable, collaboration between members of a team was recognized.

With all these changes it was a disappointing race, largely because of appalling weather. Desgrange wrote after one Pyrenean stage ridden in apocalyptic conditions that 'I have an anguished heart from all I have seen.' What caused him further anguish was the visible eclipse of French cycling and the beginning of what would be a long period of Belgian supremacy. There was even some sign of flagging interest in the race, although this proved to be a temporary phenomenon, partly connected with other distractions such as the Stockholm Olympics, where Paul Colas, another kind of crack, won two shooting gold medals for France.

It was a stormy race not only in climatic terms. The first stage was punctuated by punctures, for Lapize, Faber, Duboc, Georget among others. Odile Defraye, the Belgian, put down his marker by winning the second stage from Dunkirk to Longwy, when Brocco was badly hurt in a fall, and poor Petit-Breton retired once more after a succession of falls. Before reaching the Alps, Eugène Christophe, winner of the Milan–San Remo race two years earlier, had trimmed his large moustache *à la gauloise*. Thus lightened, he won three consecutive stages across the Alps, leading over the Galibier and making a 315-kilometre solo break. With Lapize and Crupelandt also riding strongly, Defraye held the overall lead, while Georget was taken out of the race by stomach illness, and Brocco quit after breaking a finger.

After Defraye and Lapize had slugged it out over the Col d'Allos, Desgrange wrote facetiously, 'I don't know who had the idea of adding the Col d'Allos to the itinerary. Or rather, I know very well. But I shan't pay him any compliments! From one end to the other, these seventeen kilometres were truly ferocious.' But jocosity did Lapize no good when they reached the Pyrenees. Over the Portet d'Aspet, Defraye, Christophe and Marcel Buysse escaped from a pack led by Lapize – who abruptly abandoned at St-Verons, along with the whole La Française team. It was in protest, he said, at the conduct of the leader and his team-mates and compatriots: 'They were all working for Alcyon, and all the Belgians helped Defraye whether they were in his team or not.'

This departure left the race to Defraye for the taking. After the young Belgian rider Louis Mottiat, just turned pro, won a Pyrenean stage, Jean Alavoine won three of the last five stages, and he led the field into the Parc des Princes, where the crowd huddled under umbrellas as though some Gallic providence punished this Belgian usurpation. Defraye then returned home to a hero's welcome in Brussels, greeted by the king and huge crowds.

It was the beginning of a long period of Belgian dominance, and of a truly astonishing national achievement over the whole history of the Tour. In the summer of 1914, 'gallant little Belgium' became a rallying cry in London, 'les braves Belges' in Paris, as most of the small kingdom was overrun by the German army with great brutality, and the British army fought some of its most savage battles at Ypres and elsewhere in Flanders fields where poppies grow. That was the home of Belgian cycling: the great majority of Belgian cyclists have been Flemish, with an occasional French-speaking Walloon admitted, as Geoffrey Nicholson put it, in the way a North Walian is occasionally allowed to play rugby for Wales. The Flemish dominance is startlingly illustrated by surnames: no fewer than 145 of the men who have ridden in the Tour have had names beginning 'Van', and 44 begin 'Ver', including three different Verhaegens and four Vermeulens. Since Flanders is only a part (the northern region) of the country, since the Flemings are only part (though the larger part) of the Belgian people, and since Belgium has less than one-fifth of the population of France, this makes all the more extraordinary the fact that since 1903, thirty-six Tours have been won by French riders, and eighteen by Belgian. Truly Belgian cycling has been a gallant tale, and its riders *braves*.

Whatever the original reasons for a points system, it had done the French no favours. That system could be justified as long as it produced the same result as accumulated time. But Defraye had won easily from Christophe on points, when Christophe would have won the race on time. There may thus have been some *arrière pensée* on Desgrange's part when he decided that the 1913 Tour would revert to classification by time. Desgrange had by now lost one colleague and gained one: the starter, Abran, much mocked but also feared by the riders, withdrew with illness, while Lucien Cazalis was appointed assistant to Desgrange.

Another change was geographical. The first ten races had toured France clockwise, north, east, south, west; now for the first time the Tour went round France anticlockwise, from Paris through Normandy, Brittany and thence to Bayonne, so that the Pyrenees were crossed before the Alps. After a first stage almost ruined by more saboteurs' nails strewn on the roads, the Belgian Jules Masselis won at Cherbourg from Petit-Breton in one of the sprint finishes that were becoming a feature of the race. Although the emerging French star Henri Pélissier, riding for Alcyon in his first Tour, beat Defraye to Brest, Defraye held the overall lead, as he did after the enormous 470-kilometre stage from Brest to La Rochelle.

Run in blazing heat, that stage saw one ludicrous episode. Ali Neffati was an 18-year-old Tunisian *isolé*, a protégé of Pélissier's, and easily the most conspicuous rider in the field since he rode wearing a fez. At one point Desgrange saw him from his car and thought that he seemed to be in some discomfort. Drawing alongside to enquire if he was all right, he was told, 'Oh, Monsieur Desgrange, I'm freezing!' Desgrange was never sure whether this was meant to be a joke.

By Bayonne, after only five stages, the field had been severely thinned, with only 59 riders left out of the 140 who had begun. Those who had dropped out included a sour and disenchanted Lapize. The three-times-running French champion complained that the Tour was scarcely worth his effort, thanks to the system which had now taken effect, by which prize money was shared among each team: 'If I win the Tour I don't pocket much more than 7000 francs. I win more at track racing. And so I've had enough. If I puncture, the peloton pelts off *à toutes pédales*. But if some dangerous opponent of mine crashes, no one wants to take the lead. It's me against everyone!' His La Française team-mates Georget, Crupelandt, Duboc and Brocco quit with him in sympathy, although there was no sympathy at all from the Patron. There were some *fines pédales*, Desgrange wrote the next morning, who 'don't find the Tour interesting. They would rather race twice a week in all the cycling stadiums of Europe and pick up 500 francs a time!' which was indeed exactly what Lapize had said.

Reaching the Pyrenees, Defraye held the GC lead five minutes ahead of Christophe, followed by Buysse. The mountains saw Thys, Buysse and Garrigou and their Peugeot team triumphant, but also saw disaster befall Christophe. On the Tourmalet a car ran into him and broke the forks of his bike, which he gamely carried the remaining fourteen kilometres down to Ste-Marie de Campan. There he found a blacksmith's forge and, watched by a race official, began mending the fork single-handed: the rules still insisted that such repairs must be carried out by a rider unaided. At one point he asked the boy who worked in the forge to pump the bellows for him – and for this infraction, the official pedantically penalized him, on top of the two hours he had lost anyway. A plaque stands to this day at the place the extraordinary feat was performed.

Even if he had known that, it would have been little consolation to Christophe at the time. He rejoined the race, having dropped from second to fifth place, with Philippe Thys now in the lead. After winning at Perpignan in torrential rain, Buysse took the lead, but he crashed and badly damaged his bicycle. Instead of finishing on foot, he accepted a lift in a car, for which 'discreditable action' he was put down to fifth place with Thys back in the lead, which he held across the Alps.

Over the Galibier there was a duel between Buysse and Faber, decided when Faber fell on the descent, and then another between Thys and Petit-Breton, which continued after the mountains until the penultimate Longwy–Dunkirk stage, when Petit-Breton fell on the bone-breaking road, damaging bike and knee. The riders always disliked the Nord – the department of that name and the North in general – for this reason. In French and Belgian Flanders the roads were surfaced with either cobblestones or *pavés*, stones cut the size and shape of bricks: both kinds designed very effectively to take wear and tear from heavy horse-drawn carts, but both unpleasant to ride a bike over.

Hindered in the same painful way, Thys also fell on this stage and passed out. He was dragged back to action by his teammates, and was penalized when he was seen accepting help to repair his bike. But even then, and even though Buysse won the last two stages, Thys was able to hang on and win the Tour by 8'37" from Garrigou.

For the first decade and more of its existence, the Tour de France had been run in a country increasingly prosperous, and with an astonishingly vigorous cultural life, but quivering with political and industrial unrest, and threatened, behind the glories of *arts et métiers*, by an ever more unstable international background. It is a mistake to suppose that war was approaching with complete inevitability, or that all of France, or Europe as a whole, was obsessed by that prospect to the exclusion of all other concerns. From 1912 to the summer of 1914 the English were absorbed by the Russian ballet and the first Post-Impressionist exhibition, and far more worried about labour strife, the angry movement for women's suffrage, and above all the conflict in Ulster, than with a potentially cataclysmic war. A few politically aware Frenchmen knew about incipient conflict in the distant Balkans, but in early 1914 that was less on the mind of literary Paris than André Gide's new novel *Les caves du Vatican*, of fashionable Paris than the new 'Wigwam' hat that was all the rage – and of all of Paris than the Caillaux–Calmette affair and the events of 16 March.

Madame Caillaux, wife of the finance minister Joseph Caillaux, went to the offices of the *Figaro*, the famous newspaper whose editor, Gaston Calmette, had been attacking Caillaux for his plans to tax the rich, but who had also threatened to publish compromising letters of a more intimate nature written by Caillaux. Mme Caillaux demanded the return of the letters and, when Calmette refused, she made her own forceful protest at invasion of privacy by taking out a gun and shooting him dead. It was the sort of event in which the English delighted in the days before sex scandals had become almost a monopoly of their own political class. But this was more than just another sex scandal. It had unmistakable international consequences, when awareness of the way the two great western powers were distracted – the one by Ulster and the other by the Caillaux–Calmette affair – undoubtedly influenced the German government as it edged more confidently towards war.

When the Tour set off early in the morning of 28 June 1914, the riders, the teams, the newspapermen, the fans, thus had their minds on domestic shocks, as well as the pressing question of which of the stars would win the great race, rather than more distant events. It was a very strong field, with seven previous winners in the line-up of 145, the Frenchmen Trousselier, Petit-Breton, Lapize and Garrigou, the Belgians, Defraye and Thys, and the Luxembourger Faber. Or perhaps there might be a first-time winner from among several promising contenders, Georget, Alavoine, Christophe, Brocco, Dubos or Pélissier; Marcel and Lucien Buysse, Rossius, Lambot and Thiberghien from Belgium, Constante Girardengo – 'il campionissimo', a name later bestowed on Coppi – and Vincenzo Borgarello (the first Italian to win a Tour stage, in 1912), and the Swiss Oscar Egg who held the one-hour record. There were even two Australian riders who had turned up, Donald Kirkham and Ivor Munro, to ride for Phebes–Dunlop, unfortunately dubbed 'the cannibals' by the pre-PC wags of the French sporting press (another nickname which would later be revived, for the great Eddy Merckx). The two Aussies subsequently complained of foul tactics by other riders on the Marseilles–Nice stage, and were only just persuaded to remain in the race, finishing seventeenth and twentieth out of fifty-four who completed. A very strong field meant a very open race, showing that, in its twelfth year, the Tour had arrived, that bike road racing was a great sport that could hold its own with any other, and there was an exciting future for the race in the years immediately ahead.

And so, as Thys won the first stage to Le Havre ahead of Rossius, Garrigou and Girardengo, very few of those following the race, and for that matter not many Frenchmen, even noticed that day's other news, that an Austrian archduke had been assassinated in a remote Bosnian town. Only the keenest students of politics or geography had heard of Franz Ferdinand or Sarajevo, and absolutely no one knew that this distant spark would light a conflagration to change Europe for ever and – among its far more important effects – would remove the Tour from the roads of France for five years.

After a second stage to Cherbourg won by Jean Rossius, Desgrange caused some amusement by writing ironically that only 'thanks to my friend Brocco' it hadn't been monotonous – they were never friends before – and the race continued through Brittany in tropical weather: a group of riders disported themselves in a village fountain to cool off. Rossius established himself at the head of the GC, but Egg won two stages, including the huge Brest–La Rochelle stage of 470 kilometres in a numbing 16 hours 13 minutes. But as they approached the Pyrenees, the theme of the race was 'les défaillances des cracks', the eclipse of the stars, the old order giving way to the new, with Lapize only in seventh place, and Petit-Breton and Buysse forty minutes off the pace.

Despite his reputation, the super-champion Girardengo abandoned, and the Buysse brothers, Marcel and Lucien, managed to collide with each other, before the accident-prone Marcel had one more collision, with a motorbike. Lambot led over the Tourmalet, ten minutes ahead of Thys, still heading the GC, with Pélissier behind. Petit-Breton was forced out of the race with kidney trouble, and Mottiat and Deman abandoned as well.

Reaching the Alps, Thys was a handy thirty-five minutes ahead of his Peugeot team-mate Pélissier, who attacked over the Col d'Allos and then the Galibier, but was only making up time on Thys, not catching him. This Tour had the curious feature of climbing the Ballon d'Alsace twice, between Geneva and Belfort and then again between Belfort and Longwy. On the first climb Pélissier beat Thys by 2'30" but couldn't shake him off, nor on the next stages. On the penultimate stage from Longwy to Dunkirk, Thys broke his wheel, changed it with a colleague's – and then, because of an irregularity in reporting the change, was docked thirty minutes. The regulations of the Tour were becoming more complex, and would later become more complex still, but the race authorities had found the basic device of reward and punishment, *bonifications* and *pénalités*: for a meritorious achievement of any kind, so many seconds or minutes were deducted from a rider's aggregated time in the GC; for infringements, time was added.

This proved almost decisive: Pélissier began that last stage only 1'50" behind Thys in the GC. Every French fan was desperate for him to close the gap, but it was they who undid him: the crowds mobbing him and slapping his back prevented him from making an escape that would have reversed the placings. After a final sprint Thys won the Tour by a desperately narrow 1'40" from Pélissier, himself more than half an hour ahead of Alavoine and then Rossius.

Celebrations and recriminations alike were muted by the news which, by 26 July, at the end of the race, even the most politically oblivious cyclist couldn't ignore. All the while the race had been run, the crisis begun by the assassination of the Archduke Franz Ferdinand in Sarajevo had spiralled towards international hostilities. Now the Austrian army was mobilizing, and two days later would be at war with Serbia. The great French socialist leader Jean Jaurès is commemorated to this day by *rues*, *places* and *avenues* in every other town through which the Tour passes; the day after the race ended, he was assassinated as punishment for his attempt to hold back war. Soon after that, Germany declared war on France and crossed into Luxembourg before attacking Belgium, whose neutrality England had guaranteed. And so it was that, nine days after the twelfth Tour de France ended, the great powers of Europe embarked on the most terrible war in history.

Repos

Picardy

On the fourth stage of the 2002 Tour de France the peloton was wending its way from Metz towards Rheims when the television cameras picked up a haunting sight. The cyclists were riding in front of a curious background, what appeared to be a vast field of crops, unnaturally large and regular in shape. Seen closer to, this strange fruit was in a grim sense man-made: we were close to Verdun, and the backdrop to the riders was the enormous military cemetery of Verdun-Bevaux, one of very many in these parts. The dead of the Great War – Frenchmen in this case, although there are plenty of British and German cemeteries also – are laid out in immense, awful rows, the lone and level stones stretching far away.

For centuries this was the corner of the continent where Europe let its blood. To the north, the Low Countries were traditionally the 'Cockpit of Europe', but they scarcely had a less sanguinary history than the old provinces on the French side of the border, Picardy, the Île de France, Champagne and Lorraine. If anything the names of the modern departments are still more poignantly eloquent: Marne, Somme, Ardennes, all ferocious battles during the past century. The Marne was the first great battle on the Western Front, fought in 1914 only after the end of that year's Tour.

Within those weeks France had held the German army, but had suffered horrible and devastating losses. The English think in terms of the carnage of 1916 and 1917, the Somme and Passchendaele, as they think in terms of their own losses, three-quarters of a million dead, and there are plenty of reminders of those Tommies in the cemeteries of Picardy, so well tended by the War Graves Commission whose work is one of the notable British achievements of the last century. But in the fifty-one months from August 1914 to November 1918 the French lost almost twice as many men killed, from a smaller population than the British, and their casualties were appalling not only at Verdun but much earlier, in the first months, weeks, or even days of the war, while the French army pursued its suicidal doctrine of attack *à outrance*, to the bitter end, great waves of men still in their vivid blue-and-red uniforms throwing themselves at machine guns and barbed wire. French losses in the first four months of fighting exceeded British losses in four months on the Somme; and the awful figure of 19,000 British killed on 1 July 1916, the first day of that battle, is more awfully surpassed by the 27,000 French soldiers killed on 23 August 1914. Even now one cannot follow the Tour through north-western France without being conscious of that carnage.

Not all here is grim, although this north-eastern corner of the *hexagone*, where Flanders and Flemish spill over from northern Belgium, has a sort of unspoken reputation for dourness, and its virtues are reputed stolid rather than romantic. As Michelet says, 'the genius of our stout and worthy Flanders is neither subtle nor sterile, but positive and real, resting on solid foundation'. For the English, Flanders, Picardy and the neighbouring provinces form in some ways the best-travelled and the least-known part of France, past whose bleak farms and mills countless visitors have for centuries sped from Calais by carriage, train and car, on their way to the fleshpots of Paris or to the warm south. The few dedicated pilgrims who choose to come here nowadays are often battlefield tourists, looking to see where so many fell in 1815, 1916 or 1944. But Picardy and its neighbours are worth visiting apart from those morbid memories, though admittedly not for culinary reasons. The map of 'Les Étoiles' in the Michelin guide illustrates one most interesting aspect of France: the unequal distribution of culinary riches. Thick clusters of starred restaurants are found in Burgundy, Provence and above all Alsace, in sharp contrast with the near-emptiness of the north-east, broken only by the odd decent restaurant like the Meurin at Béthune which makes its nearest shot at Picard regional cuisine with Somme eels and pigs' trotters.

Such visual beauties as the region has are still impaired by war. Plenty of larger and smaller towns which found themselves in the wrong place at the wrong time were so badly shelled and fought over as to be little recognizable as their former selves. Even there not everything has gone: Cambrai, scene of epic fighting in 1917, has the splendid tomb of Rubens, and St-Quentin, another name which appears in countless memoirs of the Western Front, has fine pictures. Theirs are among the names that a visitor associates with that characteristic sight of France between Seine and Rhine, the city seen from afar, its spires and towers rising out of featureless plains, islands shimmering in the haze of the sun, or more often in the mist.

Start off in the east at Metz, very often visited by the Tour over the years since 1907, with its St-Étienne cathedral, unusually tall and light thanks to an acre and a half of stained-glass windows ranging from the twelfth century to Chagall. Directly south, and another staging place from 1905 to 1988, Nancy is one of the most beautiful eighteenth-century cities in Europe. Its exquisite assemblage of buildings, breathing the air of the Enlightenment, inappropriately saw the upbringing of that very unenlightened author Maurice Barrès, Catholic reactionary, mystical nationalist, bitter anti-Dreyfusard, and exponent of revanchism after 1871. In his book *La Colline inspirée* the inspired hill of the title is Mont Sion twenty miles south of Nancy, where a Catholic community springs up and whither, in 1873, a pilgrimage journeys to mourn the loss of Alsace and most of Lorraine; a cardinal and seven bishops bless the pilgrims 'waving their banners amongst which the crowd piously acclaimed those of Strasbourg and Metz in mourning'.

West by north-west is Verdun, visited by the Tour in 1993 when none other than Lance Armstrong won his first ever stage. It was little heard of before the Great War, and its literary memorials since then are entirely military, from Valéry's exalted salute to the 'supreme consecration' of those who died to Jules Romains's documentary novels *Prélude à Verdun* and *Verdun* with their bitter indictment of the war and the commanders who sent hundreds of thousands of *poilus* to their deaths. Directly west, and very often visited by the Tour, Rheims is a shadow of the days when the kings of France were crowned in its cathedral, the last such coronation commemorated in Rossini's frivolous and jolly opera *Il viaggio à Reims*. Alas, most of its buildings were flattened in the Great War. The cathedral itself survives, including the spire at which a German artilleryman, a cousin of the English poet Robert Graves, to whom he told the story, once took pot-shots. Thirty miles to the north-west, Laon is less well known, though for some reason it absorbed Hitler when he mused on the antiquities of France, and should be much better known, an enchanting little hill city which – or whose Bannière de France near the cathedral – provides an ideal place to stay when the Tour's own voyage to Rheims fills that city's hotels.

Most parts of France have at least some happy historic and literary memories, but when we reach the farthest northern corner, every other name carries *Undertones of War*, the name of Edmund Blunden's book, one of several classic accounts of the Western Front that shaped English consciousness of the Great War. There are also overtones of another kind of strife: the *ville-étape* of Valenciennes, and neighbouring Anzin and Denain all close to the Belgian border, are where Zola set *Germinal*, his harshest novel of class conflict.

It would be pleasant to write about a bike race without mentioning politics or war, and it would be perfectly possible, but it would also be artificial. To call the bicycle the most beneficial of inventions and cycling the most harmless of pastimes is true, but not the only truth. In 1895 a man whose name epitomizes not only literary genius but ethical high-mindedness was presented with a bicycle by the Moscow Society of Velocipede Lovers. The 67-year-old Tolstoy dismayed his more pompous disciples by his sheer zest for the new machine: 'I feel that I am entitled to my share of natural light-heartedness, that the opinion of others has no importance, and that there is nothing wrong with enjoying oneself quite simply, like a boy.' It was a touching tribute from the spirit of noble humanity to a lovely new creation; and yet there was more to cycling than boyish light-heartedness and plain living, even in Tolstoy's time.

As cycling became the passion of the age, it was linked with more than one of the new species of mass politics that were also sweeping Europe, predominantly the progressive sort. Before cycling had acquired any definite radical tinge in France, it had done so in England, closely associated with the first generation of Fabian socialists, Bernard Shaw, H. G. Wells and the Webbs. Shaw was a remarkably clumsy cyclist, who recorded 'the stiffness, the blisters, the bruises, the pains in every twisted muscle,' though vowing that 'I will not be beaten by that hellish machine'. His friend Bertrand Russell sardonically recorded how Shaw and he had collided with a vehemence worthy of two Tour riders, 'with such force that he was hurled through the air and landed on his back twenty feet from the place of collision. However he got up completely unhurt and continued his ride; whereas my bicycle was smashed.' Shaw jeered at him all the way home, Russell said: 'I suspect that he regarded the whole incident as proof of the virtues of vegetarianism.' And Wells, their fellow progressive, looked back forty years later on the early cyclist's sense 'of masterful adventure, that has gone from him altogether now'.

In Yorkshire, Lancashire and London, cycling was a particular enthusiasm of the cheerful young socialist clerks and artisans who read William Morris and Daniel George, as well as Robert Blatchford's magazine *Clarion* and his book *Merry England*. A *Clarion* Cycling Club founded for these ardent spirits was celebrated in touchingly fusty Merry English:

> Knights of the whirring wheel are we
> And whither are ye wending, pray?
> We are on the road to Arcady.

So deep did the love of the whirring wheel run among London socialists that Sidney Webb had to suggest in his sour and unsmiling way that 'Readers of the *Clarion* may or may not care to give up a few bicycle rides to help canvas for the LCC elections'. A generation later, cycling was one of the pastimes *Left News* intended when it told its readers that 'even games, songs and recreation can, and indeed should, reflect and awaken a left-wing attitude to things,' a simple sport that can be 'quite different when your companions are "comrades of the left"'.

But it wasn't only a left-wing attitude that cycling could awaken; the wheel also whirred on the other political side. It is chilling to record that, as a new tide of anti-Semitism flowed through central Europe in the 1890s, the very first body or association to have excluded Jews from membership was an Austrian cycling club. This was a dark intimation of what was to come, and of the way that sport would be relentlessly politicized and exploited by the new nationalism. Morally pleasing as the bike can often seem, it wasn't quite untainted even in its early days. Those young idealists of the *Clarion* were, like all other cyclists at the turn of the century, riding on tyres of rubber gathered in one of the worst places of its or any other age, the heart of darkness that was the Congo 'Free State'.

A different kind of idealist hoped that sport would provide a means of uniting mankind in brotherly love, a hope not always fulfilled. In England playing games had been specifically identified, not with nationalism in a continental sense, but with team spirit, and thus with the duties of an imperial caste; a process inevitably associated with the public schools that so rapidly expanded in size and number during the century before 1914. Schoolmasters were explicit about this. Edward Lyttelton of Eton thought that 'a boy is disciplined by athletics by being free to put the welfare of the common cause before selfish interests and to obey implicitly the word of command and act in concert with the heterogeneous elements in the company he belongs to', a most dubious description of team games as played at English schools, or anywhere else, but a significant one. Another master made a still more telling contrast: 'You may think that games occupy a disproportionate share of the boy's mind. You may be thankful that it is so. What do French boys talk about?' to which one answer might have been that at least some of the time they thought about football and bicycles, as well as all that horrible manner of things intended by that master, who could not have known of James Thurber and 'Six-Day Bicycle Racing as a Sex Substitute'.

More explicitly still, J. E. Welldon, the headmaster of Harrow, saw sport not merely as a sex substitute or a means of making a common cause but a way of building a warrior elite: 'The pluck, the energy, the perseverance, the good temper, the self-control, the discipline, the co-operation, the *esprit de corps*, which merit success in cricket and football, are the very qualities which win the day in peace or war.' In the history of the British Empire, he believed, England had owed her strength to her sports. This will be smiled at today, and it wasn't a sentiment universally shared even at the time. Radicals pointed out that the British Empire had not, in fact, been won by 'playing up and playing the game'.

On the other hand, the greatest bard of empire himself angrily claimed that his countrymen had been softened by 'trinkets', and allowed their souls to be contented by 'the flanelled fools at the wicket or the muddied oafs at the goals'. At the time, Kipling's words were bitterly resented. 'The unmanly envy and immoral calumnies of Continental slander' were bad enough, one critic indignantly wrote; they had now been provided 'with fresh materials for insidious and cowardly campaign of aspersion of England and the British Empire'. And the headmaster of Loretto, the most sporting of Edinburgh public schools, said just as angrily that three-quarters of his old boys who had volunteered to fight in the Boer War had previously played for the school rugby XV.

Nor was this cult of sporting, civic and military virtue by any means purely English. In 1883, on his way to the epiphany that would see him create the modern Olympics, the Frenchman Baron Pierre de Coubertin visited Rugby school and fell on his knees before the tomb of Dr Arnold, creator of the school as it now was. Although he had not, in fact, been an uncritical admirer of the religion of games, Arnold stood in Coubertin's eyes for the athletic ideal. Here, in the 'régime arnoldien', was a model for France, by which Coubertin's fallen country could be 'rebronzed' after the humiliation of defeat by Prussia in 1871, to which end he thought that French schools should take up cricket and rugby. And another unlikely convert was Theodor Herzl, founder of Zionism, who hoped that in the Jewish State of his dreams the boys would likewise be brought up on English manly sports. Like those schoolmasters, the sporting Anglophiles are easy to scoff at, but they won victories of a kind. Despite M. Godart of the École Monge in Paris, whom Coubertin persuaded to teach his boys cricket; and despite a few cricket clubs even now in Haifa and Tel Aviv, the game of Dr Grace did not catch on as they had hoped. But both the French and the Israelis play soccer fanatically, and the French play rugby too.

In reply to his critics, Kipling said that it wasn't sport in itself he objected to when he wrote of flannelled fools and muddied oafs, so much as professionalism, the jumped-up members of the lower classes who were now paid too much to hit or kick a ball, and, what was worse, the loafers who paid to watch them. This was a prejudice he shared with Robert Baden-Powell, founder of the Boy Scouts, who thought that games were grand 'for developing a lad physically and morally', teaching him to play with unselfishness, 'to play in his place and "play the game"', but that 'games were vicious' when drawing crowds 'to be merely onlookers at a few paid performers . . . Thousands of boys and young men, pale, narrow-chested, hunched up, miserable specimens, smoking endless cigarettes, numbers of them betting, all of them learning to be hysterical as they groan and cheer and panic in unison.'

That was a description he would doubtless have applied to the men in any café in France when the Tour was being run, and a comparable prejudice against proletarian professional sportsmen could be found in France also, though mitigated by the republican traditions of equality and fraternity. Rugby had been introduced to south-western France by English businessmen, notably in the wine trade, to become the national sport of Gascony, and France joined the 'home countries' in an international championship, though the players of Brive and Dax and Pau were artisans and farmers rather than the public-school men who played for Blackheath and Harlequins. The question of professionalism simmered quietly away, to come to the boil in the 1930s. But no one expected all cyclists to be amateurs; for all those aristocrats or prosperous bourgeois who were seen racing earlier, a distinction between 'Gentlemen and Players' would have seemed far-fetched on the Tour.

In 1914 gentlemen and players alike, amateurs and pros, muddied oafs and flannelled fools, footballers and cyclists, all gave a dramatic answer to their detractors, entirely confirming what

Welldon and Herzl alike had believed. Across Europe football players and football fans joined up, while officers were told to learn news of their men's home teams, something cheerful to talk about when a soldier lay mortally wounded. Sport provided a higher form of comradeship across the battlefield: at Christmas 1914 an unofficial truce saw British and German soldiers come out of their trenches to play football together. Rugby football justified every hope that sporting patriots had ever reposed in its manly qualities, to an extraordinary degree. From among those who had played for the four home countries of England, Wales, Scotland and Ireland, no fewer than seventy-nine former internationals were killed in the Great War, thirty of them Scots.

And the Tour de France had its own roll of honour, in its way statistically remarkable, which likewise showed that heroes in the field of athletic contest could be heroes on the field of battle also. When the war began, Desgrange had himself joined up, though at fifty he was too old for active service, and in his pages he violently beat the drum for 'le grand match' to be played on the battlefield:

> My lads! My dearest lads! My lads of France. Listen to me! In the fourteen years that the *Auto* has appeared daily, it has never given you bad advice. Well, listen to me! Believe me, it isn't possible for a Frenchman to succumb to a German. You have a big match to play . . . Go without pity. The Prussians are bastards . . . When your bayonet is in their chest, they will beg for mercy. Don't give it to them. Drive it home without pity!

Whether or not influenced by these histrionics, extreme even by the standards of August 1914, the cyclists of the Tour did rally to the colours to fight and to fall. Of the ten men who had won the Tour from 1903 to 1914, three died in the war. François Faber was the first to go. The Luxembourger, whose little country had been overrun by the Germans at the beginning of the war, enlisted in the French Foreign Legion and was killed carrying a wounded comrade at Carency in May 1915. The 'Little Breton' from the Argentine, Lucien Petit-Breton, was serving at the front when he died in an automobile accident in June 1917. Octave Lapize became an airman, flew with the same dash and bravery that he had once shown on a bike, and was killed in combat over Verdun in the same month. They were only the most illustrious names. Among other riders who died, not all of whom have been traced, were several old sweats of the Tour, the young rider Georges Cadolle, and the brilliant Emile Engel, who had come tenth in 1910 and had won the Cherbourg–Brest stage in 1914. In Ringmer church, near Glyndebourne in Sussex, there is a little memorial to the men of the local cricket club who fell in the Great War. There are their three names, and the words, 'They played the game.' Those men of the Tour had also played *le match* as Desgrange had hoped.

All were part of the great blood sacrifice that Europe offered up. Peace would return, and the Tour with it, but no bike racing ever run in this part of France would ever be quite so innocent again, amid the blasted earth, the ossuaries, the vast memorials of Picardy and Lorraine. Nor would France be the same, a country that eighty-five years later is still scarred by the catastrophe of those years.

3

Braves Belges

1919–1924

'Everyone suddenly burst out singing,' when the guns fell silent, Siegfried Sassoon wrote, but that was sadly far from the truth. Europe was prostrate and despairing, in mourning for its millions of young men, so weakened nervously as well as physically that a Spanish flu virus could sweep through the continent just as the war had ended and kill another 20 million. And few countries were as sombre as France, much of whose land was devastated, whose coffers had been emptied, and a million and a half of whose men had been killed.

As soon as the war ended, Paris seemed a city of light again, its cultural life flowering once more with amazing vigour, in art, music and letters. Gide and Proust – whose *À l'ombre des jeunes filles en fleur* was published in 1919 – had been joined by the young Raymond Radiguet and Jean Cocteau, and a new school of composers had sprung up, graced above all by Poulenc. Before long, English and American lotus-eaters would find in Paris the moveable feast of hedonistic frolicking recorded for posterity by Hemingway.

And yet the mood of Paris, and of France as a whole, was very far from the gaiety of *Le Diable au corps*, *Le Boeuf sur le toit*, 'Les Six' and *The Sun Also Rises*. Or maybe that manic celebration spoke for itself about the horror and despair it tried to conceal. Every street in every city, every town and village in the country, still counted its dead. Across Europe war memorials were built, deeply revealing of different national moods. In defeated but defiant Germany, the memorials were exalted and aggressive, with strident martial figures angrily looking to the future, and by implication looking for revenge, often above the chilling words 'Not one too many died for the Fatherland'. In England memorials were startling in their realism, every boot, buckle and helmet captured as if the memory must never be lost. And in France the overwhelming mood is one of sorrow, a desolate Marianne grieving for her lost sons. A most moving example of that exalted grief, and an extraordinary piece of folk art, is found in the church at Valloire nestling in the shadow of the Col du Galibier; I visited the church just after the Tour had crossed the great pass. Next to the altar is a painting in truly naive style, showing the battlefield of Verdun where a dying soldier receives the last rites from his chaplain while the Blessed Virgin looks down. In one other little town near Anjou, grief is mixed with anger on a memorial whose inscription – 'À nos chers enfants. Maudite soit la guerre' (To our dear sons. Accursed be war) – caused bitter controversy, and might even help to explain what happened in 1940. France was far from a happy country when the guns fell silent.

For Henri Desgrange, this was his greatest challenge, and it proved his finest hour. Conditions were severe throughout France, but in the north and east they were desperate, hundreds of square miles of broken landscape where the front lines had been, thousands of miles of roads in barely passable condition, tens of thousands of cars and motorbikes still under military requisition, many hotels still occupied by the army, not to speak of the millions of *poilus* who, as 1919 began, had not yet been demobilized. During a war when armies had raised bicycle battalions and used cyclists as messengers, racing bikes had scarcely been the manufacturers' first priority. There was a shortage of bikes, and an even more acute shortage of tyres. It could not have been a less propitious time to begin the great contest again, let alone make important changes, but that is what Desgrange now did.

We have seen how much he had always disliked the influence of the bike-makers and the operation of the team system, and now he took the new beginning of the Tour as an opportunity to suppress those teams, and what proved to be a final and forlorn attempt to make the Tour an individual competition. Cyclists would compete as single riders, categorized A or B, and they would compete strictly on their own account: no cyclist could help another. Feeding would now be provided by the race officials rather than laid on by teams or foraged for by the riders.

And during the course of the 1919 Tour there was to be one other innovation, a stroke of genius that gave a phrase to the language. Newspapers, mostly but not only sporting papers, were often printed on coloured newsprint: the *Sporting Times*, with its mixture of racing news, reactionary opinions and dirty jokes, was known in every club and mess in the British Empire as 'the Pink Un'. The *Auto* was the yellow un, and its colour would soon be famous far away from France.

At 4 p.m. on 28 June 1919 a huge crowd at Versailles greeted the news that Germany had accepted, without much choice, the terms imposed by the peace conference that had been convened in Paris for months past; a treaty intended to bring eternal peace to Europe. Just eleven hours later, at 3 a.m. on 29 June, and a few miles away at the Parc des Princes, the field of sixty-nine riders, forty-four classified in category A, departed on the thirteenth Tour de France. The field had been severely depleted by the toll of war and by the five-year interruption in cycling. Many old names had departed, and there were as yet few new names to make up: Robert Jacquinot was one, and Francis Pélissier another, making his pro debut to join his brother Henri with striking fraternal success.

After Henri had won the second stage to Cherbourg, Francis won the third stage, to Brest, with the elder holding the GC lead ahead of Christophe. But Desgrange's idea that combinations and tactical alliances could be removed from the Tour was always an impossibility. The peloton now ganged up on the brothers, and when Henri and Francis tried to get back at the field, it was they who were officially rebuked for collusion; when the third stage reached Les Sables d'Olonne, the brothers abandoned in protest, impulsively and sourly: 'Tout le monde est contre nous.'

The race was the longest to date, 5560 kilometres, with one enormous 482-kilometre stage from Les Sables to Bayonne; what with that and the state of the roads, the field was rapidly reduced. After the Pyrenees, where Honoré Barthélémy gave a fine climbing performance, there were only sixteen riders left, two of them, Jules Nempon and Aloi's Verstraeten, in the new category B, and Verstraeten was disqualified before Montpellier for grabbing a lift. Other casualties included Emile Masson, winner of the Tour of Belgium, who pulled out after a fall. Barthélémy was brilliant again in the Alps, winning the stages to Grenoble and Geneva, although there was also a fine display in both mountain ranges by Luigi Lucotti, an Italian rider almost unknown in his own country let alone in France.

When the remaining riders left Metz on the antepenultimate stage, he was twenty-eight minutes behind Christophe in the GC; that is to say behind the man now wearing the *maillot jaune*. As Desgrange liked to tell it, this hadn't been planned before the race but had come to him as an inspiration while it was being run. On any given day, one rider held the lead in the race, although he was not always, or even often, to be seen at the head of proceedings as the field rode by. If he could be marked out so that no spectator could fail to see him, it would add to the thrill of the race. It would add a new lustre to the leader himself. And it would be a brilliant promotional coup for the paper.

Desgrange telegraphed to Paris to ask for jerseys to be run up in the *Auto*'s distinctive yellow. The race had reached Grenoble, whose civic virtue and spirit of equality Michelet extolled: 'Bonaparte knew Grenoble well when he selected it for his first stage on his return from Elba: he sought to restore the empire through the republic.' Maybe Desgrange knew Grenoble well when he chose to award the first yellow jersey there to Christophe, a man who had ridden his first Tour in 1906 and who had been so unlucky in 1913. If only the jersey had brought him better luck now. On that stage from Metz to Dunkirk he crashed and once again broke his front fork. This time a workshop was nearer to hand, but he still had to carry out his own repairs, and lost more than an hour.

But he had a unique place in the history of the Tour, and Desgrange had pulled off a coup on a scale he could not possibly have envisaged. Very soon the *maillot jaune* had entered the language, or languages: yellow jersey, *maglia gialla*, *gelbes Trikot*. Other jerseys adorned the race. Former French national champions were allowed their purple jersey with tricoloured sash during the Tour, and World Champions their rainbow jersey, although not always to general gratification: later on, a cycling superstition developed that a rainbow jersey in a team brought bad luck, like a woman in a boat.

In the fullness of time the Tour added other jerseys of its own, green for the leader on points, 'red peas' for the *meilleur grimpeur* or King of the Mountains, white for best younger rider. And at the end of every stage today there is a faintly comical ritual when the day's leader in each category steps up to the rostrum to be kissed by a couple of pretty girls, to receive a bunch of flowers, and to don his garment. Somewhat absurdly, this 'jersey' is now purely for show rather than to be worn, not a pulled-over-the-head jersey as was the original *maillot jaune* Christophe wore, not a light yellow blouse zipped up the front which the GC leader actually wears now on the road, but a symbolic vestment, opening at the back like a straitjacket for ease in slipping on and, once the ceremony is over, off again. Later the other great three-week races would follow suit, with the *maglia rosa* or pink jersey for the leader in the Giro d'Italia, and the gold jersey in the Vuelta a España. But none of the others has ever achieved the special *réclame* of the one introduced in 1919. Today, when a publishing imprint specializes in sports books, it naturally calls itself the Yellow Jersey Press; when a great historian like Richard Cobb collected his essays under the title *Tour de France*, a critic praising him could instinctively say that 'in his own field there's no doubt who wears the *maillot jaune*'. It remains the greatest of all cycling trophies, maybe the greatest of all sporting prizes.

For all of his being the first man in the jersey, a succession of punctures for Christophe on the last stage to the Parc meant that he finished third, behind Jean Alavoine in second and a distinctly lucky Firmin Lambot as winner, an able and thoughtful rider, if one more admired than loved. He continued the Belgian dominance, and the years to come showed that he wasn't an unworthy winner. But Christophe remained, at least until the advent of Poulidor forty years later, the saddest of all Tour riders, the unluckiest, the best cyclist who never won.

By the following year, the best place that French riders could manage was eighth, with Jean Alavoine, Henri Pélissier and Christophe all falling by the wayside, and 1920 saw Belgian dominance become complete supremacy. Belgians won twelve of the fifteen stages, and the first seven places on the podium. In New York Carpentier beat the American boxer Lewinsky (no kin of 'that woman' whose exploits electrified the world seventy-eight years later, so far as can be established); in the Antwerp Olympics Suzanne Lenglen won a tennis gold medal; and in Dublin the French rugby XV beat Ireland 15–7 to win its first ever away match. These were consolation prizes of a sort for a France whose cyclists certainly needed consoling, undone as they were by every kind of woe, self-inflicted or otherwise.

First of their big names out of the race was Alavoine, who suffered no fewer than ten punctures on the first day. Christophe was laid low, like Petit-Breton before him, by kidney trouble, Bellenger collapsed after drinking icy water in the Pyrenees. It was there that the Belgians took control of the race, after Pélissier had won two western stages, to Brest and Les Sables. But he was penalized in a curious incident, accused of having thrown an inner tube on to the road, and left the race in fury. Unforgiving as ever, Desgrange said that Pélissier 'does not know how to suffer, and he will never win the Tour'. Not for the first time, the *patron*'s words would return to haunt him.

After three Belgian riders, Firmin Lambot, Philippe Thys and Jean Rossius, had dominated in the Pyrenees, the Belgians remained in control through the Midi and over the Alps. If nothing else, Barthélémy showed that he certainly knew how to suffer. On the Perpignan–Aix-en-Provence stage he had a gruesome fall, broke his shoulder and dislocated his wrist. In later years he would never have been allowed to continue, but in those tougher days he was back in the saddle and finished eighth overall, the best of the French. It was still a Belgian triumph, with Thys becoming the first rider to win the Tour three times, 57'21" ahead of Hector Heusghem and then their compatriots, Lambot, Léon Scieur and Masson. But it was Barthélémy who was carried shoulder-high by the patriotic throng in the Parc des Princes on 25 July.

Another sport, English Thoroughbred racing, is rich in worldly-wise maxims – 'Always trust the handicapper on top of the ground', 'Back a two-year-old until it's beaten and then back the horse that beat it' – which look clever when they come true, and are forgotten when not. 'Fourth in the Guineas, first in the Derby' is another old saw that occasionally looks good; and in the 1921

Tour de France, 'Fourth last year, first this' proved the way to bet. The pattern of the race was much as in the preceding years, anticlockwise through Normandy, Brittany and Gascony to the mountains, although stopping at the great Mediterranean naval port of Toulon for the first time since 1905.

Once again the Belgians were in charge from the beginning, with Mottiat taking the first stage to Le Havre. After the French rider Romain Bellenger won into Cherbourg, Léon Scieur, who had been fourth a year earlier, took the yellow jersey, and held it for the rest of the race. Scieur reinforced his position in a duel with Lucotti over the Aubisque, but fared less well on the next Pyrenean stage to Luchon, suffering a bad fall and barely holding the lead from poor Barthélémy, who had done his best to recover from a calamitous first day when he had punctured eleven times. The whole race was cursed by silex, flints that saw twenty riders get through eighty tyres on the second day. Some Tour officials blamed the quality of tyres, but the quality of the roads, still in the shadow of war, is as likely to have been the cause.

This was the year when Alphonse Baugé, head of La Sportive, the consortium for which Scieur rode, named the great mountain climbs 'les Juges de la Paix', after the magistrates who sternly adjudicate in French commercial cases; and the judges of peace were not merciful in this race. Both ranges were ridden in intense heat, which slowed the field over the Alpine stages. Goethals won a sprint finish into Geneva, after Barthélémy had led narrowly over the Galibier. Asked whether Bayonne–Luchon or Grenoble–Geneva was the tougher stage, he said that, although the Galibier wasn't child's play, it seemed easy compared with the five successive southern passes ridden under a scorching sun: 'C'est indigeste' – it's hard to stomach.

The stage to Strasbourg was won by Henri Pélissier with Heusghem on his wheel and the others forty-two minutes behind. Desgrange now announced one more arbitrary innovation: to try and enliven the pace, lower-placed riders would leave two hours ahead of the leaders. With this change in place the last two stages were won by Goethals again, but Scieur finished the Tour a handy 18'36" ahead of Heusghem.

The winner was a 32-year-old protégé of Lambot, and like him came from Florennes. An agricultural labourer who had never ridden a bike until he was twenty-two, Scieur had turned professional just before the war, and taken fourteenth place in the 1914 Tour. Garlanded with flowers, he accepted his victory with becoming modesty: 'In Florennes, you know, it'll be quite something that Léon has won the Tour de France.'

In Paris it was quite something that French riders had had one more disappointing Tour. The angry Pélissier brothers were in excellent form away from the great race, Francis winning the French championship, Henri beating Francis in the Paris–Roubaix, while Christophe won the Bordeaux–Paris. But none of them made any showing in the Tour, and the best French performance came from Barthélémy in third with all his indigestion. National failure inflamed Desgrange, who lambasted the riders for having feebly surrendered to Scieur.

And still the French couldn't get back onto the winner's podium in 1922. This was despite a fine performance by Jean Alavoine, who finished runner-up thirteen years after his third place in 1909, and a touch of heroism from Christophe, now aged almost forty, who won the yellow jersey into Les Sables d'Olonne and held the lead over the Pyrenees. But again fortune didn't favour the brave. In the mountains, Honoré Barthélémy had a terrifying fall, arse-over-tip off a small bridge to drop twenty feet into the icy stream below, but he managed to continue as far as Briançon before abandoning. There were several impressive breakaways, from Jacquinot on the first stage and from Alavoine thirteen minutes clear over the Aspin.

In an extravagant contrast to the previous year's heatwave, the Tourmalet was still snowbound and had to be bypassed. There were two 'stage hat-tricks': Alavoine won three on the trot to Bayonne, Luçon and Perpignan, and Thys won into Toulon, Nice and Briançon. The last town was being visited for the first time, in place of Grenoble, and at the end of a stage which included the new – and, according to the riders, monstrous – Col d'Izoard. In all, Thys won five stages, but he was plagued by acute toothache and finished the race well down the field. Scieur had abandoned early with a broken fork, the very misfortune that had befallen Christophe twice before. 'Jamais deux sans trois,' the saying goes, and this time Christophe was on the Galibier when his fork broke, and he came down the great pass on foot. Mishaps of one sort or another continued, with Alavoine puncturing six times on the stage to Metz. As Portier said of this race, 'On conjugua, à tous les temps, le verbe crever' – the verb 'puncture' had to be continually used in all its forms – and one more crash removed Barthélémy.

By Strasbourg the yellow jersey had passed from Jacquinot, Christophe and Alavoine to Hector Heusghem, runner-up for the last two years, who now thought he had victory in his sights. But he damaged his bike in a tumble and borrowed another without obtaining official confirmation that his was unusable. For this technical infringement he was docked an hour, and it cost him the race: his compatriot Lambot reached Paris to win his second Tour, a back-to-back victory for Florennes, and the seventh win in succession for Belgium, which provoked bleats of 'we was robbed' in the French press. It was true that Jean Alavoine seemed desperately unlucky: he had forty-six punctures in all and his chain came loose fifteen times. But the roads were the same for all, and, if nothing else, the Tour taught the nursery lesson that life isn't fair. It was also true that Lambot had achieved the apparently tricky feat of winning the Tour without winning a single stage, just as it's possible to win without ever wearing the yellow jersey until the final podium.

Though that might seem obscure, the mathematical principle is simple enough. In a three-week road race, twenty different stages might in theory be won by twenty different riders, with a rider called Dupont second at a minute in each, in which case Dupont will certainly be the overall winner on accumulated time. Or Dupont might, again in theory, work his way up the GC to win on the last stage without having worn the jersey. Or he might take the GC lead and the jersey and then lose the lead, or hold it to the end, in either case without winning another stage. Or he might win the race without either wearing the yellow jersey or winning a stage. To be sure, the scoring and regulations for the Tour are of terrifying complexity, but the possibilities here outlined are not arcane in themselves, not even President Bush's 'fuzzy math', just straightforward arithmetic that stems from the nature of the race.

Less than two weeks after the 1922 Tour ended, Italy erupted. The previous autumn the sometime left-wing socialist Benito Mussolini had proclaimed himself Duce or Leader of the newly formed Fascists, and saviour of his country from Bolshevism. By August he seemed to make good his claim when a Communist-led strike in Milan was ferociously broken by Fascists, who then in October set off to march on Rome. It looked a piece of opera buffa at first, but there was nothing comical in the outcome when Mussolini took supreme power, to the delight of many Italians, and the horror of many others. The latter included a young artisan, a carpenter or bricklayer or horse-dealer – he was vague about his background – and part-time cyclist called Ottavio Bottecchia.

For two years the Pélissier brothers had ridden in many races wearing jerseys of French champions, but they hadn't ridden in the Tour since Desgrange had dismissed Henri as a man who would never win the race because he didn't know how to suffer. But they were both back in the starting line-up of 139 riders in 1923, and Desgrange was about to be made to look silly as well as insulting. While the field was once again thinned by punctures, Jacquinot won the first stage to Le Havre, and the next was won by Bottecchia, of whom few fans had then heard but who was to be the revelation of this Tour, and the first Italian to win the yellow jersey. He autographed his *maillot jaune* and loyally gave it to Henri Pélissier, his Automoto team leader, and the gesture seemed to do the trick: Pélissier won the next stage to Brest.

Alavoine dominated the Pyrenean stages, though as much through luck as skill. The unfortunate Jacquinot rode brilliantly over the Tourmalet to take a ten-minute lead at the summit and then increased his lead up the Peyresourde in fierce sun, until he suddenly swayed on his bike and keeled over into a ditch where he groaned, 'I'm dying . . . I've had it.' Alavoine shouted sympathetic words as he passed, and Jacquinot called back 'Gars Jean, je te salue!' (roughly speaking, 'Come on, Jean, my son'), but Alavoine took advantage to win the stage, with Henri Pélissier far behind and fuming after he had been knocked down by a car.

Luck deserted Alavoine in the Alps, when he had a bad crash descending the Izoard. Told by the doctors to abandon, he said bitterly and understandably that fate was against him: 'I'll never win a Tour, never. It's all over.' It was on this stage that Henri Pélissier seized the advantage, distancing Bottecchia by half an hour, and then won the next stage also, crossing the Galibier and the Allos ahead of his brother who loyally supported him throughout. Henri hung on to the lead until Paris, where an ecstatic crowd greeted the first Frenchman to win in twelve years.

There were others who could be accounted winners. Conveniently forgetting what he had said before about Pélissier, Desgrange was at his fruitiest in greeting him: the stage win to Briançon had been achieved with 'the beautiful regularity and classicism of the works of Racine'. The *patron* could afford to be gracious. More confident than ever, and carrying a new daily column on the Tour, 'Avec eux sur la grande-route' by the future stage director Henri Decoin, the *Auto* saw its circulation shoot up to 600,000, and on Monday, 23 July 1923, the day after the Tour ended, sales broke through the million mark. After twenty years, the Tour had wholly justified its original *raison d'être* as a money-making device for the paper, and although Desgrange liked to speak grandiosely of the honour of the Tour, he might in honesty have quoted the regular and classical Racine: 'Sans argent l'honneur n'est qu'une maladie.'

Riders had been divided into First and Second classes from 1920; in 1923 a new class of *touristes-routiers* had been introduced, independent riders outside the team organization, some of them real freelancers, semi-pros who turned up in Paris on the off-chance of competing. In that year also a new bonus system modified the scoring, with an additional two minutes for the winner of each stage, increased to three minutes in 1925. These innovations helped to change the character of the Tour, along with one other more important change in 1923, by which riders could now replace damaged parts of a bike rather than carry out repairs single-handed as before, like Christophe in his forge.

All of these details paled by comparison with the arrival of a truly great cyclist. After winning the Tour Pélissier had said simply of the runner-up, 'Bottecchia will succeed me.' He did so a year later, in quite dramatic style, and in circumstances Pélissier most definitely did not envisage. Bottecchia won the first stage of the 1924 Tour from Paris to Le Havre, and the last stage back to Paris from Dunkirk four weeks later. Far more to the point, he wore the yellow jersey throughout the race, from the first evening in Le Havre. This start-to-finish feat would be matched by Nicolas Frantz in 1928 and Romain Maes in 1935, but never since then.

At Coutances, on the third stage from Cherbourg to Brest, the Pélissier brothers abandoned melodramatically along with their team-mate Maurice Ville, with Henri only three minutes behind Bottecchia. The occasion was trivial or even ludicrous, on all sides. For the long night-time stages Desgrange issued each rider with two official jerseys. After the sun rose and began to warm him, Henri Pélissier took off one jersey and threw it aside.

This was seen by people following in the 'caravan', who reported Pélissier to the commissaires; an official took the opportunity when he finished to lift his jersey and check whether he was wearing another; Pélissier was enraged and demanded an apology. Failing to receive it, he rode as far as Coutances where he, his brother and Ville ostentatiously dismounted and sat at a café and watched the rest of the field go by.

Although that jersey question seems footling by today's standards, some of Henri Pélissier's other foibles weren't so trivial, and anticipated later tendencies all too exactly. He was, it was recorded, a veritable mobile pharmacy – far from the last time that phrase would be heard on the Tour – who carried in his jersey pocket aspirin for his migraine, chloroform for his knees, and a bottle of cocaine 'for his eyes'. The fact was that many if not most of the riders were by now using stimulants of one sort or another. Various narcotics that would later be seen as evil poison were not then even illegal. And if Pélissier took cocaine, for his eyes or otherwise, he had at least that in common with both Sherlock Holmes and Sigmund Freud.

His departure was nevertheless a setback Desgrange could have done without. The *Auto* accused the trio of deserting the Tour 'on an incomprehensible whim', though it also – under the headline 'C'est embêtant' – extended an open invitation to Pélissier to give his side of the story. He did just that, but not to Desgrange. The muck-raking journalist Albert Londres was writing for the *Petit Parisien* and befriended the trio, whose version he luridly reported, with Henri saying 'I'm called Pélissier, not Azor' (the name commonly given by French families to pet dogs). Londres compared the Tour with the last story he had covered, the penal colony on Devil's Island where Dreyfus had once been sent: the riders were the 'forçats de la route', convicts of the road.

After all these alarums and excursions, the rest of the race was almost an anticlimax. Bottecchia crushed the field in the Pyrenees, crossing the Aubisque almost five minutes ahead of

Frantz, and then took the Tourmalet and Aspin. Frantz turned the tables in the Alps, winning stages to Gex and Strasbourg after conquering the Col de Vars and the Col d'Izoard, but it wasn't enough to stop Bottecchia, who had a comfortable lead of more than half an hour over Frantz when they reached Paris. Some of the gilt was taken off Bottecchia's victory by the aggregate time: at an average speed of 22.89 k.p.h. (14.85 m.p.h.) it was the slowest Tour ever run.

And it was overshadowed also when the Olympic Games opened in Paris ten days after the Tour finished. This was the 'Chariots of Fire' Olympics, in which Eric Liddell switched from the 100 metres to 400 metres to avoid competing on a Sunday, Harold Abrahams won the 100 metres, and both were eclipsed by Paavo Nurmi, the 'Flying Finn', who won five gold medals, all despite the intense heat (the 40-kilometre cross-country was run in a temperature of more than 40°C, nearly 110°F, and half the field failed to finish).

If it had been an unsatisfactory Tour, Bottecchia proved all the same a great and ultimately tragic champion. French fans and journalists had been sniffy about this obscure but self-confident Italian, who had asked for trouble when he said that 'You don't have to be any good' to win bike races. He had showed them better. There was one footnote to the 1924 Tour that seemed trivial at the time and might have been entirely forgotten. Bottecchia had been stalked, in later parlance, by a female fan who was evidently obsessed by him. Whether or not he was really serious, he seemed to show some interest in her; whether seriously or not, Henri Pélissier said that he feared for Bottecchia's life, if the business came to bother his jealous wife. There was more to it than a potential spot of adultery. Bottecchia was known to be a socialist and an opponent of Mussolini. On several occasions during this Tour he had found his bike with the tyres flat, and he had found a threatening note one day denouncing him as an 'anti-Fascist'. He may have shrugged it off, but it was a sinister omen.

4

Convicts of the Road

1925-1929

By the 1920s sport had become more than ever a ruling passion
in advanced or capitalist countries, so much so that some mal-
contents saw it as the new opiate of the people. For one British
Communist, Jack Cohen, sport was 'one of the strongest ideo-
logical weapons of the bourgeoisie', for another, Palme Dutt, it
was 'dope to distract the workers from the struggle'; and they
might just have had a point. Certainly the people were distracted.
In America this was the decade of Babe Ruth, the greatest baseball player there had ever been and maybe there ever would be,
while in England it saw the last flowering of Jack Hobbs: in the
summer of 1925 he scored a record 14 centuries in a season and
surpassed Grace's 126 in all. Stern moralists continued to frown
at professionalism and lament the way its standards could corrupt
amateur sport, as seemed to happen that January, when for the
first time ever a player – the New Zealand captain Cyril
Brownlie – was sent off for foul play in a rugby international.
Amateurism still had its heroes and heroines, some risible, like the
Oxford crew who sank in the 1925 Boat Race; some exalted,

like the now aged Baron Pierre de Coubertin, who finally retired this year as chairman of the International Olympic Committee; and some glamorous, like the two French players who won the singles titles at Wimbledon, René Lacoste (of alligator-embroidered sportswear ill-fame) and Suzanne Lenglen.

For France the tennis players' victories were a much-needed balm, since French cyclists would remain conspicuous by their absence from the winner's podium in the Tour for the rest of the decade, during which lustrum the race was won by an Italian, by two Belgians, and twice by a Luxembourger. In 1925 not only did Bottecchia win his back-to-back victory, there were, as the year before, no French names in the first five. Bottecchia only narrowly failed to repeat his feat of wearing the yellow jersey from start to finish after winning it on the first stage to Le Havre. He yielded the lead to the Belgian Adelin Benoit in Brest after the third stage, won it back in Bayonne, yielded it again for a day but then took the lead in the next gruelling stage to Perpignan, ridden in driving rain.

If French riders were to come back, it would have to be the Pélissier brothers, riding for Automoto–Hutchinson, but they both abandoned, Henri following a crash, Francis after he had unsuccessfully chased Bottecchia over the Aubisque, and their team-mate Thys left the race as well. More frightful weather made the Nice–Briançon stage tougher than ever, but even though his compatriot Bartolomeo Aimo won the stage and took ten minutes off him, Bottecchia was still in control, and remained so to the Parc des Princes, where there was a dramatic sprint finish in which Romain Bellenger was squeezed out by two Italians, Aimo, who came third, and Bottecchia, who won the Tour by fifty-four minutes from Buysse. Those last moments summed up a race in which Bellenger had been the only Frenchman to win a stage.

That year's Tour had seen a modification of the *parcours* (the race distance), with shorter stages and more of them, eighteen in all; the 1926 race had one stage fewer, but it was the longest ever run in the history of the Tour at an enormous 5745 kilometres. For the first time it began outside Paris, leaving Evian at 2 a.m. on 20 July. Desgrange hoped this would enliven the race after what had been seen as a disappointing running in 1925, but his disputatious manner helped to ensure that a number of stars were absent, including the three Pélissier brothers – Charles, the youngest, had now joined Henri and Francis on the circuit – who were still sore over their endless disputes with the *patron*. Other brothers were present, Jules and Lucien Buysse, as well as some surprising entrants who included the first Japanese rider ever to take part in the Tour. Sadly Kisso Kawamuro got no further than the first stage, which was won by Jules Buysse, twenty-five minutes ahead of Lucien.

It was Lucien who would prevail at the end, having taken the Tour by the throat in the Pyrenees. Once again, conditions in the southern mountains were appalling, knocking one rider after another out of a race in which only 41 out of 126 starters would finish; Bottecchia and Benoit were among those who departed. The stage over the Aubisque, Tourmalet and Aspin was ridden in torrents of icy rain which made much of the road almost impassable. But Lucien was Baudelaire's 'roi d'un pays pluvieux'. He reached the summit of the Aubisque 1′43″ ahead of two Belgians, Omer Huyse and Léon Parmentier. The weather overcame Tailleu, who succumbed to an attack of cholic while Buysse crossed the climb eleven minutes ahead of Aimo, increased the lead to twenty-two minutes by the Peyresourde, and then, in an icy deluge but still king of a rainy country, arrived at Luchon 25′28″ ahead of Aimo. The rain had completely disrupted the race timetable, with poor Gustaaf Van Slembroeck, who had begun the stage wearing the yellow jersey, losing almost an hour and a half, and others hours further behind, almost all the riders arriving one by one, miserably strung out by the elements, some not even making it by bike but brought in morose and bedraggled by car.

That grim and dramatic stage effectively decided the race. Lucien went on to win into Perpignan from brother Jules, Frantz won two stages to Toulon and Nice but then fell ill and couldn't keep up, and Lucien Buysse was 1h2'25" ahead of Frantz at the finish. Buysse had ridden a methodical and brave race, and had demonstrated the way the Tour would very often from now on be won, the method Lance Armstrong still uses three-quarters of a century later, by maintaining a steady pace on the road stages and then striking in the mountains, with such ferocity that, thirty years later, Tour writers could still acclaim Buysse as the best climber Belgium ever produced: which is to say before Eddy Merckx.

The failure of the regular attempts to suppress teams and prohibit collaboration between riders illustrates Horace's saying '*Naturam expellas Furca, tamen usque recurret*', that you can drive Nature out with a pitchfork but it always comes back. With all racing sports, from athletics to horse racing to cycling, collaboration between those taking part may not be precisely natural, but it is certainly fruitful. The instinct towards collaboration stems from a simple and unavoidable fact: if three riders of equal ability take part in a race, two of them working as partners will beat the third. The question then arises how far this co-operation should be recognized as legitimate.

Sometimes collaboration is plainly illegitimate, when reduced to ignoble absurdity. When the Ferrari driver Rubens Barrichello pulled over on the final lap of the 2002 Austrian Grand Prix to allow his team-mate Michael Schumacher to win, it made the sport look contemptible in the eyes of every fan alive. In other cases the distinctions are nicer. The Rules of Racing say that every horse shall be run on its merits, meaning that it should run to win if it possibly can. In practice everyone knows that some horses have no chance, and the owner of one horse will often run another as a pacemaker. If everyone knows that this is happening, the results can be reputable, and riveting. In the enthralling

King George VI and Queen Elizabeth Stakes at Ascot in 1975, Bustino had not one pacemaker but two in his attempt to crack Grundy's stamina. The stewards knew this, and so did the other trainers, and the bookmakers, and the punters, and everyone was happy. Racegoers may be less happy when, as sometimes happens, the pacemaker wins at long odds, ahead of its stable-mate, the short-priced favourite. In France, this is taken account of by the stipulation that horses in the same owner's colours or from the same stable are coupled in the betting, so that both have to be backed together.

Then again, when a race meeting like the Shergar Cup at Ascot in 2002 was specifically organized as a competition between teams, British Isles jockeys against the Rest of the World, and then actually ridden as one, with jockeys collaborating, it caused protests not only from the stewards, with one saying that the jockeys had to ride within the Rules of Racing, but from at least one trainer. The comparison with cycling was fascinating. In a two-mile race, Kieren Fallon kicked on his horse Jasmick to force the pace against the other team, and then, having cracked the opposition, let his own team-mates through to win. Jasmick's trainer was Hugh Morrison, who didn't see the funny side of things. 'My horse has been used as a pawn,' he complained. 'They've created a team game and Kieren has played it.' Fallon himself said drily that 'They told me that it was an individual team thing. I know I'm from the west of Ireland but someone is going to have to explain that to me.' Morrison's puzzlement was understandable – he wasn't used to seeing in a horse race tactics identical to those used in the Tour, with one rider sacrificing himself for the team – while Fallon's Irishism, 'an individual team thing', admirably described the Tour.

Collaboration in other sports has been outlawed. One day in May 1954, at the Iffley Road track in Oxford, the 25-year-old medical student Roger Bannister ran a mile in 3'59.4", beating Gunder Haegg's existing record by two seconds but, far more to the point, breaking the magical four minutes for the first time ever. It was a wonderful day, still remembered by anyone who was a small boy at the time, but there was nothing spontaneous about it. The historic run had been meticulously planned; Bannister didn't have competitors trying to beat him, he had colleagues trying to help him, with Chris Chataway and Christopher Brasher setting the pace. At the time, pre-planned running of a series of laps by different pacemakers, in order to 'tow' a selected runner to a record time, raised some eyebrows in the athletics world, but today it is all part of the entertainment in the track-and-field 'circus'.

Some form of co-operation tends to take place in cycling even when there are no recognized teams. Although riders in the earliest Tours were identified by the make of bikes they rode – Garin winning the first Tour for La Française, Henri Cornet the second for JC, then Peugeot taking four and Alcyon the next four – they weren't grouped in teams until the seventh Tour, and from 1909 to 1914 the leading cyclists rode for bicycle manufacturers' teams. We have seen that, after the Tour returned in 1919, Desgrange hoped to suppress teams, but they were allowed again from 1925, with Bottecchia, Thys, the Buysse brothers and the Pélissier brothers riding for Automoto–Hutchinson, others for J.-B. Louvet–Pouchois, or Alcyon–Dunlop, Meteore–Wolber, and with Jean Alavoine quaintly comprising the one-man team Alavoine–Dunlop. In 1928 regional teams were added to the commercial groups, though not to much effect: the first three that year, Frantz, Leducq and Dewaele, were all riding for Alcyon–Dunlop, and the first two dozen at the finish were all from company teams, with Paul Filliat of Sud-Est the best of the regionals at twenty-fifth, before Desgrange suppressed teams once more, for another year, but as it turned out for the last time. From 1930 the leading riders rode for national teams, later supplemented by regional teams, through to 1962 when commercially sponsored teams returned, and, after another short interlude of national teams in 1967–8, are with us still.

Under whatever guise, team work is rooted in the efficacy of pacing. In the early days of bike racing, riders were artificially paced by other cyclists who were not taking part as competitors, and then by cars or motorbikes; later in the twentieth century, 'Derny-paced' bike races enjoyed some popularity, with the cyclists following a little moped-like machine, a cross between bicycle and motorbike, a form of competition which had shocking results on one occasion involving Eddy Merckx. In team racing the pacing is both continuous and subtler. It can be seen in pure form in team time trials, of which there is now one in each Tour, when the lead endlessly rotates between riders, each setting the pace for no more than twenty seconds at a time. On road stages, the same thing happens in less structured form, with riders leading on behalf of their team, one rider pacing others, and *domestiques* serving their leaders like worker bees serving the queen. They literally wait on him, fetching and carrying *bidons* of water, they faithfully stay with him if he punctures to relay him back to the peloton, they accompany him if he attacks, and, if a rival rider attacks, they set off and stick to his wheel: all in the service of the team and its leader.

Just how much of a co-operative team sport cycling had become, the next Tour would show. In 1926 Buysse had been riding for Automoto; in 1927 Nicolas Frantz was riding for Alcyon, much the most powerful team, and he duly won. For all his mixed feelings about manufacturers, Desgrange now encouraged the development of their teams with an innovation that was soon regarded as the worst mistake he ever made. There were twenty-four stages to be ridden in twenty-nine days, of which sixteen were split stages, run as team time trials with separate departure times at quarter-hour intervals. The avowed object was partly to put an end to the way that the race was decided – as so conspicuously the year before – in the mountains, and partly 'pour lutter', as it was bluntly put by one journalist, 'contre l'indolence des coureurs'. There was, it was widely agreed, a problem of idle riders resting on their pedals; the new arrangement of the Tour was meant to make them do some work. At the same time, Desgrange returned to tradition in the form of a departure from Paris, now at a civilized hour, 7 a.m. rather than 2 a.m. the year before. Only 37 of the 142 starters who left for Dieppe on 19 June were *groupés* in teams, the rest riding as individual *touristes-routiers*.

But the line-up did not include Ottavio Bottecchia. On 14 June, five days before the Tour began, he had been found beside an Italian country road where he had been cycling, covered in blood and his head and body battered, groaning, 'Malore, malore' – it hurts. Since his bike was undamaged, it didn't require Holmes or Poirot to see that he had been attacked. But by whom? The question became far more pressing soon after when Bottecchia was taken from the scene of the crime to a church and given the last rites before dying of his injuries; though not so pressing that it was ever answered.

He is the only Tour winner ever to have been murdered, a crime that remains unsolved to this day. Had he been set upon by peasants he had somehow angered – because he was stealing their grapes, in one not very probable story – or by common bandits? Or had he been deliberately whacked, in the later language of the American mob? Some years after his death an Italian hoodlum was stabbed in a fight on the New York waterfront, and is said to have confessed with his dying words that he had murdered Bottecchia as a contract killing for a gangster called Beto Olinas, but no one of such name has ever been traced. Those who remembered Pélissier's words about the stalker may have thought of a *crime passionel*, though given the circumstances of his death it seemed far-fetched to imagine any woman scorned or husband cheated tracking him down on that country road.

That left politics. Bottecchia was a known socialist and opponent of the Fascist government. Although a veritable gentleman compared with his contemporaries Stalin and Hitler, Mussolini wasn't above whacking opponents himself. After Mussolini had apparently won the 1924 election in a landslide, the socialist leader Giacomo Matteotti made himself a marked man by denouncing the election as a fraud, and in 1926 he was killed by a Fascist gang. A story went round that Bottecchia had likewise been liquidated as a troublemaker: the priest who was with him at his death expressed his view, very many years later, in 1973, that it had been a political murder. Against that, any demagogue of the age like Mussolini would most likely have wanted to protect a national sporting hero who, while he may have been a political dissident, was still conferring lustre on the name of Italy. At all events, after more than seventy-five years, we still we don't know who killed the great Ottavio Bottecchia, and most likely we never shall.

When the Tour began in this shadow, it was the teams who set the pace as intended, with the Dilecta team winning the first stage and Francis Pélissier taking the yellow jersey, but like many other riders he disliked the brutal pace now dictated by the flat-out time trials, or what he called 'go the whole way' racing, and he abandoned on the sixth stage. The lead was taken by Ferdinand Le Drogo in his native Brittany, before the Belgian Hector Martin, riding for J.-B. Louvet, took the yellow jersey from Vannes to Bayonne, leading by twenty-three minutes. Now Alcyon was about to show its strength, and to show why it had hired Frantz.

Once again the field reached the Pyrenees in wintry rain, and the riders, though grateful for a respite from the hated time trials, didn't face the mountains with any enthusiasm, either. Albert Londres's phrase 'convicts of the road' sounds melodramatic. No one was forced to become a Tour rider as poor wretches were sent to Devil's Island. But it should be remembered that, for many professional sportsmen, their trade has always been just that: a way of making a living, and often a harsh and comfortless one. Even county cricket, major-league baseball or professional soccer can seem a hard life, offering until recently, and for some even now, few lavish rewards and much drudgery. This is something well captured by the cricketer Simon Hughes in his book *A Lot of Hard Yakka,* and even better by the footballer Eamon Dunphy in his brilliant memoir *Only a Game?*

For little boys, and even for adult fans, racing cyclists may be heroes, but their own life rarely strikes them as heroic. Suffering from all sorts of ailments brought on by riding a bike, covering great grim distances across the plains, and even grimmer climbs up mountains that would have been thought literally impassable when the Tour began, riding sometimes in unbearable heat, sometimes in horrible cold and rain, they lead a life which, as Samuel Johnson might have said, has more to endure than to enjoy.

To make it worse, as they slogged up the first Pyrenean climb, the peloton heard that the Italian Michele Gordini had made an astonishing escape and was forty-five minutes ahead. He didn't stay there for long. He led over the Aubisque, but soon after was found beside the road disconsolately repairing his chain, and Frantz took the lead ahead of Pé Verhaegen and the little French rider Benoit Faure, 'The Mouse'. Frantz increased his lead over the Tourmalet and Aspin, to win at Luchon by 11′40″ and take the yellow jersey from Martin, whom he now led by a crushing two hours.

The excitements of the race were from then on provided by two French debutants, André Leducq and Antonin Magne. A quite short stage from Marseilles to Toulon was won by Magne, acclaimed by some reporters as a new Petit-Breton, before Frantz came into his own once again in the Alps. He escaped over the Col de Vars and the Izoard with the Belgian Julien Vervaecke, whom he allowed to win the stage: Frantz said that he didn't want to risk falling on the descent, and he was anyway far ahead in the GC. One consequence of the development of more sophisticated tactics was that, as long as a rider knew where he stood, he could afford to let others who offered no larger threat make long escapes or even win stages.

Those tactics still needed to be employed with care. On the Briançon–Evian stage, the Swiss *touriste-routier* Charles Martinet made a long escape across the Galibier, to lead by eighteen minutes at one point, before he was caught by Verhaegen, who won the stage twenty-two minutes ahead of a very tired Frantz. But Frantz won the stage to Metz and finished the Tour almost an hour and a half ahead of Dewaele in second. Although it was the second victory for Luxembourg, and another 'home defeat', there was a sense of French optimism. Behind Belgians in second and third came three Frenchmen, Leducq, Benoit and Magne.

All the same, France would have to wait. Frantz not only went on to win a back-to-back victory in 1928, he did something that had never been done before and has never been done since. Bottecchia in 1924 and Maes in 1935 led the whole length of the Tour by winning the lead on the first day and never losing it. But only Frantz has ever literally worn the yellow jersey throughout, since he came to the *Départ* at Le Vesinet on 17 June wearing the jersey as the previous year's winner, held the GC lead by winning the first stage to Caen, and never surrendered it before the Parc des Princes on 15 July.

He was much helped by his team-mates: Alcyon took the first five places, and this race dramatically confirmed the dominance of the team system. The 162 starters were categorized in a more complicated way than ever, 86 of them in teams, but the remaining *touriste-routiers* also divided into regional teams and individuals. Among the smaller groups was a four-man Australian team sponsored by Ravat–Wonder and led by Hubert Opperman. He had been sent to Europe under the aegis of Dunlop, and shown good form earlier in the year. But 'Oppy' and the Aussies made only a modest impact on the Tour: at the halfway point of one stage they actually led from Alcyon, but they couldn't match the hardened, ten-man European team. Although Opperman may have been *parti pris*, he was speaking for many others when he denounced the team time-trial system as 'a crime which should never have been perpetrated on the roads of France'.

For all such strictures, Desgrange 'persevered in error', as Portier magisterially put it, when everyone else thought that the time-trial stages with separate departures were a demonstrable mistake. That was the way the race was run, whether they liked it or not, and it only helped the 'bleu ciel' of Alcyon and thus Frantz. They showed their superiority from the first 'clm' – *contre la montre*, against the watch, as the French more nicely call time trials – despite Luducq, who finished ten minutes behind after puncturing. Eight stages through Normandy, Brittany and the west brought them to Gascony, where a local hero emerged. Victor Fontan was a 36-year-old Béarnais, said to look like a smuggler, who had been racing since he was fifteen. He had won the Toulouse–Bordeaux race as long ago as 1913 and the Tour du Sud-Ouest in 1922, was highly regarded by those who knew him but had never taken part in a race outside his own part of the country before. He now won the stage to Bordeaux, and left the town on the next stage surrounded by a huge and elated crowd, before he excelled in the Pyrenees.

On the Hendaye–Luchon stage Camille Van de Casteele made a long escape, leading at the Aubisque by twenty-seven minutes, but lost his lead on the Tourmalet where Fontan took over. He reached Luchon seven minutes ahead of Frantz, but it was Frantz who was still leading the GC by forty-one minutes. Others had their day, notably the two Magne brothers: Antonin won the great Alpine stage from Nice to Grenoble and the penultimate stage to Dieppe, while Evian–Pontarlier was won by Paul, but Frantz kept his lead. He had a sticky moment fifty-three kilometres out of Metz on the road to Charleville when his fork broke on a level crossing, but he acquired another machine – a ladies' model – at a bike shop. Under the latest version of the constantly changing rules, such a replacement was allowed as it would not have been in other years, and Frantz was helped back into the race by three *domestiques*, so that he only lost twenty-eight minutes from his lead, and iced the cake by winning the last stage to the Parc.

It was a famous victory, but an ambiguous one. Very likely the best man had won, but he had without doubt been hugely helped by riding with the strongest team. It was now almost impossible for a strong rider to win with a weak team, as poor Fontan empirically demonstrated. He had ridden superbly in the mountains, only to see his lowly team give away hours in the time trials, and one reporter wondered out loud whether, if Fontan had ridden for Alcyon and Frantz for the Pyreneans, it might not have been Fontan who had won the Tour.

At any rate, everyone but Desgrange was agreed that the formula of team time trials and split stages was the worst ever devised for the Tour de France. And even the *patron* himself, stubborn as he was, and for all that he hated to be told what to do, recognized the military maxim: never reinforce defeat. Although the previous team system remained in force in 1929, the time trials were scrapped. Even then, Desgrange characteristically felt obliged to add a minatory note that he would reintroduce them if the average speed fell below 30 k.p.h.

Whatever the sequence of cause and effect, the contrast with Frantz's yellow-all-the-way the previous year could not have been more striking. No fewer than sixteen different riders won stages in 1929, with only two men winning more than one, two for Frantz, four for Leducq. And the lead changed hands repeatedly, with the one curiosity that at Brest three riders were on equal time and Frantz, Fontan and Leducq all wore yellow jerseys. The shake-up came in the Pyrenees. Poor Fontan was a few miles out of Luchon when his front fork broke. He borrowed a spectator's bike, rode to the next village with his own bike on his back, and effected the repairs, but he had lost too much time to stay in contention; his spirit as well his machine broken, he abandoned in tears.

That stage to Perpignan was won by Jef Demuysère, where the lead was taken by Dewaele, but the pace slowed across the Midi, and Desgrange enforced his threat by introducing a time trial to Cannes as a punitive measure. Dewaele had a hard time over the Alps, and at Grenoble he talked of abandoning, but he stuck it out. Evian–Belfort was a triumph for the debutant Charles Pélissier, youngest of the brothers, who won the stage by 14′30″ to finish his first Tour in twenty-fifth, but, after Desgrange had imposed further punishment drills, the second of which time trials was won by Dewaele and Alcyon, and although Frantz took the last stage to Paris, it was Dewaele who stood on the winner's podium on 28 July.

If he thought that his triumph would be an occasion of universal rejoicing, he was soon disabused. The choleric Desgrange surpassed himself in denouncing this 'victoire d'un moribond', and went away to brood about the hated Alcyon team. It was a mark of the surly chauvinism of the *patron* and his paper that the *Auto* headlined the result 'LE 23 TOUR DE FRANCE CYCLISTE', only mentioning the winner's name in smaller type, and gave equal billing on the front page to the victory of France over the United States in the Davis Cup. It was indeed a wonderful French tennis team, the 'Four Musketeers', Borotra, Brugnon, Cochet and Lacoste, but the Tour was the paper's very own baby.

Just over thirteen weeks later, on 24 October 1929, the Twenties ended dramatically. That was 'Black Thursday', the day the New York stock market collapsed. Its effects would soon reach Europe, ushering in the great depression with many catastrophic social and political consequences. For France especially there was a clear caesura here: the decade from 1919 to 1929 was unmistakably post-war; from 1929 to 1939, just as unmistakably pre-war. The next ten runnings of the Tour would take place in the shadow of unemployment, hunger and approaching war.

Repos

Gascony

'When was Wales?' the Marxist historian Gwyn A. Williams asked in the title of a book about his native land. The same question could be asked of many other countries, not least of France; and not only, When was France? but, What was France? or even, Where was France? How to define this country of which the great race makes its Tour, the *hexagone* that's such a well-worn part of the vocabulary of cycling journalese, and which the *grande boucle* buckles? Answers fade from the page at first glance.

That somewhat irregular hexagon has six sides, four of them formed by nature, the Channel from Dunkirk to Brest, the Atlantic from Brest to Bayonne, the Pyrenees from Bayonne to Perpignan, and the Mediterranean from Perpignan to Nice. The other two, landward sides – from Nice north to Strasbourg, and then north-west from Strasbourg to Calais – are found on no map of France in the time of Louis IX or Henri IV. Until quite recently France took a decidedly different shape; and many of those parts that were formally included in its territory 500, or 300, years ago, were French only in the most dubious or tenuous sense.

That includes the south-west. The brave but unlucky Fontan came from the Béarnais, on the western edge of the Pyrenees, and rode for a Pyrenean team; or he was sometimes called a Basque, like several other good cyclists, from either side of the Franco-Spanish border; or he was a Gascon; and he was a citizen of the French Republic. But how French is Gascony, and when was it? At different times in its history it belonged to the kings of England rather than the kings of France, and very many centuries after it became French in a full political sense, it was not French culturally and linguistically, not at least in the view of Parisians.

At the time the first Tour crossed Gascony, much of south-western France was far less well known than today. It was unknown even to most northern Frenchmen, let alone the English, who had not as yet come to explore the lovely valleys of the Lot and Garonne, nor made a cult of Périgord and Quercy and especially Dordogne, whose very name now produces a frisson of excitement in the educated upper-middle classes greater even than 'Provence' or 'Tuscany'. The classic text here is Cyril Connolly's readable if risible *The Unquiet Grave*, written in wartime London amid blackout and intolerable shortage of such necessities of life as French cheese and wine. It daydreams of 'a golden classical house, three storeys high, with *oeil de boeuf* attic windows and view over water . . . a sheltered garden, indulgent to fig and nectarine,' a room within 'book-lined like that of Montaigne, wizard of the magic circle, with this motto from him: "La liberté et l'oisiveté qui sont mes mâitresses qualités."' And Connolly (who most certainly and sincerely loved freedom and sloth) provided a map of that magic circle, from Brive in the north to Toulouse in the south, Rodez in the east to Tonneins on the confluence of Lot and Garonne in the west before they meet the Dordogne. The very first Tour crossed the south-west corner of the magic circle on its way from Toulouse through Agen to Bordeaux, and occasionally the race has penetrated deeper into the circle, nine times to Albi between 1953 and 1999, to Rodez in 1984, to Cahors in 1994 when the great escapologist Jacky Durand won the stage.

Bordeaux itself has been visited by the Tour more than any other apart from Paris, seventy-eight times between 1903 and 2003, and is one of the handsomest in France, with its lovely squares and its great theatre, which can still produce the feelings Arthur Young experienced more than 200 years ago: 'Much as I had read and heard of the commerce, wealth and magnificence of this city, they greatly surpassed my expectations.' Apart from the wine trade, and a number of fine restaurants (including the wonderful Chapon Fin with its *soupe de potimaron* and its cod poached in chervil, distinctly nicer than it sounds, and the splendid Tupina with an array of regional dishes), it has particularly rich literary resonances, of Montesquieu, of François Mauriac – who was born in the old city and who set many of his novels in the region, either in Bordeaux, like *La Pharisienne*, or like *Thérèse Desqueyroux* in the Landes, or like *Le Noeud de Vipères*, in Verdelais – and above all the incomparable Montaigne, hero to Connolly and so many of us. He was born in the eponymous family chateau of Montaigne thirty-six miles west of Bordeaux, and after his travels returned there to spend the last two decades of his life, and to write the essays that changed the way Europe thought about itself. You can stay there, at the Jardin d'Eyquem, and adventure eastwards into the magic circle to do as Connolly would have done and eat *foie de canard* and duck with truffle sauce at the manoir de Bellerive in Le Buisson-de-Cadouin.

But as Michelet says, 'Rich and beautiful as is this valley of the Garonne, we cannot linger there; the distant summits of the Pyrenees are too powerful an attraction.' On the way is the strange watery waste of the Landes, haunting rather than lovely, if no longer quite as savage as French soldiers found the region in the 1840s, when they described it like something out of the remotest corner of Asia. And then there are 'the fleas that tease in the high Pyrenees', which had bitten Hilaire Belloc on his tour through the Gavarnie, before the cyclists reached those great mountains already beloved of walkers like him, and of climbers, and more recently of skiers.

Although Michelet is quite right to speak of the fantastic beauty of the Pyrenees, this most distant corner of France may be said to be richer in scenic grandeur than literary associations, or gastronomy for that matter. As John Ardagh observes, the Béarn and Basque countries are curiously lacking in writers well known even in France, let alone outside. Biarritz itself is a special case, once one of the grandest and most famous resorts in Europe, surprisingly visited only twice in a hundred years by the Tour but much more often by royalty and writers: Edward VII sojourned there every spring (and in 1908 even summoned Asquith thither, with what many thought grave lack of constitutional propriety, to kiss hands on his appointment as prime minister), Shaw stayed there, and so did Kipling.

A lovely country, then; but is it France; or when was it? Not 2000 years ago, before France was born or named; nor in the twelfth or thirteenth centuries, when Aquitaine belonged to the kings of England; and nor, plenty of Parisians would have said, as recently as Napoleon's time, or when the Third Republic was born, or even when the Tour de France was, a race that casts a fascinating light on these very concepts of France and Frenchness. Although the origins of the Tour lay in a political crisis, the race had no specific political object, not in the way that sport has often had, from the circus of Byzantium onwards. Even now when sport is held to be at worst a harmless (if commodified) distraction for the depoliticized or deluded masses, there are still soccer clubs in Scotland that shiver with sectarian – which is to say communal, which is to say in some degree political – animosities, Rangers and Celtic in Glasgow, 'Hearts' and 'Hibs' (Heart of Midlothian and Hibernian in Edinburgh): in either case the Orange–Protestant club first, the Green–Catholic second. And Israeli football clubs have names – Betar and Hapoel – deeply rooted in turbulent Zionist history.

Other sporting projects were even more avowedly political. The Gaelic Athletic Association, founded at much the same time as the Gaelic League was with the intention of reviving the Irish language, though with much more success, was a naked assertion of national distinctiveness, responding to Archbishop Croke of Cashel's complaint that England had imposed on Ireland not only her manufactured goods and 'her vicious literature' but also her games and pastimes 'to the utter discredit of our own grand national sport and to the sore humiliation, as I believe, of every genuine son and daughter of the old land'. The GAA's ban on playing with 'forces of the crown' and on those who played 'foreign games' like rugby and soccer made the most important single vehicle for advanced or republican nationalism, and one of the most aggressive manifestations of that *Trotzreaktion* that was so much a part of modern nationalism in Ireland.

If it wasn't as overtly political as the GAA or Betar, the Tour de France had patriotic overtones in its very name. For centuries the story of France was its gathering in of territories under royal control; then its expansion physically, until its present borders were achieved, more or less, in the eighteenth century; then and no less importantly the process in the past two centuries by which all of 'France' became 'French'. Other European countries saw similar stories, as when Cavour said that it was not enough to unite Italy, 'now we must make Italians'. The French version of that process is the title of Eugen Weber's admirable book *Peasants into Frenchmen*, which tells the story of how those peasants, backward, barely aware of the state that ruled them, and unable to speak its language, were turned into French citizens as rural France was modernized between 1870 and 1914. And in this the *grande boucle* would play at the very least a symbolic part, by circling and buckling what, when Desgrange began his race, was a country, but as yet by no means obviously a nation.

Whatever the rhetoric of nationalism says, few European countries have 'natural frontiers', and very few have had permanent borders. Many have expanded over the ages, though they then sometimes contracted. Between the eleventh and nineteenth centuries England conquered and absorbed all the outlying parts of the British Isles, Wales, Scotland, Ireland, and then began to lose them again in the twentieth century. The expansion of France was no less remarkable, but was a much later development: even in the early sixteenth century, when Henry VIII first united Ireland as a kingdom and brought it under the crown, later to be united in turn with Great Britain, many of the present-day departments of France, from Haut-Rhin to Haute-Corse, had no political connection whatever with Paris and the French kingdom. In 1066 William of Normandy took over a kingdom of England (or at least of the English, Rex Anglorum) stretching from Cornwall to Northumberland, at a time when no such kingdom of France stretched even from Nantes to Lyons, to take two of the towns visited by the Tour in both 1903 and 2003. Even the name was ambiguous: in any document from the twelfth century, 'France' or 'Francia' is as likely to mean the Île de France, the royal appenage surrounding Paris, as any larger territory; later still, 'France' was understood to stop at the Loire.

It was possible to claim that the *hexagone* always platonically existed – 'une certaine idée de la France,' in de Gaulle's phrase – and this was attempted ambitiously by Michelet in his *History of France*. He begins with a 'Tableau de France', a bravura description of the country all of whose component parts had characteristics that, when combined, produced the essence of the country itself. And yet he knew perfectly well that many of those components had not been French at all in the Middle Ages, or indeed later. In its early years the Tour kept to the west of the Saône and Rhône, and its first stops were Lyons, a city of the kingdom of Burgundy in the time of St Louis, and Marseilles, a city of the county of Provence.

As the race expanded it visited other 'French' provinces that, like the Dauphiné or Venaissan, had been quite independent of France in the thirteenth century; or, like the Franche-Comté and Savoy, in the sixteenth; or, like Alsace and much of Lorraine, in the eighteenth. (The duc de Choiseul, Louis XV's minister, was born in Lorraine and was thus not even a French subject by birth at the time.) That first Tour stopped in Nantes, capital of what in the tenth century had been the county of Brittany, a dependency of the duchy of Normandy, before passing under English suzerainty in the twelfth, to become an autonomous duchy in the thirteenth. And the riders had cycled thither from Bordeaux in the duchy of Gascony, which for much of the later Middle Ages belonged to the kings of England, until the Hundred Years War finally saw them depart, leaving only an English toehold at Calais – visited by the Tour in 1994 and 2001 – until it was lost and engraved on Mary Tudor's heart. And even though provinces like Périgord and Toulouse, Champagne and the duchy of Burgundy (to the west of the Saône, rather than the palatinate or Franche-Comté to the east) may have been French in the sense of wanting to belonging to the regnum, there was no way in which the royal writ could be said to have run there.

By the sixteenth century most of what was held to be the kingdom of France had at any rate come under royal authority, but much of what is now part of the République Française wasn't as yet French at all. Even after the Peace of Westphalia in 1648, such hallowed *villes-étapes* of the Tour as Besançon, Nancy and Lille belonged to independent principalities or bishoprics, and were part of the Holy Roman Empire. The borders were ruthlessly pushed westwards by Louis XIV, but the *hexagone* only took its present hexagonal form when the dust settled after Revolutionary and Napoleonic wars.

In the British case the absorption of the Celtic fringe came to be seen as a form of benighted monarchical imperialism, the 'Ukanian' hegemony of Tom Nairn's coining. But in France it was republicans who were much keener to centralize authority, and to gallicize Brittany, Alsace or Corsica, than royalty had ever been. In the seventeenth century men from the capital spoke of the darkest south as a remote continent. When Racine had visited Uzès, not far from Arles, he had needed 'an interpreter as much as a Muscovite would need one in Paris', and much later

Parisian visitors to the outlying provinces were still complaining about the natives' incomprehensibility and sheer barbarism. Even in the nineteenth century, by when almost all of what is now France was unquestionably ruled from Paris, much remained very remote to Parisian eyes and ears. In 1831 the prefect of Ariège – the Pyrenean department that contains the Plateau-de-Beille *étape* and the Col de Port climb – said that the population of the place was 'as brutal as the bears it breeds', while one of Balzac's characters says in his 1844 novel *Paysans*, 'You don't need to go to America to see savages,' since here – in the depths of Burgundy – 'are the Redskins of Fenimore Cooper'. All of this was akin to the language in which educated Englishmen at the time were wont to describe the primitive backwardness of Scotch Highlanders or Irish peasants, except that the fastidious Parisians don't even seem to have found any redeeming touch of the lovably quaint or picturesque.

No doubt they were they right by their lights: the evidence is that, by urban standards, much of outlying France was indeed very raw until quite recently. Early in the nineteenth century, when Georges Haussmann – he who later rebuilt much of Paris – visited Houeillès in the south-west corner of Lot-et-Garonne, today a matter of minutes from the D932 road where it takes the Tour from Bordeaux to Pau, he found no roads or signposts and had to be guided by a man using a compass. His complaints were still being echoed at the end of the nineteenth century.

There was more to metropolitan disdain than physical backwardness. These 'savages' in Gascony or Brittany or remoter Limousin, were savage not least because they simply weren't French. That is, they didn't speak the language of Racine, of Voltaire, and of the republic. The revolution had not only promoted Liberty, Equality and Fraternity, it had claimed that France was 'one and indivisible', even if it had done so at a time when this simply wasn't true. Many people who lived in the First Republic, or even the Third, may have lived under French law and administration, but they had no common culture, apart from that catholicism that was precisely what republicanism defined itself against. Plenty of citizens didn't so much as know which country they lived in. An inspector of education touring the Lozère mountains in 1864 was baffled and angered to find that most children at a village school could not name their country, or answer his irritable question, 'Are you English or Russian?'

Above all, most 'Frenchmen' didn't speak French until well into the nineteenth century, or many of them into the twentieth. This was something of which the Jacobins had been aware, and which they bitterly resented. One of the harshest accusations made against those who ruled the United Kingdom of Great Britain and Ireland from London was to be that they had wilfully neglected or even persecuted the Celtic languages, Welsh, Scots Gaelic and Irish. But no administrators in London could have been more hostile towards smaller languages than were the French revolutionists of the 1790s, with their rallying cry: 'Citizens! Join in holy emulation to extirpate from every region of France these jargons which are the surviving tatters of feudalism and slavery.'

The 'jargons' in question were the smaller languages or patois or dialects – themselves fighting words – of France. Some were entirely distinct, like Breton, sister-tongue to Welsh, in the far north-west, and Basque in the far south-west. Some others spoken on the fringes of the *hexagone* were branches of neighbouring larger languages, like Flemish, which is a version of Dutch, or 'Alsatian', which is audibly a German dialect, or 'Corsican', which is audibly an Italian dialect, or the language of Pyrénées-Orientales, which is simply Catalan. But others, above all in the land of the tongue of Oc – 'Languedoc'– from Gascony to Provence, were romance tongues comparable with, but different to the point of incomprehensibility from, the French of the Île de France.

Not all those peasants had become Frenchmen by the first

decade of the Tour, at least not in quite the way that good republicans wanted. The Catholic Church was still hugely strong, waging what was by no means just a forlorn rearguard action against liberalism and laicism. A great national *Kulturkampf* was waged in miniature in villages throughout France, until the very end of the Third Republic, with the pious *curé* and the free-thinking schoolteacher, a Radical, or later often a Communist, fighting their own little skirmishes. Almost the decisive events in this story came after 1914. There was the war itself, which took millions of peasants away from their *pays* for the first time in their lives and afterwards returned them, those that survived, as Frenchmen for the first time. And then after the war came the new mass media. Cinema had reached France before 1914, but it was in the 1920s that it began to be a part of national culture; appropriately the Tour played its part. In 1925 what may have been the first cycling film was made, *Le Roi de la Pédale*, starring the popular actor Biscot, and with scenes shot on the Tour. It would be followed by plenty of others as talkies replaced silent film: in 1939, *Pour le Maillot jaune* was shot during the Tour, starring Albert Préjean and Meg Lemonnier, sister-in-law of Jacques Goddet, who later succeed Desgrange as director general of the Tour.

And there was the 'TSF', wireless or radio, the other captivating mass medium that dominated popular culture in the west until another arrived, which would combine the hypnotic visual power of cinema and the immediacy of radio. Sport was given a new dimension, albeit an unlikely one, by radio. Broadcasters became national figures: in the case of one American football commentator Ronald Reagan, the beginning of a career that would end in the White House. Even now there are elderly men who can remember listening to World Series or to soccer matches before the war (one bizarre notion of the BBC commentators' – dividing the pitch into imaginary squares so as to indicate verbally to listeners, referring to a grid printed in the *Radio Times*, where the man with the ball was – soon lapsed, leaving behind only the phrase 'back to square one'), or boxing matches, as when much of England, and all of Wales, sat up till the small hours one August night in 1937 to hear Tommy Farr go the distance with Joe Louis.

In 1929 the Tour was covered on radio for the first time, on a modest scale, but the beginnings of what would one day be transmissions listened to by tens of millions of Frenchmen at home or in cafés and bars. Those listeners became familiar with 'La Houppa' singing 'On tourne autour du Tour', one of a flurry of popular songs about the Tour, before 1938, when the commentators included Préjean, a still greater movie actor in Jean Gabin, and Georges Carpentier. And although Gabin may have spoken with a strong Parisian accent, French was what he spoke, and so did the others: as with English in the British Isles, radio was a more powerful force for linguistic and cultural centralization than anything governments had done.

It may have been the final blow against the contrary movements for regional distinctiveness and for the revival of those 'jargons', from Breton to Provençal, which had sprung up in outlying parts of France in the nineteenth century as in Wales, Scotland and Ireland. In Brittany and Provence, as in the Celtic fringe, it was too late. As Weber truly says (in words equally applicable to the British Isles as the French Republic) the revivalists could not deal with the decline of their beloved tongues, because they could not deal with the causes of the decline. By the later twentieth century, such revivals appeared to enjoy some success, but it was illusory. Although famous *villes-étapes* from Nantes to Nice now have bilingual street signs, just as there are in Swansea or Cork, in the local language (jargon or patois) as well as the language of the state, this is unmistakably a touch of folklorique colour rather than an authentic expression of an everyday tongue. As can be seen by anyone who follows the great race around the republic, for better or worse, all of France within the *hexagone* is French at last.

5

French Renaissance

1930–1934

For all the greatly increased popular success which the Tour enjoyed in the 1920s, Desgrange remained as farouche and dissatisfied as ever. He was dismayed by the long line of French failure in the great French race, angered by the continuing grip of commerce in general, vexed by the dominance of Alcyon in particular. It seemed to him that his brainchild had been kidnapped. And so he resolved to break the trade teams at a stroke. The 1930 Tour, he announced, would be contested by national teams – eight riders each from France, Belgium, Italy, Spain and Germany – as well as sixty *touristes-routiers* grouped in regional teams. This was linked to two further innovations, the use by all riders of 'anonymous' or standard bikes, provided by the Tour and painted the *Auto*'s own yellow, and the arrival of the *caravane publicitaire* to provide an alternative source of finance. The caravan is now such a feature of the Tour that it's hard to imagine France in July without that great parade, floats, cars and vans topped like heraldic helmets with the manufacturers' emblems for instant coffee, processed cheese, chocolates, Crédit

Lyonnais in yellow, PMU in green, which precedes the riders by an hour or so. For 'La Vache qui Rit', Graf, Delft *biscottes*, Esders, Noveltex, the caravan trumpeted their wares around the corners of the *hexagone*; for Desgrange, it answered his central financial problem.

'Anonymous' bikes seemed a logical change, although as it proved not a permanent one. Sport remains contradictory when it comes to equipment. Whereas no one serving at Roland-Garros, pitching at the Yankee Stadium or bowling at Lord's uses balls of his own choice, but takes what he's given, players at St Andrews and Augusta do use their own golf balls. This has plausibly been called an absurd anomaly: quite apart from the way high-tech balls, as well as clubs, are making a nonsense of the sport, by allowing all the best golfers, and not only Tiger Woods, to drive much further and reach the green much more easily than intended when the courses were built, it must be wrong that different balls should give different chances. Golf would be a better game if every player in a major tournament took a dozen balls from an identical batch at the first tee.

This analogy both does and doesn't apply with bike racing. At Longchamps or Newmarket, the horse is the competitor, not the jockey, whose neutrality is emphasized by the way that all weights are equalized, even if every racegoer knows that a brilliant jockey can be worth several pounds in a hard finish. At Silverstone or Indianapolis both driver and car are competitors. A great driver may be able to win with one team or another, but the technical competition between manufacturers to improve their machines is an essential or even the principal part of the sport. The Tour is a race between bicyclists, not bicycles. And yet improvements in bike technology have been regularly spurred on by the sport, albeit with little enthusiasm from those who run it and who have often, over a hundred years, given the impression that they would like cyclists still to be riding the machines of 1903.

At any rate, and whatever his motives, the immediate outcome of his latest change was gratifying for Desgrange. The

1930 Tour was dominated by the French team, with five of its eight riders in the top ten finishers, including the first Frenchman to win the race since 1923; and it was indeed a triumph for national team spirit. After stages in Normandy and Brittany won by Charles Pélissier, André Leducq won the stage to Les Sables, took the yellow jersey into Luchon, and held it for twelve more stages into Paris, supported all the way by his team-mates. It was sweet revenge: Leducq was a very able rider who had already enjoyed eight stage wins and had come fourth in 1927 and second in 1928. But, so far from being supported by the trade teams he had been riding for, he had served as an underling riding to orders and had never yet had the opportunity to achieve his potential.

Even now he needed luck as well as his courage and strikingly equable temperament, which saw him through one of the heroic rivalries of Tour history. He was an adequate climber but a much better descender, with a mastery of that blend of delicate balance and steel nerve needed to gain time turning and leaning at high speed downhill. This he was doing down from the Galibier on the long Alpine stage from Grenoble to Evian, still ninety seconds off the lead, when he took a terrible tumble, arse-over-tip twice, breaking a pedal and cutting himself badly on the gravel. Tough as he was, Leducq wanted to abandon, but his comrades Charles Pélissier, Antonin Magne and Marcel Bidot urged him back into the saddle even though he had lost fifteen minutes.

Having won the previous stage, Learco Guerra now led an escape to make up as much time as possible over Leducq, and could never have been caught on a present-day Tour, with stages as much as 150 kilometres shorter. It was the remaining 65 kilometres out of a 331-kilometre stage which gave the Frenchmen their chance. In an extraordinary performance, they gradually caught up with the leaders and raced for the finish in a thirty-man sprint amid screaming crowds, won by a bloody, bold and resolute Leducq from Pélissier in astonishing fashion. 'Dédé', one reporter wrote of Leducq, was 'gueule d'amour, muscle d'acier', a lover's smile and steel muscles.

After that the Tour was almost all theirs. The Belgian Frans Bonduel won the next stage from Evian to Belfort, but the brave roadman-sprinter Pélissier won the last four stages in a row, while Leducq never lost his yellow jersey, with Guerra taking second place at the finish. The French had won the first team prize, which meant 51,900 francs. It was scarcely more a triumph for Leducq than for his team-mate: Pélissier had been in the first three for a truly remarkable eighteen of the twenty-one stages, and the last four stages which he won on the trot gave him eight in all, a record since equalled only by Eddy Merckx in 1970 and 1974 and Freddy Maertens in 1976, and never yet surpassed. As a result he picked up even more lucrative contracts than Leducq himself. Other nations enjoyed their cycling successes that year, with Alfredo Binda winning his second rainbow jersey as road World Champion in Liège, to follow his first in 1927, but the Tour was a French triumph. 'Football's coming home,' the English players sang in 1996; in 1930, cycling had come home – and it remained there for five years, with French riders winning every Tour from 1930 to 1934.

But this period was distinguished by more than just a national resurgence. The whole character of the race was changing. As Portier put it in his history of the first half-century of the Tour: 'The physiognomy of the contest was modified. Racing by team, co-operation between team-mates, self-sacrificial assistance to the leader – whom it became difficult to shake off even after an accident – meant that more and more riders finished in the peloton. Stages lasted six hours instead of the fifteen or sixteen of the heroic age. Cyclists no longer rode all night. The Tour was humanized.'

And Desgrange's self-interested humanizing of the Tour paid dividends. The *Auto*'s circulation rose by half, from half a million to three-quarters. The Tour was now a central part of French life, and so was the paper.

By the following summer, sporting France needed something to cheer it up. Over the winter the great scandal had erupted that saw France brutally ejected from international rugby and the championship in which she had been the fifth nation, the only one outside the British Isles. There may have been an element of nationalism and class resentment in this. The English public-school men who ran rugby in London and tried to guard its absolute amateur purity had always had mixed feelings about Welsh miners, or for that matter Gascons and Basques from the south-west – which was and is the home of the French game. Those rough farmers and artisans, very much not public-school men, were never quite above suspicion, and when clear evidence emerged that some of *les rugbymen* had been accepting discreet payment, France was kicked out of the competition with alacrity, not to return until after the war.

And so another French triumph in the Tour was healing balm, when Antonin Magne, third behind Leducq the previous year, won the 1931 Tour for France, a feat 'Tonin' accomplished despite taking no more than one individual stage. Honour if not prize money was divided between him and two *routiers-sprinters*, Charles Pélissier and Raffaele di Paco, who jousted from Vannes to Montpellier to Grenoble and Paris, taking five stages each. Neither made it into the top ten in the final classification, but if the 'points' or sprinters' green jersey had yet existed, one of them would surely have won it.

Along with that humanization of which Portier spoke, the general standard of the riders was rapidly improving, and also levelling: hence the way most of the field rode together, and hence also the much shorter intervals between finishers. In 1920 Thys in first place had finished ten hours ahead of Vandaele in tenth; in 1933 Speicher and Stoepel in the same positions were separated by no more than forty-six minutes. But this generally improving standard produced its own problems. The best riders were more and more of a muchness, who were hard to split at a finish. When the 1931 Tour riders reached the Pyrenees, an almost indistinguishable group of ten finished in a bunch, with barely a minute between them and Vervaecke in nineteenth place. The race began in earnest only on the ninth stage. Leducq, Camusso and Benoit-Faure battled up the Col d'Aubisque, along with a gaggle of gifted younger climbers, Alfons Schepers and Julien Vervaecke from Belgium and the Italian Antonio Pesenti.

But the man who struck was Magne. Born in 1904, twelve days before Leducq, stubborn, level-headed, unflappable, hard as nails, Magne may have been the first truly professional rider to win the Tour by means of dedication and training rather than courage and flair. Thirty years later he was Poulidor's *directeur sportif*, and reproached that great if fallible sportsman for his indiscipline in training, telling him that the work of preparing for the Tour and riding in it is as intricate as a spider's web. Every May Magne used to take himself to the Pyrenees, to acclimatize himself to racing at altitude and to practise up and down the gradients.

In July 1931 it showed. He climbed the mist-shrouded Tourmalet grimly and calmly, and then left the field for dead on the descent, reaching Luchon five minutes ahead of Pesenti, who was winning his spurs on the Tour, and who was in turn three minutes ahead of Demuysère. Magne took the yellow jersey, and held it to the end, demonstrating his own adage that 'Wearing the yellow jersey doubles your strength.'

All the same he needed more than his own strength. On the stage from Nice to Gap Magne had problems with his chain, and Demuysère and Pesenti pulled far ahead while the peloton caught up with Magne. Then Pélissier heroically performed single-handed for Magne what the whole French team had done for Leducq. He slipped free from the peloton, taking with him Magne and also Di Paco, though the latter with mixed feelings as they were bitter enemies. By the finishing line in Gap, Demuysère was barely two minutes ahead of these three musketeers.

A grim stage over the Galibier was ridden through rain and mud and harsh unseasonal cold, and then the ding-dong sprinting duel between Pélissier and Di Paco resumed. Pélissier won a sprint in the Charleville velodrome on the antepenultimate stage, but only by outmanoeuvring his rival so ruthlessly that the stage was awarded to Di Paco by the officials after Italian protests. One last road stage across the stones of the Nord, still in foul weather, was won by the tough Frenchman Gaston Rebry: points that helped towards his national team's victory in the Tour, but couldn't stop Magne winning. He and Pélissier were carried shoulder high by the crowd, all of them soaked through by the rain. In case Magne didn't know what to do with his prize money, Leducq told him laconically that 'You'll be able to buy some fine big-dugged cows.'

Although the green jersey was not inaugurated for another nineteen years, the 1932 Tour saw an innovation that was a precursor of it – the award of time bonuses. If a stage winner won by more than three minutes, he picked up an additional three minutes, and the first three received an additional four. This system, had it been in force two years earlier, would have taken an hour off Pélissier's aggregated time. The object of the exercise was once more to combat indolence, to shake up the pack and 'urge the riders to fight hard', a phrase that might sound brutal but addressed a persistent truth. There is an ever-present temptation for cyclists in a long, exhausting race, if they aren't going to win anything, to go through the motions, pedalling steadily without pushing themselves to the utmost. By way of unintended consequence, the change encouraged a new breed of points specialists, sprinters who could put in a fierce finish.

Like the preceding five, this Tour took an anticlockwise route with a first stage from Paris to Caen, although with a distinct change: several stages in the north and west were dropped, and the race reached the Pyrenees in no more than four long stages as well as two much-needed rest days. As a whole it was notably shorter than the year before, twenty-one stages instead of twenty-four, 4479 kilometres, down from 5091, although the longest individual stage was a gruelling 382 kilometres from Nantes to Bordeaux, substantially further than the previous year's longest.

As it proved, it was on that third stage that Leducq took the yellow jersey from the German Kurt Stoepel when he pipped Raffaele di Paco at the line, and held on to it for the next eighteen days. They weren't plain sailing, for all that. The field left Luchon in a storm which an old hand thought presaged 'a nightmare day', and they made their way painfully up what seemed a more than usually flinty and pot-holed road to the Col d'Aubisque, with the little Spanish rider Trueba (inevitably 'The Flea') in the lead. By the end of the day Pesenti had won the stage, though there were other fine performances, uphill from Maurice Archambaud, showing his quality as a climber, and downhill from Georges Speicher, who showed his own strength as a *descendeur extraordinaire* by moving from fifty-first place atop the Tourmalet to twelfth at Luchon. Leaving the Pyrenees Leducq had three minutes over Stoepel, nine over Pesenti and eleven over Benoit-Faure.

And then Leducq and Archambaud gave another demonstration of team work when Leducq punctured on the stage to Perpignan but Archambaud stuck by and helped him back to the peloton and eventually to second place for the day, behind the Belgian Frans Bonduel, who had problems of his own. That year's Belgian team looked formidable on paper, but, in striking contrast with French co-operation, was riven by dissension. Jean Aerts, the team leader, accused his colleagues of leaving him in the lurch, and one meeting in the team hotel almost ended in physical violence.

On the stage from Cannes to Nice it was the turn of the Italians, who came into their own with a team performance that would eventually put Camusso in third place on the podium. But Leducq held his place throughout the Alps, crossing the Galibier in snow, where he won the approval of a discreet spectator, none other than Henri Pélissier. 'Celui-là, c'est un costaud', he said of Leducq: that's one tough guy. By what was becoming well-nigh a Tour tradition, Leducq beat Di Paco into Charleville but was declassed. From there to Malo, Demuysère and Rebry reprised their duel of the preceding year, Rebry finishing more than fifteen minutes ahead of the field, but with little effect on the GC. Leducq took the last two stages, having anyway cleverly used the new points system to make the lead he had established in the Pyrenees unassailable, and 'the joyful Dédé' reached Paris as one of the most popular champions ever to win.

That race prompted one French writer to eulogize the joy of this most beautiful of international sporting contests, but before the next running of the Tour joy and beauty were perceptibly put in the shade by political events. In January 1933 Germany had a new leader, and the European stage darkened. It wasn't until the Berlin Olympics three years later that Hitler showed his full, masterly understanding of the new uses of sport for political purposes, but any idea that sport transcended national rivalries was already less realistic than ever, and the French team at the very least knew that they were in some degree riding for national glory. That was made easier by their quality: by 1933 France had a stellar *équipe*, one of those glorious conjunctions of great athletes in one team that now and again grace one sport or another; as it might be, the late 1930s Yankees of DiMaggio and Gehrig, the late 1940s Middlesex of Compton and Edrich, or the late 1950s Real Madrid of Puskas and Di Stefano. Under André Leducq the team comprised Antonin Magne, Charles Pélissier, Georges Speicher, Roger Lapebie, Maurice Archambaud, René le Grèves and Léon le Calvez. The Italians were captained by Guerra, who would finish second, the Belgians by Aerts, who came ninth. Both Guerra and his team-mate Binda had been reckoned favourites by some, but no team proved a match for the French, and it was always likely that a French rider would win.

What was not pre-ordained, however, was which of the team it would be. Archambaud won the first stage and held the yellow jersey to Digne in the Provençal Alps, at the end of the ninth stage. Archambaud was tiny for a cyclist, and in those more robust days, before correctness and 'sensitivity', his press nickname was 'Le Nabot', the dwarf. Whatever his size he was strong enough to win over the *pavé* from Paris to Lille, heading a group of Belgians into Marcq-en-Bareuil racecourse and leaving Magne in fortieth place, sixteen minutes off the pace. Just to confirm how unsettled the form was, the great Di Paco finished the second stage into Charleville as *lanterne rouge*, and Benoit-Faure was eliminated. On the next stage, to Metz, Charles Pélissier had a bad crash, and finished the stage with his right arm dripping blood, to be eliminated also.

This was the year which saw a new prize, the Grand Prix de la Montagne, awarded to the *meilleur grimpeur* – best climber or King of the Mountains – on a comparatively simple formula of points measured by performance on climbs, although 'comparatively' is, as it were, a comparative word where anything to do with the regulations of the Tour is concerned. As the years went by the scoring was refined and climbs were graded by difficulty, from 1 to 4 and, above 1 (like Premier Grand Cru claret), the *hors catégorie* climbs. Category 4 means gentle hills in Normandy or Lorraine which any weekend cyclist could potter over; 'outside category' means awesome Alpine passes like the Galibier, which are frightening even to look at. As the rules in 2002 stipulated, scores ranged from 1 point for the third rider over a category 4 climb to 10 for the fourth over a category 2, to 40 points for the first over an *hors catégorie*.

In that first year the mountains leadership was seized on the Ballon d'Alsace by Trueba, who confirmed his place as best climber on the Galibier, although that stage into Grenoble was won by Guerra, now second overall to Archambaud. The next stage to Gap had been reconnoitred by Magne on behalf of the French team. Duly aware how tough the later part of the course was, he launched an attack after only twenty kilometres: Georges Speicher won the stage and moved into fourth place. The whole stage was so brutal that Machuery, the timekeeper, allowed additional time, but ten riders were eliminated even so. Poor Archambaud rode to the limits of his endurance, and although Leducq and Lapébie helped him on the Col de Vars, he reached the summit completely exhausted, and his yellow jersey was taken over by the Belgian Georges Lemaire.

The mountain stages Grenoble–Gap and Gap–Digne were won by the 26-year-old Speicher, an enthusiastic swimmer who had never ridden a bike until he was seventeen, had only turned pro the previous season, and was only in the French team as a substitute. He turned into a fine rider, and in particular a brilliant descender, though technology as well as courage and skill played a crucial part: he was riding a bike that for the first time had a brake clamping the rim of the rear wheel. A front brake alone, even – or especially – when assisted by the rider's foot applied to the wheel, had been unsatisfactory on all stages, tending to make the bike rear up, but was particularly perilous downhill. As Speicher showed, the descents could now be handled much more adroitly, and hence that much faster.

It was Speicher's skill downhill that won him the next stage into Marseilles. Although tensions inside the French camp were reported, Archambaud stiffened his upper lip to say the next day, 'Speicher or me, it's all the same' – a contrast to the Belgian team with its continued intestine squabbling.

Through the Pyrenees Trueba again dominated the climbs, while Speicher nearly lost his yellow jersey, left behind up the Tourmalet by Guerra and Martano. But he too showed great skill as *dégringoleur* or downhill artist, catching the two Italians to take second place. Speicher then held the overall lead through

Gascony, Brittany, Normandy and at last into the motor-racing course at Montlhery. He had won three of the year's twenty-three stages, in itself less impressive than Jean Aerts's six, including three consecutively from Bordeaux to Rennes, and Guerra's five, including the last stage.

By now Europe was shivering with political fevers, and few countries were spared. Although the Third Republic didn't experience revolution, or totalitarianism, or the small-scale civil war Austria endured in July 1934 when Dollfuss was assassinated in an attempted putsch by the National Socialists, that year saw violence in France also. In October, three months after the Tour had ridden into Marseilles, King Alexander of Yugoslavia landed there to be greeted by the French foreign minister Louis Barthou, and as the pair drove from the harbour they were assassinated by a Croat nationalist. And the year had begun with the explosive Stavisky scandal, with the suicide of the fraudster Alexander Stavisky and the resignation of a government minister who was implicated in his swindles, and then in February there was a one-day general strike, violent clashes in Paris between Right and Left and widespread rioting.

Sport was not excluded from the effects of politics, quite apart from the irrelevant but teasing coincidence that, on the very day Stavisky was found dying in his chalet in Chamonix, a boy called Jacques Anquetil was born in Rouen. In the month before the Tour the new football World Cup was staged for a second time, in Italy. It had been created four years earlier to link the two great centres of soccer at the time, Europe and Latin America. That first competition in Uruguay had been something of a hollow victory for the host nation, as England and Scotland were in dispute with the world governing body and most other European countries had boycotted the competition for reasons of their own, with only France, Belgium, Yugoslavia and Romania sending teams to Montevideo. In 1934 the host nation again won – and Mussolini turned the World Cup into a propaganda circus, with the Italian players giving the fascist salute before beating the Czechs in the final.

By that standard the Tour, which began in Paris on 3 July, was a more elevating occasion. French supremacy was confirmed, with a French rider beating an Italian once more, but there was no orgy of nationalistic triumphalism. And the French really did dominate, winning nineteen of the twenty-three stages, five won by Roger Lapébie, holding the yellow jersey from start to finish, and taking three out of the first five places.

In addition to the national teams, twenty individual riders were invited by the race organizers; the system of time bonuses was modified; and scoring for the Mountains prize in its second year was refined by grading the great climbs over the Ballon d'Alsace, Galibier, Vars, Allos, Peyresourde, Aspin, Tourmalet and Aubisque. There was also a *contre la montre individuel* or time trial over eighty kilometres from La Roche sur Yon to Nantes, a discipline that would become a specialism.

In the brilliant French team there were two new names, the national champion Raymond Louviot, 'Laripette', and the *cannois* René Vietto, only twenty but already with a reputation as a climber, and destined to be the year's true hero. Both were urged on by Leducq, who was now following the race by car. The early stages were eventful, with plenty of crashes on the northern *pavé*, and Archambaud abruptly abandoning after he fell badly crossing tram lines just after leaving Belfort, to break his collar bone. Even then – and even when Charles Pélissier, their best sprinter, abandoned – the French were in complete control, taking the first six stages, before Vietto came into his own across the Alps, winning from Aix-les-Bains to Grenoble. He was made to fight all the way up the Galibier by the brilliant little Spanish rider Federico Ezquerra, but he tore away downhill and had three minutes in hand over Martano and Magne at the line. Over the Vars and Allos, and then again on the Gap–Digne stage, Vietto leapt further up the GC from sixteenth place to sixth, before winning the stage from Nice despite a fierce attack by Martano. He rode into his home town of Cannes to an ecstatic reception from a huge crowd, cheering even as it was brutally driven back by police truncheons.

By the Pyrenees Magne was still in the yellow jersey, but he kept it only through Vietto's self-sacrifice, which entered the heroic annals of the Tour. Descending from the Hospatilet, Magne fell badly. Vietto was not far behind. Told that Magne had broken his wheel, he immediately took a wheel off his own bike to give it to Magne, and then waited in tears for the *car balai*, the broomstick van.

The next day Vietto led over the Col de Port and then lost the lead. Magne was back in the peloton, wondering how far his chances had been damaged, when Vietto joined him again as *fidus Achates*, and they caught Martano together. On top of that, Martano drank bad milk on the evening before the stage from Luçon to Tarbes, and spent most of the night in the latrine. Magne won the stage from Trueba, twenty-two minutes ahead of Martano. Then a last mountain stage saw a huge crowd at the Tourmalet to cheer on Vietto at the head of the field. He crossed the Aubisque, and then reached Pau, ahead of Lapébie and Martano.

Leaving the Pyrenees Magne had the race at his mercy, but he recalled the year when Leducq was almost caught on the line, and said, in what would become ritual fashion for the leader, still echoed by Lance Armstrong sixty-eight years later, that 'the Tour is never finished until the last turn of the pedal'. In the event Magne only emphasized his dominance in the time trial in Brittany ahead of Lapébie and held the overall lead to the end, when Leducq heavy handedly told him that he could now afford half a dozen of his big-uddered cows. Magne himself was less whimsical in explaining his success in unexceptionable terms. 'You need to be able to stay the trip, economize your strength,' he said, 'and be as strong at the end of the race as at the beginning.'

Some of his glory was shared with others. The last stage into the Parc des Princes was won by Sylvère Maes, and his compatriot Félicien Vervaecke took fourth place overall, the more impressive since both of them were competing as individual riders. Vervaecke was rewarded by inclusion in the Belgian national team for the following year.

And there was Vietto, who became the first of what remain, remarkably enough, only four Frenchmen to have won the Mountains prize in more than sixty Tours, to be followed by Louison Bobet, Raphael Geminiani and Richard Virenque. The prize later became something of a prerogative of men either from hilly Spain, led by Federico Bahamontes, maybe the greatest climber of all, and, less explicably, from the lowlands of Belgium. A Belgian would take the Mountains prize in 1935, while two others, and an Italian, would bring to an end those years of ceaseless French triumph.

6

'Raisons Politiques'

1935–1939

Over its first century, one of the themes of the Tour's story has been the regular flowering of Belgian cycling: before and after the Great War, in the late 1930s, and then the total dominance of Merckx in the early 1970s. By an improbable coincidence, the Tours of 1935 and 1936 were won by Belgian namesakes but no kin – Romain Maes and Sylvère Maes merely and coincidentally shared a common Flemish name – but it was the first of these who achieved the more memorable feat. Romain won the yellow jersey on the first stage from Paris to Lille on 4 July, and he was still wearing it as they returned to Paris and the Parc des Princes on 28 July. It was the third time that this feat had been accomplished, and the last. It may now be one of those sporting records, like Ted Williams's .406 in 1941, Jim Laker's nineteen wickets at Old Trafford in 1956, or Lester Piggott's nine wins in the Derby, that are almost certainly never to be matched. But there was a sombre note, and Maes's feat took place in a race marred by tragedy.

On a Tour that followed almost the same course as the preceding year's, although now with six half-stage time trials, Maes's romantic exploit began when he escaped in the unromantic mining town of Bruay on that first stage to Lille, and reached the line at the Croié-Laroch racecourse all alone, nineteen minutes ahead of poor Vietto who had made a sorry start. A further toll was taken on the next stage to Charleville where bad roads wrought havoc on the peloton; Archambaud punctured half a dozen times and Martano was eliminated. By Belfort, Maes held a six-minute lead over Magne. The first time trial, from Geneva to Evian, was ostensibly won by Di Paco, but only by means of grabbing a lift on to a car, for which he was penalized and lucky not to be disqualified.

The race began in earnest in the Alps. Vietto came into his own over the Col d'Aravis, easily beating Maes. A reporter who consolingly told Maes that he would have ridden a fine race even if he lost the yellow jersey the next day was told, 'Who said that I'm going to lose the yellow jersey?' and he didn't lose it. The Alpine stages were notable for a grimmer reason. A series of collisions between riders and vehicles had begun on an earlier stage, and a publicity car had already become entangled with the peloton before Magne ran into the back of a car that had braked suddenly. He fell, nastily impaling his left calf on a pedal. Although Leducq stopped to try to help him, it was soon clear that the Tour was over for him.

But it was on the next stage that disaster came, and on the descent from the Galibier where the Spanish rider Francesco Cepeda had a horrible fall, dying from his injuries. He was the first fatality claimed by the Tour, to be followed by Simpson in 1967 and Casartelli in 1995. 'One is too many' is easily said, and true enough, but if anything it may seem surprising that no more than three riders have been killed in a hundred years. To watch riders in a bunch sprint finish, or swerving on wet *pavés*, or negotiating narrow pass roads, or descending from a great col at hair-raising speed, is to witness what by any standards is a dangerous sport. The cyclists who ride in the Tour are brave men.

Although Vietto won the stage from Gap to Digne, he wasn't riding as well as the previous year, and it was Vervaecke and Benoit-Faure who slugged it out over Vars and Allos. Romain Maes was still in the lead by Nice, but with no more than thirty-five seconds over Camusso, the Belgians' great foe, with Speicher five minutes behind, and Romain won the next stage to Cannes ahead of his namesake Sylvère Maes. On the next stage from Cannes to Marseilles there was another nasty accident, mercifully not fatal. Jules Merviel made an escape, while the field stopped at a water fountain to drink and douse themselves. 'Julou' was almost twenty minutes ahead at Cogolin, but nearing Hyères he was overcome by dizziness in the intense heat, ran into a station-ary car, and collapsed with blood pouring out of his left eye. He was lucky to be taken in time to hospital at Hyères, and luckier that he had sustained only a fractured collar bone and partial damage to his eye. In those unhappy circumstances Charles Pélissier and Honoré Granier reached Marseilles first. Nor did the casualty list end there: Lapébie had a torn muscle and aban-doned, as did Di Paco.

A diminished and sombre field rode on to the Pyrenees, where Speicher broke down, though he still managed to take sixth place in the Tour. Poor Vietto never got back into the race, despite attacking gamely on the Perpignan–Luchon stage, and the Italians were in disarray, with Camusso suffering a fall and most of his team also abandoning, to leave three Belgians in the lead, Romain Maes, Félicien Vervaecke and Sylvère Maes.

On the next stage the heat was still overpowering but made slightly more bearable by a quantity of bottles of beer lining the road, so that the riders, in the freer and easier conditions of the age, were able to stop for a 'thirst truce'. Or so they thought: the beer was in fact a ruse arranged by Julien Moineau to distract his rivals, and he reached Bordeaux fifteen minutes ahead of the field, chortling at his wheeze. Even so, he made little impression on the general classification. The Belgians only consolidated their position in a series of time trials, and by the end took four of the first five places. Romain Maes won the last stage from Caen to Paris to win the Tour from Morelli, followed by Vervaecke.

Any lingering idea that sport could exist above politics was ended in 1936. On the day before the Tour ended the Berlin Olympics began, to become an awesome display of sport as theatre as politics recorded for posterity by the slickly repellent film-maker Leni Riefenstahl and with an orgy of Nazi flag-waving, gratifyingly spoiled for exponents of 'racial science' by the brilliant victories of the black American Jesse Owens in the 100 and 200 metres and long jump.

Political events were ominous enough. In March Hitler defied Europe by reoccupying the Rhineland, then Mussolini's armies stamped out the last resistance in Abyssinia in April. And in July, while the Tour cyclists descended from the Alps, and shortly after the 'Republican Olympics' were due to be held in Barcelona, the Spanish Civil War began, a war that among less trivial consequences would halt the Vuelta a España. Just as the European Left had persuaded itself that an anti-Fascist Popular Front was a noble cause uniting all decent men and women, Stalin complicated matters in August by staging the first Moscow Trial, when sixteen of his colleagues where shot after confessing to imaginary crimes. The times were not dull.

France was caught up in the turmoil. As the year opened, Pierre Laval was prime minister, but he resigned in late January, another step on the path that would take this former Communist towards the Vichy government, energetic support for Hitler's New Order, and execution as a traitor. Just a month before the Tour began, Léon Blum became prime minister at the head of a left-wing coalition determined to give the workers a shorter working week and paid holidays. In the midst of this fervent atmosphere the 1936 race really did deserve to be called the Popular Front Tour.

As if to emphasize this age of anxiety, the Italian cyclists were absent, it was said, 'pour raisons politiques', but there were teams from France, Belgium and Germany, as well as smaller national teams of four or five riders from Holland, Spain, Switzerland, Luxembourg, Austria and, for the first time, Romania and Yugoslavia. A Swiss rider wore the yellow jersey, again for the first time, when Paul Egli won the initial stage from Paris to Lille. If that suggested that the smaller teams would play a large part, it was illusory. The absence of the Italians meant that the race – over much the course of the previous year, from Paris to the Nord, to Alsace, over the Alps and through Provence to the Pyrenees and home by the west coast and Normandy – would be dominated by the Belgians led by Romain Maes and the French led by Magne. Sixty team riders were augmented by thirty *touristes-routiers*, who included Vietto. After Egli's brief moment of glory, Archambaud took the overall lead, lost it to Arsène Mersch of Luxembourg, took it back over the Ballon d'Alsace into Belfort. Despite a bruising fall, he kept the lead between Evian and Aix-les-Bains, on which stage poor Vietto abandoned. It was a miserable summer, and most stages were ridden through the rain, until the Galibier, which was bathed in sunshine, though covered in snow. The Spaniards Ezquerra and Julian Berrendero dominated the climbs, but the stage was nevertheless won by the Dutch sprinter Theo Middelkamp.

For some years the Tour hadn't visited Briançon, and renewed acquaintance proved unlucky for Archambaud. He was taken ill with a vomiting attack, and his overall lead passed to Sylvère Maes, who never thereafter relinquished it. Magne fought out a duel with Maes on the next stage to Digne, but the Belgian won with a ferocious climbing performance on the Izoard.

They crossed the Col de Vars, past its quaint refuge, really a barracks built during the reign of the absurd Napoleon III, with those same two Spaniards leading from Sylvère Maes and Magne, before Maes punctured on the descent. There was then a bizarre incident at St-André-des-Alpes when the local post-man threw a beer bottle at a rider, who failed to catch it. The bottle shattered in front of Magne's bike, and he lost minutes to the resulting puncture. Maes increased his lead when his Belgians won the team time trial from Nîmes to Montpellier. Not that the teams were entirely unchallenged: another freelance, Sauveur Ducazeaux from Bayonne, won the first stage in the Pyrenees from Perpignan to Luchon with an escape before the Portet d'Aspet. Mersch joined him, and they came back to the field, but escaped again rather undeservedly when not only the peloton but the officials were held up by a train at the Pont-de-Cazeaux level crossing.

While it rides along 'Les jolies routes de France et de Navarre', as the song has it, the Tour passes scores of level crossings every year. Whereas the roads it uses are ruthlessly cleared for many hours by the gendarmerie, the trains continue to run, sometimes holding up the field, or groups of riders, or a single man; and the race regulations covering how *passages à niveau* can affect the race are of a Cartesian intellectual rigour – 'When a rider(s) with less than a 30-second advantage is (are) held up at a railroad crossing the fact that the barrier is down is considered a mere race inci-dent' – which it may require an education at the École Normale fully to elucidate.

Bad weather still dogged the Tour. On the crucial stage over the high Pyrenean passes, thick fog meant that the field could only see a few yards ahead, to be followed by driving rain. Magne had been waiting for this day to mount an attack, but he punctured again, found himself cut off from his team and gloomily watched others pass him, led by Maes who won the stage into Pau and sealed Magne's fate for the year. It was 27 July, Sylvère Maes's twenty-seventh birthday: as he said himself, a very happy one. Mersch led the last day into the Parc des Princes, but the overall lead was still comfortably held by Maes, who won from Magne and Vervaecke, with the *touriste-routier*

Léon Level, who had been second to Maes on the Luchon–Pau stage, a very creditable tenth. Less creditable was the performance of the French team, so triumphant for the past three years, but now placed behind Belgium, Spain and Luxembourg. There was modest compensation for France and Archambaud the following year when he beat the world hour record by covering 45.767 kilometres; and there was another French star in the ascendant: Roger Lapébie won the Paris–Nice race and the Critérium National. But his truly heroic performance came in the *grande boucle*, regrettably overshadowing another country's participation.

Although England had some claim to be the home of the bicycle, and although cycling has been a hugely popular sport among the British, it has never been one in which they have excelled at the highest level. To date, only fifty-two British riders have competed in the Tour, and only twenty-three have finished. None had taken part in the race until 1937. That was the year when a new king was crowned in Westminster Abbey (and the coronation was the new-born BBC television service's first outside broadcast), with the shy and awkward George VI providentially succeeding his glamorous but shallow brother Edward who had abdicated the previous December, and whose presence on the throne would have been disastrous when war came; the year Neville Chamberlain succeeded Baldwin as prime minister; the year George Orwell wrote *The Road to Wigan Pier*.

And it was the year Charley Holland and Bill Burl entered the Tour de France as the first British riders, in a three-man team with the French-Canadian Pierre Gachon. It was not an auspicious debut, and their participation had little impact on the great field in a race that was both unusually dramatic and historic. Gachon was eliminated by time on the first stage, Burl abandoned on the second after crashing twice, and Holland was relegated to last place after the stage over the Ballon d'Alsace for holding on to a car.

More important than any national participation, this was the first year when the *dérailleur* gear was generally used by Tour cyclists. Although the appearance of handlebars has varied, and of wheels, as has the materials from which frames are made, both strengthening and lightening bikes, the brilliant simplicity and effectiveness of the original diamond-shaped design means that it has changed very little in basic appearance in more than a hundred years. During the whole time the Tour has been run there has been in fact only one truly radical change, and that is the gear. The coming of the derailleur (to anglicize it) was akin to the change from hand-set type to machine composition, or from piston-prop aircraft to jets. And as with other technical revolutions, it was strongly resisted: many of the bike companies claimed that the new gear was too expensive and troublesome.

It was surely ingenious. Until then, gear ratios on a bike could be changed by turning the rear wheel round, as Tour riders did when beginning a climb, or with a simple three-speed hub gear on a city push-bike. The derailleur was operated by a switch on the frame of the bike beneath the handlebar (much later the switch was moved on to the handlebar), operating a wire which moved an articulated arm holding the chain by the rear wheel. As its name suggests, this gear derails the chain to move it from one cogwheel to another. Now riders could choose from four or five gears, later doubled by the simple expedient of having two sets of cogged wheels at the pedal end of the chain. Oddly enough, this revolutionary innovation appeared at first to make little difference, at least as measured in basic statistics: the winner of the 1936 Tour covered its 4442 kilometres at an average of 31.108 k.p.h., the winner next year covered 4415 km at 31.565 k.p.h. But cycling was transformed all the same.

France was not quite transformed. A great International Exposition held in Paris in 1937 gave a misleading appearance to a country that was in reality in woeful economic difficulties, and politically still very tense. The Popular Front government came and went, leaving behind one other legacy for which hundreds of millions of travellers would be grateful, the creation of the SNCF. The nationally owned railway network covered a total of 42,500 kilometres at the time of its formation. Sixty-five years later a correspondent covering the Tour, especially if he came from England with its third-world railways, could only be awe-struck by a country where trains still cover most of the country with comfort and punctuality and stunning speed. After the first rest day in the 2002 Tour, it was possible to catch up with the race by taking a train from Paris to Bordeaux, a distance of 580 kilometres, in 3 hours 40 minutes, leaving and arriving on the second. An equivalent (or rather, at 350 miles, a shorter journey) from London to Berwick-on-Tweed takes just under five hours, if you're lucky. They order some things better in France, from railways to movies: 1937 was also the year of *La Grande Illusion*, the first part of Jean Renoir's incomparably moving 'War and Peace', followed two years later by *La Règle du Jeu*.

The rules of the game for the 1937 Tour saw ninety-eight cyclists grouped in national teams, as well as individuals who would 'for the first time be treated and cared for like the aces'. In the early stages the lead changed hands, with Majerus, Archambaud, Kint and Bautz – Luxembourger, Frenchman, Belgian and German – successively wearing the yellow jersey, until it was taken by a 22-year-old Italian. Gino Bartali had already twice won the Giro, but this year had been told by Mussolini to skip the Italian race in favour of the Tour for reasons of national prestige. He rode brilliantly over the Galibier, reaching Grenoble eight and sixteen minutes ahead of Sylvère Maes and Lapébie.

Here the drama began to unfold. First, Archambaud collided with an official car, wrecking one of his wheels. He took over Le Grèves's bike, which was too big for him, but crashed again and abandoned, followed by Speicher after another tumble. Then disaster struck Bartali as he descended from the Col du Laffrey, accompanied by Jules Rossi, his team-mate. Crossing a bridge, Rossi suddenly fell, forcing Bartali into the parapet, and over into the icy stream beneath.

In the local doggerel, 'Parlement, Mistral et Durance sont les trois fléaux de Provence', and this tributary of the Durance was quite enough of a scourge for Bartali. Helped by Camusso, he heroically rejoined the race even though his bloody and muddy body was almost seized up with cold. Amazingly enough he still held the yellow jersey at Briançon. A famously pious Catholic, Bartali claimed to be sustained by his faith and by the intercession of the Blessed Virgin, but even she couldn't make up for the effects of his terrifying accident. Although Bartali reached Marseilles, it was clearer to the Italian cycling authorities than to him that he couldn't go further, and he was ordered to abandon.

That Toulon–Marseilles stage was a team time trial, won by the Belgians, who were plunged into a violent row when the race director arbitrarily decided to change the rules in favour of single riders against teams, ostensibly 'to equalize chances'. A nasty situation grew nastier in the Pyrenees when Lapébie's handlebars broke after they had been sabotaged; the Belgians accused Lapébie of taking unauthorized food for his brother Guy; and then Lapébie was given an illicit push, 'despite his vehement protests', and was penalized ninety seconds. On the next stage it was Maes who punctured, was helped illegally by his team-mates and by two individual countrymen, Gustaaf Deloor and Adolf Braeckeveldt, and was penalized in turn. Much worse, an angry mob in Bordeaux, enraged by the treatment of their local hero Lapébie, attacked the Belgians, throwing pepper in their faces. Just before the next stage began, the Belgians announced that they were withdrawing in protest and would not take part in the Tour in future, with one of the team saying sarcastically that they didn't want to be lynched in Paris.

As it all too often does, violence worked: Lapébie was able to win the stages into La Rochelle and La Roche sur Yon, before winning the Tour seven minutes ahead of Vicini, with the Swiss rider Leo Amberg in third. Displaying singularly little magnanimity in victory, Lapébie poured scorn on the Belgians: 'I was the fastest. Sylvère Maes knew he was beaten.' Orwell may not have been entirely right when he said that, far from a mark of human brotherhood, sport is 'an unfailing source of ill-will' between peoples; but there are times when he doesn't seem to have been so far wrong.

Despite their threats, the Belgian 'black squadron' (from the colour of its team jerseys rather than its mood) did return in 1938, and despite his disaster, Bartali was back stronger than ever, amid a deeply ominous national and international scene. In January, after the resignation of the French premier Chautemps, Blum first tried and then failed to form another government, then briefly succeeded, his four weeks in office coinciding with an event that shook Europe. In the 1930 and 1931 Tours there had been German teams; in 1932 this became 'Deutschland–Oesterreich', adumbrating in cycling terms the Anschluss, Hitler's absorption of Austria in March 1938.

Although it would be far-fetched to suppose that there were any conscious political forces affecting the Tour, this mood of heightened nationalism was echoed in the new rules: no more individual riders, only national teams. France was in fact represented by not one but three teams, the first squad, captained by Magne, and two supplementary teams, the Pernod Cadets captained by Leducq, and the Bleuets. The *bonifications* were simplified and reduced, a minute's bonus only for a stage winner, and the Briançon–Aix-les-Bains stage included for the first time the Col d'Iseran, with the race run anticlockwise for the first time since 1932.

And so, as the field rode through Normandy, Brittany and Guyenne, the yellow jersey changed hands from Oberbeck to Majerus to Leducq, an unexpected leader when they reached the Pyrenees, but with no more than twelve minutes in hand over Sylvère Maes, who was forty-second in the GC. The only incidents by then were sundry misfortunes. Paul Maye, a French sprinting champion, had had a bad fall even before the Tour began. He managed to finish the first stage to Caen with an agonizing broken shoulder-bone before abandoning. Vietto seemed out of sorts even before he collided with a motor-coach on the second stage; the Toulouse rider Sylvain Marcillou came a cropper at St-Georges-de-Didonne and cracked his head against the edge of an old well, was helped back into the saddle by Jaminet, and rode on until the blood blinded him and his team had to leave him by the roadside. He nevertheless forced himself to continue to the finish, arriving half an hour behind the field at Bordeaux, where he collapsed. It was a moving episode, and yet almost absurd. The story of the Tour is quite often one of heroic but fruitless sacrifice.

Towards the end of the Pau–Luchon stage, Bartali attacked. He was already one of the great climbers of the age, though with a completely distinctive technique. Instead of a steady incremental advance uphill, he stuck to the other climbers' wheels until they approached the summit, then attacked and broke away from the field with something as close to a sprint as the gradient permitted. Then on the descent from the Col d'Aspin he skidded on a tricky corner and broke a wheel. But he repaired and recovered and began to tighten his grip with every mountain stage, where the new system of bonus points for climbers worked very much to his benefit. Leducq had lost his appetite or his aptitude for climbing and finished badly in the mountains. As for the victor of five years earlier, Speicher was caught cadging a tow from a car and was ignominiously disqualified.

The next stage in driving rain from Luchon to Perpignan was won by Jean Fréchaut, usually reckoned a sprinter; Félicien Vervaecke won the Narbonne–Béziers time trial; and Magne showed that he wasn't finished, by winning the stage to Montpellier, though not with much help. The French team was fractious and jealous, not even sure whether to follow Magne, Jean-Pierre Goasmat or Victor Cosson, the last of whom was the leading French rider when the Tour reached the Alps, in third place, 8′45″ behind Vervaecke and Bartali.

Even then there was a lull before Bartali launched the attack everyone had been expecting, between Digne and Briançon, crossing the line on his own 5′18″ ahead of his team-mate Vicini, followed by Mathis Clemens. Now Bartali had the yellow jersey, and he meant to keep it, despite a fierce attack by the Belgians after the Galibier and over the 2769-metre Col d'Iseran. On the descent to Bourg-Madame the whole Italian team managed to puncture except for Bartali on whom fortune was smiling and who was left racing with Belgians and Frenchmen. But they couldn't hold him, there or all the way to Paris. On the last stage Magne and Leducq escaped together. The two near twins, who had both ridden the Tour for the first time in 1927, who had both finished in nine races and who had won it twice each, entranced the crowd from Vallangoujard to the Parc des Princes. The officials hesitated before awarding the stage to them both 'ex aequo'. It was a sentimental occasion, the more so in hindsight since neither man was to ride in the race again. But no amount of sentiment could stop Bartali, who won the Tour by eighteen minutes from Vervaecke, with Cosson in third place.

This was the first Italian victory since Bottecchia's second Tour thirteen years earlier, only the third in all. It sent Italy into raptures and was inevitably milked for political purposes. A fund was set up for Bartali, to which Mussolini was ostentatiously the first subscriber. When Italian fans had crossed the border for the Briançon stage and begun to mob Bartali, an Italian cycling official shouted, 'Don't touch him. He's a god!' He wasn't, in fact, for all that the grudging chauvinist Desgrange had said the year before that 'I have never seen anything as wonderful as Bartali on the Ballon d'Alsace'. He was indeed a wonderful rider, as well as one of the more attractive Tour winners, a simple Tuscan, a generous man who, in Italian races, had been known to let another rider win ahead of him when the man's *promessa sposa* was waiting at the line. His sense of duty and piety was what everyone wrote and writes about Bartali: he made the pilgrimage to Lourdes, he ate with a statuette of the Madonna on the table, he thanked her for his successes. Maybe what's significant here is that his behaviour was thought noteworthy. The very fact that open devotion seemed quaint or amusing in a man from the homeland of Catholic Europe may have adumbrated the implosion of the Catholic Church a generation or two later, not least in Italy. At any rate, Bartali's piety would add a piquant element to one of the great duels in the story of the Tour, with his impious young countryman Fausto Coppi.

By the following summer the most politically ignorant cycling fan could not be unaware of the direction in which Europe was heading, and the 1939 Tour was a shadow of itself. A field of 79 riders began the race, not in itself a huge reduction from the 100 of 1930, but for *raisons politiques* both obvious and ominous, there were no German or Italian riders, and no Spaniards either in the harsh aftermath of the Civil War that had just ended. One French rider entered for the race was André Bramard. He was even allocated 69 as his *dossard* number, but by July he had been issued another number by the army, was already in uniform, and couldn't take part.

Partly in order to give a depleted race some fresh flavour, there was a second 'B' team from Belgium, along with teams of eight each from Switzerland and Luxembourg, and four regional French squads. The provinces of France thus had home teams to cheer, Ouest fans when the race went from Lorient to Nantes, Sud-Ouest from Bordeaux to Toulouse, Sud-Est from Montpellier up into the Alps. In this respect the new formula proved a considerable success. As if pre-ordained, the stages through Brittany were dominated by Breton riders: Jean Fontenay took the yellow jersey, Eloi Tassin won Vire–Brest, Pierre Cloarec won Brest–Lorient. But the year was more notable for Vietto's comeback after years in the doldrums following his fine races in 1934 and 1935. Riding for the South-East team, he overcame the jinx that had seemed to dog him in the earlier stages of the race, and had won the yellow jersey by the Pyrenees.

They were crossed in appalling weather, violent storms and heavy rain, with Vietto attacking on the Tourmalet and then battling with Maes on the descent through thick fog. Maes pulled away on the Col d'Aspin, but Vietto fought back and still led the GC into Toulouse, and then through his home town of Cannes to an ecstatic welcome. And yet he was only 1'49" ahead of Sylvère Maes when they reached the line at Monaco, with no more than twelve minutes over Vlaemynck, Vissers and Archambaud.

Instead of torrential rain they now raced through scorching Alpine sun. The Belgians struck, with Maes dropping Vietto and increasing his lead approaching the Col d'Izoard. And Vietto was stricken. All racing cyclists dread pole-axing *défaillance*, or what English riders call 'the bonk': not the mellow tiredness that a game of tennis, golf or rugby can bring, nor yet the deep fatigue that any professional athlete sometimes knows, but a terrifying, paralysing collapse, when the blood sugar is exhausted from the rider's metabolism and he can find neither energy nor will to use his muscles at all. Vietto was bonked. He recovered, and managed to reach the summit, but was now a hopeless 17'25" behind Maes, who took the stage into Briançon and the yellow jersey. It was a heart-breaking day for Vietto. His decline was only confirmed on the stage over the Col d'Iseran, which – 'par un sorte de sadisme', as one reporter put it – had been made a time trial. Maes rode the sadistic thirteen kilometres in 47'39", more than eight minutes faster than Vietto in twenty-first place.

Although Archambaud again showed the qualities that made him the one-hour record holder by winning the Neuens–Dijon time trial, covering the 59 kilometres at a nippy 42 k.p.h., and another title-holder, the previous year's road racing champion Marcel Kint, won the last stage into the Parc, Maes won the Tour more than half an hour ahead of Vietto.

A few months later 'Il faut en finir' was the slogan repetitiously drummed into the French: we must finish the war that had by then begun, as indeed France did finish it the following summer, though not in the way the sloganeers had hoped. 'Il faut en finir' might have been Sylvère Maes's maxim, as he drove himself to the end of a gruelling race, an ordeal he didn't pretend to have enjoyed: 'The contest was too hard. I shan't take part again.'

But far more poignant was Vietto's fate. 'Dramatic irony' in its strict sense means that the audience knows something the protagonist doesn't. In Greek drama the storylines were familiar to every Athenian from childhood, and only the characters on stage were unaware of what was coming. All of history must in that sense have an ironic quality, since we can only view it with hindsight and the knowledge of what came next. In Paris on 30 July that year, Vietto thought that he had ridden a superb race, as he had, and that he had been vanquished as much by illness as by his opponent, which was also true. He would still only be twenty-six the next summer. If ever he was going to win the great race, it would be the Tour de France of 1940.

Repos

Normandy

On its fifth day in 2002 the Tour finished in Rouen, a town often visited by the race since 1949 though oddly not before then, and which was the *Départ* in 1997, when the Prologue there was won by the honourable and scrupulous Chris Boardman. Rouen is famous for its cathedral and the church of St-Ouen, for its luscious cream-heavy cooking, for the journey round its streets in the horse-drawn cab in which Emma Bovary committed adultery with Léon, and for the death of Joan of Arc. A few hundred yards from the finishing line is a huge monument glorifying her, whose mortal remains were lost for ever in the fire that consumed her but who lives in the hearts of those who love her. Not that everyone loves her equally, not even in France, where her cult and her canonization had a very clear – and a very divisive – political message. For many, she was the embodiment of 'a certain idea of France', which is to say of Catholic France fighting its fierce battle against the laical republic. And against other dark forces, too: it wasn't until 1949 that the Tour first visited Orléans whence the Maid took her name (though she was born in the little village of Domrémy-la-Pucelle in Lorraine, no distance from Nancy). Not many years earlier visitors could have bought a postcard on sale there, comparing Orléans in 1431, exalted by the pure and saintly Joan, with Orléans in 1931, in the hands of the Jews.

We have heard the ominous political echoes of sport, louder in the last decade than ever; sporting or otherwise, France had not been a happy country in the 1930s, and less happy in 1940 than ever before in her history. Five weeks after the 1939 Tour ended, France was at war with Germany. Only weeks before the 1940 Tour should have been run, the German armies swept into France, crossing the Meuse on 10 May and reaching the Channel at Boulogne seventeen days later to cut off the British army and a large part of the French. That beleaguered garrison was evacuated, but the Germans moved through Normandy and south to the Loire, and on 16 June the new leader, Marshal Pétain, sued for peace, signing an armistice on the 22nd. Germany had played one of the most devastating 'return matches' in history to avenge the defeat of 1918, and cruelly confute Desgrange's former boasting that 'a Frenchman will never succumb to a German'. A new regime under Pétain was installed at Vichy (visited by the Tour surprisingly soon after a war in which it had became the name of ill-fame, whose bottled water Claude Rains eloquently discards at the end of *Casablanca*). Some Frenchmen, led by Brigadier-General Charles de Gaulle, refused to accept the verdict and raised the standard of Free France in London, though their cause wasn't immediately helped by the British. Dunkirk and Strasbourg lie at different points of the *hexagone* and both have often been *villes-étapes*. Shortly after the fall of France the French fleet, including the eponymous battleships *Dunkerque* and *Strasbourg*, lay across the Mediterranean at Mers-el-Kebir on the Algerian coast. When they refused immediately to surrender to the Royal Navy they were sunk on Churchill's orders with heavy loss of life, *pour encourager les autres*, even if it wasn't quite clear who the others were meant to be in this case.

All of France north of the Loire became an occupied zone, including those two great nurseries of cyclists, Brittany and Normandy, where English riders have often come to base themselves in the hope of making a career. No one visiting Normandy today can miss the undertones of war, from very long before the 1940s, or the long connection with England, very nearly a thousand years old. In Bayeux is the great tapestry stitched to commemorate the conquest of England by William the Bastard, Duke of Normandy, in 1066. Less than 400 years later, Henry V of England was back, besieging Harfleur north of the mouth of the Seine before marking his great victory at Agincourt by massacring the French prisoners.

Not so very far from there, on the first Friday of the 2002 race, I stayed literally en route for that day's stage, at Evreux where the peloton rode past its fine cathedral, one of a dozen great churches between Rheims, where the third stage had ended on Tuesday and Mont St-Michel, in whose shadow the seventh stage ended on Saturday: a route which takes you close to the cathedrals of Beauvais, Lisieux and Bayeux. And the visitor to Normandy can intersperse beautiful buildings with sumptuous meals.

Nothing about Norman cuisine is in any way *nouvelle* or *minceur*. This is a landscape of pastures, meadows and chalk streams, offering some of the best trout fishing in Europe. Its farms produce beef, which means the tripes to be cooked *à la mode de Caen*, *pré-salé* lamb, pork for *andouille de Vire* (a very distinctive and distinctly acquired taste), the Rouennais duck stewed in its own juice, the butter and cream that almost every Norman dish, such as sole *dieppois*, uses in copious quantities, Livarot and Camembert cheeses, chickens, and the eggs for the omelettes Mère Poulard which are something of a culinary cliché of Mont St-Michel. Not by accident the province also gives us the *trou normand*, a slug of calvados apple brandy taken between courses to settle the stomach and prepare it for more assaults on the digestive juices.

Needless to say, Normandy is now swept up in the exhausting enthusiasm for *la mode rétro*, for invented tradition, and for institutionalizing writers and artists by turning anywhere they lived or worked into tourist shrines. Not that this is purely French, as visitors can find out who go to Wessex – 'Hardy country' – or to Mayo – 'Yeats country' – or to Eastwood in Nottinghamshire, the whole of which former mining village has been turned into a kitschy monument to D. H. Lawrence. With Marcel Proust this has happened twice over, in the village of Illiers near Chartres where he grew up, which he imagined in literature as 'Combray', and which is now 'Illiers-Combray' (as it were, 'Dorchester-Casterbridge') in case anyone forgets; and at Cabourg on the Normandy coast, not far from Caen, which he imagined as 'Balbec'. Lest we forget, the Grand Hotel at Cabourg is now called 'Le Balbec', it serves a 'Cocktail Proust', and breakfasters are obliged to eat a madeleine, with or without tisane.

Not every cyclist who has ridden in the Tour will have read *À la Recherche du Temps Perdu* or will know the luminous passage on the front at Balbec, where the narrator first sees Albertine, the captivating temptress who will bewitch and torment him for several hundred thousand more words, 'a girl with brilliant, laughing eyes and plump matt cheeks, a black polo cap crammed on her head, who was pushing a bicycle with such an uninhibited swing of the hips', whose saucy gamine manner makes him think that she and her girlfriends frequented the racecourse, or 'must be the very young mistresses of professional cyclists'. Possibly there are professional cyclists who still have mistresses, though they will count themselves unlucky if any of these ladies is as tricky as Albertine.

Other literary shades in Normandy include Flaubert's, not only in Rouen but in Pont-l'Eveque, where the cheese comes from and where he set *Un Coeur simple*; Maupassant, who set stories in Fécamp, Tôtes, and Yport; and Gide, with *Isabelle* at La Roque-Baignard and *La Porte étroite* at Cuverville. Le Havre may seem, even when the Tour calls, one of the least beguiling ports in France, or anywhere, but it inspired Maupassant's *Pierre et Jean*, Sartre's *La Nausée*, and Queneau's *Un rude Hiver*. And further up the coast to Dieppe and beyond are other memories, of Oscar Wilde's sad last days in exile, and then of another though voluntary literary exile. P. G. Wodehouse lived at Le Touquet where he was found by the German army in 1940, with such unhappy consequences.

And so, while France licked her wounds, there was no Tour that July, nor for the duration of the war, though that wasn't for want of trying. No one who has followed this story so far will be under many illusions about Desgrange, with his dictatorial manner, his habit of arbitrarily, and often foolishly, changing the rules before a Tour began or even when it was in progress, his astonishing capacity for abusing riders in print. He had been an anti-Dreyfusard in the 1890s, and was no simpering liberal ever after. But he was a French patriot, and he had lived to see the utter humiliation of his country. Overshadowed by this catastrophe, Desgrange died on 16 August.

Despite all his faults, I have called him one of the great Frenchmen of his century, and he was certainly one of the most influential. To borrow and adapt words from another country and a quite different sphere, what Sir Rudolf Bing said about John Christie, the founder of the Glyndebourne opera festival, may be adapted and fit very aptly. Henri Desgrange was difficult as well as eccentric, he was sometimes tactless and overbearing, and at times 'could be megalomaniac'. But he was also a man of remarkable judgement and energy, while in the end 'all his boasting came back to the fact' that he had created the Tour de France, 'and nobody else could have done it; and on that matter he was entirely right'.

After his death Desgrange was formally succeeded as Directeur de la Course by Jacques Goddet, whose finest hour was his first in this role, when he resisted all blandishments to stage the race under occupation. Sport was disrupted in most countries that were at war, with no first-class cricket played in England, and a diminished football season in most continental countries, although in America sport continued full-blast until Pearl Harbor – 1941 was the season when Joe DiMaggio of the Yankees hit in 56 straight games and Ted Williams of the Red

Sox batted .406 – and even in Europe some events were continued as a means to entertain and boost morale. For totalitarian countries sport sometimes posed problems when the wrong side won. After Germany was beaten at ice hockey by a team from the satellite rump Czech state, Himmler complained that inferior races should not be given such opportunities to humiliate their betters, rather as Desgrange had felt about Major Taylor, the black cyclist.

In Italy the Giro was held in attenuated form in 1940, when it saw the beginning of a great rivalry between Bartali and Coppi, and competitive cycling continued elsewhere on a reduced scale, with one-day races in various countries. There was indeed an attempt to stage a 'tour' race in France in 1942, but without the stamp of authority that only Goddet could have provided this 'Circuit de France' was a sham. The following year the *Auto* announced a 'Grand Prix du Tour de France', but this was no more than a totting-up by points of nine of the races that were still being run. At the other end of the earth, in what was still technically a French colony though occupied by the Japanese, a true curiosity was held in the form of a Tour of Indo-China, using whatever bikes could be scraped together, an event worthy of the pen of Graham Greene rather than Proust.

Back at home the *Auto* covered itself with little glory during those years, although admittedly not many French institutions did much better. It was a subsequent *fable convenue* that most Frenchmen or women were *résistants*; what was true was that, as one Englishman concerned with the resistance well said, most of the French were resisters in the sense that they wished the German occupation to be over, and most were collaborators in the sense that they accepted it. Even men of the Left like Sartre and Camus spent the war writing in Paris, where a great film like *Les Enfants du Paradis* could be made cheek by jowl with the 'occupying' Germans, whose forces in truth ruled France with a light hand.

For most people, that is; and the story of French cycling has one indirect but peculiarly sombre pendant. Of all the stadiums that had sprouted in and around Paris at the end of one century and the beginning of the next, one had a special fame within and without the sport. The 'Vel d'Hiv' – Vélodrome d'Hiver, winter stadium – on the boulevard de Grenelle had opened in 1909 and had long been used for conventions and political rallies as well as its original purpose. On one famous occasion in 1937, *le tout Paris* of the Left turned out there to support the Spanish Republic in its war with Franco's insurgents and to hear the famous fulminating agitatress 'La Pasionaria' give one of her harangues.

But then something else happened within five years of that rally with which the name of the stadium would always be associated. In 1942, in a huge sweep by French police, acting under German supervision but with no lack of enthusiasm, the Jews of Paris were rounded up, and many of them held at the Vel d'Hiv, before being sent on a fatal final journey to Auschwitz. There were 4000 children among them. For the great Catholic writer François Mauriac, this was a moral landmark: 'The dream which Western man conceived in the eighteenth century, whose dawn he thought he saw in 1789, and which, until 2 August 1914, had grown stronger with the process of enlightenment and the discoveries of science – this dream vanished finally for me with those trainloads of little children.'

Two years later, too late to save those victims, the greatest seaborne invasion in the history of warfare sailed to Normandy and hit the huge stretch of beaches running west and east between the Vire and Seine estuaries, and the British on the left flank would fight their way grimly towards Caen, visited many times by the Tour over the years, although between the stage there won by Fournier in 1939 and the stage won by Diot in 1947, there wasn't much of it left. They then fought their way gruellingly through the *bocage* which seems comparatively easy going to cyclists, but not to infantry and armour facing stiff opposition.

On 25 August Paris was liberated by a French army under de Gaulle, amid scenes of mass rapture and mass copulation, followed by the dubious *épuration* in which many collaborators or supposed collaborators were savagely punished, often by people who had little to be proud of themselves.

One man who had very much to be proud of never mentioned it in his lifetime. It only transpired months before the centennial Tour that Gino Bartali, hero of the 1938 and 1948 Tours, had shown still greater heroism in 1943–4. Working as courier for a secret network, he smuggled documents to create false identity papers, and thus enable several hundred Italian Jews to escape deportation and death. Bartali did many good and brave things in his life, but nothing better or braver than this.

Slowly French life returned to normal, which required a good deal of conscious forgetting of the past. The degree of enthusiasm or acquiescence with which so many of the French had accepted defeat and collaboration was quietly forgotten, as was, thanks to those troops of de Gaulle's and General Leclerc's fighting under the Cross of Lorraine, the awkward fact that, during the course of the war, more Frenchmen had borne arms on the Axis side than on the Allied. Some acts of oblivion applied to the press. Newspapers that had continued publishing under the occupation were suspended by the new government, and then after a decent interval reappeared in new guise. Thus the tainted *Temps* and *Auto* re-emerged as the *Monde* and the *Équipe* respectively, to this day two great and flourishing papers, with the *Équipe* still one of the sponsors of the Tour.

In 1946 a Petit Tour was held with no pretence that it was the real thing, but still a proper stage race of 1310 kilometres from Monte Carlo to Paris in five days. It was won by the young Jean Lazaridès, 'Apo', from his middle name, or 'L'Enfant Grec', a protégé of René Vietto who himself came third, with Jean Robic between them in second. Now France was once again ready for something like former life, including its greatest sporting event.

7

Italian Duel

1947–1951

Even after peace returned at last to Europe, two years were
needed before a liberated but physically shattered and emotionally confused France could stage the full-scale Tour again.
Running the race would have been impossible in 1945, and even
in 1946 would have looked an indecent luxury in a country still
destitute and hungry, although also strangely beautiful away from
the scarred battlefields. Compared with many of the great cities
of Europe, Paris itself was pretty well untouched, apart from
some bombing of factories on the outskirts. The learnedly passionate Richard Cobb, Oxford professor, ardent francophile and
great historian of France, had come to know and adore Paris
before the war, went back to spend the post-war decade there,
and was overcome with pleasure when an eminent French
scholar told him that he spoke French *comme un titi parisien*, like a
Paris cockney. Cobb had first returned to Paris in late 1944 in the
unconvincing guise of a British army corporal, and he used to say
that the city was never lovelier than that autumn, freed from the
Germans but also from two of his greatest dislikes: there was

barely any motor traffic, because there was no petrol, and there were no dogs, 'because they'd all been eaten'.

Before long Paris was once again an exhilarating *ville lumière*, now the city of existentialism and modern jazz, Suzy Delair in *Quai des Orfèvres*, Juliette Greco, Jean-Paul Sartre and his as-yet-friendly rival Albert Camus (a former footballer rather than cyclist, a goalkeeper like Nabokov), whose haunting *La Peste* was published in 1947. Holding the Tour was controversial enough in this year, in a country threatened by political instability, beset by strikes – Tour business that year had to be conducted by telegram during a national postal strike – and still hungry, with continued food rationing. Acting on the principle that people should have circuses even if they couldn't have bread, the government nevertheless agreed that the race should be staged, and, as a relaxation to prevailing austerity, even arranged to make provisions available for the riders: a ton of meat, eighty kilos of sugar, and several hundred bananas, a luxury which for most Europeans had for years past been as exotic as caviar. The Tour was organized jointly by the newly named rather than new-born the *Équipe*, by the *Parisien Libéré*, and by the Parc des Princes. As in the last two pre-war years, the race was open to national and regional teams, placed for the first time under the authority of technical directors.

For Desgrange's successor Jacques Goddet, the resumption of the Tour was 'an act of faith'. Before the war he had been editor of the *Auto* and very much Desgrange's protégé. He now paid an act of homage to the *patron*: the initials 'HD' were embroidered on the shoulders of the yellow jersey, where they remained until years later when they were removed to make room for yet more advertising logos. The new boss inherited some of the old man's foibles, not least the taste for grandiloquent editorial prose. Goddet once wrote of a rider 'accepting gallantly the delay forced on him by the celestial handicapper', and he marked the resumption of the race in tones worthy of his predecessor: 'We are living through a cruel time in the life of society in which, if we fail to resist it, selfishness will become the dominant passion. We will fight in the name of solidarity against such a threat. "Team" [i.e., the paper's new name, the *Équipe*] – the very word exercises a noble influence on the health of our group – an influence that was exerting itself during a time of rage and hope when our collective will was placed in the service of the Resistance.' In itself this is a fine example of the way French history was being rewritten, with an invented tradition of universal defiance.

Over the years, Goddet became as much of a larger-than-life figure as Desgrange, and promoted himself quite as consciously. During the Tour he took to dressing like a white hunter, at least when the weather permitted, khaki shirt and shorts and solar topee, in which get-up he would stand in his car imagining himself as a commander of some Free French unit chasing the Afrika Korps across the desert. He said himself that he had donned this apparel by chance, but kept it permanently when it proved popular. 'It was certainly cooler and it added colour to the race.' To adapt F. R. Leavis's phrase, the Tour was an episode in the history of cycling, and of publicity.

In the *patron*'s high-flown manner, Goddet said that the reborn race would send 'a message of joy and confidence . . . across all the radiant landscape . . . a heroic adventure from which hatred is absent'. In truth, most stages of the 1947 race echoed the great conflict that had ended two years before. The first three days from Paris to Lille, Brussels and Luxembourg followed the path of the Allied armies in late 1944. Then, after their long loop round the country, the riders returned to Paris by way of an antepenultimate stage into St-Brieuc, where the American army under General Patton had broken out from Normandy, and a penultimate stage into Caen, where the British army under General Montgomery had fought their grim slogging match: a town still crushed flat amid a landscape still trashed and poisoned.

The wartime hiatus inevitably meant a lost generation, as it did in all sports, or at least a generation whose careers were gravely disrupted. The Yorkshire and England batsman Len Hutton sustained an injury (albeit in an army gym rather than on the battlefield) followed by an operation that left him with one arm shorter than the other. But for that, and the missing years, he used to say, 'I could have been as great as Bradman.' And when Ted Williams returned to the Red Sox from the United States Army Air Force he was never quite the man of his *annus mirabilis* in 1941. As if to emphasize that hiatus, only 10 of the 100 riders in the 1947 Tour had ridden before the war, the *brisquards* or old soldiers. Supreme among them was René Vietto, hero to the crowd of 300,000 that cheered away the riders from the Arc de Triomphe as they were sent off by Marcel Cerdan. Hoping that experience would compensate for ageing muscles, Vietto attempted to dominate the race from the beginning. On the second day he took the yellow jersey into Brussels with an individual 130-kilometre escape, and was 1'22" ahead of Roncini when they reached the Alps.

But there were new stars waiting in the wings. The West of France team was led by the brilliant young Breton cyclo-cross champion Jean Robic. According to a hallowed story, he had told his young bride before the race, 'I've no dowry, but I'll offer you the first prize of the Tour.' Robic won from Lyons to Grenoble, but Vietto struck back on the Briançon–Digne stage, helped by his faithful young team-mate Apo Lazaridès who took on Robic in the Alpine passes. Robic was riding fiercely over the Galibier when he punctured, and was still behind the leaders as they reached his native Brittany after Vietto had regained the yellow jersey into Digne.

So many people desperately wanted Vietto to win after his pre-war disappointments, and he was still wearing the yellow jersey when a brutal 138-kilometre time trial began from Vannes to St-Brieuc. It was won by Raymond Impanis of Belgium, but with Robic second and edging ominously close to the lead. The penultimate stage to Caen was won by the Parisian Maurice Diot, riding for the Île de France team, and won very bravely, since boils had erupted all over his body, even his hands, which had to be lanced before he could grasp the handlebars through bandages. On the last day the Italians thought the Tour was theirs. Their team was leading, and Brambilla and Roncini were in first and second, with Robic third at 2′58″, more than three minutes ahead of Vietto. Robic hadn't yet worn the yellow jersey, but he now gave a magnificent performance. One group escaped before, at about halfway, on the Bon Secours climb, Robic attacked, accompanied by Edouard Fachleitner of Luxembourg.

Briek Schotte, Bernard Gauthier and Jean Diederich reached the Parc first, but were followed soon after by Fachleitner and a French trio of Lucien Teisseire, Edouard Muller and Jean Robic, who took the Tour by 3′58″ from Fachleitner, with Vietto fifth at 15′23″. Italy won the team prize and Brambilla was best climber, but Robic's victory was a much-needed fillip for French spirits.

Few years in the twentieth century were as dramatic and pregnant with significance for the future as 1948, whose repercussions the world was still grappling with more than half a century later. Outside Europe, it saw the establishment of the state of Israel and the accession of the Nationalist apartheid regime in South Africa. Within, it was the year when the Cold War sank to freezing point, with the Communist putsch in Prague, the Berlin blockade and airlift, and a crucial election in Italy. More than a third of the Italian people were voting for the Communist Party, and it looked as though the Communists might actually and unwontedly take over a European country at the ballot box. The Italian CP was supported by the Soviet Union's huge intelligence and propaganda service, its Christian Democrat opponents by the State Department and the CIA. This battle wasn't only political but cultural, and even sporting. In the 1930s the famous classical sculpture called *Discobolus* or the Discus Thrower, revered by Hitler as an expression of the athletic ideal, had been legitimately acquired from Italy by a German buyer. Now in 1948, on American instructions, it was returned to Italy with little pretence of legality, all to flatter the Italians on behalf of the anti-Communist cause. Not perhaps because of that, the Christian Democrats won the election in April, but the situation in Italy remained very tense.

Nor did the Tour escape from politics. Ten years after he had become only the second Italian to win the Tour, Bartali was now the *capo*, the undisputed master. In 1940 he had ridden in the Giro as the star of the Legnano team, on which the 20-year-old Fausto Coppi rode as a *domestique*, brilliantly precocious after turning pro in his teens. In an echo of the very first Tour, Bartali had a nasty crash after colliding with a dog. The resulting knee injury ended his chances in the race, and Coppi was told by the team boss to go for it, which he duly did, taking the *maglia rosa* – the pink jersey, the Giro's *maillot jaune* – and winning the race. In Italy you either loved or hated Coppi for the way he had snatched victory in this manner, a debate that ended only when Mussolini's boastful but parasitic entry into the war gave the country something else to think about.

The Tour introduced several changes for the 1948 race. The first prize had been increased from 500,000 francs to 600,000, although for foreign competitors that would have been more impressive if the franc hadn't been devalued in January from 480 to the pound sterling to 864 (from 1152 to the dollar to 3312). Mountain climbs were now categorized A or B, and they included three new passes, Turini, Forclaz in Switzerland and Vue des Alps. The race visited several other places for the first time, Trouville, Dinard, Biarritz, Lourdes, as well as taking three hops across the frontier, to San Remo in Italy, Lausanne in Switzerland and Liège in Belgium. And a ruthless new rule said that the *lanterne rouge*, the last rider in each day's GC, would be eliminated.

That last didn't affect Gino Bartali, but the prize money very much did, and the story of the race was his superb comeback, in more than one sense. It was remarkable enough that he had returned at all after the long hiatus of the war at an age when many riders had retired – he turned thirty-four during this race – or that he won the first stage, from Paris to Trouville; it was less surprising that he then subsided. France had her own rising star, the 23-year-old Louison Bobet, who won the Bordeaux–Biarritz stage, but even though Bartali won the next two Pyrenean stages, he seemed a very forlorn hope at twenty minutes down when the Tour reached Cannes.

Just across the border, Italy edged towards disaster in the aftermath of the election, with the attempted assassination of Palmiro Togliatti, the Communist Party leader, and talk of incipient civil war. The day after the shooting of Togliatti, Bartali took a telephone call in Cannes. It was from Alcide de Gaspari, the Christian Democrat leader, a founding father of what would become the European Union, and one of the great Italians of his age. This was by no means the first time that sport had been invoked for patriotic purposes, or that politicians had intervened in sporting contests. After the 'Bodyline' crisis during the Test series in 1933 had severely blighted relations between England and Australia, the Dominions Secretary in London, J. H. Thomas, insisted that Harold Larwood, the principal offending bowler, should be dropped from the team; or, as A. J. P. Taylor put it, this was 'the only occasion on which a cabinet minister has chosen a cricket eleven, even negatively'.

For de Gaspari, the purpose wasn't to salve relations between countries but to give a boost to national pride: it would be of huge benefit to Italy, to Christian civilization, and in particular to the Democristiani, he told Bartali, if he could just win one more stage. Bartali replied, 'I'll do better than that, I'll win the Tour.' The next day he rode one of the heroic stages in Tour history, ten hours through the Alps over the passes of Allos, Vars and Izoard, to reach Briançon more than six minutes ahead of Schotte. Bartali was still a minute down on Bobet, but he won the next

two stages, taking seven in all out of twenty-one, and rode into
the Parc on 25 July to win his second Tour de France, and much
the more remarkable of the two.

As he entered the Parc, Bartali was also riding towards another
sign of the post-war times, something never before seen on the
Tour: a television camera. This invention had been conceived
decades earlier, born in England shortly before the war closed down
transmission, had now left its infancy, and was beginning to sweep
America. It would take over France and the rest of Europe more
slowly, but one day would transform life there, for better or worse,
and transform sport as much as anything. The Tour de France had
always been a curious spectator sport. Millions of people would,
and still do, wait all day to see the riders approach, go by, and vanish,
all in a matter of seconds. The only way to follow the progress of a
race had been, first, to read the papers the next morning, and then,
to listen to radio commentaries. Today we can watch the continuous
television coverage for which cycling is perhaps more apt than any
other sport. Apart from steeplechasing and snooker there's nothing
quite so telegenic as the Tour, with the coverage of peloton, of Alpine
climbs, of bunch sprint finishes, of team time trials: all beginning
that day in Paris in 1948.

This was the year of Vittorio de Sica's *Ladri di Biciclette* (*Bicycle
Thieves*), that touching masterpiece of Italian neo-realist cinema;
another Italian had just as movingly stolen the great bike race. By
winning two Tours a decade apart, Bartali achieved a feat no one
had ever accomplished before and no one is ever likely to repeat.
Bobet in the end could only manage fourth place, behind Schotte
and Roger Lapébie, but he was the revelation and the rider
who had caught every eye, including the eye of Alfredo Binda,
technical manager of the Italian team. With no great loyalty to
his own champion, Binda said that, 'If I'd managed Bobet, he
would have won the Tour.'

He did win, but not for some years yet. Bartali's challenger in
1949 was another Italian. Even if Gino Bartali and Fausto Coppi

weren't conscious figureheads, the two great Italian cyclists personified their culturally and ideologically riven country. Bartali was handsome and wholesome, a good scout and straight arrow, a devout and dutiful Catholic. Coppi was sinister in the literal – of the Left – and maybe the looser senses, a self-proclaimed radical and atheist whose liaison with another man's wife caused a national scandal. In training methods also, one was a traditionalist and one a progressive iconoclast.

That iconoclast was a butcher's son from Piedmont, who fell in love with cycling as a boy. Young 'Faustino' told his uncle, a merchant seaman, also a Fausto, how much he longed for a Legnano, the bike of his dreams. He even said that to get it he would give years from his life, a light-hearted but unhappily prophetic turn of phrase. From far away in Ceylon the uncle sent 400 lire, asking the family to make it up and 'buy Faustino the bike he deserves. Who knows, one day he might become a real racing cyclist.' Both wishes were granted, nephew's and uncle's. By the age of eighteen Coppi had won his first race as an amateur, the Castello d'Orba, and the next year he collected a hatful of prizes. In 1940 he won the Pursuit Championship of Italy – a form of track racing he would make a particular province of his – and that Giro which split the nation, before another clutch of victories in 1941 and 1942.

If all those races might seem to suggest a rather frivolous attitude to the war Italy had entered in the summer of 1940, reality wasn't far away. There was no Giro in 1941, and the following year Coppi was called up into the army. 'Fausto' means lucky, and it may have been good fortune in disguise when Coppi was shipped to north Africa shortly before the Axis forces there capitulated in 1943: he was soon taken prisoner and spent the war safely in British hands, driving a lorry rather than riding a bike. He liked to tease his fellow prisoners by saying with a straight face that Churchill had contacted him from London: 'Once the war is over he wants me to take over the job of restructuring English cycling.' In the event there was another job for Coppi when the war ended. He was repatriated to Italy early in 1945, and then, after a spell as batman to an RAF officer near Naples, was allowed to depart. He found a bike and rode it home to the north through a war-battered landscape. Despite all his alarms and excursions, he returned to competitive racing that July, winning a race in Milan, and then married Bruna, the sweetheart who had been waiting for him. All was set for the second act of a great career.

In that year's Giro, which Bartali won, Coppi crashed, but in the Milan–San Remo race he made a daring 147-kilometre escape to win by fifteen minutes, with Bartali battling for third place, and the rivalry that had begun in 1940 was now more bitter than ever. The writer Curzio Malaparte, who had seen a thing or two in the Balkans and Russia during the war, described the difference between them: 'Bartali is for the orthodox, his talent is spiritual, the saints look after him; Coppi has no protection up there. Bartali has blood in his veins, Coppi has petrol.' In another of the Tour's unhelpful sobriquets, Pierre Chany called Coppi 'The Heron', and he was certainly a slight figure, five-foot-ten and ten stones, an unimposing body on spindly legs. But Chany saw how this delicate creature could perch seemingly weightless on his bike, 'untroubled by the dead weight and useless muscles which make others seem like mules crawling to the mountain passes'.

If they were rivals, Bartali and Coppi were also team-mates. Two tough and canny technical directors faced each other, Georges Caviller newly appointed as head of the French team and Alfredo Binda, of the Squadra. Coppi had just won the Giro from Bartali, as well as the Milan–San Remo for the third time and a fourth consecutive Tour of Lombardy. Relations between them needed to be cemented, which Binda duly did with the 'Pact of Chiavari' only two weeks before the Tour began. At least, it was a pact for armed neutrality. Shortly before, in the winter of 1946–7, England cricketers had toured Australia, strained by what was said to be a frosty relationship between Walter Hammond and Len Hutton, captain and opening batsman. Many years later a journalistic acquaintance asked Hutton if this had been true. 'Not at all, not at all, perfectly cordial. The first morning of the tour I said to him, "Good morning, Walter," and he said, "Good morning, Len." D'you know, for the rest of the tour we never exchanged another word, and our relations were perfectly cordial.' Hutton's dry Yorkshire wit might have applied to the perfectly cordial relations between Bartali and Coppi in 1949.

Sport everywhere enjoyed a golden age in that post-war lustrum, with great crowds at baseball games in New York and Chicago or at soccer matches in Italy and Brazil. British sport flourished as rarely before and almost never since. In 1946 some 300,000 watched the Grand National at Aintree (on a Friday), while 143,470 watched Rangers play Hibs in the 1948 Scottish Cup semi-final at Hampden Park, and Sheffield Wednesday thought nothing of playing League matches in front of 80,000 at Hillsborough. Bike road racing was no exception, busting out all over France. A new race was born in 1948, the Grand Prix du Midi Libre, named after the Montpellier newspaper that sponsored it, and destined to become a hardy annual which many riders used each May to tune up for the Tour until a cold economic wind snuffed the race out in 2002.

A few more novelties marked this year's Tour, which controversially crossed the frontier into Spain at San Sebastien, at a time when Franco was still much of a pariah, as well as into Italy to Aosta. The cols were now graded into three categories, and they included four new climbs, Montgenèvre, Mont-Cenis, and the two St-Bernard passes, great and small. In his calculating and canny way, Coppi had deliberately missed the first two post-war Tours, and hadn't planned to ride until 1950. But he made his debut after all in 1949, and he triumphed. The race went from

Paris to Brussels and then back westwards through Normandy and Brittany and down to the Spanish frontier, with the yellow jersey changing continually, to Marcel Dussault, Roger Lambrecht, Norbert Callens and then 'The Parakeet', the little Parisian Jacques Marinelli, despite a bad fall early on.

Cool as ever, Coppi won the two time trials, and then annihilated the field in the Alpine passes, not so much climbing the Vars, Izoard and Galibier, it was said, as flying over them. He left Bartali for dead below the Izoard to win the stage by twenty minutes and then raced over the Galibier, past a memorial to Desgrange that had just been unveiled there in the presence of André Leducq. Coppi crossed the line at the Parc a comfortable 10'55" ahead of Bartali, with the young Frenchman Jacques Marinelli, the year's revelation, in third. In a newspaper column describing his victory, Coppi was at his most laconic. It was perfectly easy, he said: 'We all have two legs.'

Very likely he would have taken the 1950 Tour as well had he not broken his pelvis in the Giro, enforcing his absence. Every year some notability, savant or charlatan, was chosen to start the race. This year it was Orson Welles, more revered in France at the time than in his own country. 'Don't believe everything you read in the newspapers,' Citizen Kane sarcastically told a reporter, but what appeared in the papers this summer was all too true. It caught the eye of Evelyn Waugh. 'I read with interest', he told his ardently francophile friend Nancy Mitford, 'how the politest people in the world treated the Italian cyclists.'

What had happened was worthy of his derision. Through the north and west towards the Pyrenees, the race was comparatively uneventful. But on the Col d'Aspin the crowd grew out of control and rabbled the riders. When Bartali and Robic fell in the mêlée, the French mob, some of them drunk, set upon Bartali and beat him up. Even though he managed to get back on his bike and win the stage, while his team-mate Fiorenzo Magni took the yellow jersey, the whole Italian team withdrew in protest.

Ferdi Kubler of Switzerland took the lead by embarrassing default. In the circumstances it seemed impolitic to cross into Italy as planned, and so a stage which was meant to go to San Remo went no further than Menton on the border. Bobet won the stage into Briançon, and the next day he attacked by way of skipping the feeding station at Pont-de-Claix. But the race was now Kubler's, with Bobet in third behind Constant Ockers of Belgium.

There was another Swiss success the next year, but not from Ferdi Kubler. He and Hugo Koblet were competitors as well as team-mates and compatriots, like Bartali and Coppi; all unlike the two Italians, the two Swiss were great friends and helped each other whenever they could, although that could not include the 1951 Tour in which Kubler didn't take part. Coppi was in the field when the race started at Metz on 4 July but was out of sorts in every way. Following his previous injury, he had fractured a clavicle early in the season, and, worse still, had lost his brother Serse, also a cyclist, who died after fracturing his skull in a race not long before the Tour began.

They were racing round a new map: not only was Paris not reached until the fourth day, not only were Ghent, Le Tréport, and Avignon all visited for the first time, but the Tour left the periphery of the *hexagone* to plunge into the very heart of France, darting to Limoges and then east to the Massif Central and Clermont-Ferrand, returning to the south-west by way of Brive, Agen and Dax, all new *étapes*. There was also an important modification of the scoring, with new bonuses for the first three finishers on each stage.

Auspiciously enough, the first stage was won by a Swiss rider, Giovanni Rossi, before the Luxembourger Jean Diederich escaped on the next stage from Rheims to Ghent over the grim cobbled climb of the Mur de Grammont. A couple of stages were taken by riders with the Ouest-Sud-Ouest regional team, before the Ghent–Le Tréport stage was marked by a ludicrous incident. Abdel-Kader Zaaf of Algeria, one of eight riders in a team from French north Africa, suddenly made an individual escape and found himself well ahead of the field. It was a scorchingly hot day, and when he tried to quench his thirst with a *bidon* of wine he was carrying, the drink knocked him out, and he was found unconscious in a grass patch beside the road. He later recovered and rejoined the peloton, though only to end the Tour as *lanterne rouge*.

On the Paris–Caen stage there was a more successful escape. The leading riders were fooling about, with no one setting a serious pace, when two Italian *domestiques*, Angelo Colinelli and Serafino Biagoni, broke away. Colinelli flagged, but Biagoni stayed in front not only to win the stage by ten minutes but to take the yellow jersey. It was suspected that the star riders had been dawdling in preparation for the time trial, and it was indeed the stars who excelled in it. Bobet appeared to win, but there had been a timing error and he was demoted behind Koblet, who was beginning to look very good, with poor Coppi languishing. Thanks to the new race route the first mountains this year were the Massif Central. Geminiani won the stage from Limoges to Clermont-Ferrand, his home town, after crushing climbs over La Moreno and La Ceysatt, taking him to third in the GC. But on the next stage it was Koblet who made a superb 135-kilometre escape. Wim Van Est won the stage to Dax to become the first Dutchman to wear the yellow jersey, but his luck deserted him in the Pyrenees where he crashed twice, fell into a ravine on the Aubisque, and abandoned.

After Diederich led over the Tourmalet, Coppi came back to lead over the Aspin and Peyresourde, but he was only narrowly ahead of Koblet who sprinted into Luchon to win the stage, take the yellow jersey and, as it proved, win the Tour. Coppi was still in contention, but was taken ill on the Carcassonne–Montpellier stage and, although his team loyally kept him going, Koblet only increased his lead. Although he held it through Avignon,

Marseilles and to Gap, the starring role was played by the mighty Mont Ventoux, which was being climbed for the first time, and to whose story we will return.

But it was then that one of the heroic exploits of Tour history was witnessed, on the Gap–Briançon high passes. Coppi escaped on the Col de Vars, taking the Est-Sud-Est regional Roger Buchonnet with him, and rode with matchless skill and courage to lead by forty seconds at the summit, with Koblet more than eight minutes away. Koblet fought back grimly to cross the Izoard only three minutes behind, but Coppi held on to win the stage. He had left it too late for the race, even though that wonderful display had taken him from seventeenth to tenth in the GC. Others were still worse off: Marinelli abandoned after severe injuries in a fall on the Col de Vars, and Bobet was laid low with food poisoning.

The last climbing stage was won by the Spaniard Vittorio Ruiz, before Koblet won the subsequent time trial, not very far from his home town of Geneva. But although there was an *échappée fleuve* or group breakaway of ten lesser riders on the penultimate stage, Koblet finished the race first by a comfortable twenty-two minutes from Geminiani. It was a very popular win. Koblet had enjoyed one technical edge, though not his alone: along with Bartali, Coppi and four others, he had a bike fitted with the new Campagnolo derailleur available that year, using handlebar controls, heavy to today's eye but decidedly better than any existing gears. But he also had the advantage of his own courage and skill, not to mention a very pleasing manner. One reporter saw the race won by 'the domination, the personality and the elegance of Koblet', while the singer Jacques Grello, writing for the *Équipe*, called the winner 'the pedaller of charm'. His charm captivated an 18-year-old trainee metal-worker and amateur cyclist from Rouen, who had watched the stage from Paris to Caen, won by Biagoni with Koblet in fourth, and had been fascinated by the Swiss rider, a man he dreamed of emulating. He was called Jacques Anquetil.

After six years of peace, France was stable, and increasingly prosperous. The Fourth Republic may have seemed politically erratic, with its multiplicity of parties and its notoriously short-lived governments, but the future was bright compared with the dark past. Just how dark their recent history had been, the French had been reminded six days before the 1951 Tour reached the Parc des Princes, by the death of Marshal Pétain. A burden of memory had been lifted.

8

Bobet Divides France

1952–1957

If France was a much calmer country at home in the early 1950s than twenty years before, she was still much troubled by the ebbing tides of empire. One French army was mired in a bitter war in Vietnam, and in April 1952 it launched what was meant to be, but wasn't, a decisive attack against the communist Vietminh (the background for *The Quiet American* by Graham Greene). Disaster wasn't far away, and a French win in the Tour would have been more welcome solace than in most years. It wasn't to be, not just yet, and France could manage no higher than fifth in the 1952 Tour.

Even then, the narrowest Gallic chauvinist couldn't deny that this was one of the greatest Tours there have ever been. The race was a modified version of the previous year's but in the opposite direction: leaving Brest to cross Brittany, Normandy and the north, it turned south through Belgium to Lorraine and Alsace, traversed the Alps, headed to the Pyrenees and then turned from Bordeaux into the Massif Central to reach Paris by way of Vichy. Once more to discourage the field from resting on their pedals, there were two new prizes introduced, one for teams, and the other a prime of 100,000 francs for the rider *plus combatif*, designed to encourage escapes and attacks. As further tests of toughness, the race for the first time climbed both Mont Ventoux and the Puy de Dôme, the latter geographically part of the Massif Central but dramatically standing all on its own at 1582 metres to overlook Clermont-Ferrand, an unjustly neglected industrial city with an interesting old quarter and two fine churches worth seeing, the cathedral and Notre-Dame-du-Port.

At first the race seemed to lack competitive edge because of the absence of Koblet, Kubler and Bobet, but there were plenty of other cracks and rising stars – and for the first time they could be seen on television not only at the finish but while they were riding road stages, with Henri Persin as the intrepid cameraman perched on a motorbike and Georges de Canes as travelling commentator. Partly thanks to the new team prize, which had revved up the Belgians, the first stage was taken by Rik Van Steenbergen, whose victory in this year's Paris–Roubaix race ahead of Coppi showed that he was in fine fettle. But the Belgians subsided after that start, or at any rate devoted them-selves to supporting Ockers. The fifth stage from Roubaix to Namur was won by Diederich, but more to the point Coppi flexed his muscles for the first time to follow him home, before winning a sixty-kilometre time trial by thirty-four seconds from the Belgian Roger Decock.

This was a fairly extraordinary feat in itself, given that Coppi punctured his front tyre, and then, as he was trying to change the wheel, lost additional time when his mechanic absent-mindedly handed him a spare rear wheel. Anyone standing close to them could have learned some interesting colloquial Italian. Over the Ballon d'Alsace it was Geminiani's turn to strike, but the race had barely begun before the Alps, where Coppi reigned supreme. There were two stages finishing at altitude, l'Alpe d'Huez, and Sestrières the next day. Coppi won them both, with poor Robic floundering in his wake, eighty seconds behind him at l'Alpe d'Huez.

But it was the next stage that people would still talk about fifty years later. Over the Cols de Croix-de-Fer, Télégraphe, and Galibier, Coppi was in a class of his own. No one who saw it ever forgot the way he accelerated past the field up the steepest of slopes. Nor did Robic forget it, or the young French rider Jean Le Guily, who gave what would have been an unbeatable climbing performance on any other day, nor Ruiz, who finished in second place eight minutes behind Coppi, now with a twenty-minute lead in the race.

It had been supposed that Bartali was riding in the Tour for old time's sake, and certainly not for friendship's. To everyone's astonishment both suppositions proved wrong. On the stage to Monaco, Coppi punctured once, then his rear wheel broke. And Bartali stopped to hand his own wheel to the man who was supposed to be his bitter enemy. It was a knightly deed, and one of the most touching gestures in the history of the great race. Maybe providence rewarded virtue two days later. Robic rode explosively up Mont Ventoux to win by 2 minutes from Bartali, who was now third overall, 49 minutes behind Ockers, who was 25'27" behind Coppi. The first of the Pyrenean stages was won by Raphael Geminiani after he had failed to escape over the Peyresourde, but then managed to do so over the Aspin.

All of that was eclipsed by Coppi's breathtaking ride to Pau the next day. He was already sure of winning the Mountains title as well as the Tour, but he accumulated even more climbing points by leading over the Tourmalet, Soulor and Aubisque. And even that wasn't the end of it – nor the greatest moment in his victory. When they reached the Puy de Dôme, he did it again, and more. The mark of the great *grimpeur* is the ability to climb a slope with the gradient of a ski run, which would exhaust most people on foot, and to overtake a field of cyclists as if they were standing still. On the Puy Coppi sized up the field from the rear, and he then cut down his rivals one by one, Ockers, Robic, Geminiani, Bartali, until only the Dutch rider Nolten was still ahead. Then he too was passed, as Coppi reached the summit to win by a bare second, and quite brilliantly.

On the last two stages to Vichy and Paris (two names with unhappy political overtones when linked together) Coppi took it easier. He could afford to. He ended in the Parc with the Mountains prize and at the head of the winning Italian team, as well as winner of the Tour by almost half an hour from Ockers, then Ruiz, Bartali and Robic.

Over the course of a century the Tour's *palmarès* have developed as it were by compound interest. Petit-Breton won the fifth and sixth Tours back to back, but it wasn't until Thys in 1920 that a rider had won three Tours. By 1939 only Bottecchia and Frantz had followed Petit-Breton to win consecutive Tours, and truly great cyclists like Leducq and Coppi won no more than two Tours each. By contrast, the distinctive feature of the race in the second half of the century was the increasing dominance of successive generations by one rider. That's to say that a rider won the first hat-trick of consecutive victories in 1953–5; another won the first four-timer in 1961–4, and then became the first to win five in all for the first time; both those records were matched less than a decade later in 1969–72; then in the 1990s a rider won five successive Tours; and, as the race reaches its centenary, another rider has won four on the trot, and few would bet heavily against his making that not only a record-equalling five but a record-breaking six.

This consistency represented by those post-war champions – Louison Bobet, Jacques Anquetil, Eddy Merckx, Bernard Hinault, Miguel Induráin and Lance Armstrong – may be a reflection on the technical improvement of bikes, which reduced some of the elements of chance, on increasingly efficient training, on ever-greater fitness and more sophisticated medical treatment of one form or another. At any rate, the fiftieth anniversary Tour of 1953 saw Bobet stamp his authority on the race. Apart from taking in three new stages, at Cauterets, Albi and Montluçon, and bidding an emotional farewell to Bartali, riding in the race for the last time after an astonishing twenty-six years, the Tour saw one more historic innovation, the *maillot vert*.

This green jersey is often called the sprinters' prize, which is a simplification of a complex truth. It is an award 'by points', themselves allocated on a system whose complexity would tax the combined talents of a senior wrangler and a Chancery Silk. Points are awarded *inter alia* for 'hot-spot' sprints interspersed on the road stages, and for consistency at the finish, which itself, given bunch sprint finishes, favours specialist sprinters. And so the green jersey, although not literally a sprinting prize, is usually won by sprinters. The first green jersey was won by the Swiss rider Fritz Schaer, who finished sixth overall, and Kubler won the second (four years after he had won the Tour) while finishing second. Then Ockers's double in 1955–6 announced that the points jersey would become something of a Belgian benefit: from 1955 to 1988 Belgian riders took the green eighteen times in thirty-four races.

But the Tour winner of 1953 was a Frenchman, albeit the victor more of a French civil war than an international contest. The 1947 winner Robic was locked in a sharp dispute with the national team, and rode instead for Ouest. After the lead had passed from Schaer to Roger Hassenforder and back, Robic took the yellow jersey. But the French team were biding their time until the Pyrenees. Robic had caused surprise and amusement by turning up for the race in a new white-rubber helmet. For more than fifty years cyclists had ridden the Tour in *casquets* or cotton caps, and many hated – some don't much like even now – the idea of hard headgear. Helmets were thought wimpish, which they may have been, and uncomfortable, as they certainly were. Robic was no wimp, but he was accident-prone, his regular falls earning him the unkind nickname of 'glass head' from the Italians. He angrily responded to mockery of his new titfer by defying his team-mate François Mahé to hit him on the helmet with a screwdriver handle, which Mahé cheerfully did, until he drew blood.

It was not a good augury. Robic tried another quaint wheeze on the Tourmalet, filling a *bidon* with lead so as to add weight – and hence speed to – his downhill run, which was less impressive than alarming. Indeed, if the climbs weren't quite as hairy as the journey Yves Montand and his comrades made in *Le Salaire de la Peur*, this year's spine-tingling movie, the riders counted their own wages of fear. After Koblet had fallen on the Col du Solour, Robic fell in the Fouremont, and the lead passed to his team-mates, Mahé and then Jean Mallejac. On the Albi–Béziers stage the Tricolores struck. But, although they had taken over the race, the French team now fell out among themselves. During that stage Robic made a mess of his sprints; there was an unseemly squabble between him and Geminiani over bonus points; and it took the best efforts of the team manager Marcel Bidot to reconcile them.

It was the sixth Tour in which Louison Bobet had ridden, five years after he had captured the imagination of France, and he finally came into his inheritance over the Col d'Izoard, with a superb performance that delighted Bidot and was applauded by one inconspicuous but illustrious spectator: standing on the roadside in shorts and with a camera round his neck was Fausto Coppi. Bidot said that Bobet had found 'la bonne carburation', his body firing on all cylinders and pumping in perfect harmony like a motor; Coppi said with meiotic eloquence, 'He looks good.'

At the Parc everything had been done to make the Cinquentenaire a sentimental occasion, already marked by the government with a special 12-franc stamp. Fifteen former winners were present, including the very first, Maurice Garin now a ripe eighty-two, as well as Garrigou, both the Maes, Leducq, Magne, Lapébie and Kubler, and Christophe who had worn the very first yellow jersey thirty-two years before. All of this famous crowd cheered home Bobet, 14'18" ahead of Mallejac. There were other heroes besides: two riders had shown what they where capable of, Hassenforder wearing the yellow jersey on behalf of Nord-Est-Centre over three stages from Caen to Bordeaux, Darrigade winning a stage for the first time, and the boy star of the race, Charly Gaul of Luxembourg, riding in his first Tour at only twenty.

No one who had ever seen Louison Bobet in his infancy, would have supposed him to be born a hero. For a great athlete he was very highly strung, not to say a bundle of neuroses, who was angered by the smallest irritation like a grease mark on his front tyre or the colour of the wrapping of his spare tyre. A *domestique* of his was once sent off to get him a bottle of mineral water from a bar, haggled at length over payment (or perhaps hoped not to pay at all, as riders often enjoyed free drinks), finally and desperately caught up with the peloton which had left him far behind to hand the water to his boss, who said angrily, 'You know very well I don't like that brand.' Foibles like that, and his distinctive personality in general, helped explain why France was by now divided into two camps, Bobetiste and anti-Bobetiste: not quite as seriously as the Dreyfusards and anti-Dreyfusards whose schism had indirectly brought the Tour into being, but fiercely partisan enough.

If the antis wanted to see Louison get his come-uppance next year, they were to be disappointed. At least the Tour provided some relief for a France which was wading deeper into its late-imperial struggles. Although 1954 was the year when Charles de Gaulle published the first volume of his exalted *Mémoires de Guerre*, it was also the year that would leave far grimmer memories of war, with the humiliating French defeat at Dien Bien Phu and withdrawal from Vietnam, and the beginning of the Algerian uprising that would poison France for years to come.

Winning the Tour this year was made easier by the absence of the Italians. Their attempts to drum up publicity outside cycling led to an acrimonious row with the Tour organizers, who had themselves found a new sponsor or *partenaire officiel* in the car company Peugeot. And for the first time the race began outside the borders of France, in Amsterdam. The first stage to Antwerp was aptly won by the Dutchman Wout Wagtmans, who held the yellow jersey for two more stages, but from early on it was clear that the race was never likely to be won by anyone but Bobet. He had a tussle with Gilbert Bauvin, riding for Nord-Est-Centre, who won the Bordeaux–Bayonne stage, but Bobet had taken the lead by Millau on the way to the Massif Central, and seized complete control of the race over the Col d'Izoard. Robic and Koblet both fell and were eliminated, and Bobet added a time trial at Nancy before crossing the line at the Parc comfortably ahead of Kubler, who took the green jersey as consolation. Beside them on the podium was a young Spaniard: Federico Bahamontes had won the Mountains prize for what even he couldn't have guessed would be the first of six times.

Even his two victories in the Tour, to which he added the World Champion's rainbow jersey, couldn't make all of France love Bobet, and even respecting him was made no easier by his behaviour. In the early summer of 1955 he was afflicted by a hardening of his skin, which created acute saddle sores. Although it was painful, it wasn't unique or irreparable, but Bobet always gave the impression that he could turn a problem into a drama into a disaster; or to be more charitable, his physical malady accentuated his psychological malaise, and as a crisis of self-confidence gripped him he talked of pulling out of the Tour, for all that he was on a hat-trick, as cricketers would say. Few of his colleagues warmed to him, any more than much of the public, what with his brusque manner and self-absorption and tightfistedness, but Bidot knew how badly the French team, and France, and the Tour, needed Bobet. And so he enlisted the support of Raymond Le Bert, Bobet's *soigneur*, and between them they talked him out of quitting.

A clockwise race started at Le Havre and went into Switzerland and as far as Zurich before reaching the Alps, where the action really began. When it did it took the unexpected form of a dazzling display by Gaul. Still only twenty-two, the Luxembourger annihilated the field over the Cols du Télégraphe and Galibier and had a thirteen-minute lead on the stage into Briançon to take third place in the GC. He outstripped Bobet again towards Monaco before crashing on a wet road and surrendering third place to him.

Other casualties included the first British team to take part in the Tour. Sceptics had wondered whether the British were yet up to it, even if there were plenty of good English cyclists with achievements to their credit in track events: this very year Norman Sheil was the first British rider to win the World Pursuit Championship, from his countryman Peter Brotherton. The team comprised David Bedwell, Tony Hoar, Stan Jones, Fred Krebs, Bob Maitland, Bernard Pusey, Brian Robinson, Ian Steel and Bev Wood; and their names joined those annals of gallant failure that adorn our island story. It was a tough race, and only 69 of 130 starters finished. Those who abandoned included all the British cyclists apart from Robinson, who finished twenty-ninth and thereby began a continental career of some distinction, and Hoar, who ended the Tour as *lanterne rouge*, the last to finish, just over six hours behind the winner. It mattered not that he had won or lost but that he had played the game.

Being an English fan in many sports has long been a spiritual exercise, or an education in disappointment, which takes the form of elation when our lads flatter to deceive, do well against each other, and then less well against foreigners. Tim Henman can beat most British tennis players, but not so many Europeans or Americans, cricketers who look good in county matches look double-plus-ungood against the Australians. And in late 2001, when Arsenal were about to follow Sir John Moore to Corunna and play Deportivo, one football correspondent asked plaintively why the team with much the best away record in the domestic league had such a poor away record in Europe. His question brought to mind the cruel saying of the great historian Sir Lewis Namier that, since the fifteenth century, no Italian army has ever beaten anything apart from another Italian army.

After Lucien Lazaridès had won the stage to Marseilles came what proved the decisive day of the race, from Marseilles to Avignon over Mont Ventoux. Despite that tumble, Gaul was another king of a rainy country who actually liked racing in cold wet weather, and he didn't enjoy what turned out to be a blisteringly hot day even for Provence in July. Bobet did. He climbed the great peak relentlessly, with Bidot shouting encouragement from his car alongside, and with his rivals falling away one by one. This was the first year that the Tour used a photo-finish camera to separate riders, but no snapshots were needed in Avignon: even after a puncture, Bobet entered the papal city alone.

The yellow jersey was still held, from Briançon, by his teammate Antonin Rolland, Miguel Poblet having already taken it – the first Spaniard ever to do so – as well as Wout Wagtmans and Van Est. But Rolland was about to lose the lead. Gaul won one more stage, from Albi to St Gaudens, and it was here that Bobet took the overall lead and held it despite a challenge from Jean Brankart. And despite his own condition. Those who failed to warm to Bobet's personality couldn't fail to recognize his courage. As he had feared, his sores grew worse as the race wore on, he looked ungainly and even comical with his backside waving up in the air as he tried to keep it out of the saddle.

The penultimate Châtteleraut–Tours stage was a time trial, and a time of trial it was for Bobet, who was now in acute pain. It was won by Brankart, a deserved second overall when they reached the Parc, but not as deserving as the winner. Bobet's saddle area was so seriously afflicted that later in the year it required surgery. He won other races, Paris–Roubaix and Bordeaux–Paris, but he said that he was never the same rider again after that July, and he may have been right. He retired in 1961, and, like all too many winners, died before his time, in 1983 aged only fifty-eight.

If the rule of the second half-century of the Tour has been for one outstanding champion to consolidate his position over several years, and for form to be confirmed, then rules are defined by exceptions. Few years have ever seen such a surprise as 1956. Roger Walkowiak won a race which was full of oddities, not least his repeating the curious feat of Cornet in 1904 and Lambot in 1922 by winning the Tour without finishing first in a single stage. The yellow jersey changed hands eight times and was worn by six riders; Darrigade and Walkowiak both won it, lost it and won it back. A French citizen, but not even riding for the national team, 'Walko' (his nickname a little more forgivable than most) had been drafted into the Nord-Est-Centre team directed by Sauveur Ducazeaux who discerned his quality despite his reputation for useless impetuosity in the form of the cyclist's forlorn hope, the *échappée bidon* or doomed breakaway.

Many a rider of strength and spirit can escape from the peloton, sometimes by a good distance, sometimes for a large part of a day. The question is whether such an escape is going to endure and have a serious impact on the race or whether it's a gallant but empty gesture. In recent years Jacky Durand has been the master of the *échappée bidon*, making long lonely escapes to while away the time well ahead of the field and often winning the daily award for *combativité*, as most aggressive rider. But he rarely seems to end very high in the GC, and the great escape too often has a ring of the RAF officer in *Beyond the Fringe*: 'We need a useless sacrifice at this point.'

Like treason in Talleyrand's phrase, road racing is a matter of timing. That's peculiarly true of *contre la montre* stages, time trials where the successful rider is the one, as used to be said of Lester Piggott on the racecourse, with a clock in his head. But throughout the Tour individual riders and teams need to have an acute sense of time, of who stands where in the table. Riders are kept informed of their and others' relative positions, formerly by *directeurs sportifs* shouting the news from cars, or by signs at the roadside with timings chalked on them, nowadays less romantically by the earpieces of the radios tucked in a jersey back pocket to which all riders are constantly tuned in. Hence other riders can watch with detachment as Durand or any other escape artist sets off on his foray, simply because he is so far behind in the overall classification. But occasionally the break succeeds, and the escapers actually establish a commanding lead.

In this respect also, 1956 was exceptional. Going anticlockwise from Rheims through Belgium, Normandy and Brittany, the race took fire between Lorient and Angers when a group escape of thirty-one riders got eighteen minutes ahead of the peloton. The group was led by Walkowiak but also included the man who would prove his main rival, Gilbert Bauvin of the French team. A climbers' contest developed in the Pyrenees among Walkowiak, Bahamontes, Ockers (who would finish with the green jersey) and Gaul (who weeks earlier had won the Giro with an epic ride through the snow on Monte Bondone, and would finish the Tour with the Mountains prize). Walkowiak made another – individual and brilliant – break over the Croix de Fer to take the overall lead into Grenoble and keep it through Lyons and Montluçon, reaching the Parc 1'25" ahead of Bauvin and then Adriaenssens and Bahamontes.

Although Walkowiak never won the Tour again, it was no freak result. Jacques Goddet called 1956 'one of my favourite Tours', and its quality was simply demonstrated by a record average speed of 36.268 k.p.h. A final prize for good loser and good humour should have gone to Roger Chaussabel, the Marseillais rider who finished as *lanterne rouge* more than four hours behind Walkowiak. 'I don't ride, I don't climb, I don't sprint,' he wryly said. 'I'm a complete racer. Donc un homme du Tour.'

If the French rider who won the Tour wasn't in the national team, it was still a good year for the French, on bike or on foot: far away at the Melbourne Olympics, Alain Mimoun won the Marathon gold medal while, of French cyclists, Jean Forestier won the Tour of Flanders, Bobet won Paris–Roubaix, and André Darrigade – who showed well in the Tour to win the yellow jersey at Pau – won the Tour of Lombardy. And there was young Jacques Anquetil, who hadn't yet ridden in the Tour but who won a fourth consecutive Grand Prix des Nations, and broke the one-hour speed record with 46.393 km. He was the man to watch.

His speed record lasted only until the following year when it was broken by Roger Rivière, but that was small worry for Anquetil when he made his Tour debut. Born in Rouen in 1934, the son of a small farmer who grew strawberries and apples, he had been sent to technical school before he got a low-paid job at a metal factory. But his heart was never in it. Anquetil loved cycling, and he dreamed of the rewards it would bring: even before he had the means to gratify them, Jacques had luxurious tastes in food and wine. He became an independent, the stepping stone between amateur and pro, was soon established as a brilliant time-triallist, and in 1952 began winning races by the fistful.

Before long, he had caught the eye of a member of a famous family. Henri Pélissier, winner in 1923 and greatest of the three brothers, had died in 1935 aged only forty-six, but Francis Pélissier had survived and prospered and was now *directeur sportif* of La Perle. He saw in Anquetil at first a potential champion time-triallist, and he offered him a two-month contract at 30,000 francs a month. When Anquetil duly won the 1953 Grand Prix, he became a national hero. Journalists flocked to the family farm at Quincampoix, where Pélissier managed to get in on the act, photographed with cigarette in lips and thumbs hooked into waistcoat.

The young champion was now living high on the hog, dining out and buying an expensive car, a Renault Frégate in bright red (or 'crushed strawberry' as it was jocosely suggested). But there was one thing no fame or money could avoid: military service. A couple of years later another famous young star was drafted into the United States Army, but Elvis Presley's career was not more inconveniently interrupted than Jacques Anquetil's. The French army even insisted on following regulations and sending him to Algeria, a good deal more of a trouble spot at the time than Elvis's Bavarian posting, but he was sensibly allowed to spend his time here riding a bike, before returning to civilian life and competitive cycling. After an astonishing *palmarès* in shorter-distance races in 1956 – French Pursuit championship, six Criteriums, and two top time trials, the Grand Prix of Geneva, and that Grand Prix des Nations, for the fourth out of six in succession – he made his still more astonishing debut in the Tour in 1957.

This new ace was one of the least romantic or beguiling men to have ridden in the Tour, and he never became the best-loved winner, but he was one of the most admired, and was certainly one of the most intelligent. Those who knew him well said that he was essentially shy (that useful excuse for any form of ill humour or bad manners), and he was doubtless solitary by disposition. In later years he didn't get about much any more, but stayed on his Norman estate, eating and drinking on his own and looking at the stars. Even when he was one of the most famous men in France, a seemingly *farouche* and arrogant manner annoyed colleagues, and alienated fans. Some of it was deliberate, as when he summoned a reporter one evening during the Tour to watch him consume a large plate of seafood washed down with Muscadet, knowing that this would be recorded and would incense rivals whose digestive systems barely allowed them more than liquid rice. Still, if other riders were modest men, then many of them had a good deal to be modest about, and if Jacques Anquetil was a proud man, he had a good deal to be proud of.

At first, Anquetil had said that he wouldn't ride for the French team alongside Bobet, but that problem was resolved during the

Giro when Bobet said he would not be taking part in the Tour. A year that saw the death of Maurice Garin, fifty-four years after his victory in the first Tour, also saw the Tricolores dominating the Tour almost from beginning to end of a sultry July. They won between them thirteen stages, with André Darrigade, René Privat and Jean Forestier successively wearing the yellow jersey, interrupted only by Nicolas Barone of the Île-de-France regional team, until Anquetil took command.

From Nantes to Rouen to Belgium and then down to Alsace, he bided his time, before striking in the mountains. Or rather, he struck a first blow on the Roubaix–Charleroi stage with a brilliant climb over the Grammont 'Wall', before beating a group of eight, more than ten minutes ahead of the field, in a sprint finish to Thonon-les-Bains. He then rode fiercely over the Galibier, challenged by the tough Gastone Nencini – who would end with the Mountains prize – until shaking him off.

But Anquetil's finest moment in this Tour came in the Pyrenees. He had a severe *défaillance* and seemed near collapse on the Aubisque, before fighting back into the race by pure willpower, holding the yellow jersey in the end all the way from Briançon to Paris, and reaching the Parc disdainfully more than fifteen minutes ahead of Janssens. Tragedy marred Anquetil's first great victory. As the race had dipped into Catalonia and back, on the Barcelona–Ax-les-Thermes stage, the press motorbike in which the famous Tour reporter Alex Virot was being driven by René Wagner crashed, and both were killed. It was Virot who, not long before his death, had given Anquetil a piece of advice: 'If you concentrate on making money you'll lose races, if you concentrate on winning races, you'll make money.' This was the cycling version of Pushkin's maxim, 'Write for pleasure and publish for money,' and it was one that Anquetil took to heart.

If anyone was keen on making money it wasn't the riders but the organizers: 1957 saw the baleful innovation of commercial *affiches* – advertising logos – on cyclists' jerseys. The appearance of riders was slowly changing. In photographs until the Second World War they look heavier: heavier bikes with sturdier tyres, cork-topped tin *bidons* on the handlebars, chunky dust goggles worn over strong cotton caps, heavy cloth shorts and woollen jerseys with one large pocket for food, emblazoned with the team name, Alcyon or J.-B. Louvet, as Jean Brankart and Stan Ockers are still grinning in post-war races above the modest Elve-Peugeot strip on their chests. Now Raphael Geminiani took the initiative in drumming up advertisers, and Anquetil rode to victory bearing the name of the aperitif St-Raphaël. It might have seemed a small step but it might, forty-five years later, also seem a sad one: 'Gem' didn't foresee the day when cyclists', footballers' and racing drivers' clothing would be so heavily covered with commercial names that their colours were barely visible, when the *patron*'s initials 'HD' were discreetly removed from the yellow jersey to make room for other names, and when only baseball teams – surprisingly but admirably in the home of advertising – remained ad-free.

Repos

Burgundy

When Desgrange began the Tour, he had seen it as little more than a publicity stunt, a circulation-booster, a way to dish his rivals. Even when the success of the race saw the *Auto*'s circulation rapidly increase, he had no idea that he was creating a national institution and a world-famous event. It was scarcely intended to last for ever; but then we have seen how the story of the Tour from the beginning illustrated the truth that 'ce n'est que le provisoire qui dure'. Quite soon the race had become a permanent fixture, part of French life and culture, and, in the best spirit of invented tradition, it had become a 'national property', as Georges Rozet of the *Temps* called it as early as 1908.

Fifty years later the Tour organizer Xavier Loy could call the race even more grandiosely, though not quite absurdly, an 'objet du patrimoine nationale'. As the historian Georges Vigarello put it after nearly ninety years of the Tour, within only a matter of decades the race had been rooted in national ritual to the extent that its origins seemed remote and forgotten. It was more than a race, Vigarello thought, it addressed itself to the national consciousness, 'it played with geography, provinces, frontiers'. It was like a great theatrical production whose stage scenery was the country itself.

Part of that country visited by the Tour almost every year was Burgundy, although a part that again shows the equivocal concept of Frenchness and even of France. Burgundy was once a kingdom, one of the three into which Charlemagne's empire was divided, then for much longer an autonomous principality, or collection of principalities. The Free-County to the east of the Saône was never part of France at all in the Middle Ages, and to the west, was briefly absorbed by the French kings in the eleventh century, and was then made autonomous under a cadet line of the Capetian dynasty.

After a certain amount of further dynastic *va-et-vient*, Burgundy's time of greatness came when King Jean II of France made his son Philip the Bold hereditary ruler, and Philip adroitly used the devices of purchase and marriage to extend his dominions. By the fifteenth century 'Burgundy' included not only Burgundy, Lorraine and Bar but Flanders – one day to be a great nursery of cyclists – and most of the rest of what are now 'Benelux'. In 1420 the Burgundians allied themselves with Henry V of England: it was they who helpfully burned Joan of Arc at the stake in Rouen. There is maybe just a hint of that distant connection in the English (and also Belgian) wine trade with Burgundy, and in the 1949 English film comedy *Passport to Pimlico*, in which that district of London discovered that it was really a dependency of the old duchy of Burgundy, and could thus escape rationing and the other oppressions of the Attlee Terror.

But before the end of the fifteenth century the duchy had been acquired by France as a marriage dowry, along with the Free-County and Artois as well, while paradoxically the name survived far away in the 'Burgunder Kreis' or Burgundian Circle of the Holy Roman Empire, Brabant, Limburg and Gelderland. Burgundy as we now think of it became another military governorship of the French kingdom, with a somewhat vestigial *parlement* at Dijon, under the presidency of the Bishop of Autun, representing the clergy, and with the Mayor of Dijon representing the Third Estate. It was an ironical reflection on past grandeurs that as the *ancien régime* ended it was the Bishop of Autun – the cynical sceptic Talleyrand – who said that no one would ever know how sweet life was who had not lived before the Revolution. 'Duke of Burgundy' became any other title, bestowed by Louis XIV on his eldest grandson in 1682, and Burgundy became one more province, then divided into the departments of Saône-et-Loire, Ain, and Côte-d'Or, a heroic name, redolent of the sublime wines of Pommard, Beaune, Pernand Echezeaux and Chambertin.

South-west of Macôn is strictly the Lyonnais rather than Burgundy, valleys covered with the vineyards of Beaujolais and dotted with small towns and villages any one of which might have been Clochemerle-en-Beaujolais, the setting of Gabriel Chevallier's surprisingly sharp and amusing 1934 novel, in which lecherous priests enjoy the favours of their housekeepers while cynical local notables intrigue over the all-important question of where a public lavatory should be sited in the town, and the old feud of *curé* and radical mayor goes on. Needless to say, one town does claim to be the original: Vaux-en-Beaujolais now has an Auberge de Clochemerle, where Chevallier used to stay, not to mention 'Clochemerle nouveau' with which you can fill your bladder, and a Pissotière de Clochemerle where you can then empty it.

To the north, stretching from Macôn to Dijon, is that truly golden *côte* of ripening grapes and fine kitchens, strewn with excellent restaurants in pretty villages bearing noble names, Santeney, Puligny-Montrachet, Savigny-les-Beaune, Aloxe-Corton, at Mercurey. But by some quirk of fortune, this historic and handsome province, with so many vinous and culinary riches, is less richly endowed with literary associations. More characteristic of the *terroir* is Colette, born in St-Sauveur-en-Puisaye, south-west of Auxerre, in the department of Yonne in the northerly corner of Burgundy, with her intense feeling for nature, animals and flowers, as well as the complexes of human affection and physical passion. Auxerre itself, six times a *ville-étape*, has its wonderful cathedral and the Abbey of St-Germain, as well as an astonishing cluster of good restaurants, although Barnabet's Burgundy truffles in potatoes is an autumn dish, alas not served when the Tour is being run.

Quite apart from its wine, its mustard and its regular visits by the Tour, Dijon is the great city of Burgundy, and one of the handsomest in France, with wonderful churches, the cathedral of Saint-Michel and Saint-Jean now like so many churches through-out Europe used as a theatre, a telling illustration of the way that Culture has taken the place of religion. Besides, there are the many memories of the glorious years when Burgundy was a power among the lands, the ducal palace and numerous lesser but lovely noble town houses, like the Hotel de Vogué, distantly connected with the boy seen bike racing in Paris many centuries after Philip the Good.

By reclaiming the name of the Duke of Burgundy, Louis XIV was making a political statement, and earlier kings had long made another kind of statement, with regular progresses around their domains. In this sense, as Vigarello says, the Tour lay in a long tradition of such tours of France, 'the royal tour taking pos-session of the land and displaying sovereignty; the tour of companions, with its initiations and *gestes de formation*; even the educational tour, with its scholarly apprenticeship and its literary pastimes. The race which the *Auto* had invented was a bit of all of these.' It was a processional display, a good labourer's journey, an educational device.

Absorption with the Tour as *événement* and epic links popular culture with academic analysis. Songs about the bike go back to the nineteenth-century music hall, in England – 'You'll look sweet upon the seat of a bicycle made for two' – and France: 'Viens, viens, Mad'leine sur ma p'tit' reine' (the *petite reine* or little queen was an old sobriquet for the bike). Songs about the Tour itself begin after the Great War. 'Charlot' – not Charlie Chaplin but Charles Pélissier – was hymned: 'Les meilleurs des coureurs,/ C'est le géant Charlot,/Fameux en tour de piste/Il veut avoir le maillot' ('The best of the riders is the great Charlot, famous around the tracks, he wants to win the jersey'), while Perchicot sang 'Les Tours de France' in 1927: 'Je suis allé/Les voir passer/Les "Tours de France",/Ils pédalaient,/Et leurs mollets/Rythmaient une belle cadence,/Qu'ils étaient beaux!/Sur leurs vélos/Dans leurs maillots pleins d'élégance' ('I went to see them pass, the Tours de France, they pedalled and their calves put rhythm into a beautiful motion. They were so handsome on their bikes, in their elegant jerseys', though this may lose something in translation). The Provençal *chanteur* Marcel Darcelys made his record 'Le Tour de France' in 1929, and there was a series of 'Official Marches' of the Tour by popular singers like Koval, La Houppa, Frédo Gardoni and Monty, a great favourite in the 1930s, not least with his 1936 Tour song 'Ah! Les Voilà!' saluting the riders as they appear along the road.

In the middle years of the century France had no more popular singer than a Corsican who overshadowed all his rivals, to a degree one of them ruefully acknowledged. Just as destiny had chosen Poulidor to arrive in the same generation as Anquetil, Luis Mariano said, 'I arrived in the generation of Tino Rossi.' In 1937, a year after Frédo Gardoni had sung 'Le Maillot Jaune' ('C'est le maillot du vainqueur'), Rossi recorded 'Doux secret d'amour', which sweet secret of love was a *valse chantée du Tour de France*. Although popular songs of this kind rather went out of fashion in the post-war years, Marcel Amont could still release 'Il a le maillot jaune' in 1960, ending with an up-to-date touch: 'Il a le maillot. Vite à la maison/Pour voir son triomphe à la télévision' ('He's got the jersey, let's get home quick to see him win on television').

At the other end of the intellectual scale, as it were, the concept of the Tour as myth and epic was elaborated by Jean Calvet in his remarkable book published in 1981, *Le Mythe des géants de la route*, but he wasn't the first. In the second half of the twentieth century France produced not only great writers and historians but a number of theoreticians, rhetoricians and 'public intellectuals', who gave the world existentialism, deconstructionism and what-not, writing with varying degrees of plausibility and sanity. Most of these – Sartre, Foucault, Derrida, Lévi-Strauss, Althusser, Lacan – evinced little interest in sport, but the exception was Roland Barthes. Born in Cherbourg, he moved with his war-wid-owed mother to Bayonne, and may have been conscious as a little boy of the Tour passing through in the years after the Great War, before they moved to Paris, where he was educated at the Sorbonne, to become an eminent theorist of structural linguistics and analyst of the 'science of signs'.

But he had already shown himself an acutely intelligent and entertaining analyst of myth and ritual in popular culture and, how-ever it might be with academic theory, Barthes was an outstanding journalist. His idea that contemporary culture – from wrestling to wine-drinking to striptease – could be dissected in terms of sign and myth was perfectly valid, and he never wrote more interestingly than on 'Le Tour de France Comme Épopée,' his essay looking at the Tour as epic published in his 1957 collection *Mythologies* (though lamentably and inexplicably not included in the later, much abbreviated English translation under the same name).

It might have been a little far-fetched to see the names of the riders as hailing from an ancient tribal age – 'Brankart le Franc, Bobet le Francien, Robic le Celte, Ruiz l'Ibère, Darrigade le Gascon' – or to see the names of Geminiani and Rolland as 'algebraic signs of courage, loyalty, treachery or stoicism'. And his belief that the mythic qualities of the cyclists was enhanced by their nicknames or abbreviations (so that one could see Raphael Geminiani as a hero both good and brave from the way that he was sometimes called 'Raph' and sometimes 'Gem') is not shared by this chronicler. If such journalistic pet names were 'part tender and part servile', then that was true of every 'Becks' who ever played football for England.

But Barthes was surely right to see echoes of epic myth in the Tour. When Bobet, during one stage in Brittany, had publicly offered his hand to Lauridi, who had just as openly refused it, there was a ring of Homeric quarrels, which were, as Barthes said, matched by the manly sentimentality of the race, with Bobet telling Koblet 'I miss you', or the perennial kissing: Marcel Bidot kissing Geminiani after a stage win or Rolland just as fervently kissing 'Gem's' cheek. More recent exponents of gay studies and Queer Theory would doubtless see this tenderness in their own terms, but Barthes rightly preferred to compare it with the male bonding and comradeship of the arena or the foxhole.

Maybe Barthes the gifted journalist was a little too sentimental himself about journalism, or journalese. He had a soft spot for the way that the geography of the Tour had become part of the epic essence in every typewritten account, the landscape personified so that 'man is naturalized and nature is humanized'. In the sports pages one stage or another would be hairy, sticky, fiery, prickly, 'all adjectives which belong to an existential order of categorization and which suggest that the rider is at grips not with some natural difficulty or other but with a real question of existence, a question of substance, where he engages his understanding and judgement in a single movement'. Or it might just be that's the way newspapermen write.

Behind these flights of fancy, Barthes perceptively descried heroic duelling as the essence of the Tour. Even more than foxhunting, the Tour fits Surtees's phrase, 'the image of war without its guilt': in terms of the number of its personnel and the importance of its materiel, the Tour can be compared to an army, its warriors eulogized in martial terms Napoleon or Hugo would have understood. And its dynamic, said Barthes (somewhat to simplify him), had four aspects: *mener, suivre, s'échapper, l'affaissement.*

Mener – to lead – was the hardest act, and the least useful; the leader at any moment was usually acting sacrificially, and he wasn't likely to enhance his own chances. *Suivre* – to follow – seemed on the contrary a little cowardly and a little sly. The opportunism of the *suceur de roues*, the wheel-sucker, was a form of

Evil. *S'échapper* – to escape – was a kind of poetry and an act of individual destiny, not the less so because the escaper was almost always caught. It was glorious because of its useless honour (think of the *fugue solitaire* of the Spanish rider Alomar, with the Castilian distance and haughtiness of a Montherlant hero). And *affaissement* – extreme *défaillance*, the bonk, or collapse – usually prefaced abandoning the race. It was always grim to watch, and at its most terrible, on Ventoux too often, it could be called *hiroshimatique*.

Although Barthes wrote as a fascinated outsider, the Tour had just acquired the greatest of all its chroniclers from the inside. Antoine Blondin was a dazzlingly gifted writer, as can be seen in novels like *Un singe en hiver* (*A Monkey in Winter*); a sardonic reactionary contemptuous of the leftist domination of French intellectual life, a self-destructive boozer; and a passionate devotee of the Tour. His despatches for the *Equipe* from 1954 to 1982, apart from showing how well a man can write even when half-drunk half the time, are an uncommon example of truly fine sports writing. If countless music-hall songs, newspaper columns, cartoons and *affiches* showed how deeply the Tour had become engraved in French popular consciousness, Blondin, Barthes and Vigarello showed how it was a subject worthy of serious and intelligent analysis. Apart from its more exalted aspects, they also had something to say about the role played by *dopage* in his great epic. But that must await its sombre context.

9

Anquetil's Apotheosis

1958-1962

After that astonishing debut, 1958 was an anticlimax for
Anquetil's fans, but the race didn't lack for drama otherwise. In
that year Rivière broke the one-hour record once more despite
puncturing, Baldini won the Giro, as well as the World
Champion's rainbow jersey ahead of Bobet, and Jean Stablinski
of France – a man who rode in twelve Tours but never came
higher than thirtieth in 1962 – won the Vuelta. For football this
was a year of grandeur and misery. A glorious Brazilian side won
the World Cup, graced by a wonderful boy called Pelé, but
another superb team of young players was martyred when the
plane carrying Manchester United home from Zagreb crashed at
Munich. Three officials and eight journalists were killed along
with seven players, including Roger Byrne, Duncan Edwards
and Liam Whelan, their names even now like a knell for anyone
who was aged twelve that winter. And the Tour saw splendours
and miseries of its own.

Although Anquetil had been in good form, the first blow was
struck by André Darrigade before a steady turnover of the lead

while they made their way from Brussels to Brest by way of Versailles and St-Nazaire. These two were both new stops, the latter still showing signs of the heroic British commando raid commemorated in the name of the rue du 28 février 1943. Charly Gaul won a time trial unexpectedly from Anquetil, and then another up Mont Ventoux. Refreshed by his advertising ventures, Geminiani had been chosen by Adolphe Deledda to ride for his Centre-Midi team, and he justified the choice by taking the GC lead on Mont Ventoux and holding it for two more stages, while Bahamontes won Gap–Briançon on his thirtieth birthday, and would finish with the Mountains prize.

A still more extraordinary stage from Briançon to Aix-les-Bains, one of the epics in the history of the Tour, was ridden in indescribably frightful weather, so bad that the usual time limit was remitted. While Gaul was the one rider who relished the conditions, Anquetil was flagging badly, and by the end of that stage had lost 22 minutes to Gaul, who replaced him in third place. Favero still led the GC by more than half an hour, having replaced Geminiani. For some reason Geminiani was convinced that the French team had betrayed him, and screamed 'Les Judas!' at them. As for poor Anquetil, he wasn't just flagging but ailing, and abandoned on the next stage with pulmonary congestion. Gaul seized and held the lead, to become the third Luxemburger to win the Tour, thirty years after Frantz had completed his double.

Between the finish of one Tour at the Parc des Princes on 19 July 1958 and the departure of the next from Mulhouse on 25 June 1959, France was turned upside down. The bitter war in Algeria led to a military coup there, and then to the sudden return to power in Paris of General de Gaulle after years of internal exile at Colombey-les-deux-Eglises. He became president under the constitution of the new Fifth Republic, although the unprecedented powers it gave him didn't as yet enable him to resolve the conflict, or heal the bitter rifts within the French nation.

On a more trivial level, the French cyclists were also divided, with sharp rivalries between Anquetil, Rivière and Bobet which threatened the collective will of the whole French team. But now, ten years after Binda had made peace between Coppi and Bartali with the Chiavari pact, another accord, the Pact of Poigny-la-Forêt made peace between the Frenchmen. Like de Gaulle's return, this did not bring immediate tranquillity, certainly not for Bobet. It turned out to be the last Tour for both him and Robic, the one abandoning at the top of the Col d'Iseran, the other eliminated at Chalon-sur-Saône after the antepenultimate stage. And although both Anquetil and Rivière performed well, far from collaborating, they wore each other out. Anglade rode a brilliant stage from Albi to Aurillac, but they none of them could hold Bahamontes. The Spanish rider won the Tour with a quartet of Frenchmen behind him, Anglade, Anquetil, Rivière and Mahé.

If no Spaniard had won the Tour before, that wasn't from a shortage of skill, especially in the mountains. Federico Martin Alejandra Bahamontes, harmlessly if unilluminatingly dubbed 'The Eagle of Toledo', came from a line of Spanish mountain men, of whom he was the greatest. He had already won the King of the Mountains prize in 1954 and 1958, he won it again this year, and he would win it thrice more in successive years 1962–4. Good judges, like the French journalist Pierre Chany, insist that climbing was then far harder work than it later became: the condition of the roads was worse and the gears were much tougher. Bahamontes was certainly a man of astonishing mettle, wiry and tense, although his mental resilience had one flaw. He had had a nasty downhill crash when riding as an amateur, landing in a cactus as the story went, and he never quite recovered his nerve as an enthusiastic descender. So little did he like going downhill without any support that he once reached the summit of a col on his own and stopped to eat an ice cream until the next riders joined him. His last Mountains prize came on his last but one Tour. On the Bagnères-de-Bigorre–Ax-les-Thermes stage in 1965, in his beloved Pyrenees, he abandoned and went home, for good as it proved.

A pall hung over the 1960 Tour before it began. In recent years Fausto Coppi had had a troubled career and an equally troubled romantic life, even given his reputation as a rake. He had been photographed with a lady not his wife, but unfortunately someone else's, and the white coat she was wearing added 'La dama in bianco' to the language of Italian popular journalism. She had a name of her own, Giulia Locatelli, and she offered him something he did not get from his devout but mousy wife. Bruna was forever telling him to give up cycling, but Giulia adored him as her hero, the white lady's white knight. Although the affair embroiled Coppi in sundry unsavoury rows, not least with Giulia's husband, and was followed in lurid detail by the press, it was a true romance, and Coppi was devoted to the son she bore him. Alas, it did nothing for Coppi as a cyclist. He never rode in the Tour after 1952, and his magnificent career petered out while he went on riding elsewhere long after he should have stopped.

Promoters of Criteriums shortened them to a derisory 45 kilometres just so that he could take part with some prospect of finishing. He was still riding in the Vuelta in 1959, but, like an ageing heavyweight humiliatingly floored over and again, he was the first rider to be dropped every day, and only kept going at all by doping himself to the gills. Although he had amassed a huge fortune for a cyclist, leaving $1.5 million at his death, he was a sad shadow, 'a magnificent and grotesque washout,' in Chany's words, 'a weary and disillusioned man' wrapped in impenetrable melancholy. In late 1959 he went to take part in some exhibition races in Upper Volta (now less well known as Burkina Faso) where he contracted malaria. Maybe weakened by whatever he had ingested over the years, he died on 2 January 1960. He was forty. According to one lurid rumour which surfaced more than forty years later he had been poisoned by an African rival, but his own doctor discounted this. According to another (which also sounds *ben trovato*, since it couldn't have been substantiated without abuse of elementary ecclesiastical ethics), a priest only gave him absolution and the last rites when he agreed, if he survived, to leave Giulia. But she was at his funeral, with their son Faustino, along with Anquetil, Bobet, his enemy and friend Bartali, and thousands of others, as the line of wreaths stretched for hundreds of yards. Goddet wrote that everyone in cycling had wanted to tell him to stop, but that 'as nobody dared to, destiny took care of it'. Flawed, magnificent, he was one of the greatest riders ever to win the Tour de France; even though he won no more than twice, some still think him the greatest of all.

One sign of de Gaulle's new regime was monetary: Tour prize money of 47.7 million francs, 2 million to the winner, in 1959 became 400,000 and 20,000 in 1960 – but these were New or 'heavy' francs, which had replaced the ailing and ever-inflationary old currency. Judged by a simple test, the first prize now bought 32,258 kilos of bread, and was thus worth more than four times as much in real terms as the 3000 francs won in 1903. Whatever the prize or the currency or the value, the French still couldn't get back into the race in 1960. Indeed they had a dismal year, after initial promise. Anquetil had just become the first French rider to win the Giro, from Nencini and Gaul, but he didn't take part in the Tour, and more misfortune followed for the Tricolores. Three riders wore the yellow jersey before Anglade took it, but from St-Malo to Lorient a four-man break by Rivière, Nencini, Junkermann and Adriaenssens left the field over fourteen minutes behind, disrupting Anglade's chances. Rivière was still in with his own chances, but in the Cevennes he had a horrible fall, which ended his career and left him in a wheelchair; he died of cancer aged only forty in 1976.

This was the year the French boxer Halimi beat the Irishman Gilroy, and was reported a little implausibly to have said, 'I've avenged Joan of Arc!', words that might have pleased the general at the Élysée Palace. Gaullism wasn't as shameless in exploiting sporting glory as different totalitarianisms had been. Even so, the Tour field was still obliged, as it neared Paris on the penultimate Besançon–Troyes stage, to stop at Colombey-les-deux-Eglises. De Gaulle shook hands with Nencini and Anglade, and the peloton saluted him. Though not an ardent sports fan, de Gaulle could recognize a great national institution when he saw one, and his successors in the Élysée Palace have been happy to appropriate the Tour as expressing their own 'certain idea of France'.

That ceremony was missed by Pierre Beuffeuil because of a puncture, and he then adroitly used the opportunity to escape and win the stage. But it was Nencini who stood on the first place in the Parc. He had held the lead through eleven stages from Pau onwards, despite repeating Walkowiak's curious trick of winning the Tour without winning a single stage. His compatriot Graziano Battistini was in second and the Belgian Jan Adriaenssens third.

Meantime the Algerian conflict was moving towards its messy conclusion, after de Gaulle had told the French Algerians, 'Je vous ai compris,' by which he turned out to mean that he understood he had to abandon those *pieds noirs* in the name of sacred egoism and for the good of the republic. He saw off the generals' coup in Algiers, subsequently obtaining the 1962 ceasefire and Evian agreement which meant the end of 'l'Algérie française' and the departure of a million *pieds noirs* for France, following the departure of the army. The Paras marched out of Algiers, where they had rounded up many a usual suspect and merrily tortured them, singing 'Je ne regrette rien'. And Edith Piaf's 1961 hit might have been Anquetil's song as well that year: if he regretted his departure from the Tour two years earlier and then his absence a year later, he kept it to himself, and determined on the best kind of recompense.

His victory this year was indeed devastating. Darrigade won the yellow jersey in the first half-stage, which was his fifth victory on the first day of the Tour, and he finished with the green jersey. In the time trial that immediately followed, Anquetil took the lead, and never lost it over the next three weeks. At the finish he won easily by more than twelve minutes, the French team also winning in a breeze. The only excitement at the end was when Gaul looked sure to follow Anquetil home, but the Italian rider Guido Carlesi snatched second on the last day. It was Carlesi's first Tour; he was nineteenth the next year, abandoned in 1963 and 1966, and never rode in the race again.

That was Anquetil's second Tour victory, the first of his unprecedented consecutive four-timer, and his last in French colours. In 1962 the Tour returned after more than three decades to the formula that Desgrange had discarded in 1930, of commercially sponsored teams. And these were truly commercial: instead of bicycle manufacturers, the new team sponsors were businesses that often had no connection with sport, or more usually several sponsors combining to back a team. Anquetil was riding for ACCB–Saint-Raphaël–Helyett–Hutchinson, generally and not surprisingly referred to as St-Raphael; one Italian team was sponsored by the domestic appliances group Moschettieri-Ignis, another by one more drinks company, Carpano. Elsewhere the commercial sponsorship of sport was also beginning – English steeplechasing already had the Hennessy Cognac and Whitbread Gold Cups – as businessmen saw an effective, and cost-effective, way to promote their wares which compared favourably with conventional advertising.

But this race was notable for something more than competing aperitifs: it was the first round of what would be one of the epic duels in the history of the Tour de France. A year earlier that last French team could have included, but didn't, a fine young rider called Raymond Poulidor. Looking back, the team manager Marcel Bidot lamented this failure. 'I'm sorry that Antonin Magne opposed the selection of Poulidor in the French team last year. Raymond could come to terms with Anquetil and . . . he could probably win a Tour, or a few. Together they could dominate cycling for ten years.' They did dominate the Tour for years, but Poulidor would remain the best rider never to win the race, the 'eternal second': more precisely, he was second three times and third five.

This intelligent and sensitive man – to the extent that he liked any nickname, he preferred 'Pouli', as the peloton called him, and detested the infantile 'Pou Pou', which the press inflicted on him for good – was a couple of years younger than Anquetil, born in 1936 in Léonard-de-Noblet near Limoges, the son of *métayeurs*, poor sharecroppers at the bottom of the French rural ladder. Poulidor grew up fit as any peasant's son from hard manual work, rode a bike when young from village to village, followed Anquetil into the army, took up cycling seriously, turned pro in 1960. His first big race was the World Road Championship that year, in which he was in the lead when he punctured, but he picked up more prizes before the 1962 Tour in which, by now twenty-six, he was chosen to ride for Mercier–BP–Hutchinson.

It was the beginning of a magnificent and melancholy career, which captured the hearts of the French. Nobody could express that chagrin and disappointment better than Poulidor himself. There have been other autobiographies published under unforgettably sad titles redolent of self-effacement or disappointment, from the Finnish composer Einar Englund's *In the Shadow of Sibelius* to Vyvyan Holland's *Son of Oscar Wilde*. Neither of those is more poignant than Poulidor's *Gloire sans le Maillot Jaune*, and it was, astonishingly enough, true that he never once held the *classification général* lead to wear the yellow jersey. Between the first time he took third place in the Tour and the last time he did so was an interval of fourteen years, a superbly consistent record; but still, he never won.

He scarcely rode a better Tour than his first, leaving the start at Nancy with a hand in plaster and dropping eight minutes on that first stage. But he stuck with the field, while the lead changed hands endlessly: a record seven men wore the yellow jersey during the course of the race. One of them was Tom Simpson: first British cyclist ever to do so; fine rider; tragic hero. Another day belonged to Poulidor when he won the Briançon–Aix-les-Bains stage across the Chartreuse. But the race belonged to Anquetil, who rode with his steady, ruthless determination, winning only two stages, from the new *ville-étape* of Luçon to La Rochelle, and then, most convincingly, the time trial from Bourgoin to Lyons, where he took the yellow jersey and held it for the next two days until the finish, with Helyett–Saint-Raphaël winning the team prize. Poulidor had acquitted himself admirably in third only 10'24" off the pace. Time was surely on his side.

10

'Put Me Back on My Bike'

1963-1967

If Anquetil was one of those sportsmen easier to admire than to love, he belonged in that respect to a formidable line, a Don Bradman not a Tom Graveney, a Joe DiMaggio not a Willie Mays, a Roy Keane not a George Best, a Rob Andrew not a Phil Bennett. For one thing, his specialism of the time trial is by definition the least beguiling or most desiccated aspect of bike racing, the province of sophisters, economists and calculators. Time-triallists may stack up the minutes, and the scoring of the Tour is weighted in their favour, but what the public loves is doughty roadmen and even more the climbers who can make their case before the 'judges of peace' in the great mountain ranges.

And so, even after three victories, Anquetil hadn't captured French hearts. In 1963, he took the opportunity of the fiftieth Tour (as opposed to the fiftieth anniversary ten years before) to show what he could do. Yes, he won the two time trials as expected, 24.5 kilometres at Angers and then 55 kilometres from Arbois to Besançon two weeks later, but he did much more than that.

Even at the height of his powers, Anquetil never looked a well man, thin, drawn, almost emaciated, and appearances weren't deceptive since indeed he often was not very well. In the spring of 1963, five years after the illness that knocked him out of the 1958 Tour, he was infested by a tapeworm which left him lean and weakened, and his doctors advised him against taking part. 'Never mind your doctor's orders,' Oscar Wilde was told in the witness box, and replied, 'I never do.' Anquetil followed his principle. He left Paris under the watchful gaze of Bobet and set off with the field of 130 through Champagne, Normandy and the Limousin. With Poulidor well below his best, any challenge to Anquetil would come from Bahamontes, and would come in the mountains, or so it was supposed.

In fact, Bahamontes threw down a challenge on the first day with an escape that put him ninety seconds ahead of Anquetil; the yellow jersey was taken by Eddy Pauwels, a Belgian rider with Wiels–Groene Leuw. A team time trial at Jambes was won by Pelforth–Sauvage–Lejeune, promoting one more alcoholic beverage, and one that reflects amusingly on French taste. The late Sir Kingsley Amis laid down the dogmatic principle that no decent drink should taste like medicine, which rules out most continental aperitifs, Campari, Punt-e-Mes and indeed Saint-Raphaël. But a medicinally sour fortified wine is surely less of an acquired taste than a sickly-sweet beer like Pelforth. Could anyone but the French enjoy it? At any rate it was the prevailing theme of sponsorship. Other teams were sponsored, in cumbrous portmanteau names, by tyre manufacturers, with a prize for cumbrousness taken by VC XII–Saint-Raphaël–Gitane–Dunlop. But drinks predominated.

The following day another break was led by the Irishman Shay (for Seamus) Elliott from Anquetil's team, who had abandoned in two Tours since 1956, finished in midfield in two, and would end in sixty-third place this year, and included Henry Anglade, who gained more than nine minutes on Anquetil and looked like a real threat. Elliott then took the yellow jersey, the first Irish rider to do so, and held it for three more days. Anquetil easily beat Poulidor in the first time trial to begin a steady ascent in the GC.

In the mountains Anquetil revealed his greatness. Not at first: when they reached the Pyrenees, Bahamontes beat him over the Col d'Aubisque, but Anquetil turned tables over the Tourmalet with the sun on his back, holding Bahamontes, and then setting off in a five-man sprint for the finish at Bagnères de Bigorre to win the stage from Jose Perez Frances, Poulidor and Bahamontes. Bahamontes won one Alpine stage, from Saint-Étienne to Grenoble, to move into second place, and he took the yellow jersey at Val d'Isère when he finished upsides with the reigning champion.

'The Tour will be decided on the Forclaz,' Anquetil said. The following day they raced from Val d'Isère to Chamonix. Bahamontes broke away gamely from Anquetil and Poulidor on the Col du Grand St Bernard to take ninety seconds, but he lost the time downhill, unluckily slowed by rain and fog before finding the road broken up by building work. A group of ten riders formed to climb the Forclaz, the third of the day's cols, thirty kilometres from the finish, again in gruelling conditions over what was more a gravel track than a road. Anquetil and Bahamontes dropped the group, Bahamontes attacked to go four lengths ahead, Anquetil came back.

And then he stopped. This was a ruse dreamed up by Geminiani: pretending that he had had a mechanical hitch, he changed his bike for a lighter model, and although Bahamontes took four seconds at the summit, it wasn't enough. Anquetil had been right, and he clinched his superiority as they sprinted into Chamonix where Anquetil received the ovation of his life as he arrived to collect the yellow jersey. An even larger crowd awaited him at the Parc when he finished the race 3'35" from Bahamontes: a sad contrast with Poulidor, who hadn't coped with the mountains, finished eighth and was derisively whistled at by the Parisian crowd for his pains. He could only nurse his injured pride and wait for next year.

But still fortune didn't smile on Poulidor in 1964. Bahamontes won the Mountains prize, for the third year running – the sixth time in all, and the last time as it proved – while Janssen won the points prize, and Georges Groussard was the new star, riding like his brother Joseph for Pelforth, and leading from eighth to sixteenth stages. None of that mattered on this Tour besides the personal contest between the two rivals, one of the greatest such duels the race has ever seen. Neither won a stage of the clockwise race until after the last day in the Alps. Anquetil had come to the Tour in top form after winning the Giro. He took Briançon–Monaco, and then another stage to Toulon. Poulidor fought back. He could have won Andorra–Toulouse after beating Anquetil over the Port d'Envalira but for an accident near the finish, he could have won the Peyrehorade–Bayonne time trial but for a puncture, leaving it to be taken by Anquetil.

Then came a last climb, up the Puy de Dôme, on the day before Bastille Day and only four days from Paris; and it saw a culmination of that great duel. This was only the third time that the Tour had climbed the Puy. The recent fashion is for climbing stages to end up a mountain, at a ski resort which has paid to advertise itself thus. The Tour used to climb Mont Ventoux and then come down again, rather than, as in 2002, finishing on the peak to the great inconvenience of all those covering the race. But with Puy there's no choice: it's its own *Arrivée* because the road reaches the peak and ends there, with no other road down, after the climb turns from one 5-kilometre stretch at 1-in-14 gradient to another 5 kilometres at 1-in-8.

On that day the two men raced *coude à coude*, not in the loose sense that Tour journalists love to say 'shoulder to shoulder' for any two riders in close contention, but actually bumping elbows and thighs, Anquetil on the inside, Poulidor on the valley side, as they jostled behind Jimenez and Bahamontes. Finally Poulidor broke away to reach the peak ahead of his rival, but Anquetil was still 14 seconds ahead in the GC, which he had increased slightly before reaching the Parc to win the Tour by a cruel 55 seconds from Poulidor. It was cruel because Poulidor had been beaten by less than a minute after three weeks and more than 127 hours in the saddle, or by 0.00013 of the total time ridden, rather as though a 1500-metre track race lasting nearly four minutes was lost by a thirtieth of a second; and it was doubly cruel, because it was the nearest he would ever come to winning the Tour.

Defeat and victory weren't followed by any great show of sports-manship. Anquetil had said ungenerously at the Puy summit, 'It wasn't a great day for Poulidor or for me,' and Poulidor's *directeur sportif* Magne reacted angrily after the race: 'Raymond has lost the Tour because he lied to me.' He calmed down after a while, although Magne was at no time a warm personality, with the public, or with his colleagues, or with his Mercier riders. Sociolinguists speak of the 'T/V' distinction in most European languages, though not in English, native speakers of which have the greatest difficulty with this even when they speak those lan-guages quite well; that is, the differentiation between intimate T(u) and formal V(ous). *Bon bourgeois* eschew *tu*: two couples, General and Madame de Gaulle, and Sartre and Simone de Beauvoir, had this in common, that they called each other '*vous*' all their lives. Some groups – students and miners – will always instinctively *tutoyer*, and cyclists too, but Magne never did when speaking to his team. He illustrated the point when he said to Poulidor, 'Raymond, vous êtes insaisissable,' literally, 'You're elusive,' or, 'I don't get you.' There at least he spoke for many people.

For his part, Anquetil barely disguised the contempt he felt for Poulidor for lacking the final killer instinct, and even those who loved Poulidor and longed for him to win knew that there was something in this. I thought of his *grandeurs* and *misères* on 19 July 2002 when the stage from Lannemezan ended at Plateau-de-Beille and a vast throng made its way very slowly indeed down from the 1780-metre ski station. Sitting in the great gruesome traffic jam I turned around to look out of the side window, and realized that I was next to the Crédit Lyonnais car, and there was Poulidor, his features softened after decades of retirement but in any case always sensitive and pensive, and perceptibly sad.

If he followed the cycling news attentively Poulidor would have heard something else that year, and learned a new name. The title of amateur World Road Champion had been won by a young Belgian called Eddy Merckx. He almost didn't take part in that race because the official doctor of the Belgian cycling federation said that his heart was 'too small' for serious riding. His own doctor was called in, for a second opinion that changed cycling history. When the 1965 Tour began, as far afield as Cologne, the field didn't include Anquetil. He was much preoccupied with his life outside cycling; he had recently sold the hotel he owned in Rouen and bought a farm; he had quite enough laurels to rest on, with a Vuelta and two Giros as well as consecutive Tours; he was irritated by the way the public still preferred Poulidor to him. 'I won't be riding in the 1965 Tour de Poulidor,' he told a reporter early in the year, and when asked to expatiate, said that by reducing the number of time trials, the Tour organizers had loaded the dice in Poulidor's favour.

This wasn't actually true, as an amused Poulidor pointed out: 'Bloody Jacques' always wanted to say something controversial about the Tour, he remarked, and anyway the time trials hadn't been lengthened. As his own wife Janine admitted, Anquetil did have a knack of getting bees in his bonnet, but this one buzzed away and couldn't be dislodged. He had a fine season, winning the Dauphiné Libéré and the Bordeaux–Paris races – travelling overnight from one race to the other – as well as a stack of Criteriums, but he held to his resolve and missed the great race, almost as if to say to Poulidor, 'It's all yours, if you're up to it.'

As it proved, the man who struck first and last was Felice Gimondi, a 23-year-old Italian who had announced his arrival by winning the Tour de l'Avenir – the tour-of-the-future, or amateurs' race, run over the Tour course – the year before. Even then, he was lucky to be taking part in the big boys' Tour, as a replacement in the GS Salvarini team for Bruno Fantinato who had forfeited his place. He opened up a handy lead to win the third stage from Roubaix to Rouen, before Poulidor, in a most ironical comment on Anquetil's animadversions, won the first time trial by seven seconds from him. Julio Jimenez struck back in the Pyrenees to win the stage into Bagnères-de-Bigorre, but Poulidor bravely won ahead of him up Mont Ventoux, where Gimondi managed to limit the damage. After Jimenez had won another stage, Briançon–Aix-les-Bains in the Alps, to ensure that he would finish as King of the Mountains, Gimondi won a time trial up the newly raced Mont Revard. And then, on the very last stage, run on the *quatorze juillet*, a mere 37.8 kilometres from Versailles to Paris, Gimondi won ahead of Gianni Motta, with Poulidor at 1'08" – which was to say 2'40" behind Gimondi in the final GC.

All the talk was of Gimondi's prowess, and of Poulidor's comportment in defeat. It may be thought a linguistic illustration of the English Imposture that, whereas the English words for *chagrin* and *Schadenfreude* are 'chagrin' and 'schadenfreude', the French and German words for 'fair play' are *le fairplay* and *die Fair-play*. However that may be, it was for his fair play and sportsmanship that Poulidor was universally admired; or almost universally. 'Nice guys finish last' is an old tag, and something of a misquotation. What Leo 'The Lip' Durocher, manager of the Brooklyn Dodgers, originally said – in 1949, when the National League had seven teams – was 'Nice guys finish seventh.' If he had followed the Tour during Poulidor's career, he might have said: 'Nice guys finish second or third.'

For Poulidor there was one more bitter cup to drink in 1966, though with a slightly different flavour. The race left Nancy for

Dieppe and Angers on the way to Bordeaux and the Pyrenees, where a new climb had been added between Pau and Luchon, the Col de Mente, a handsome pass one day to be darkened by tragedy. Poulidor's decency and decorum had now made him more popular than ever. On the other hand, and whether or not he was graced with those qualities (or whether or not he cared), Anquetil's strength as a rider had never been greater. Although he was third in the Giro behind the 23-year-old Gianni Motta, he won the Liège–Bastogne–Liège race this year, along with his fifth Paris–Nice, and the Grand Prix des Nations for the ninth time in nine appearances. It seemed certain that the Tour would be won by one of the two great Frenchmen. The race was won by a French rider, all right, but not the one either pros or fans expected. In fact, Poulidor won only one stage and Anquetil none, and neither man ever held the lead.

Before the race got serious, there was drama off the road. At Bordeaux an unannounced dope test was sprung on the riders, with a court official accompanying the testers, who called first on Poulidor. Anquetil expressed his solidarity with his rival whose dignity and reputation had been affronted, and so did the whole field, who staged a token strike at Gradignan; events that gave a foretaste of cycling for a generation to come. Until that point the idea that the Tour forbade drugs was a *fable convenue*, a polite fiction, even a joke. Riders were honour-bound to abstain from narcotics, serious attempts to enforce the rules were rarely made, and, when they were, the cyclists protested vehemently at this insult to their good names.

The truth was that almost everyone was at it and everyone knew that everyone was at it. Solemn official edicts against *dopage* were rather like the scene Conor Cruise O'Brien witnessed in Accra a couple of years earlier, when Kwame Nkrumah, with a straight face, told the Ghanaian parliament that no politicians should have bank accounts abroad, and that any such that existed should be closed, while the whole assembly giggled uncontrollably. Like those legislators, the Tour riders nodded with a smile if anyone reminded them what the rules were; like them, they were outraged if anyone appeared to take the rules seriously. All that was about to change in the grimmest circumstances.

When racing resumed it was Lucien Aimar, Anquetil's colleague in the newly formed Ford–Geminiani team, and an experimentalist who had been trying out a huge new 55×13 gear, who attacked over the Col d'Aubisque and steadily moved up the GC. On its passage through the Midi the Tour paid a first visit to the agreeable and agreeably unfashionable port of Sète, Paul Valéry's 'toit tranquille, où marchent les colombes'; a stage won by Vandenberghe. Then two days later Poulidor gratifyingly beat Anquetil in the time trial at Vals-les-Bains. And yet the race was not going well for him.

On the way from Bourg d'Oisans to Briançon, Tom Simpson escaped, wearing the World Champion's rainbow jersey. He was ninety seconds clear as he began to climb the Col du Télégraphe, but Jimenez, destined to win the Mountains prize for the second year running, began to pick him up, followed by both his teammate Anquetil and by Poulidor. When Jimenez caught him, waited with him, and then went ahead, Simpson realized that he had made his break too soon. Before long, Anquetil and Poulidor had also passed him.

By this point Anquetil knew that he wasn't likely to win the Tour, but if he wasn't, nor was Poulidor, not if he could help it. He fought flat out up the Galibier to take second place at the col to Jimenez. On the descent Jos Huysmans was close behind with Aimar plummeting at dangerous speed, throwing his bike this way and that at the corners, and Simpson was catching up again until, nearing the day's finish, a television-toting motorbike skidded and brought him down. He rode into Briançon dripping with blood, barely able to use his right arm, and had to abandon the next day. His departure was followed by Anquetil, stricken once more, on the Chamonix–St-Étienne stage. And still

Poulidor couldn't take advantage. He attacked again and made a tremendous descent from the Col d'Ornon, but was too far from the lead. The race saw one last exploit, on the antepenultimate day from Montluçon to Orléans, when Beuffeuil won the stage after making an individual break of 205 kilometres, the sixth-longest in Tour history. At the Parc Poulidor finished third behind Aimar and Jan Janssen, surprisingly enough the first man ever to stand on the podium from the cycling-mad Netherlands.

If Holland had never produced a winner, nor had England. The best hopes our damp little island ever enjoyed in the Tour came in 1967, with Tom Simpson seemingly at his peak, and his country still elated after England's exciting if not wholly deserved victory in the 1966 World Cup when 'They think it's all over' entered the language, now to be joined by a much more poignant phrase; it would soon be all over for one brave rider. This was also the summer of *Sergeant Pepper's Lonely Hearts Club Band*; for many an English cycling fan, what was about to happen in Provence would be remembered 'When I'm Sixty-Four'.

The race seemed up for grabs when Anquetil, despite winning the Criterium International for the fourth time, announced that he was a non-runner in the Tour; he would never take part again. After five years of commercial *groupes sportifs*, the race had returned to national teams, three of them French, the first-string *équipe*, the Bleuets, and the Coqs de France; and it began with an innovation, the Prologue on 29 June. This was actually an additional time trial, called by another name to slip it past UCI – the Union Cycliste International, the sport's governing body – regulations. Its first running in Angers this St Peter's Day was won by José-Maria Errandonea with Poulidor six seconds away. But yet again it wasn't Poulidor's year. After the race set off clockwise through Brittany, Normandy, Picardy and Lorraine, he fell badly in the Vosges, and over the Ballon d'Alsace lost any chances. They passed instead to his Tricolores team-mate Roger Pingeon, who had staked his claim with a long individual escape between

Roubaix and Jambes. The lead passed to and fro, with the yellow jersey worn over three weeks by five riders as they crossed the Alps and headed for Mont Ventoux.

Where it happened. Simpson had been riding very well, and had come seventh in the stage from Digne to Marseilles two days before, a minute and a half behind Riotte. He was in good spirits that day from Marseilles, maybe too much so. It was still winked at if the riders refreshed themselves in bars, and when the field reached the pleasant village of Bédoin at the foot of Mont Ventoux, he was said to have stopped for a glass of whisky and maybe one of pastis also, never a good combination.

Then they set off for the great climb, along its endless succession of bends. Simpson was a few hundred feet below the summit when he swayed and fell. It was clear that he was gravely ill, and he was incoherent, except to say, 'Put me back on my bike.' If he did say that. Sceptics have wondered whether they were really his words, or the imaginative fancy of a *Sun* journalist. But then journalism has always tended to the view that when the legend becomes bigger than the truth you print the legend, or that there are some stories too good to check. Did George Hirst really say to Rhodes, in the electric last minutes of the 1904 Oval Test, 'We'll get them in singles, Wilfred'? Does it matter? As Barthes said, the Tour de France partakes of epic myth, transcending literal facts.

What's for certain is that Simpson never spoke again. He was helicoptered to hospital in Avignon, too late. Perhaps there had been an unnecessary delay, perhaps not. In either case, he couldn't be revived. The inquest found that he had died from heart failure aggravated by alcohol and drugs. After that the rest of the race was a shadow of itself. Gimondi won up the Puy de Dôme, the Swiss René Binggeli won the penultimate stage from Fontainebleau to Versailles and Poulidor the final time trial but Pingeon rode on with steady determination to keep the yellow jersey he had been wearing since the eighth stage all the way to the finish, supported by

Poulidor. Jimenez again won the Mountains prize and Janssen the green jersey. Pingeon collected his prize in the Parc des Princes, for the last time as it was shortly to be demolished. It wasn't his fault that the man whose name would be for ever associated with the 1967 Tour was one who never finished it, or any other race.

Repos

Provence

Two great mountain ranges are always traversed by the Tour, the Alps and Pyrenees, and two solitary volcanic peaks are sometimes climbed. An ideal Tour would include both Puy de Dôme and Mont Ventoux, but the ideal is rarely achieved; the two have only been climbed twelve times each, and only twice, in 1952 and 1967, did the *parcours* include both. Although not as high as the great Alpine passes, they are both frightening, psychologically as much as physically, leaping up as they do from their surroundings, almost as though defying anyone to climb them, on foot or by *vélo*.

In summer the searing heat of Provence is tempered by the winds of the Vaucluse where Mont Ventoux stands and where mistral meets tramonte with alarming effect. As Julian Barnes says, the popular etymology in which Ventoux derives from *vent* or wind is all too appropriate (though false: the roots of 'ventoux' are in the Ligurian *ven-* for mountain, so that 'Mont Ventoux' with disappointing pleonasm means 'Mount Mountain'). The strongest gust of wind ever recorded on Earth was on the peak here in February 1967, at 320 k.p.h. It is an awe-inspiring place seen from afar, let alone as one ascends it.

And it is only dubiously French. Originally a Roman province (Provincia, or the Province, giving that name to the language), it remained a highly distinctive territory for many centuries, and in some ways is so even now. Until the later Middle Ages, the

County of Provence ran from the mouth of the Rhône east to Nizza, or Nice, and north into the Alps, and the Margravate of Provence stood either side of the Rhône valley, from Viviers north to Valence: two independent principalities, separate but sharing a name, like Duchy and Free-County of Burgundy further north; while Avignon and the Venaisin, including Mont Ventoux, belonged to the Popes. This history has left the region with many magnificences, from the Classical antiquities of Orange, where I once heard *Die Zauberflöte* performed in the faultless acoustics of the Roman theatre, and Vaison-la-Romaine, to the grandeurs of papal Avignon. Even after Provence had been absorbed by the kingdom of France, it was a long way from anywhere – or at least from Paris – and it minded its own business.

Then, around 200 years ago, the English discovered the balmy calm of the Provençal coast, to be called the Riviera or Côte d'Azur (they discovered its pleasures in winter, that is, in saner days before people flocked to grill themselves on distant beaches in August). And the aristocrats and *rentiers* who gave their name to the Promenade des Anglais in Nice enjoyed a kind of literary validation, as the very name Provence acquired its own special resonance, with Keats longing for a draught of vintage tasting of Flora and the country green, 'Dance, and Provençal song, and sunburnt mirth.' Parisians also learned the delights of the south: before the Mediterranean meant 'sea, sun and sex' for trippers, Verdi's Germont could console his son by saying that he would have, if not the last, then at least the other two of those if he left his mistress Violetta for the south: 'Di Provenza, il mar, il suol . . .'

At the very time that Provence was becoming a playground, it developed almost in reaction its own literary form of national consciousness. Frederic Mistral spent his life in the village of Maillane south of Avignon writing in what he and his friends in the Félibrige thought their true Provençal language. But Provence was destined to be a resting place for the international rich and not so rich, few of them much interested in its history, language or culture. Camus lived just to the north of Aix-en-Provence at Lourmarin in his last years, Somerset Maugham lived at Cap Ferrat, D. H. Lawrence died at Vence; none was concerned with the life of the place. Even though Scott Fitzgerald set *Tender Is the Night* (with its title from that Keats poem) at Cap d'Antibes, and even though Graham Greene lived in Nice and wrote a polemical book about its politics, neither could be called so much as an adoptive Provençal writer. The final indignity came when a retired English advertising man wrote a series of bestsellers with little discernible of the texture or tang of the place except its name.

Even now coast and hinterland are infested by the rich, as can be seen by the cluster of very expensive, and sometimes even good, restaurants running from Monte Carlo west to St Tropez, and a little further inland, the Bastide St-Antoine at Grasse or Jacques Maximin at Vence, or the excellent and far from ruinous Terraillers at Biot to the west of Nice. Vaucluse is, perhaps mercifully, less luxurious, although Avignon has the delightfully unchanged Hiély-Luculus where the schoolboy Cyril Connolly ate one of the first of what would be very many meals in French restaurants. And Vaison-la-Romaine, whence the fifteenth stage of the 2002 Tour departed, has the enchanting Moulin à Huile, which came close to winning my own culinary *maillot jaune*.

From there it's no distance to what Edith Wharton called 'the sublimest object in Provence'. Mont Ventoux towers in lonesome and awesome solitude at 1909 metres over the plains. The most famous writer to live in its shadow was Petrarch, an Italian from Arezzo who was brought as a boy to Avignon when the papal court was seated there and then, after years in the service of a cardinal, settled at Fontaine de Vaucluse to the south-east of the great peak. In 1336, 631 years before Simpson's fatal ascent, Petrarch climbed the mountain with his brother, the poet bracing himself with a line from Ovid: 'To wish is little: we must long with the utmost eagerness to gain our end', words that might be held up by Tour fans.

On 21 July 2002 the crowds lined the road from Bédoin at the foot of Ventoux all the way up to the summit. Cars and camper vans had been there all night, cyclists had made their own climb hours before the racers, Belgian tricolours jostled with Basque crosses, and fans held up an array of placards and banners that deserved anthologizing and deconstructing at length. Some saluted the champion: 'Don't mess with Texas' (or alternatively and imploringly, 'Lose 8 minutes please Lance'). Dozens were addressed in grateful valediction to Laurent Jalabert, who had just announced his retirement – 'Vas y Ja Ja', or 'Ja Ja Bonne Retraite' – while others were a little more ominous or provocative. 'Il dopo ha gia un nome', said one, before libellously naming the doper, while another shouted, 'Jan ohne Dich ist die Tour Scheisse' (the Tour is shit without you) by way of saluting Jan Ullrich, whose misdemeanours with recreational drugs had enforced his temporary absence. And one more, 'Virenque – Merci pour Tout' which made me think: thanks for absolutely everything? It was Virenque, after all, who had been at the centre of the 1998 drugs scandal that brought more discredit on the Tour than anything before.

Finally as the bends climb higher and higher through the tree line comes the bleak peak itself. 'Lunar' is an easy word for any barren landscape, but here it's almost too apt. As the once and future king of the Tour, far from losing the suggested eight minutes, climbed relentlessly to the summit that day, one of his adoring compatriots stood in the distance planting a flagstaff with a huge Stars and Stripes on a high ridge of bare pumice; and there was sudden visual memory of another American called Armstrong taking one small step for man, thirty-three years to the very day before.

A few hundred feet below the observatory that stands on the pinnacle, a few minutes before the riders reach the finishing line,

1. On his trike: Henri Desgrange racing on three wheels.

2. First of the Tour champions: Maurice Garin.

3. Running repairs: Hippolyte Aucouturier fixes his front wheel.

4. Lauded with sweet flowers: Aucouturier is welcomed.

5. Let brotherly love continue: Henri and Francis Pélissier.

6. Cooling-off period: Ottavio Bottecchia sluices himself.

7. Advice from the Patron: (left to right) Raymond Louviot, Georges Speicher and Henri Desgrange.

8. Passing through the Pyrenees, 1938.

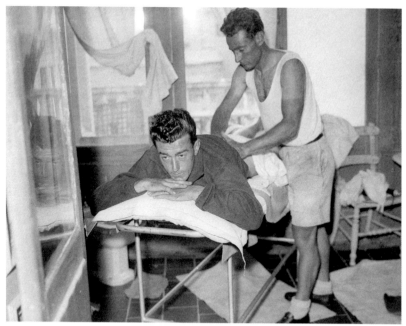

9. Massaging the master's muscles: Louison Bobet with his *soigneur*.

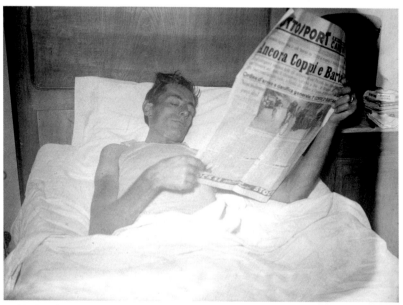

10. Good news from a far country: Fausto Coppi reads about himself and Bartali.

11. 'À votre santé!' A chef greets the tour in 1951.

12. Public men and cheering crowds: spectators at the 1951 Tour photographed by Bert Hardy of *Picture Post.*

13. The pedaller of charm: Hugo Koblet at the Parc des Princes after winning the 1951 Tour.

14. The way of an Eagle in the air: Federico Bahamontes crests the Tourmalet in 1954.

15. Maître Jacques: the enigmatic Anquetil, 1957.

16. Leaders of the pack: Bahamontes (left) and Raymond Poulidor, 1963.

17. Happy days: Tom
Simpson (left) joins
in the song, 1966.

18. And the
unhappiest:
Simpson is tended
on Mont Ventoux,
13 July 1967.

19. Bloodied but unbowed: Poulidor in 1968.

20. Looking down hungrily:
Eddy Merckx, 1972.

21. A tragic hero in his prime: Luis Ocaña, 1973.

22. 'Glory without the yellow jersey': Poulidor, 1974.

23. Invoking a higher power: Merckx, 1975.

24. Badgering the field: Bernard Hinault, 1978.

25. For this relief, much thanks: Hinault eases the strain in 1985.

26. 'By the grace of God': Miguel Induráin rides in triumph, 1990.

27. A Lance none could break: Armstrong on his way to winning his first Tour in 1999.

28. 'Oh say can you see?': Armstrong looks towards the Stars and Stripes from the winner's podium, 2000.

is the Stèle Simpson, in itself quite modest, though covered with tokens of remembrance and votive offerings to the point that Barnes calls it 'part Jewish grave and part the tumultuous altar of some popular if dubious Catholic saint'. The main inscription records Simpson's life and death as an 'Olympic Medallist, World Champion, British Sporting Ambassador', but there are supplementary plaques, the most touching of which reads, 'There is no mountain too high. Your daughters Jane and Joanne July 15, 1997.' During the Tour the tributes pile high, but flowers, *bidons*, caps, tyres are there all the year round.

This isn't just sentimentality, or guilt. Tom Simpson was a rider much liked, by peloton and public, and as far as can be judged was a genuinely likeable man. He was certainly a precociously gifted sportsman. At twenty-one he won a team bronze medal in the pursuit events at the 1956 Olympics, before turning pro in 1959. He had left England in any case when still an amateur in order to avoid his military call-up (something subsequently forgiven or forgotten) and went to St-Brieuc in Brittany, where he met his English wife Helen Sherburn working as an au pair. She tried to keep him on the straight and narrow, knowing his reputation as a *tombeur des femmes*, before they moved to Ghent, the centre of Belgian cycling and home to a British ex-pat community of cyclists, few of whom enjoyed any real success. Simpson was the great exception. In his first season he won two stages of the Tour de l'Ouest, before he joined the Rapha–Gitane team, winning the Tour du Sud Est in 1960 and a couple of criteriums. That year he rode in his first Tour and finished a very creditable twenty-ninth. He abandoned in 1961, but then in 1962, now riding for VC XII Saint-Raphaël–Gitane–Dunlop, he hit a purple patch. Riding superbly, he was ninth in the first stage, twentieth in St-Nazaire–Luçon, and stayed in the top three until Pau.

And then, on a glorious day in the Pyrenees, Tom Simpson finished in the leading group to become the first Englishman ever to wear the *maillot jaune*. He ended the Tour in sixth and then, after

missing the next year's race, came fourteenth in 1964, now with
Peugeot–BP, as well as winning the Milan–San Remo race, won
the Tour of Lombardy and the World Road Race Championship
in 1965, and nine Criteriums in 1966. He was near the height of
his powers, winning the 1967 Paris–Nice, as well as two stages of
the Vuelta.

By this time Simpson was a very popular figure on the continent, and a national hero at home, the first English cyclist of
whom that could really be said. He allowed the French to turn
him into a stage Englishman, dressing up in bowler and brolly as
'Major Tom' to echo the unfunny Major Thompson novels of
Pierre Daninos. But if he played the clown, he wasn't really one.
Chris Brasher, the famous runner, who had become an *Observer*
sports journalist, interviewed Simpson in 1960, with a stereo-
type in his mind of what this bumptious Durham miner's son
would be like, and found instead 'an impeccable Englishman in
a Prince of Wales suit'.

In 1967 it seemed that Simpson was entering his *annus mirabilis*.
He had already won a clutch of 'sportsman of the year' awards,
including one from the BBC. Accepting this in the presence of
Harold Wilson, he made a graceful and amusing speech, observing that the Prime Minister was still in the saddle, 'but I hope his
bottom doesn't hurt as much as mine', and asking British business
to realize the commercial potential of cycling sponsorship. Even
though he hadn't completed the Tour in the past two years, this
year should have been his apotheosis.

But although his health had held up through most of his
exhausting races, it wasn't impregnable, and he was riding this
year troubled by intestinal disorders, with acute diarrhoea close to
dysentery. Cycling may seem an exciting sport when viewed from
a long distance, and when the conquering champion is cheered
like a knightly hero. Closer to, it would be euphemistic to talk of
the nitty-gritty; 'down and dirty' is all too apt. A cyclist eats on
the move, sucking liquid rice from a *bidon* on his handlebar, or

snatching up a *musette* feeding sack at the *ravitaillement* feeding station, picking out the sandwiches and fruit, and then throwing aside the bag, which can become a prized souvenir. And he not only eats on the move: as Armstrong says, you never stop if you can help it, 'not even for a piss'. When a rider used to relieve himself too visibly, exposing himself in front of a crowd, it was punishable by deduction of points as an offence against the dignity of the Tour, but riders learned to urinate less indecently, if not very comfortably, without opening their Lycra shorts. They will try to void their bowels before a day's stage begins, although you can sometimes see a cyclist pull off the road for a couple of minutes, to answer a call of nature, as the commentator discreetly says. At least that means the rider is passing solid stools, unlike Simpson that year. He didn't need to stop; it was his mechanic who was obliged to begin each evening by hosing down the bike. Not everything about bike racing is glamour.

Nor all simply heroism. The death of any sporting hero is poignant, even if it happens away from the field of play. Any Englishman who like myself was a boy in the 1950s may still feel a pang of emotion at the name of Mike Hawthorn, killed in a road accident in January 1959 a few weeks before his thirtieth birthday and less than six years after his dazzling victory over Fangio in the French Grand Prix at Rheims; and still more at the names of those Manchester United players killed in the Munich air crash in February 1958. And yet, if Simpson's death was poignant, it wasn't simply noble, since it was certainly in some measure self-inflicted, through the amphetamines found in his jersey pocket. Many if not most riders took drugs at the time. In fact, the sonorous chorus of the Tour authorities inveighing against illegal substances had for years past had a comical descant in the confessions of cyclists. After his retirement, Coppi was asked whether riders had taken *la bomba*, as Italians called amphetamines. 'Yes, and those who say otherwise aren't worth talking to about cycling.' Had he taken them? 'Yes, whenever it was needed.' And when was that? 'Practically all the time.' And in the very year of Simpson's death, Anquetil told the *Équipe*, 'You'd have to be an imbecile or a hypocrite to imagine that a professional cyclist who rides 235 days a year can hold himself together without stimulants.'

In one form or another, stimulants had been used from the beginning of competitive cycling, or the day when an English rider called Linton died on the 1896 Bordeaux–Paris race, having succumbed, it was supposed, to an ill-judged quantity of morphine. Riders had always dosed themselves with alcohol, sometimes in great quantities. On that same race – a horror of endurance, 580 kilometres cycled at a stretch, day and night – a later team gave each rider an allowance of wine, champagne, port and a bottle of eau-de-vie. We have seen several times how riders in the Tour drank wine copiously, sometimes with ill effects, more often it is to be supposed without.

Novices were sometimes puzzled to hear an older rider shouting for 'la moutarde', but this was no delicate Moutarde de Meaux or de Dijon, it was slang for a *bidon* full of illicit stimulant. Tom Simpson cut the mustard in royal style. He told one comrade that his year's 'supply of Mickey Finns' had cost him £800, an enormous amount of money for a small-time pro, who might make £4 a week, or even for a successful rider. But then Simpson wanted nothing but the best. Poorer riders took Benzedrine; the stuff found on him when he died was Tonedrin, the château-bottled claret of amphetamines. Nor did he confine himself to quality rather than quantity: he once cheerfully told a friend that his principle with medication was, 'If it takes ten to kill you, I'll take nine.'

All of this has cast a pall over Simpson's memory, maybe unfairly since he was so far from alone, then or since. The question of what is the wrongful use of narcotics or performance-enhancing drugs – or how to define them – isn't ever easy to answer. At least until managers like Arsène Wenger told players to clean up their act,

alcohol was part of the culture of football, and of most professional sports. Thirty years ago, one player with a London team told
an interviewer from the *Evening Standard* (where a pompous sports
sub-editor cut it), 'We have an old saying or maxim in football:
Win or lose, on with the booze.' And there are countless tales of
cricketers drinking by day and by night. Sir Gary Sobers, of
Barbados, Nottinghamshire and the West Indies, perhaps the
greatest cricketer I shall ever see, and in his way a true knightly
figure, has described how he played one of his finest innings in a
Lord's Test. He left the pitch in the evening, not out and having
already scored a century, went on the tiles, drank until dawn, and
until anyone else would have dropped, returned to play in the
morning, almost unable to see the ball at first, gradually pulled
himself together, and then completed a brilliant innings.

And the very amphetamines that had helped kill Simpson,
after they helped him ride, help bomber aircrew keep going on
long missions, not only, as was well known, in the Second World
War, but also today, as we learned at the inquiry into how
American aircraft had come to bomb Canadian soldiers in
Afghanistan.

Later that day in 2002, after the race had finished, and when
the top of Mont Ventoux was clogged up in one of the vast traffic jams wilfully created when there is an *arrivée en altitude*,
thousands of vehicles queuing for one narrow road downhill, I
was flagged down by a young man strung with cameras, a *confrère*
as it turned out. There were no press facilities up there, and even
mobiles didn't seem to work on the peak, so that this amiable
chap needed to descend to the foot of the mountain to transmit
pics to his paper in Marseilles as urgently as I needed to get to a
telephone and ring the *Daily Mail* in London. We talked about
the day, and I compared the way the crowd had booed
Armstrong yet again – 'Dopé!'– with the way the same crowd
had actually cheered Virenque, the self-confessed culprit of the
great 1998 scandal. My companion was indignant at the idea

that Virenque should be singled out: 'They're all at it, the whole lot. *Tous!*'

And it was that emphatic '*Tous!* All of them!' that was still ringing in my ears when I returned the next morning, on a rest day, to look at Simpson's shrine without the crowds. Sporting ambassador? Certainly he was. Sporting hero? Surely, in the full Shakespearian sense of a brave man undone by his folly or misjudgement. We who write about the Tour and Tom Simpson should nothing extenuate, nor set down aught in malice, and every cyclist should visit the Stèle Simpson on Mont Ventoux: such a sublime spot, and such a touching monument to a man who loved his sport not wisely but too well.

11

Merckx Devours the Field

1968-1973

As dramatic a year as 1948 had been, 1968 saw the Russian suppression of Czech hopes of freedom and America riven by the Vietnam War, the assassination of Martin Luther King and Robert Kennedy, and the departure of Lyndon Johnson. And France had her own lurid upheavals, when the *événements* of May, originally a student rebellion, spread to parts of the industrial working class and for a moment seemed to threaten de Gaulle's regime, as he left the country to recover his position. Unlike Johnson, he didn't depart the presidency forthwith, but France felt very a different country before 27 June when the field of 110 riders left the mineral-water spa of Vittel.

Not only a new starting point, they were headed for a new destination: after the demolition of the Parc des Princes the race would now culminate at the Cipale, the Vincennes municipal stadium. There was another and more important change in a none too oblique reference to Simpson's death. Under the direction of Dr Pierre Dumas, this was to be the 'Tour de la Santé', the healthy Tour. Now there were anti-doping tests at each finishing point, as well as close medical supervision of the whole race.

Several riders who were in good form that year didn't take part in the Tour: not Gimondi, who had won his second successive Grand Prix des Nations, nor Guido Reybroeck with his third Paris–Tours race, nor young Merckx in the year he won his first Giro and the Paris–Roubaix one-day classic. Nor was there a repeat for the title-holder Pingeon, even though he made a brilliant break of 193 kilometres averaging 40 k.p.h. to win the stage from Font-Romeu to Albi; he finished at Vincennes in fifth place. And it wasn't Poulidor's year, either, as his misfortunes continued. On that same stage that saw Pingeon's escape, Poulidor was strongly placed in the GC when he crashed badly trying to avoid a motorbike. This was lamentable but it was not amazing. Anyone who has witnessed the Tour close up may well be surprised, not that there have been so many accidents over the years, but that there have been so few. The abandon with which the publicity caravan goes through towns and villages led to the death of a little boy on the 2002 Tour, the breakneck speed at which team and press cars and motorbikes cover each day's journey has caused at least one fatal accident, and could easily have caused more.

The Tour's intimacy is part of its charm. Before the race left St-Martin-de-Landelles on Bastille Day in 2002, I found myself standing next to a group of Italian riders as they sat talking and joking, and then, when they had got on their bikes, I was walking towards the start when an officious official saw the Press badge around my neck and hustled me on to the road during the 'neutralization' period (when riders are pedalling but not racing up to the start). Before I knew what had happened, I was in the midst of an as yet mercifully almost immobile peloton, trying to move away before I did them an injury, or they me. Security on the race is far from oppressive, and long may that remain so, but the cheek-by-jowl proximity of riders, spectators and vehicles can be alarming.

At any rate, Poulidor – 'poor' or 'unhappy' seem by now almost redundant – was badly hurt. Even his critics, even Anquetil, couldn't deny that he had the stuff of heroism somewhere in him. The way he finished that stage, in grave pain from serious injuries, was one of the most courageous performances of his life, and needless to say one of the most futile: he was forced to abandon the next day on the stage to Aurillac. His exit effectively ended the chances of his team, and it was an anticlimactic note for Marcel Bidot to leave on as *directeur technique*, forty-two years after he had ridden in his first Tour.

Now the Tour was wide open, and it was the Dutch who seized it. One of their countrymen wasn't surprised. Ab Geldermans, who rode in seven consecutive Tours between 1960 and 1966 and was fifth in 1962, had had a bet that Jan Janssen would beat Herman Van Springel of Belgium to become the first Dutch winner. So it proved, although it wasn't until the final time trial that Janssen established a winning lead, thirty-eight seconds ahead of Van Springel at the Cipale, with Spain winning the team prize, their Aurelio Gonzalez King of the Mountains, and Franco Bitossi of Italy the points winner in red jersey: red on this one occasion, absurdly enough, rather than green, at the demand of a sponsor; the Tour was good at 'invented tradition', but not always respectful of it.

In 1939 a Belgian had won the Tour nine months before Panzer divisions rolled across his country. Sylvère Maes died in 1966 aged fifty-seven, and didn't live to see a compatriot as successor on the winner's podium. But when he arrived, he was one of the greatest cyclists there have ever been, some would say the greatest of all. Not that Eddy Merckx had an auspicious inauguration into the race. At twenty-four he was already garlanded with honours, beginning with his amateur championship and by now including the professional road title, a batch of classics and the Giro d'Italia. In the 1969 renewal of that race, however, he was wearing the *maglia rosa* when he tested positive for illicit drugs.

He wasn't only slung out of the race, to howls about a dastardly Italian plot from Faema, his team, and from the Belgian press, he was also given a twenty-eight-day ban, which would have prevented him from joining the start of the Tour at Roubaix on 28 June.

Resentful English yachtsmen used to say about the way that the America's Cup was conducted that 'Britannia rules the waves but America waives the rules'. Something of the kind was true of cycling. A lesser rider would doubtless have been told to stay at home, but Merckx's stature was clear even before his first Tour, and the UCI conveniently found a way to lift the suspension. If this seemed a challenge, to live up to his favourable treatment, Merckx responded breathtakingly from the first stages in his own country, including the third day, a team time trial in his home town of Woulwe-St Pierre.

The CLM *par équipes* is truly a test of collective skill, and one of the most pleasing spectacles in cycling. Its exact rules have changed over the years; to describe it in twenty-first-century terms, as of the 2002 Tour, a team of nine riders races together over a measured distance, say the 67.5 kilometres from Epernay to Château-Thierry, setting off as a little peloton of their own to race and pace together. At any moment, one cyclist gives his team the lead and sets the pace, a role that is so demanding that he will stay at the head for no more than fifteen or twenty seconds, unless he is an exceptionally strong rider like Lance Armstrong, in which case he may lead for anything up to a minute, when he slips aside to let a colleague take his place. The best view of this performance is from above: seen from helicopter-born television camera, a team might be a skein of geese seen from below, holding a loose pattern that continually, kaleidoscopically, very slightly, rather beautifully, changes its shape. To qualify, at least five riders out of a team of nine must finish; the team is marked by the time of the fifth, but the winning team can then nominate any of its riders as the individual winner of the stage. Usually this will be the team leader, although if he is so comfortably ahead in the GC that he has nothing to lose he can graciously hand the prize to a team-mate.

When that time trial at Woulwe was won by Faema, they stamped their collective authority on the Tour, in which not only would they win the team prize but their whole team would complete the course. There was no question of anyone but Merckx taking the individual stage, and thereby the yellow jersey. He lost it the next day into Maastricht to his team-mate Julien Stevens, who held the lead for four days, but Merckx took it back over the Ballon d'Alsace and never surrendered it for the next two weeks and more, through the Alps, where he won Briançon–Digne, and into the Pyrenees.

He left Luchon with more than eight minutes in hand over Pingeon, and the cognoscenti expected him to take it easy, riding defensively and carefully, husbanding his resources. That's what Anquetil would have done, that's what Induráin would later do, that's what Armstrong will still do. It was not what Merckx did. Illustrating if ever anyone did the maxim that attack is the best form of defence, he rode a ferocious race over the cols. Pingeon and Poulidor were still with him crossing the Peyresourde, Aspin and Tourmalet. But he dropped them on the descent, they not quite realizing that he might steal the stage. Merckx crossed the Aubisque alone to make a 130-kilometre escape, with the thermometer in the nineties, reaching Mourenx 7'56" in the lead.

The next stage was a sentimental occasion twice over, both because the Englishman Barry Hoban had never won a stage before, and because the finish was in the old Bordeaux velodrome that would never see the Tour again. Five years earlier, Hoban should have won Bayonne–Bordeaux on the selfsame spot, entering the stadium with a fifty-metre lead, 'but André Darrigade was desperate to win in Bordeaux for the first time and caught me with only ten metres to go. It was the biggest blow of my career,' Hoban said. 'I wept.' All untearful he now won the next day's stage into Brive as well, but the Tour was effectively over. Merckx didn't need to win the last climb up the Puy de Dôme, and finished at Vincennes 17'54" ahead of Pingeon, a margin which has not since been surpassed, with Poulidor another 22'13" behind in third.

It was the beginning of an era: a new champion, and the first 'baby-boomer' born after VE Day to win the Tour. He became one of the greatest riders in the history of cycling and of the Tour, though one of the least adored, and least understood. As Merckx himself said, 'No one really knows me,' and it was quite true. None of his team-mates or opponents ever worked out what made him tick. Merckx was born in June 1945, and was a mere boy when he discovered his astonishing ability as a cyclist. He rode in a number of races when he was sixteen and seventeen, though not with immediate success: his records for 1961 and 1962 are a long list of 'fell' and 'abandoned'. But before long he was winning as an amateur. He competed in the 1964 Tokyo Olympics without great success, but turned pro the next year, and won more races, working his way steadily through the big races, winning the World Championship in 1967 and the Giro in 1968, as well as the Tour of Catalonia and the Paris–Roubaix, to be followed by his explosive arrival in the Tour.

With all his amazing achievements over the next decade, Merckx remained a mystery. More *insaisissable*, in Magne's word, than Poulidor himself, he was what his sometime team-mate Johan de Muynck called 'the biggest stranger in the peloton' where he was unloved as well as unknown. Plenty of riders profited by working with him, but few enjoyed it. He won his first Tour with other *braves Belges* in the all-Belgian Faema team; it did not pass without comment that several of them left the team before the next season. Jan Janssen said that 'he can be incredibly surly', and Merckx himself revealingly admitted, 'You have to put your own interests ahead of camaraderie.' That was what he did throughout his career; that was why, as was said of Lloyd George, 'he had no friends and did not deserve any'; that was why he won.

He was never prouder of any later Tour, or of any day than of that day on the Tourmalet, 'one of my best performances,' which Merckx didn't believe he ever matched again, and he expressed the exhilaration and exaltation that comes only rarely even to the greatest cyclists: 'I could hardly feel the pedals.' So complete had his domination of the race been, winning all three individual time trials as well as three mountain stages, that he collected a trio of first prize, Mountains prize and green jersey. It would have been better for him if 1969 had stopped at the moment he took the podium on 20 July. Instead, triumph was followed by tragedy. At an unimportant track meeting at Blois, he was riding behind a little motorbike in a 'Derny-paced' race when he and his pacer Fernand Wabst crashed horribly at full speed. Wabst was killed, Merckx was seriously injured, more seriously than was immediately realized even as he was taken unconscious to hospital bleeding from his head injuries. He also proved to have a damaged vertebra and a twisted pelvis, and he ever after said that he was never the same rider again.

At which his unfortunate rivals might have wondered what they would have had to endure without that accident. His domination in 1970 was scarcely less complete. Coming into the race fresh from winning the Giro, this time untouched by scandal, he took the yellow jersey in the first day's Prologue, allowed his team-mate Italo Zilioli to wear it after the team time trial on the third day but soon won it back, and no one else wore it until the finish where Merckx ended a comfortable 12'41" ahead of Joop Zoetemelk. He had won a thumping eight stages, including the Prologue and two time trials. One stage from Valenciennes to Forest he tried out a new gearing, a freewheel of 11 teeth and a 51×11 ratio, which wasn't so remarkable except as a reflection of his supreme confidence: no one else would have made such an experiment in the middle of the Tour. Others showed well this year. The best young rider was Bernard Thévenet, who won the St-Gaudens–La Mongie stage in the Pyrenees, and Walter Godefroot was allowed to pick up the points prize. But the race was Merckx's, and that was that.

It had begun in Limoges, but that had brought no 'home-team advantage' for Poulidor the Limousin, who faded to finish seventh. One colleague, Christian Raymond, had dubbed Merckx, not very affectionately, 'The Cannibal'; as Merckx said, it was 'a bit of a barbaric name, but it probably reflected how my rivals truly felt about me'. Poulidor might have imagined himself not so much the contents of a cannibal's stew pot as Prometheus when, as P. G. Wodehouse put it, the bird dropped in for a spot of lunch.

Whatever Poulidor felt about Merckx he at least kept to himself, unlike the French public and newspapers. After only two victories, French distaste for the unsmiling, unbeatable Belgian had quickly become more like hatred. Spectators jeered him as a matter of course, and *Paris-Match* asked, 'Is Merckx going to kill the Tour de France?', to which the answer was that the Tour was always bigger than any one champion, however great. And that was a truth the 1971 race demonstrated with superb vividness.

In 1970 Merckx had ridden for the Faema team (another all-Belgian team, but for Zilioli); for the next two years he rode for Molteni, and although they won the first stage in 1971, an experimental team Prologue that was discontinued after one year, they didn't win a team prize despite their great star. He didn't himself dominate the 1971 race as he had the previous year's. He had just missed the Giro with an injured knee (it was won by the Swedish rider Gosta Petterson) and was patently below his best. Although he was the first to take the yellow jersey, as a curiously-shaped race wandered from Mulhouse into Switzerland and back to Alsace and Lorraine and then through the north and west of France before the action really began, the GC lead fluctuated, passing to Wagtmans, back to Merckx, to Zoetemelk – and then to Luis Ocaña. The Spanish rider was in excellent form, had gathered a strong team for Bic, and was the threat to Merckx if anyone was.

So he showed by winning on the Puy de Dôme before they zig-zagged east to the Alps, and what Ocaña saw as his opportunity. Anquetil had told him: 'Keep your nerve, wait for the mountains, and then strike,' and Ocaña followed this advice to the letter. Coming down from the Col de Cucheron, with the Col de Porte still ahead of them but the finish then only thirty kilometres away, Merckx was riding in the leading group when he punctured. Merckx had two Guillaumes in his life, his *soigneur* Guillaume Michiels, and his *directeur sportif* Guillaume Driessens. Michiels was a sometime rider, known as 'The Grave' both because he had once worked for an undertaker and because of his silent and sombre manner, occasionally broken, as Disraeli said of Peel, by a smile like the silver plate on a coffin. Riders often have a rela-tionship with their *soigneur* at least as close and trusting as any golfer with his caddy, and Michiels, who had known Merckx since he was a boy, enjoyed his complete confidence, the one person of whom that could be said and on whom he utterly relied.

Which was far from true of Driessens. He had been hired by Faema almost deliberately as a balance for Merckx. The self-contained, almost depressive Merckx and the bumptious, facetious Driessens might have found the attraction of opposites, but it didn't work out like that and their dealings were always wary at best. Merckx didn't conceal his irritation with Driessens's laddish bonhomie and intermittent bossiness. During the 1969 Tour of Flanders, Merckx made an escape with seventy kilome-tres to go, Driessens caught up with him in the team car and told him he was mad, Merckx shouted back a colloquial Flemish phrase that has been reliably translated as 'Go fuck yourself,' and went on to win. He said later that 'Everything Driessens did was like a big game to him.' Eddy didn't play games.

On that occasion before the Col de Porte, everything went wrong. Driessens was helping Wagtmans and Van Springel, all at the unluckiest possible moment of Merckx's puncture. Merckx lost forty seconds before he was provided with a new bike, and then it was the wrong kind for him, he said. Even so, he didn't foresee just how wrong: descending at full speed, a tyre came off the wheel rim. After being slowed down by colliding with a safety railing, he waited for repairs, before remounting, reaching the bottom, and setting off up the next climb. Despite the bike, and despite losing his rhythm, he caught one group of riders 300 metres from the summit. But another break was some way ahead, and behind them – in front of Merckx – was a flotilla of team cars. He weaved his way ferociously through the vehicles to come upsides Leif Mortensen, Ocaña's team-mate, and meet a further problem.

The arcane Tour regulations give plenty of opportunity for tactical chicanery. If a rider had had an accident or punctured, the team cars allowed him to pass. But if a rider had just fallen behind, it was he who was required to let the cars pass towards the leaders. When the Bic team heard that Merckx was catching up, the Danish rider had dropped back to join him. And so, as Merckx sat on Mortensen's wheel, the cars overtook them, and Goddet saw no choice but to 'enforce the barrier' and hold them up for what he called 'eighty derisory metres', with Merckx enraged, and Mortensen bringing to mind Hamlet's assertion 'That one may smile, and smile, and be a villain; At least I'm sure it may be so in Denmark.'

When he could hit the road again, Merckx rode with heightened fury, but the leaders had now gone two minutes clear and rode together to stay there. Even after a frantic descent, Merckx was still 1'38" behind at Grenoble. The next day, following Anquetil's advice again, Ocaña attacked early on the Côte de Laffrey accompanied by a group of hardened mountain men from various inelegantly named teams, Joop Zoetemelk of

Mars–Fandria, Joaquim Agostinho of Hoover–De Gribaldy and Lucien van Impe of Fagor–Mercier, who would end the Tour with the Mountains prize, his first of five. Merckx only had his two *domestiques*, Marinus Wagtmans and Jos Huysmans, but they couldn't keep up with him as he tried to catch the leaders, and he was only just ahead of the peloton as he rode up to Orcières-Merlette, an *arrivée en altitude* in the coming fashion, where Ocaña took the yellow jersey. Merckx's morale was crushed, he said, as he finished 8′42″ behind Ocaña, whom Merckx ruefully compared to the great torero Cordobes dispatching a bull.

And yet the Tour recognized Merckx's stature. Goddet later looked back unhappily on the wretched ill-fortune he had inflicted on 'probably the greatest rider of all time'. The crowds who had relentlessly jeered 'Mossieu', their derisive name for the Belgian, were silenced; even the ranks of Tuscany could not forbear to cheer, or the still more chauvinistic ranks of Gaul. One French reporter gave a hint of his colleagues' shame: 'In defeat the Belgian champion has revealed an unknown and admirable side of his character.' His display of superhuman energy had shown as much as any successful day's riding 'how justly he merited the glory his victories have brought him ... As for those who whistled at and booed him, their only excuse is ignorance of his real worth and blindness of chauvinism. In truth, Merckx's behaviour in defeat offers us an exalted, a solemn lesson in the conduct of sport and in dignity.'

Solemn and exalted were the words for this tribute, but Merckx showed that it wasn't empty rhetoric. The next day he rode a blinder, setting off on a huge break in baking heat. This time Wagtmans and Huysmans managed to keep up with him to begin with, and by Marseilles Merckx had taken back nearly two minutes from Ocaña, but no more: enough to salve wounded pride but not to win the great prize. For that, luck had to swing his way. They reached the Pyrenees and crossed the 1349-metre

Col de Mente in apocalyptic weather, a thunderstorm emptying the skies. Merckx was leading the perilous descent when he skidded to one side. Trying to avoid him, Ocaña fell, and was remounting when Zoetemelk and Agostinho ran into him. The pile-up injured Ocaña's legs and shoulders so badly that he had to abandon. Even hardened observers were dismayed at the way that 'a brief storm of cataclysmic proportions', as Antonin Blondin wrote in the *Équipe* with a certain freedom of metaphor, had been enough 'to sweep our beautifully flashing blade to the ground, just when he was preparing to crown himself'.

Although Merckx reached Luchon at the head of the GC, he marked this triumph with a gesture that would be remembered a long time: he refused to put on the yellow jersey that had come to him through Ocaña's miserable mischance, waiting until he felt he had won it fair and square. A few days later he visited Ocaña in hospital, and he had a clear conscience when he took the podium at Vincennes for his third Tour victory. Whatever his physical setbacks, Merckx had a terrific year in 1971, winning the Paris–Nice, Milan–San Remo, Liège–Bastogne–Liège, Tour of Lombardy, Dauphiné Libéré, Midi Libre and World Championship as well as the Tour, but he never had a greater day than that one in the Pyrenees.

One man absent was Poulidor, who didn't compete in the 1971 Tour, though he rode the course ahead of the field for a television broadcast. By the following year time seemed to be running out for Poulidor, who was now thirty-six. And yet his form outside the Tour was still very impressive. He won a record-equalling fifth victory in the Critérium National and he beat Merckx in the Paris–Nice. But still 1972 wasn't to be his year. The 'revelation' was Cyrille Guimard, the Nantes cyclist riding in his third Tour but leaping out of the pack for the first time.

Merckx won the Prologue, but Guimard soon took the yellow jersey off him and pummelled the sprinters into St-Brieuc in his native Brittany. He and the champion jousted over the cols, fighting to the top of Mont Revard shoulder to shoulder before Merckx raised his arms in victory, too soon: it was Guimard who had won by a short head, or rather 'by a quarter wheel'. That wasn't going to deflate Merckx, who rode two of his great climbs over the Cols d'Izoard and du Galibier; and once more he showed that fortune favours the brave. Ocaña fell ill and abandoned again, and so did Guimard on the penultimate stage, suffering from tendinitis. By the end Merckx was able to claim a somewhat bloodless victory, from Gimondi at 10'41" and none other than Poulidor at 11'34": once more, near but so far.

By the following year the race had a new organizing body, the Société d'Exploitation du Tour de France, a new starting point in The Hague (the second time the race had begun in Holland, after Amsterdam in 1954), and a new winner. Although Merckx won a string of victories in 1973 – the Paris–Roubaix, Liège–Bastogne–Liège, Paris–Brussels, the Grand Prix des Nations and two out of the great three-week road races, Giro d'Italia and the Vuelta a España – he missed the greatest of all and left the field open to Poulidor, Ocaña and younger challengers like Van Impe and Thévenet.

After the Low Countries, where Zoetemelk won the Prologue by less than a second from Poulidor, the race turned south through eastern France, and numerous new *étapes* that had bought themselves publicity if not glory. Ocaña won his first stage this year from Divonne to Aspro Gaillard, crossing a new pass over Mont Saleve, as the race went on to a succession of ski resorts: Thévenet won at Meribel, Ocaña at Les Orres. Ocaña was said to be riding à la Merckx, with brutal no-prisoners determination, but there was a technical reason for his superiority besides fitness and willpower.

Although the basic design of the bicycle hadn't changed in ninety years, and hasn't to this day, its shape can be made out of any kind of metal (or anything else), and the revolution of this period was in materials, some developed from aviation technology, some even from space exploration. Ocaña had met an engineer from the Sud-Aviation company, who suggested that a bike could be made from titanium, until then only used in airframe manufacture. It was with this advanced bike, stronger but much lighter than any before, that Ocaña now floored the field.

The Pyrenees were Poulidor's undoing when he fell descending from the Col du Portet d'Aspet, and by Paris Ocaña had no serious challenger. Having taken the yellow jersey on the seventh stage, he held it until the twentieth and last. Winning six stages in all, including a time trial, and imposing victories down into Luchon and up the Puy de Dôme, he crossed the finish in the Vincennes stadium an almost insulting 15'51" ahead of Thévenet and then Fuente at 17'49", compared with the 3'09" that separated Aimar in first and Poulidor in third in 1966.

After the wretched crash that had taken Ocaña out of the race in 1971, Blondin had written that although he hadn't necessarily been the best rider in the race, 'he was the shining star, who with the sun' – i.e. Merckx – 'had dazzled us for four days,' and he seemed very much a worthy winner two years later. He was a man and a rider greatly liked for his simplicity and generosity, as well as a certain panache, playing the stage Spaniard like Simpson the stage Englishman. Instead of bowler and brolly, Ocaña allowed himself to be got up as a toreador, which was corny but apt enough, the very image Merckx had once used, and his victorious Tour had a tang of the arena. 'It was a massacre,' Pierre Chany said in the *Équipe*, 'a sort of collective annihilation.' It was the fifth Tour of the eight in all in which Ocaña would ride, before his early retirement, and his lamentable death, in 1994 at only forty-eight.

12

Heart and Nerve and Sinew

1974–1980

But there was no return match between Merckx and Ocaña in 1974: this time it was the Belgian's turn to come back to the podium, and the Spaniard's turn to sit out the race, along with the unfortunate Joop Zoetemelk, second in 1971 and fourth in 1973, who was badly injured in a fall during the Midi Libre. The first curiosity this year came two days after Merckx had won the Prologue in Brest, when the Tour crossed the Channel. Although it had often left French soil since 1906 (or, if the French considered Alsace-Lorraine occupied French territory, since crossing into Switzerland in 1907), to visit at one time or another all of the countries with which France shared a land border, Belgium, Luxembourg, Germany, Switzerland, Italy and Spain, as well as the toy-town principalities of Andorra and Monaco, and then the Netherlands, the Tour had never before left the European mainland. But on 29 June 1974, having reached St-Pol-de-Léon, the field crossed the Channel, bikes by sea, riders by air, to ride a stage fro and to Plymouth, before returning to Brittany.

All the riders detested the Devonian divagation, which meant, as Geoffrey Nicholson recorded, 'two early starts, one late night and a long unforeseen delay at Exeter airport on the homeward journey', utterly disrupting the routine of eating, riding, eating, massage, and sleep. It was a good example of how commercial interests could buy stages of the Tour, even if to the detriment of the race itself. For many years the choice of *villes-étapes* had been partly decided by backstairs bartering, with one place or another putting in discreet bids to buy some Tour glory. A town like Angers, for example, paid a reported 93,000 francs, or £9300, to begin the 1967 Tour, a seaside resort like Merlin-Plage bought itself into the race for years, and each year ski stations competed to see which could bag a stage.

Even by those standards, the Channel hop was embarrassing. If the Tour was going to cross the sea, it made sense – before or after the Channel Tunnel was opened – to do so at the narrow end, where the white cliffs of Dover and Cap Gris Nez look at one another and plucky fellows swim between them, rather than with a substantially lengthier and more tedious passage at the western end. The commercial interests concerned weren't even English: it wasn't the Devon tourist board, although Plymouth did make a contribution of £40,000, nor yet some West Country light industry, but the market-gardening business of Brittany which had paid for the stage as a stunt. From humble beginnings, with those other bicyclists of happy memory, the beret-wearing Bretons with strings of onions draped on handlebars who pedalled and peddled their way through the suburban streets of London, growing and exporting vegetables had become a big business in Brittany, which could afford to put up £180,000 for the 1974 Tour to finance the Prologue in Brest, two more local stages, and the frankly fatuous stage up and down the Plympton by-pass, all to publicize the new Roscoff–Plymouth ferry and to persuade the British to eat more Breton artichokes. The Tour had perennial and real problems of finding how to pay its way, but didn't always find the right answers to them.

Back in France, normal service was resumed, with stages to Caen and Dieppe and into Belgium. A stage with sombre military echoes from Mons to Châlons-sur-Marne led towards Besançon and the Alps, and another mountain duel between Merckx and Poulidor. It was Poulidor who most unexpectedly struck first, with what was nicely called a *coup de jeune* as the 38-year-old dropped his younger rival over the Col du Chat. Merckx fought back over the Galibier, where Poulidor cracked. In fact, Merckx fought back again and again, as the yellow jersey was taken from him by his Molteni team-mate Joseph Bruyère, then, after he had regained it, by Gerben Karstens, a Dutchman riding for Bic and ballpoints, and Patrick Sercu, a Belgian riding for Brooklyn and chewing gum, before Merckx won it yet again. Although Poulidor had one more moment of glory, crossing the Pla d'Adet to take the Seo-de-Urgel–St-Lary-Soulan stage, it didn't take him into the first three in the GC.

He made it to third after the next stage. The Tourmalet was climbed twice in two days, the second time when a stage finished on the summit. Jean-Pierre Danguillaume made an escape, and was followed by three French riders, Poulidor, Alain Santy and Mariano Martinez, who took the first four places at the summit, leaving Merckx in their wake, before he rode a blistering stage from Vouvray to Orléans averaging 48.352 k.p.h. As the last time trial began, Poulidor was still in third place, 2'16" behind Lopez-Carril, but by beating him so easily in that Orléans trial he ensured himself second place once more, at 8'4" from Merckx, when they reached 'La Cipale', the Vincennes stadium, for the last time.

A film was made this year about Eddy Merckx, *Le Cours en tête*. Neither Joel Santoni who made it nor its star knew that the movie would mark Merckx's last win in the Tour. Though not his last race: in 1975 his form still looked good enough after he won the

Liège–Bastogne–Liège for the fifth time, as indeed he won his seventh Milan–San Remo the following year. Poulidor had been pleasingly honoured by the Belgian government, which made him a Chevalier of the Order of Leopold. Maybe with some tincture of shame about Merckx's treatment by French fans and press (or the nearest thing the French official class can come to shame), the honour was reciprocated and, at Charleroi before the race began on 26 June, the reigning champion received the insignia of a Chevalier of the Légion d'Honneur from the hands of Pierre Mazeaud, secretary of state for youth and sport.

Alas, the gong didn't bring Merckx further victory, and France regained the Tour through Bernard Thévenet, riding for the Peugeot–BP team in a hard-fought race. Francesco Moser won the Prologue in Charleroi and held the yellow jersey until the fifth stage as the race ran west into Brittany. Then Merckx gave one of his best performances in a time trial to take the lead and hold it to Bordeaux, through the Pyrenees, winning another stage over the mountains from Fleurance to Auch. The Puy de Dôme stage was won by Van Impe, who ended with the Prix du Meilleur Grimpeur – which is to say the new 'polka-dot' jersey for King of the Mountains which was introduced this year, more nicely called the *maillot blanc à pois rouges* by the French, the white jersey with red peas. This was seen at the time as an experiment or even an expedient, not to say as an embarrassment which would probably be dropped. Yet again *le provisoire dure*, and the red-peas jersey is with us still, alongside yellow and green. In its first year it was won by Van Impe but also by high-tech: he was riding the first racing bike made of fibreglass. This miraculous new substance, strong, powerful and flexible as needed, would transform everything from space rocketry to fly-fishing.

That Puy de Dôme stage saw a grotesque episode when Chevalier Merckx was hit in the kidneys by a spectator who jumped out of the crowd and from whom he subsequently collected a token franc in damages out of a large fine. It was one of the more remarkable displays of Merckx's toughness that he finished the stage third behind Van Impe and Thévenet. Even then, Merckx still led by 1'58" from Thévenet as the Tour took a rest day to be transferred from Clermont-Ferrand to Nice. Here the race began in earnest, with a gruelling stage over five climbs, finishing with a last climb up to Pra-Loup. Thévenet attacked up the Col des Champs, a new, 2191-metre climb, with his teammate Raymond Delisle beside him. Merckx fought back with the help of his Molteni comrades Edward Janssens and Jos de Schoenmaecker, before descending at a speed the strong but careful Thévenet couldn't have matched even if he hadn't punctured at this point; so fast, in fact, that Merckx almost ran into the flotilla of press and team cars. Although he had managed to avoid coming to grief in the mêlée, the Bianchi car didn't. As it swerved off the edge of the road, the doors flew open, manager and driver were miraculously ejected, and they watched their car with its load of spare bikes on the roof perform that balletic display beloved of movie special-effects men, turning head over heels down the slope. By an odd touch of symmetry, it was a Bianchi rider, the 1965 winner Gimondi, who was on Merckx's heels as he headed for the 2240-metre Col d'Allos.

Only twenty-four kilometres from the finish, Merckx lost it. It was one of the most dramatic *défaillances* in the history of the Tour. Not a complete collapse: poor Merckx fought gamely on, but he had lost rhythm, energy, speed. Maybe the kidney punch had done more harm than had been realized, or maybe it was the medication he had then been given, or maybe he had some sort of fever. Whatever the cause, this great, brave, immensely strong rider seemed broken, slumped in intense pain. It was no disgrace when Thévenet caught him very near the finish and then passed Gimondi, to win the stage to Pra-Loup and, more to the point, take nearly four minutes for the day from Merckx and thus capture the yellow jersey, 1'56" ahead of him in the GC. Merckx was chivalrous in defeat: 'I tried everything and it didn't work. Only the strongest can win. And Thévenet is the strongest' – or he was that day.

He consolidated his lead with another cracking solo climb over the Col d'Izoard. And then the day after, sorrows coming not in single spies but in battalions, Merckx collided with the Danish rider Ole Ritter. This was in the 'neutralization', the period defined in the rules when riders are pedalling but not racing before the start (the race can also be *neutralisé* if interrupted by a demonstration, or very severe weather), and so the crash wasn't at great speed but enough to throw him from his bike head-first on to the road, breaking his maxilla and sinus bone. His face was wired up so that he could only ingest liquids; he was in acute pain; his doctor told him he must abandon; he rode on; he even, unbelievably, made up some time in a climbing time trial. The Tour finished in Paris on 20 July in the Champs-Élysées, which was now and henceforth its thoroughly appropriate new *Arrivée*. Thévenet won, but by no more than 2′47″; Merckx had won five out of the last six Tours, but he never rode a braver race than to be second in 1975.

> If you can tell your heart and nerve and sinew
> To serve your turn long after they are gone,
> And so hold on when there is nothing in you
> Except the Will which says to them: 'Hold On!'

Much loved by clergymen and housemasters of yore, and voted the most popular of all poems in a recent London newspaper poll, Kipling's 'If' is engraved over the players' entrance at Wimbledon. It is sometimes denigrated, even by Orwell in his fine essay on Kipling, and by Kipling's excellent latest biographer David Gilmour, who calls it a parody of the public-school spirit. Certainly it is hackneyed by repetition and misuse, so that few people now understand why (or indeed know that) it could have been translated by the Marxist writer Antonio Gramsci, who called it a great anticlerical and revolutionary poem. Those words about 'the Will which says to them "Hold On!"' applied to Gramsci imprisoned in Mussolini's jails; they were no less apt for Eddy Merckx at his finest.

His wasn't the only grim courage the race had seen. Poulidor was suffering from bronchitis and also had an excruciating Tour, which he could finish in no better than nineteenth place, almost an hour off the pace. By now it was openly said that he had ridden too many Tours for too long and was too old, to which he defiantly replied, 'I'll be back next year to mount the podium,' and he meant it. For Thévenet, victory was a one and only. He had to abandon in 1976, Merckx forfeited, and neither of them was among the several heroes of this Tour.

First of all there was Freddy Maertens, the Belgian sprinter who won the Prologue at St-Jean-de-Monts, held the yellow jersey for nine days, won eight stages in all – a record he shared with Charles Pélissier and Merckx – and easily won the green jersey at the finish before going on to win the World Road Championship. Then there was José-Luis Viejo, who made an epic solo break of 160 kilometres to win the Alpine stage from Montgenèvre to Manosque by 22′50″. There was Delisle, who took over the yellow jersey from Van Impe in the Pyrenees, and there was Van Impe himself, who then won the lead back.

But behind him was his director, Cyrille Guimard. The role of trainers, coaches and managers is an interesting and contentious one. Hans Keller used to posit the idea of the 'phoney profession', which he defined as a job which had not previously existed, and whose invention created more problems than it solved. Two of his illustrations were the opera producer and the viola player. A hundred years ago, operas were put on by stage managers, ideally under the broader direction of a conductor who was a great theatrical musician, like Mahler at the Vienna Hofoper or Toscanini at the Scala. Not only did the stagings serve as hand-maiden to the work (a contrast indeed to many opera productions today) but by all accounts they were vivid and engaging in themselves. And there were likewise no viola players as such, only violinists playing the viola. This doctrine might have been applied to managers in sports, including the football Keller loved so passionately: soccer, baseball and cricket teams used to get along somehow before managers took control, and before anyone foresaw the day when Sir Alex Ferguson would be the most important man with Manchester United.

All the same, the contrary idea that the manager plays a crucial role is sometimes given colour, by Ferguson on occasion – and in the 1976 Tour, when Guimard played a masterly game by working out an intricate strategy for Van Impe. Hitherto he had been a pure climber, who had won the Mountains prize the year before but seemed to have few chances in the GC. Now Guimard allowed Delisle to take the lead after Maertens had won the Prologue in St-Jean-de-Monts, 'sacrificing' the yellow jersey or *reculant pour mieux sauter*, against everyone else's advice. After lulling Delisle and his team all the way through the north, Alsace and the Alps, Van Impe struck again ferociously over the Col de Portillon to reach the Pla d'Adet alone. In a masterpiece of tactical bluffing worthy of a great poker player, as was said, Guimard saw his man back into the yellow jersey, which he was wearing in Paris at the finish. There he took first prize, which meant just over a million francs in cash and an additional new prize in kind, in the shape of an apartment in Merlin-Plage, the popular if unromantic seaside resort on the west coast: one new direction sponsorship was taking.

At the end Delisle finished not only behind Zoetemelk in second, he finished behind Poulidor in third. At the age of forty Poulidor had ridden a truly excellent race, keeping Delisle at level-pegging up the Puy de Dôme two days from the end and then shaving the needed points off him in the final *contre la montre* round the Champs-Élysées. It was the last Tour he rode, and he finished as he had promised he would on the podium.

All of this was narrated by a new voice: Daniel Mangeas became this year the official onsite race commentator for the Tour. For more than a quarter-century, *la voix du Tour* would become familiar to scores of millions of Frenchmen and women. Cynics in the press room sometimes smiled at his puppyish enthusiasm, and he was certainly a man who never had a bad word to say about any cyclist. Introducing a stage, he will always find some words of praise – one man has won a Criterium in Slovenia, another a stage of the Tour d'Anjou, a third was the revelation of last year's Giro di Pantelleria – but is all the same a great commentator, and those media sophisticates who smile at him also depend on him.

Thanks to the Tour's esoteric scoring system, Van Impe won the Mountains red-peas prize both in 1975 and 1977, when he finished the race itself in third place, both times behind Thévenet in winning place, but not in 1976, when he won the race but when the King of the Mountains was Giancarlo Bellini. The next year Thévenet now returned triumphant, but after a puzzling race. It began for the first time in the deep south-west and began climbing the Pyrenees on only the second day. The Prologue in Fleurance was won by the young German Dietrich Thurau making a remarkable debut: he not only took the yellow jersey from the start but held it for two weeks, crushing the field over the Tourmalet and Aubisque and then again in a thirty-kilometre time trial at Bordeaux when he rode at 46 k.p.h. to take fifty seconds off Merckx and more than a minute off Thévenet.

He ended with the white jersey for the best younger rider, an award now in its third year, having previously been won by Francesco Moser and Enrique Martinez-Heredia. These names illustrate incidentally the way the team system was now shaping itself. Teams were commercial rather than national, but they were inevitably recruited from riders who knew each other and wanted (or were prepared) to work together, and so in practice they tended to be predominantly made up of riders from one country. Thus Moser was one of the eight Italians in the 1975 Filotex team (along with a Swiss and a Dane), while Martinez-Heredia rode for the all-Spanish 1976 Kas–Campagnolo team. Nationality of riders did not have to correspond with nationality of company: in 1977 no fewer than seven out of ten riding for Fiat – that is, Fabbrica Italiana Autonomo di Torino – were Belgian, while TI–Raleigh had seven Dutchmen, a Belgian (José de Cauwer), an Englishman (Bill Nickson) and a German (Thurau).

Only when the *boucle* had circled most of France clockwise, through Limousin, Brittany, Normandy and down to the Alps, did the race begin in earnest. Besançon–Thonon-les-Bains was won by Bernard Quilfen with a huge escape of 222 kilometres to finish more than three minutes ahead of the field. More to the point, Thurau finally flagged over the Alps, where Thévenet decisively overcame Van Impe, and then confirmed his lead in a time-trial at Dijon. Even then he reached the line in the Champs-Élysées with no more than forty-eight seconds over Kuiper.

This was the race which unmistakably marked Merckx's eclipse. He was ill again, and if anything he rode bravely to finish even as high as sixth. And it was the year which saw a new name on the scene: the Liège–Bastogne–Liège, the Dauphiné Libéré and the Grand Prix des Nations were all won by a brilliant young Breton called Bernard Hinault. His reputation preceded him into the 1978 Tour, but there has never been less of a 'talking horse', flattering to deceive. To the contrary, the old order gave way to the new in dramatic fashion. Certainly the greatest cyclist of his generation, and quite possibly of all time, Eddy Merckx, retired, just as a man who was to dominate the next generation arrived. And the 23-year-old Hinault didn't just win his first Tour, he completely dominated it, on the flat, in the mountains, and against the clock.

He bided his time, not winning a stage for the first week through Holland, Belgium and northern France, until the riders reached Ste-Foy-la-Grande on the Dordogne, when he won his first stage. It was not a happy Tour. A dispute with the Tour officials led to a strike by the riders on the stage into Valence d'Agen, where they dismounted and crossed the line on foot, and the stage was annulled. After beating Hinault into l'Alpe d'Huez to take the yellow jersey, Michel Pollentier was caught trying to deceive the doping check with a urine sample which wasn't quite all his own work, and was ejected from the race. From the moment doping checks had been more or less seriously introduced, cyclists had been trying to find ways of circumventing them. More recently, a man giving a sample is expected to strip first, although this undignified proceeding isn't always enforced. But unless he is naked, it doesn't take much ingenuity or dexterity for a man to appear to be making water while in fact squeezing a pipette he has placed inside his shorts after filling it with the product of someone else's bladder. Hence the story, cherished by cyclists and possibly even true, of the rider who was congratulated that his specimen had tested negative, but warned that he was pregnant.

Having waited through the Pyrenees and then the Alps, Hinault finally pounced in the twentieth, penultimate stage, the Metz–Nancy time trial, where he snatched the yellow jersey from Zoetemelk, leading from him by just under four minutes at the end. It was perfectly characteristic of how Le Blaireau, 'the Badger', liked to win, an earnest of the way Hinault would ride all his races, badgering away at his rivals with devastating effect, even if it enchanted few fans. When Bill Shankly was manager of Liverpool football club, and told that his team weren't playing in entertaining enough style, he memorably replied that 'If people want entertainment, they can go to the fucking circus.' Hinault was a sportsman after Shankly's own heart. 'I race to win, not to please people,' he said bluntly. 'I'm the one who rides. If somebody thinks he can do it better, let him get a bike.'

He rode in that same spirit in 1979, which saw another duel between Hinault and Zoetemelk. After Gerrie Knetemann had won the Prologue, again in Fleurance, Hinault won the third stage into the Pyrenees, and thereafter it was only one of the two stars who ever held the GC lead, Hinault taking it, ceding it for a time to Zoetemelk, pacing himself with his usual icy calculation, and regaining it when he needed to, taking the yellow jersey back on the fifteenth, Evian–Avoriaz stage. Riding for Renault–Gitane, he was using a new Profil bike, and it suited him. He won seven stages in all, including the last two, Auxerre–Nogent-sur-Marne – after Zoetemelk had had a taste of glory on the antepenultimate Dijon–Auxerre stage – and then into Paris to win by 6'50". Zoetemelk had his other triumphs that year, in the Milan–San Remo and the Vuelta, but Hinault had even more, the Dauphiné Libéré, the Tour of Lombardy, the Flèche-Wallonne, and a third consecutive 'Nations'. If nothing went wrong for him, he wasn't going to be easy to beat.

Next year, something went wrong. The management of the Tour had been reorganized, with the Société now under the aegis of the 'Amis du Tour de France', and the management had chosen to start the race in Frankfurt before it visited Wiesbaden and crossed Belgium, taking almost a week to reach French soil and then loop westwards to St-Malo and Bordeaux. Hinault won the Prologue with his usual unsmiling dedication, then two more stages. He ceded the yellow jersey to Yvon Bertin and then Rudy Pevenage, before reclaiming the lead. He had dominated the race, and was still wearing the yellow jersey when they reached the foot of the Pyrenees at Pau. And there he was stricken. There could be none of the heroics Merckx had displayed five years before: Hinault's knee had gone. By sheer will power a cyclist can fight fever, boils or even a broken shoulder, but a crocked knee leaves him as helpless as a batsman with a broken finger or a footballer with a fractured toe, and he had no choice but to abandon.

The heroics were left to Raymond Martin, who made a long solo escape over the mountains from Pau to Luchon and, more to the point, consolidated his position so that he took third place when the race finished in Paris on 21 July. But it was the year of the Dutch. Zoetemelk rode with increasing confidence as well as his habitual perseverance and consistency, taking two time trials, and winning at the end from his countryman Kuiper by 6'55". Or more or less Dutch: married to a French girl, the daughter of Jacques Duchaussoy, he lived at Meaux, and to salve their feelings, the French press greeted Zoetemelk as 'le plus français des Hollandais'. Hinault had to make do with the Giro and the World Championship, nursing his knee for the next time.

Away from the Tour, 1980 was a year of arrivals, for better or worse, with Ronald Reagan elected President in the United States, Lech Walesa founding Solidarity in Poland, and the outbreak of what would prove an appalling war between Iraq and Iran. For cycling it was a year of farewells. Several notable riders died, including three former winners of the Tour: André Leducq, who had at least lived to the good age of seventy-six after his victories in 1930 and 1932, Jean Robic, the 1947 winner, and Gastone Nencini, only twenty years after he had shaken General de Gaulle's hand at Colombey-les-deux-Eglises on his way to victory in 1960. Those two died respectively at fifty-nine and forty-nine: the great race exacted a cruel tribute.

Repos

Brittany

Although the Tour sometimes visits Brittany, it doesn't do so every year, which is sad but maybe nowadays inevitable. The difficulties of boxing the whole *hexagone* have been amplified by the commercial pressures to stop at seaside resorts and ski stations that have done little to deserve the honour except pay for it, and in 1976 the Tour came no nearer the historic duchy than a first stage from St-Jean-de-Mont on the Vendée coast to Angers, up the Loire valley from Nantes. The following year the cyclists rode deeper into Breton country, with a stage from Lorient to Rennes; and Brest, the other great harbour of Brittany, has been visited twenty-eight times over the years. Sad to say, neither port had much of its former glories left after the war. Lorient was a purpose-built city and a company town named after its line of business, founded by Colbert in 1666 as a port for the East India trade, and Brest is one of the home ports of *la royale*, as the French navy still calls itself, but Brest and Lorient were so badly smashed up that they had effectively to be rebuilt after 1945.

Both Nantes and Rennes were luckier, at least in the past century. The historic capital of the duchy, Rennes was largely destroyed by fire in 1720, and although a number of earlier buildings survived, their chief effect is to offset the classical *hauteur* of the late eighteenth-century cathedral. The seventeenth-century Parlement was the most important older building to survive the fire, only to be burned out in another calamitous fire in 1994, which may have been caused by, and at any rate followed, a demonstration by Breton fishermen demanding larger subsidies, one of the less happy examples of the French taste for direct action. Strictly speaking, Nantes isn't on Breton soil, but the dukes of Brittany used it as a capital, and Duke François II built the fifteenth-century castle where Henry IV of France signed the Edict of Nantes in 1598 granting religious toleration (not for very long as it turned out).

In any case true Brittany lies further west even than Rennes. One reason Brittany should be part of the itinerary is that it has been the nursery of so many great riders, right up to the greatest of them all who erupted on to the stage with Bernard Hinault's devastating debut in 1978. Another reason is that this is one of the loveliest corners of France, though perhaps the most melancholy, because of a turbulent history, and until recently because of isolation and sheer poverty. It has been said that the Bretons haven't matched other Celtic people, Welsh or still more Irish, in literary prolificacy and brilliance, though this comparison is misleading. Ireland was a poor country, but with a richer colony; most great 'Irish literature' has been in English, and many great Irish writers have stemmed from the Protestant Saxon colony who knew nothing of Gaelic language or letters. Brittany was simply poor and backward, or regarded as such in the eyes and ears of Parisians, or indeed Nantais, for whom Breton was as much a barbarous dialect as Irish in the eyes and ears of Londoners, or indeed Dubliners, and we have seen that the Jacobin republican tradition was even more ruthlessly unsympathetic to backward 'jargons' than Whiggery or Utilitarianism in the British Isles, in the Celtic fringes of which the language revival came significantly earlier than in Brittany.

As with the tension between Welsh-speaking West Wales and the Anglophone east, there was a rivalry amounting to hostility between Lower and Upper Brittany, the Celtic west that spoke

Breton, sister-tongue to Welsh, and the eastern part that spoke French (or a form of it), with even greater animosity further east. Only thirty years before the Tour began, a group of Breton pilgrims visiting Mont-St-Michel in Normandy was physically attacked by the locals outraged by this primitive incursion. And such writers of eminence as were born in Brittany had little cultural connection with the province. Chateaubriand may have been born at St-Malo, the splendid island port seven times visited by the Tour, and lived on his nearby country estate at Combourg, but he was scarcely more Breton than Swift was Irish; nor, though he was born further to the west on the coast at Treguier, was Ernest Renan, author of a once-famous sceptical life of Christ, and author also of the penetrating definition that to be a nationalist requires ignorance of your history and hatred of your neighbours.

Surprisingly few books have even had Breton backgrounds. Pierre Loti came from the Charente, but set his morose seafaring novel *Pêcheur d'Islande*, remembered ungratefully by a generation of French A-level candidates in the early 1960s, in Paimpol close to Treguier, on a coast scattered with crosses mourning lost sailors including those, as in the title, who fished off Iceland. Jean Genet's *Querelle de Brest*, which gives new meaning to 'Hello, sailor', is set in that port, and describes it rather beautifully amid the lengthier descriptions of unsafe sex, but is scarcely a contribution to folkloric Breton writing. The most notable recent literary distinction of Rennes wasn't French at all: after Milan Kundera had been driven out of Prague in 1975, he spent some years teaching at the university there, where he wrote *The Book of Laughter and Forgetting*.

Wisest of all was the greatest of French novelists. In 1875, 107 years before Vershuere won the only stage that has ever finished at Concarneau, Flaubert spent several weeks there. While his friend the naturalist Georges Pouchet, with whom he was staying, dissected the 'fruits of the sea', Flaubert consumed them. He wrote letters, he took dips in the briny, and he ate lobsters, as the sensible visitor still does. Today there are fine restaurants in Brittany, and there are expensive restaurants, and there are some which are both, like Patrick Jeffroy's at Carantac or the Moulin de Rosmadec at Pont-Aven, which achieve astonishing things with crustaceans. But the best thing to do in Brittany is to go to any one of dozens of good little places along the coast that serve wondrous platters of *fruits de mer*, a dozen different kinds of shellfish, and whatever such other bounty of the seas as has survived over-fishing and tanker spillage.

Sitting in imagination, as it were, over such a plate with a glass of muscadet, this is a good point at which to look back at the Tour de France in its modern maturity, after almost three-quarters of a century and sixty-four runnings. As it happens, we have a particularly vivid snapshot of the race at that time in Geoffrey Nicholson's *The Great Bike Race*, still one of the best books about the Tour. Nicholson was a Welshman, educated at Swansea university in his home town. There he met his wife Mavis when they were both taught by Kingsley Amis, who dedicated his novel *Take a Girl Like You* to them. With such an auspicious literary inauguration, Nicholson had something to live up to, and he did. Over the years he wrote for several papers, but his true home was the first, the *Observer*, from the 1950s to the 1970s. It was then enjoying a golden age under David Astor's editorship-proprietorship, not least in the sports pages, which were consciously intended to be as well written as the political or literary pages.

Good sports writing has a distinguished lineage, from Hazlitt on prizefighting onwards. Ring Lardner and Ernest Hemingway gave it their own stamp in America, and many other writers have been fascinated by sport, quite apart from the two great literary goalies Camus and Nabokov. If Samuel Beckett is the only winner of the Nobel Prize for Literature to have appeared in *Wisden*'s Cricketers' Almanac (he played for Trinity College, Dublin) then V. S. Naipaul is at least one other Nobel laureate who has written about the game, which has inspired its own

corpus of poetry from Lionel Thompson to Harold Pinter. Since
literature begins with the – ideally lucid and lively – narrative of
an event, sport ought to be attractive to imaginative writers as
well as journalists: a match, a race or a fight is pre-eminently a
story waiting to be told.

When Nicholson began writing about bike racing in 1959, he
was struck by this very narrative aspect. Even a quite ordinary
and long-since-forgotten stage of the long-since-defunct Milk-for-
Stamina Tour of Britain (its name not chosen by anyone with a
keenly developed sense of the ridiculous), which he had been sent
to cover, had all the elements that make road racing attractive:

> . . . the adventure and suspense of the long escape, the surprising
> speed – over 20 miles an hour along twisted roads that rose from
> sea level . . . and continually dipped and rose again. The change
> of scenery. The unpredictable factors, not just of wind and
> rain . . . The tactical variety: the riders didn't just put their heads
> down and their bottoms up and pelt from A to B, they attacked
> and chased, flagged and rallied, formed instant alliances for
> immediate ends, and broke them without another single thought.

And even more compelling was the dramatic quality of the sport.
A race is 'a rounded, self-contained story with complex relation-
ships, sudden shifts of action, identifiable heroes, a beginning, a
middle and an end', and a stage in a six-day or three-week race
was 'another chapter in a picaresque novel which each day introduced new characters in a different setting'. Other sports –
different species of football maybe, baseball certainly, cricket
above all – offer the chronicler a dramatic narrative that he can
unfold, and have all attracted writers of high quality, as bike
racing had found in Blondin. It was then awaiting, in English, its
Hazlitt or Lardner, and in Nicholson it found him. Even then he
found difficulty in getting newspapers to let him write about
cycling as fully and vividly as it deserved. He covered the Tour of

Britain for *The Times*, but was only asked to file on alternate days; after he had reported one extraordinary day on the Black Mountain, with crashes and escapes, punctures and recoveries, the paper headlined his story 'Cyclists Traverse Welsh Valleys'.

When he came to cover the Tour de France, he discovered, as others have, its *misères* as well as *grandeurs*, all the difficulties and disappointments involved. The reporter from a Lyons paper in whose car he had hired a seat would drive to a quiet spot to type the morning interviews and, at the first sign of the approaching riders, would drive on to the finish where Nicholson was allowed to see the final sprints: 'The whole experience was like seeing the Second Coming from the top of a passing bus.'

All the same, he was captivated by the colour and majesty of the Tour. By the 1970s it was without question the greatest sports event on earth. Its only rivals were the Olympics and the World Cup, in some ways bigger but each quadrennial, and each peripatetic from one country to another. Yearly and in one place, the Tour is in a class of its own, not least in scale, of time and distance. Every Tour between 1906 and 1970 was not less than 4000 kilometres long, reaching the terrifying 5745 of 1926, before dropping back. By the 1970s the rules of the UCI – the International Cycling Union or Union Cycliste Internationale, invariably initialized from the French version – held that the race could have no more than twenty-two stages, a maximum of 269 kilometres each, but it no longer came anywhere near the 5720 kilometres that would theoretically have permitted. In 1976 it was 4017, and the 1980s saw the *parcours* shrinking right down to 3285 km in 1989; no race has reached 4000 km since 4231 in 1987, and the following year saw a sharp truncation to 3286, which was, with the next year almost identical, the shortest since 1905; the centennial Tour of 2003 is a modest 3350, only three-fifths the length of Buysse's great race seventy-seven years earlier. There is no ideal length for the Tour, and it would be cruel and unusual punishment to expect riders now to emulate their forebears of 1926, with an average of

337 kilometres a day. All the same, it's hard to escape the feeling that, when the daily average is, as in 2003, only 167 kilometres, the race has lost something of that epic quality Barthes descried.

In 1976 the 130 riders who began the Tour were accompanied by around 1800 camp followers, officials, technicians, press, publicists, moving like a small army (again, Barthes's own comparison) across the country and filling all hotel beds every night in each stage town and for about forty kilometres around. The mobile force itself was dwarfed by the numbers who served it on its journey, not least by around 26,000 policemen – local *agents*, national gendarmerie, and France's magnificent riot police, as Auberon Waugh used to call the Compagnie Républicaine de la Sécurité – who clear the way. For several hours each day, several hundreds of kilometres of French roads are closed to the public, and only those whose cars sport official stickers rear and aft are waved through, past the 15 million or so spectators who are said to watch the race in the flesh.

That's the figure that has been given for thirty or forty years. It is pretty much a 'guesstimate', and computing the numbers of any large crowd is as hazardous in France as anywhere else, but the number has been repeated so often as to have taken on a factual life of its own, and is plausible enough. A majority of French people never see the Tour, many are quite indifferent to it, and a fair number greatly resent it. It certainly disrupts normal life wherever it goes, and almost inevitably its commercialization became a focus of radical student protest. A sarcastic broadsheet handed out at Lacanau-Océan in 1976 said that, thanks to the Tour, the French cycle industry was selling 2.5 million bikes a year: 'Bravo! Sport is neutral and disinterested.' The heavy irony was misplaced. Of course sport wasn't disinterested, and couldn't be. The Tour has been concerned with money since the beginning. But it is true that its commercial aspects were complex, and sometimes dubious.

The bike-manufacturing industry had had an obvious and not necessarily unhealthy relationship with the race. Nor was it inherently corrupting for commercial sponsors unconnected with cycling to back Tour teams, whether an Italian sausage company like Molteni, to whom Merckx transferred his affections, or at least his services, in 1971, winning in their colours in three of the next four years, or a ballpoint-maker like Bic for whom Ocaña won in 1973. In fact, accusations of profiteering are perhaps the least fair of any made against the organizers of the Tour. It isn't a charity, and the various forms of sponsorship or inducement are needed to break even. In the mid-1970s the annual budget was around 8 to 8.5 million francs (£800,000–850,000) and when Félix Lévitan said that 'we try to balance expenses and receipts, without always managing to do so,' there was no reason to doubt him.

Given the principle that towns pay for the privilege of being a *ville-étape*, it wasn't improper that Angers should have bought its 1967 *Départ*, although the Plymouth stage in 1974 was another matter. So was the increasing tendency for mountain stages to finish in ski resorts which had paid to secure the *Arrivée*. As Nicholson said, 'The only way to a ski resort is up,' but his view that the demands of commerce more or less coincided with those of sport – 'since a summit finish effectively divides the flock of valley sheep from the individual mountain goats' – needs to be qualified: these high finishes put the descender's art at a discount.

By now those bike racing specialisms, which barely existed in the first years of the Tour, had sorted themselves out, and some were better loved than others. The old orchestral jingle, 'Brass for drinkers, woodwind for thinkers, strings for stinkers,' applied to cycling *mutatis mutandis*. If not necessarily drinkers (although some of them certainly were), the climbers were the tough guys of the race. That does not mean that they were big or burly. Often they were slight and spare, with Julio Jimenez, King of the Mountains in 1965–7, a notable example. In Nicholson's words, 'he was also balding, grey-faced and never looked particularly well, but in the first steep slopes would prance away as though he had springs in his calves'. Jimenez's native Spain had an extraordinary record, especially in the third quarter of the century, winning the King of the Mountains prize thirteen out of the twenty-two years from 1953 to 1974, but the Belgian record has also been remarkable, while in the past decade, thanks to Richard Virenque and Laurent Jalabert, the red-peas jersey has tended to be French cycling's one consolation.

Like clarinettists and flutists, time-triallists are the thinking men, with the most precise sense of their and their rivals' abilities, as well as that clock in the head that tells every *contre la montre* expert exactly how fast he is going and how he needs to pace the rest of the stage. And sprinters are stinkers, at least in the eyes of many fans, and a good many other riders, because their craft so often seems parasitic. By nature they have to conserve their energy for the hot-spot sprints and for the finishes; another way of putting it is that others do the work while these wheel-suckers, slip-streamers, jackals or opportunists – some of the epithets traditionally hurled at them – live off the energy of their rivals.

Such parasites (if they are that) were well rewarded for their work: the green points jersey was by now the most valuable after only the winner's yellow jersey. In 1976 the Tour winner received 100,000 francs (£10,000), with £2500 to the second, £1550 to the third and so on down to the thirty-fifth with a modest £65. The green jersey holder won £100 a day during the course of the race, and £1200 at the end, while the red peas winner – as he had just become – collected £900. Nicholson was one of several commentators who found the *maillot blanc à pois rouges* something of an embarrassment, a temporary stunt which he predicted would probably be dropped, but the polka-dot jersey is with us still.

All of these came on top of the daily prizes, £310 for a stage winner, with those who followed him home collecting something all the way down to thirtieth. There were losers as well as winners: the daily computations included a cut, in golfing terms: riders who had failed to complete a stage within a certain percentage of the winner's time were eliminated, although the Tour continued Desgrange's own tradition of arbitrary justice, the prince dispensing punishments and pardons, and passionate pleas for clemency married to plausible excuses sometimes won a reprieve.

Even those were only some of the bonuses and *primes* awarded. The green jersey was calculated by points, 25 to the winner of a stage, 20 for second, 16 for third, down to 1 point for the fifteenth finisher. Fewer such finishing points were awarded on mountain stages, since the green jersey was intended to reward sprinters, who also collected daily primes of £40, £20 and £10 for the hot-spot sprints, besides which were the informal primes of £20 or £10 offered by towns and villages. Tour etiquette, sometimes but not always observed, says that a local rider should be allowed to go ahead and pick up these, and the accompanying cheers from his friends and neighbours.

Finally came the team prizes, one worth £8450 awarded on time, won by KAS in 1976, and another worth £4000 awarded on points. Those were by way of consolations. It was a curiosity of road racing as an individual sport which was also a team sport that the team for which the yellow-jersey winner rode so rarely won the team prize: in the eight years following the return of commercially sponsored teams, this happened only twice, with Merckx and Faema in 1969 and Ocaña and Bic in 1973. Given the choice of riding in a team that won the *classement par équipes* or a team whose leader won the Tour, any *domestique* would always choose the yellow jersey, since not only the *réclame* but the rewards – the winner's purse divided among his colleagues, the sponsorships and invitations – are greater.

And it was by this time that Tour racing, and Merckx in particular, had developed team tactics to a degree where this was held to be spoiling the sport by stifling competition. Rather than merely rely on a multifariously gifted team's support, as Magne certainly had with the French team in the early 1930s and Coppi with the Italian twenty years later, Merckx seemed to have assembled a team whose only real purpose was to help him win. Maybe the criticism was just; maybe what had happened was inevitable; maybe it was the pattern of the future.

13

The Yanks Are Coming

1981–1987

Another quinquennium of French victories awaited as the new decade began, but it proved to be the last such years of success during the first century of the Tour, followed by a striking national *défaillance*: no Frenchman has won France's great race since 1985. Maybe it really was a turning point in French history. If 1981 saw the deaths of René Clair and George Brassens, most brightly enchanting of film directors and most saltily mordant of singers, it saw also the election of François Mitterrand as president, to the elation of the French Left (I was with a party of reporters in the deserts of Namibia when we heard the news, and the South African correspondent of the *Monde* could scarcely control his rapture), and a grand slam by the French rugby team. At least one of those triumphs proved illusory, as Mitterand's career slowly dissolved in a puddle of scandal. The one lasting French success of these years was the opening of the TGV, which cut the journey from Paris to Lyons to two hours; by the time I took the train from Mâcon to the Gare de Lyons after the penultimate day's time trial in the 2002 Tour, the journey on that magnificent line had been reduced to ninety minutes for almost 400 kilometres, in shaming contrast to my own country's contemptible trains travelling at half the speed if they're running at all.

One of Brassens's songs, for which the word salty is inadequate, is about the novice tart and her talents, or lack of them: 'L'avait l'don, c'st vrai, j'en conviens,/L'avait le génie,/Mais, sans technique, un don n'est rien/Qu'un' sal' manie.' Or roughly, I know it's true she had something, genius even, but without technical skill no gift like that's any better than a dirty habit. These are words with which any cyclist might agree in his own context, and they applied notably to Bernard Hinault. He had both, the *génie* and the *technique*, as he showed yet again in 1981 with the second of his two back-to-back victories in the Tour. The race directors Jacques Goddet and Félix Lévitan had been joined by three assistant directors, and once again the *parcours* was much meddled about with, beginning in Nice, with a Prologue won by Hinault, before riding westwards to the Pyrenees. Knetemann took the lead from Hinault and then ceded it to Phil Anderson, who made his own footnote of history as the first Australian to wear the yellow jersey.

These were mere pleasantries. The seventh stage was a time trial from Nay to Pau. Hinault won it, grasped the GC lead, and never relinquished it again, all the way north to Le Mans, northeast to Brussels, down to Mulhouse, on to the Alps, and then turning for home. A fine ride by Freddy Maertens gave him five stage wins and the green jersey at the end, while Van Impe won the red-peas jersey as consolation, but he was very decidedly runner-up, almost quarter of an hour behind Hinault at the finish. The winner received both cash and kind, 30,000 francs and what was by now the traditional apartment in Merlin-Plage. Since Hinault won in all five of these riparian retreats, it's to be supposed that he realized their sale value, now given at 120,000 francs. Jacques Tati died in the year of Hinault's fifth and last

Tour victory, and Monsieur Hulot himself might have had a comical holiday trying to juggle the five at once.

At any rate, Hinault had no difficulty in claiming the prize: 1982 was his most uneventful Tour, though echoing the previous year's in several respects. Hinault won the Prologue in Basle, let the lead pass to Ludo Peeters and then Phil Anderson, but racked up four stages and held the yellow jersey for ten days before finishing ahead of Van Impe. The only event that disturbed the somewhat placid course of this race was a demonstration at Fontaine-au-Pire, a new *ville-étape*, which led to the annulment of that stage, a team time trial, and its replacement by another from Lorient to Plumiec. Otherwise Hinault hacked up, crushing the field in a time trial at St-Priest when he covered the last kilometre in a minute, and again in the final Champs-Élysées sprint. Bernard Vallet of France won the red-peas jersey, Sean Kelly of Ireland the green, and Anderson of Australia the white, awarded since 1975 to the best young rider, but it was Hinault's year, as the dour Breton took the Giro–Tour double, and his fourth Grand Prix des Nations.

By now Hinault had overtaken Thys and Bobet with their three victories, and looked as if he would equal the five of Anquetil and Merckx. But he sat out the 1983 Tour, for reasons about which he was a little evasive. He had been suffering from tendinitis, but he suffered also from a blunt or even surly disposition. His career was lived in a series of rows with rivals, colleagues and managers, and most reporters attributed his absence to a row with his Renault team. It was thus an open race, and in more senses than one: amateur riders were invited, and indeed took part in the form of a team from Colombia. They were accompanied by a conspicuous phalanx of thirty-two Colombian journalists, two of whose papers, the *Tiempo* and the *Espectador*, daily devoted three pages each to their heroes' progress.

The race left Fontenay-sous-Bois outside Paris on 1 July, to loop across the Belgian border and then turn back westwards towards Nantes, then south to the Pyrenees. The lead passed from Eric Vanderaerden to Jean-Louis Gauthier to Kim Andersen to Kelly – who followed his stage win in 1978 with two in 1980, one each in 1981 and in 1982, when he won the green jersey and was the first Irishman to wear the yellow jersey – before Pascal Simon took the GC lead at Bagnères-de-Luchon, after a stage won by Robert Millar of Scotland. Simon then had a bad fall and fractured his shoulder, which should have taken him out of the race. But with remarkable courage he rode on for another six days, up the Puy de Dôme and into the Alps. It was only when he was finally overcome and had to abandon on the La Tour-du-Pin–l'Alpe-d'Huez stage, still wearing the yellow jersey, that the Parisian novice Laurent Fignon was able to take the lead.

On the preceding stage from Issoire to St-Étienne there had been another curious episode. Michel Laurent and Henk Lubberding made an escape together and were racing to the line when Lubberding veered into Laurent, knocking him off his line until he crashed; he could only manage seventh after remounting. As they might have said at Newmarket, it was a clear case of bumping and boring, and a stewards' enquiry did something most unusual, disqualifying Lubberding for dangerous riding and promoting Laurent. But the Tour was Fignon's. He held that lead to the finish, where he won what was then a unique double of yellow jersey and white as best young rider. It was hail to the young and farewell to the old; or not so old: the year also saw the deaths of three former Tour winners, Antonin Magne at seventy-nine, Romain Maes at sixty-nine, and Louison Bobet at only fifty-eight.

Even then, Fignon hadn't quite set the Seine on fire. He was a former dental student, and looked the part, a bespectacled swot with a fixed grin. Although he had never ridden in the Tour before, Cyrille Guimard, *directeur sportif* of Renault–Gitane, discerned his quality and chose Fignon along with Marc Madoit as key players in his team after Hinault's defection. As the race was nearing its end, detractors pointed out that Fignon had yet to win a stage, to which he duly responded by winning the Dijon time trial on the penultimate day. But if he never quite shook off his nerdy image, he answered his critics still more convincingly in 1984. Hinault had been hired by the lurid and dubious Bernard Tapie for his new La Vie Claire team, funded with what was then the enormous sum of 10 million francs, and they had made an explosive start together, with Hinault winning the Flèche-Wallonne and Vuelta in 1983, and the 1984 Grand Prix des Nations (his fifth). In the Tour he began as he meant to continue by winning the Prologue at Montreuil-sous-Bois on 29 June. But the lead soon passed to a Low Countries trio of Vanderaerden, Jacques Hanegraaf and Adri Van Der Poel, before Fignon took the lead.

He was helped by his new bike. The Giro had just been won from Fignon by Francesco Moser, who was riding an up-to-the-minute machine which Fignon asked his team's experts to match. They duly provided him with the Delta: fin-shaped handlebars and streamlined body. Riding this, he brilliantly won three stages up to Alpine ski resorts. At La Plagne he wasn't so much confident as exalted: 'My physical condition means that I can cycle to the maximum and keep going to the limit with no risk. Bike racing in these conditions is enchantment.' Fignon was no less enchanting when he won the three time trials, and at the finish he easily beat Hinault by 8'58".

More remarkable was the man in third, Greg LeMond. When he had won the 1982 Tour de l'Avenir, his name as yet scarcely registered with fans or press, who barely imagined that American riders would ever play any serious part in the Tour, and under-standably so, since they were completely unknown quantities. In the 1976 Tour the sixth stage to Nancy had left from Bastogne and from the place McAuliffe, a resonant American name. Less than twenty-eight years earlier, in a desperate last throw of the dice just before Christmas 1944, Hitler had launched an attack in the Ardennes, the 'Battle of the Bulge'. In that Belgian town the line was held by 'the battling bastards of Bastogne', the 101st Airborne Division of the United States Army under Brigadier General Anthony McAuliffe. For generations of genteel French ladies, 'le mot de Cambronne' was the only way to allude to the unspeakable expletive 'Merde!', General Cambronne's contemptuous reply at Waterloo when ordered to surrender. The *mot de McAuliffe* was 'Nuts!' in reply to the same demand in 1944, a great moment in the history of America in Europe.

And yet there was no American rider in the place McAuliffe in 1976, and none took part in the Tour until 1984. By reaching the podium in his first Tour, wearing the white jersey as best young rider, LeMond announced in the most dramatic way that a new nation had appeared on the scene. Jean-Jacques Servan-Schreiber had startled France in 1967 with his book *Le Défi américain*, about the economic and political challenge posed by the United States; seventeen years later, another American challenge had arrived unmistakably. The Yanks were coming.

After a two-year absence from the winner's place, Hinault returned there after winning the Giro in 1985, but this Tour was eloquent of the future and not of the past. The man who had beaten Hinault a year earlier was absent hurt, as Hinault had been in 1983: the misfortune this time was Fignon's, undergoing an operation on his Achilles' tendon. It was altogether a good year for younger sportsmen, with the unknown seventeen-year-old Boris Becker brilliantly winning the Wimbledon men's singles; it was a wonderful year in the Tour for Ireland, with heroic performances by Stephen Roche and Sean Kelly; and it was an ominous year for European cycling.

By winning the Prologue, Hinault immediately reclaimed his yellow jersey. Another rider, the Belgian Alfons de Wolf, finished more than two minutes down on Hinault, after he had turned up five minutes late for the start, and suffered the unusual indignity of being ejected from the Tour on the first day for not trying. One other rider didn't do quite so badly, finishing 100th in the Prologue and abandoning three days later. Any failure was only temporary: Miguel Induráin would be back for more. From Brittany the race wound north and east to Lorraine and south towards the Alps, while the lead passed to Vanderaerden and then the Dane Andersen. Hinault won another time trial from Sarrebourg–Strasbourg to take the yellow jersey again, and looked to be in control until the fourteenth stage out of Autrans.

In Fignon's absence the challenge had turned out to come from one of Hinault's own team-mates in La Vie Claire–Wonder–Radar (to give it its not very catchy full name), none other than young LeMond, who had transferred from his previous team. Hinault was leading from him in the GC when a sprint finish into the Cours Fauriel at St-Étienne ended in a collision between Hinault and Anderson riding for Panasonic. Hinault fell and was badly injured, his nose broken by his sunglasses, blood pouring from his head, and rows of stitches needed. If he had abandoned he couldn't have been blamed by anyone, except himself. Instead, he rode on with indomitable courage, holding his three-minute lead over LeMond intact until the Pyrenees.

The turning point of the race came on the exceptionally tough Toulouse–Luz-Ardiden stage, and it came in unheroic and displeasing fashion. Hinault's wounds had taken their toll, and he was suffering. Unable to breathe easily, he was dropped over the Col du Tourmalet, while LeMond was riding more strongly and smoothly than ever, palpably cutting into the lead of his captain Hinault, and 'strong enough to attack', as he said later. At which point Paul Koechli, team manager of La Vie Claire, quietly stepped in and told a mortified LeMond to take it easy. It was quite close to telling a boxer to throw a fight, and LeMond's reaction echoed Marlon Brando's 'I coulda been a contender' in *On the Waterfront*. As the American said bitterly, 'The team lost me the Tour.'

This cast a vivid and questionable light on the Tour as at once an individual and a team event. A *domestique* isn't there to win but to 'follow my leader' and serve him loyally, in a way that distinguishes cycling from other team sports. Of course a football manager can take a player off, a baseball coach can retire a pitcher, a cricket captain can declare an innings closed even when a batsman is on the point of making a century, all for the good of the team. But what happened to LeMond in 1985 was different in kind from those. There had also been an altercation between Hinault and Joel Pelier, Hinault ticking the young French rider off for attacking pointlessly, wasting effort in suicidal escape bids. That was one thing, a rebuke by a much more experienced and successful rider to a younger for wasting his substance, though the rebuke might have been better delivered in private. LeMond's 'suicide', in contrast, was more like Seneca's or Rommel's, acting under orders, and it clearly confuted any idea that each rider should at least have the opportunity to do his best.

Whatever his feelings, LeMond did as he was told, although on the penultimate day of the Tour at Lac du Vassivière he seemed to be making a point rather sharply when he won the time trial – and the first Tour stage ever won by an American – to leave him only 1'42" behind his boss at the finish a day later. In third was Roche, who had ridden a splendid race to become the first Irishman ever on the podium. His compatriot Kelly was fourth, winning the green jersey for the third of the four times he would take it.

For British Tour fans the year was notable for one other novelty: television reports were carried daily for the first time, needless to say on Channel 4 rather than the BBC, which has rarely shown any very lively interest in cycling. I have called the Tour a curious spectator sport, and that goes for the press corps. They will watch the *Départ* of each day's stage, then get into their fleet of cars and set off, very often at hair-raising speed, to the *Arrivée*, seeing next to nothing of the race itself but relying on the

Tour's own running radio commentary to tell them what's actually happening. Then at the finish they will see the cyclists arrive, although nowadays they are less likely to do this *en plein air* than in the exceptionally well-appointed press centres, where hundreds of laptops are plugged in at tables, and where the finish can be watched on large-screen television, followed by the daily routine of interviews with stage winners and jersey wearers.

During the course of the 2002 Tour I was obliged to return to England for a few days, and thereby made an interesting rather than amazing discovery: if you merely want to know what's going on, the best place to watch the Tour is at home in front of a television. Even if it has failings of its own – for all the advances of technology, the camera still sometimes misrepresents what it shows by foreshortening distances – television gives the viewer a more complete picture of the race at any moment than is enjoyed by anyone on the road. It may be that the very idea of the privileged 'ringside seat' is now doubtful in other sports also, from football to baseball, and not just in sports. Years ago some of us made another simple discovery when covering party conferences, that this is best done by staying in one's hotel room and watching the debates on screen before setting out for lunch. And a friend who was given unique 'access' to Tony Blair during his triumphant 1997 General Election campaign – travelling with him by road and air, sitting in his various offices and his constituency home morning and evening, never hearing a radio or watching a television – says that at no election he has ever covered did he know less about what was actually going on. The Tour de France is a quite extraordinary *événement*. Watching it close up is a delight, and covering its whole length is a wonderful experience. All the same there is a paradox, that you need the broadcast media to learn the progress of the race.

By an allusion no one can have deliberately intended, the 1986 Tour began on the Fourth of July. That proved astonishingly apt:

this race would truly mark a declaration of independence for American cycling. The prize was there to be taken. Hinault was now thirty-one. After his victory in 1985, he had said a little grandiloquently, and not quite accurately, that 'My only real rival was the ghost of my former self which insisted that I equal my previous performances.' Although he recognized that he hadn't been in the physical shape of ten years earlier, 'I had a wealth of experience and my enthusiasm was undimmed'. It was scarcely more dimmed a year later, but if the spirit was still willing, the flesh was weaker. Hinault announced that he would retire late in 1986, on his thirty-second birthday, and intimated also that this year he would pass on the torch to his young team-mate: now he would work for LeMond, and not the other way round. Having said that, he confused the issue by wondering out loud whether he might not after all go for a last Tour victory: 'I said I'd help LeMond win the Tour but he's got to earn it. He must be worthy of the yellow jersey.'

The Prologue was in Boulogne-Billancourt, the industrial suburb of south-west Paris, famous as home of the Renault motor works, and notorious for Sartre's saying in a different context, 'Il ne faut pas désésperer Billancourt' (sc. we mustn't dishearten Billancourt, or disappoint the working class, by telling them the truth about Soviet Communism). Hinault's fans were disheartened, not only when Thierry Marie took the Prologue, on a bike with an *appui dorsal*, a new kind of saddle, or when the yellow jersey passed to Alex Stieda, the first Canadian ever to wear it, but by the later outcome of the race. On their way through the north-west and south-west to the Pyrenees, it seemed that Hinault's second thoughts had prevailed. He attacked repeatedly and wilfully to wear out the climbers even before they began climbing, so that they 'had nothing left', as he said himself. 'You have to attack them until they can't recover. It's not hard to do.' LeMond evidently agreed, and told journalists that Hinault was out to do him down, an impression reinforced in the

Pyrenees. On the first mountain stage from Bayonne to Pau over the Col de Marie Blanque, Hinault attacked alongside Pedro Delgado. The Spaniard took the stage but Hinault took the yellow jersey. LeMond was provoked into actually winning the next stage into Superbagnères, one of the rather few stage wins in his career, and began to whittle away at the lead. By the Alps he had taken the yellow jersey.

But not without difficulties. For one thing, LeMond never really got inside the way the European team system worked, or the peloton: on the one hand, samurai fealty by *domestiques* to leader, on the other, continually changing tactical alliances. It was one thing for riders from different teams to combine against another team leader, but in one race in America, the 1985 Coors Classic, LeMond had actually worked with riders from another team to attack his team-mate Hinault, a shocking assault on European concepts of *esprit de corps*, not to say *omertà*. Maybe it was a sign of American individualism, but he couldn't emotionally grasp the idea of a rider serving his liege master as a page served his knight, and he would never have done what Merckx did in lordly fashion in 1968, when he handed a race to Guido Reybroeck for services earlier rendered, or Hinault himself had done on one stage of the 1980 Giro when Jean-René Bernaudeau helped him up the Stelvio climb and, at the finish, Hinault waved his colleague through to take the stage.

At any rate, the Colombian Luis Herrera led over the Col du Galibier in 1986 alongside Guido Winterberg, from La Vie Claire, followed by a group including Hinault. LeMond had been dropped, but he caught up on the descent and then towards the Col du Télégraphe, where Hinault and LeMond broke away together and stayed clear over the Col de la Croix de Fer and the Col du Glandon, with Hinault always keeping a perceptible upper hand. He took the stage into l'Alpe d'Huez – but he did so clasping hands with LeMond alongside him. If the gesture looked rather artificial, that was no more than the case. There was still little love lost between the two, and little mutual sympathy. Hinault congratulated the American, saying that he had thrown everything at him for days and put him under as much pressure as possible. This was true, and was recognized by the award to Hinault of the short-lived Prix de la Super-Combativité ('extra aggressive') at the end of a hard race.

What looked like a coming American supremacy was interrupted by Spanish success, and before that a glorious Irish triumph. It has never been necessary to be Irish, or to have any sympathy for the nastier manifestations of Irish nationalism, to be a vicarious Irish sports fan and to find Irish sporting achievements very endearing. Jackie Kyle, Tony O'Reilly, Willie John McBride, Paul Wallace and David Humphreys put a dash and a delight into rugby that eluded even the best English players, and the feats of the Irish football teams in recent World Cups have, as the great Myles na Gopaleen would have said in his 'Catechism of Cliché', imparted heat to many an obscure coronary mollusc ('Sure, it warms the cockles of me heart'). Every such mollusc was heated by the triumphs of Stephen – never 'Steve' – Roche.

The 1987 Tour started further from France than ever before or ever since, in a Berlin still separated from West Germany, though not for much longer. After three days of Prologue, road stage and time trial, which left the Polish rider Lech Piasecki in the yellow jersey, the riders hadn't left the once and future German capital. It was indeed an odd race. A largely new team was in charge after Félix Lévitan had departed from the Société du Tour de France, leaving Phillipe Amaury as administrator alongside the managing director Jacques Goddet, Jean-François Naquet-Radiguet as director-general – and the new *conseilleur technique* in the form of Bernard Hinault, retired at last from the saddle. Whichever of them was responsible, or whatever commercial pressure had been applied, it was curious and unsatisfactory for a Tour de 'France' not to reach French soil until the end of the first week. Just as awkwardly, the race then circled the country anticlockwise and only reached the mountains after two weeks.

Until then it was an uneventful race, with the Swiss rider Erich Maechler holding the yellow jersey for six days, from Stuttgart to the Loire, where Roche won the Saumur–Futuroscope time trial, as it proved his one and only stage of the race. Martial Gayant took over the lead at Chaumeil before Charly Mottet took it for five days. Then, after a time trial up Mont Ventoux, the action began in the Alps. Several Spanish climbers were in their element, with Pedro Delgado taking Valréas–Villard de Lans, when Roche finally gained the yellow jersey, only to cede it to Delgado on the next stage from Villard de Lans up to l'Alpe d'Huez won by Delgado's countryman Federico Echave. The next stage, a tough 185-kilometre ride from Bourg d'Oisans to La Plagne thus began with Delgado twenty-five seconds ahead of Roche. It was won by Fignon, making something of a comeback after his years of greatness, and destined for seventh place in Paris. But the real duel was a minute behind him.

Up and down the Galibier went Roche, and he attacked with a group of riders to put ninety seconds between them and Delgado. But Delgado didn't run down his flag. He relentlessly pursued them and caught them after fifty kilometres. The foot of the last climb to La Plagne, with less than fifteen kilometres to go, found Roche and Delgado upsides. Fignon and Anselmo Fuerte attacked and broke away and Delgado followed, but Roche kept his counsel and kept his cool, knowing the overall position, and knowing that he had one more time trial to come. Delgado fell back from the two leaders, but still had two minutes on Roche, who cleverly lulled him, until the cheers at the finish were audible: 'I decided to wait until four kilometres to go and then give it everything.' By the four-kilometre sign, he had whittled Delgado's lead down to 1'15", and then 'went into overdrive'. He saw the cars following Delgado, and knew he had done it: by the line, he was only four seconds behind the Spaniard.

And then he collapsed. Suddenly pole-axed by exhaustion and white as a sheet, Roche was stretchered to an ambulance and taken to hospital, with just time to say, 'I'm okay, don't worry.' Delgado was still twenty-nine seconds ahead of him in the GC, which became thirty-nine seconds when Roche was penalized for having scoffed an illegal feed. Astonishing as it may seem, Roche was cleared by the medics the next morning, and rode another fine stage in the last day in the mountains to finish second, eighteen seconds ahead of Delgado. All Roche needed now was to hammer Delgado against the clock in Dijon, which he duly did. The stage was won by Jean-François Bernard, victor of the Mont Ventoux time-trial, in 50'1", with Roche at 21", and Delgado at 1'2": a gap that decided the Tour. Roche reached Paris in triumph to take the race from Delgado and then from Bernard and Mottet. He had won by the same forty-second margin of the Dijon time trial, the second-smallest margin in the race's history, but quite enough.

A British trade team called ANC hadn't prospered in the Tour, with only four riders finishing, led by Adrian Timmis in seventieth. For French cycling the death of Jacques Anquetil at only fifty-three seemed a melancholy mark of national eclipse, while France had once more to look elsewhere for sporting consolation when the rugby team won its fourth grand slam. But Irish eyes were smiling. In a gloriously polychromatic triumph of yellow, pink and rainbow jerseys, Roche won not only the Tour, he won the Giro and the World Championship, a feat only Merckx had accomplished before. And yet in the official UCI world rankings he finished the year second – to his compatriot Sean Kelly, who had crashed in the Tour and broke his collarbone but had won his third Critérium International.

The man who capped this Irish year of triumph was a Dubliner, son of a milkman who had encouraged his son to stick to cycling even when grave injury early in 1986 in a six-day race in Paris had almost persuaded him to give up. Modesty as well as bravery made Roche popular not only in his own country but in France, where the *Équipe* saluted his victory with the excruciatingly punning headline 'TOUR: UNE NOUVELLE EIRE'. There was in fact to be no prolonged Irish domination. A *nouvelle ère* or new era was dawning, to be sure, but the men who would rule over it were Spanish and American.

14

Induráin in Excelsis

1988–1994

Although Sean Kelly won not only the Milan–San Remo classic in 1988 and his seventh consecutive Paris–Nice race, there was to be no Tour double for Stephen Roche, who was plagued by his recurring knee injury and missed most of this season. The way was left open for Delgado to take his revenge. Jean-Pierre Courcol, editor of the *Équipe*, had become director of the Société du Tour, with Jean-Claude Hérault commercial director, and yet again they fiddled about with the pattern of the race: the Prologue replaced by a 'Préface' at La Boule in Brittany, four new *étapes*, at Machecoul, Ancenis, Wasquehal and Santenay, and the *Village-Départ* newly born. This was a happy innovation, and is still with us, a stationary publicity caravan, as it were, where punters can relax, trough and sluice before the race.

The said Preface was won by Guido Bontempi and his Weinmann team, Bontempi covering a measured kilometre in 1′4.11″ or at 48.576 k.p.h., before the yellow jersey was taken by the Canadian Steve Bauer. As the race headed up the Loire, through Normandy and east towards the Alps, the lead passed to three flying Dutchmen, Teun Van Vliet, Henk Lubberding and Jelle Nijdam, until Bauer reclaimed it. Then Delgado struck in the Alps, taking the lead in the Morzine–l'Alpe-d'Huez stage won by Steven Rooks, one more rider from the Netherlands. Delgado won from Grenoble to Villard de Lans and now had a firm grip on the race. There were one or two upsets, as when the rank outsider Juan Martinez-Oliver took a time-trial stage at Santenay, when Rooks came second in the GC and took the red-peas jersey (he won a stage the following year and came seventh), and when Eddy Planckaert – one of five riders from that prolific family – took the green jersey, although his final GC position was no higher than 115th out of 151 who finished, and this was the only Tour he ever completed. There were hard-luck stories on the Blagnac–Guzet-Neige stage: Bouvatier and Millar were both in contention for the stage when they were mistakenly directed off the course.

And there was one distinct good-luck story. Delgado tested positive for probenicide, beyond question a performance-enhancing drug but one which had not yet been included in the UCI's list of banned substances. The whole peloton stood by him, delaying the start of the next stage in protest, and in the end no action was taken. Justice may have been done in a technical sense. The maxims that a man is innocent until proved guilty, and that it is better for any number of guilty men to go free than for one innocent man to be convicted, echo nobly through legal history. But by letting Delgado off, the race officials almost parodied what remained an excessively indulgent attitude towards doping on the part of cycling in general, and the Tour in particular. It cast a slight pall over his victory in the Champs-Élysées on 24 July, and it would return to haunt the Tour. Not that *dopage* was a problem confined to cycling. On the other side of the world a Canadian sprinter won a gold medal in that year's Seoul Olympics, and then lost it when he tested positive. O rare Ben

Johnson? All the evidence suggested that he was far from rare, in athletics or in many other sports.

By now the American challenge had unmistakably arrived. Greg LeMond had become the first rider from his country to stand on the Tour podium, then to win a stage, and then the following year to win the Tour itself. Not long after that historic victory he sustained a sporting injury in California: not hurt in a bike crash but peppered with shotgun pellets in a shooting accident that he was lucky to survive. He thus missed the 1987 and 1988 races, but was back to win one more in 1989, though by the barest of margins, in an exceptionally exciting race. Jean-Pierre Carensio was now director general of the Tour, with Dominique Pasquier as administrative director, and they devised a course from Luxembourg to Brittany to the south-west and the mountains, with 198 riders selected on international rankings, divided into twenty-two teams of nine men each, eighteen teams invited in advance, joined by four 'wild card teams' (the French for which is – despite the best efforts of the Académie Française and all other foes of Franglais – 'les wild cards'), which selected themselves on merit before the Tour. Fiat was now an official partner; Bernard Thévenet rejoined the Tour as a journalist; and although there was still a prize for best young rider, won by Fabrice Philipot as it proved, his white jersey was mysteriously abolished.

If ever there was a year when France would have loved to win, it was this, the *bicentenaire* of the French Revolution. From a race whose total length was 3285 kilometres, it was calculated with magnificent meticulosity that the field would reach exactly the 1789-kilometre point at Martres-Tolosane, between Luchon and Blagnac, where the first rider to cross the line received a special prime of 17,890 francs. But the sentimental anniversary brought France no luck. Any idea that it would be a rerun of the previous year almost vanished at the start, now once again called a

Prologue, when Delgado managed to turn up late in his champion's yellow jersey, saying sadly, 'I didn't notice time passing.' He wasn't disqualified, but lost almost three minutes, which he never recovered.

By the fifth stage, a time trial into Rennes won by LeMond, the race had become a duel between him and Fignon. And what a duel! LeMond had made himself conspicuous in more ways than one by turning up with triathlon-style handlebars, which the commissaires had eventually if irritably allowed him to use. He now held the yellow jersey for five days into the Pyrenees, where a stage to Pau began from La Bastide d'Armagnac; or rather, and reverently, from the church of Notre Dame des Cyclistes, founded by the Abbé Massie. Two days later the Cauterets–Superbagnères stage was won by Millar. It was this Scotsman's lucky airt – he had won stages close by in 1983 and 1984, when he was fourth in the Tour – and he rode a blinder. The race hotted up on the Tourmalet, when Pascal Richard of Switzerland attacked, and then Millar and Charly Mottet dropped him before the summit. They were twenty-eight seconds ahead of LeMond and a pursuing group before Delgado joined them with an alarmingly fast descent, got away from them less than a mile from the line, only to be heroically caught and just passed by Millar.

But Fignon took the GC lead, and held it across the Midi to the Alps and Gap. Asked his opinion at this point, Leblanc showed rather more acumen than many sports officials by saying that LeMond and Fignon had nothing between them in the mountains, 'but I think LeMond will beat Fignon in the time trial and win the Tour.' LeMond soon regained the yellow jersey, but Fignon hadn't given in. Two days later he climbed into l'Alpe d'Huez and back into the lead, which he held for four more days, until the final time trial from Versailles to Paris: no more than 28.5 kilometres to ride, but all-important. LeMond now knew precisely what he had to do, to beat Fignon by fifty-one seconds.

Riders in a time trial set off in reverse order – bottom of the GC first, yellow jersey last – so that LeMond left just before his rival. He blistered his way to the Champs-Élysées on a ferocious 54 × 12 gear and crossed the line in 26'57".

As Fignon approached, his ponytail bobbing behind the yellow jersey, the huge crowd was in unbearable suspense to see if he could match LeMond's time. He couldn't. He lost that lead, and eight more seconds besides, to leave the smallest margin by which the Tour was ever lost and won. A crestfallen Fignon conceded defeat gracefully if a little platitudinously: 'I have nothing against LeMond. Sport is made up of victories and defeats. Life does not stop here.' But there, in terms of his own career, he was sadly wrong. He was never in the big time again, and retired in 1993.

What neither he nor the gloomiest French fan could have guessed was that no French rider would win the Tour again before it reached its own centenary in 2003. An American, an Irishman, Spaniards, a Dane, a German and an Italian; but still no Frenchman has won since Hinault. Fignon's victory in the 1989 Milan–San Remo was a last French flourish, for male cyclists at least. The national hero of the bicentennial year was a heroine: Jeannie Longo won a clutch of women's titles, including the French championship, a third Tour de France, and fourth road World Championship.

After his heart-stopping victory over Fignon, LeMond won his third and last Tour in 1990 less excitingly, and more decisively. The lead was taken at the Prologue by Thierry Marie – who had won a couple of stages in previous races and worn the yellow jersey in 1986 – before Bauer took over, followed by Ronan Pensec and Claudio Chiappucci. LeMond didn't win a single stage, but gradually worked his way to the head of the GC. Poor Fignon abandoned on the fifth stage, and LeMond's victory seemed foregone, despite a brave race by the Italian Chiappucci, whose chances were blown away on the penultimate day in another time trial; he finished the Tour second at 2′16″. A notably international Tour saw Raul Alcalá, who had the previous year been the first Mexican to win a stage, win another, the Vittel–Epinal time trial; and more happily still, the fall of the Berlin Wall the year before and the implosion of the Soviet empire were marked by the presence of east European riders, and the first ever Russian stage victory, Dmitri Konishev winning Lourdes–Pau.

A year later Chiappucci won a well-deserved King of the Mountains prize, and was third overall, but there was nothing that he or anyone else, including LeMond, could do in 1991 to stop the inexorable, the invincible, the incomparable Miguel Induráin, as he began what would be the first run of five consecutive victories in the history of the Tour. Other riders had their days. Marie won the Prologue in Lyons and then, after the race had ridden north to Dijon, Rheims and Valenciennes, he won the sixth stage from Arras to Le Havre with a solo escape of 234 kilometres, one of the longest in the history of the Tour. He had retaken the lead from LeMond and then the Dane Soerensen when the luckless Soerenson fell at Valenciennes and experienced the very unusual misfortune of being eliminated while wearing the yellow jersey. LeMond regained the lead at Alençon, though not for very much longer.

Two days after Mauro Ribeiro had become the first Brazilian to win a stage, there was more drama on the Quimper–St-Herblan stage, when the whole PDM team fell ill and abandoned. From there, or more precisely from Nantes, the whole race transferred to Pau by air; or more precisely the riders and teams officials did, while a tail of more than 600 journalists and 140 photographers, representing some 350 papers and 20 television channels, pelted down the coast by car. And so did Urs Zimmermann, for which infraction of not flying he was pedantically ejected from the race, until a protest by other riders had him reinstated.

The race was decided in the Pyrenees. LeMond faltered on the Tourmalet, the lead passed to Luc Leblanc, Induráin seized control on the thirteenth stage into Val Louron, and he never looked back through Midi, Alps and Burgundy, winning the penultimate stage to Mâcon before sealing victory the next day in Paris. A last dramatic flourish was provided by the Russians, with Konyshev winning the last stage and Djamolidine Abdoujaparov – a Soviet rider until his native Uzbekistan became independent – winning the green jersey, despite taking a tumble in the Champs-Élysées. At the end, Induráin won comfortably from the Italians Gianni Bugno and Claudio Chiappucci, both of whom, as well as Leblanc in fifth, had acquitted themselves admirably.

There was nothing sudden about the great Spaniard's arrival on the podium. Anquetil and Fignon had each won the Tour on his debut. Induráin had already ridden in the race six times in six years between 1985 and 1990, failing to complete twice, then rising steadily through 97th, 47th, 17th and 10th places, a tribute both to his determination and still more to the wisdom of his mentors. Born in 1964 in Villava, close to Pamplona where the bulls run, Miguel Induráin Larraya – to give him his name in the full Spanish form – had won the amateur road-race championship of Spain before he was twenty, and before he was taken under the wing of the remarkable José Miguel Echávarri. Induráin had been a track athlete, 400-metre champion of Navarre, at a time when Echávarri was running a bar in Pamplona and working part-time as a coach. His talents being noticed, Echávarri was hired as *directeur sportif* of the all-Spanish Reynolds team, in whose colours Delgado was riding when he won the Tour in 1988, and he took Induráin along with him. Their compatriot, the journalist and novelist Javier García Sánchez, who knew them both well, described Echávarri as the diametrical opposite of Induráin, 'talkative, seductive, a lover of understatement, elaborate turns of phrase and wordplay'. Those of us who lack the language of Cervantes and Quevedo must take that on trust, just as we must suppose that Hispanic under-statement includes Echávarri's comparison of Induráin with a religious building, or his saying that 'It has been by the grace of God that this land of pastures and healthy cork trees has enjoyed Miguel's skills.'

However that might be, Echávarri was a splendid tutor, whose thoughtful and protective coaching was a contrast to the way some more grasping men in his position would have behaved with a rider as good as Induráin. Echávarri saw the young man as an 'apprentice' on his first two Tours, and it was he who told the apprentice to abandon before he took too much out of himself. On his second Tour, when the race reached Pau, Induráin was keen to go on, but Echávarri didn't want him to tackle the Pyrenees as yet, and discreetly summoned his father from across the border. Induráin described the scene: 'I was in my pyjamas when my father arrived. "Come on," he said, "we're going home. I need you for the harvest." So I got dressed, picked up my things and we returned to Villava by way of Arnéguy and Roncevaux.' That was before he carefully worked his way up the GC year by year, until his first victory and then his second.

Aptly enough, the 1992 Tour began in Spain, just across the border in San Sebastian with a Prologue just as aptly won by Induráin. He shortly ceded the yellow jersey to the remarkable young Swiss Alex Zülle, while French hopes were raised by a whole new crop of 'revelations': Richard Virenque, who next took the lead, and Pascal Lino who succeeded him and wore the yellow jersey for all of eleven days, from Bordeaux to St-Gervais, all the way through west, north, Belgium, Luxembourg and Alsace. The next stage to Sestrières was won brilliantly by Chiappucci, who finished the race in second, with the Mountains prize, and for the second year running that quaintly named Prix de la Combativité (it may be just as well that no such prize for 'most aggressive' competitor is awarded in other sports; the

Arsenal back four and the Leicester front row need no encouragement).

But it was there that Induráin took the lead, and held it for more than a week to the finish. Another American had come to the fore, Andrew Hampsten winning an Alpine stage, to finish in fourth. A young French star rose who would capture, if sometimes break, his country's heart, when Laurent Jalabert took the green jersey. Roche was ninth and nearing the end of his career. As a consolation prize he received another curious award, the new and as it proved short-lived 'Trophée du Fair-play', won the next year by Gianni Bugno before it silently lapsed, leaving cynics to suppose that fair play had only been seen in two out of ninety runnings of the Tour.

It might have sounded cynical also of Hinault to say that 'Induráin is the best cyclist of his generation, but he won this Tour without any worries or any great opposition. If his rivals continue to let him get away with it, there's a chance that his reign is going to last a while.' But that was just as it proved. Almost repetitiously, Induráin came to the 1993 Tour from winning the Giro, and again began by winning the Prologue, in Puy-du-Fou, before the race headed north through Brittany and Normandy. He lost the yellow jersey, which passed from one rider to another, before the Châlons-sur-Marne–Verdun stage, which was momentous and portentous: it was won by the young Texan Lance Armstrong, who also won the World Championship this year. But this Tour was decided by the following stage, the Lac de Madine time trial. Induráin won despite a puncture to regain the lead and hold it thence to the finish.

The only rider who came near landing a blow was Tony Rominger, who won a couple of stages in the Alps, and then won a time trial on the penultimate day by a whopping forty-two seconds from Induráin. But the Swiss had very unluckily had time docked after that time trial because of a penalty imposed on his team, and Induráin had 4′59″ on him at the line in the

Champs-Élysées the next day. Rominger had to be contented with the Mountains prize, of which he was the first Swiss winner. Honourable mentions also went to Zenon Jaskula in third, the first Pole ever on the podium, and Johan Bruyneel, who from Evreux to Amiens rode the fastest stage in the history of the Tour, at an average of 49.417 k.p.h. (Elsewhere in the cycling calendar great acclaim was showered on two riders who broke the hour record, Graham Obree at Hamar and Chris Boardman at Bordeaux.)

Otherwise it was all Induráin again – and little for French comfort. Only one stage in the 1993 Tour was won by a Frenchman, Pascal Lino from Montpellier to Perpignan, and the highest French rider in the final placings was Philippe Dojwa in fifteenth. There appeared to be some salve for national pride when Olympique of Marseilles beat AC Milan to win the European Cup, but even that soured when a bribery and match-fixing scandal erupted around the club and Marseilles was ejected from the competition.

Nor was there much French joy in 1994, when cycling had a notably multinational flavour. Russia had her triumphs, with Andrei Tchmil winning the Paris–Roubaix and Evgeny Berzin the Giro, and England had hers with Chris Boardman winning the Prologue, and Yates also wearing the yellow jersey in Rennes. In between these two English successes the Tour had visited England through the new Channel tunnel to ride stages from Dover to Brighton and to Portsmouth. The next stage was historic in another sense, from Cherbourg to Rennes by way of Utah Beach. Nearby at Saint-Lô there was special memorial prime to mark the fiftieth anniversary of the D-Day landings, won a trifle ironically by a German rider, Olaf Ludwig.

Before the Pyrenees Induráin had already won the Périgueux–Bergerac time trial to claim the yellow jersey. A stage to Cahors was won by Jacky Durand, who had finished well down the field the two previous years. Although he didn't complete this year, it marked the beginning of his hugely popular career as an escapologist, delighting the French public with his long lonely breaks. The next stage from Lourdes gratified the pious when, forty-six years after the God-fearing Bartali had won there, another devout Catholic did so, with Luc Leblanc heading Induráin, before Virenque made a splendid solo escape the next day to win into Luz-Ardidien. One more such stirring exploit saw the Italian Eros Poli, a stalwart of the peloton, make a glorious 171-kilometre escape to lead over Mont Ventoux and into Carpentras, before the Alps bestowed more prizes, two of them, Moûtiers–Cluses and Cluses–Avoriaz, on Letton Ugrumov (Soviet when his career began, then Latvian), who also rode a smashing last stage from Disneyland to the Champs-Élysées. But he was still more than five minutes behind the untouchable Induráin. The previous year's form wasn't confirmed: poor Rominger, second in 1993, had abandoned in exhaustion on the thirteenth stage, and Dojwa, the best French rider that year, also pulled out. Even sadder misfortune had early befallen the other young French hero, when a bad fall on the first stage took him out of the race. But Jalabert would be back.

This was Induráin's fourth Tour out of the five he would win, and it should have been an exalted moment for his country. And yet, the Tour had begun under a dark shadow, tragic especially for Spanish cycling. On 19 May, less than seven weeks before the race had begun, Luis Ocaña had been found at his home where he had settled at Caupenne d'Armagnac, south of Bordeaux and not far from the Pyrenees and Spain, with a bullet wound in his head and a gun beside him. A doctor couldn't revive him, and nor could the staff at the hospital at Mont-de-Marsan when he was rushed there. He was forty-eight. Two decades after his victory in the 1973 Tour, things had not gone well for him. He had taken up wine-making but had recently experienced serious financial difficulties, he had separated from his wife, he had contracted hepatitis C, the treatment for which had debilitated and depressed him, and he had been obliged to pull out of his job as a radio commentator on the Vuelta while it was being run.

Whatever the reasons, the suicide of a second Tour winner, just over eighty-seven years after Pottier hanged himself, shocked every cyclist, including his great rival. 'I couldn't have had worse news,' Eddy Merckx said. 'He had told me about his financial difficulties and his family problems, but I didn't think it was as severe as that. He was a fighter, an honest and courageous man.' Decent words, but grim words, by one man who knew what the Tour could exact, about another who had paid a far higher price.

Repos

Savoy

Rather more than two hundred years ago, the English discovered Nature, and at just the same time they invented tourism. In the eighteenth century young noblemen made the Grand Tour through France, Germany and Italy, and the word was then extended: 'tourist' appears for the first time in 1780, as such enthusiasts found contemplation of the new-found beauties of lakes and fells in the north-west of England. Maps of the Lake District in the 1790s were engraved 'for the Tourists', and by 1811 a reference to 'Cockney Tourism' suggests that the word had already acquired its sometimes opprobrious modern overtones.

Keener tourists looking for grander views had already moved further afield than Cumberland, and the Alps had begun its new career as Europe's greatest scenic attraction. No one then could have foreseen the day when 'alpinism' or mountain-climbing would take so many muscular Christians, or indeed muscular agnostics in Leslie Stephen's case, from Oxford and Cambridge to explore those peaks. Later in the late nineteenth century tobogganing would be invented (by English sportsmen, of course) at St Moritz, before the previously utilitarian gadgets called skis would be adapted for downhill sport (English again to the fore), and from modest beginnings become a multi-billion-Euro business bringing tens of millions to the Alps each winter.

Nor did anyone guess the thrill and the thrall of the world's greatest bike race crossing a series of now-hallowed passes in the great mountains every summer: not in 1816 when Byron first visited the Alps, to find 'the music of the Cows' Bells . . . in the pastures (which reach to a height far above any mountains in Britain) and the shepherds' shouting to us from crag to crag & playing on their reeds where the steeps appeared almost inaccessible, with the surrounding scenery . . . pure and unmixed – solitary – savage and patriarchal – the effect I cannot describe,' which was the way that scenery would take many people from then until now, making them feel superior in the process. His banal words about 'any mountains in Britain' didn't stop Byron sneering at a commonplace Englishwoman who was gawping over the 'rural' scenery as if it were no more than Hampstead or Highgate.

In his own tour surveying the components of the national genius, Michelet traversed the Dauphiné towards Savoy, the modern departments of Isère, Savoie and Haute-Savoie. Some of what he said could sound a little fusty or sententious:

> The virile genius of the women of the Dauphiny has often exercised irresistible power over men; as for instance, the famous Madame Tencin, d'Alembert's mother, and that washerwoman of Grenoble [Claudine Mignot], who married husband after husband until she at last married the king of Poland. There is a frank and lively simplicity, a mountaineer grace, about the people of Dauphiny, which charms one at first sight. As you ascend towards the Alps, you meet with the honesty of the Savoyard, the same kindness, but with less gentleness. Men, here, must love one another perforce, – for nature seemingly loves them but little.

And yet this particular generalization may not seem so silly to those who know and love that corner of the *hexagone*. There really is a friendliness about the Savoyards, which one encounters over and again, winter and summer; and Michelet might have had a point about human nature reacting to the threat of the harsh environment, as seafarers and miners are warmer and more companionable than city folk. The Alps may be a playground today, but that could only happen once wild nature had been tamed: the contemplation of natural beauty only became possible when it no longer represented a mortal threat. For most of history these mountains had not been sublime but terrifying, offering only the most scanty, hard-fought-for living to those who lived among them, and always echoing with sudden death.

For most of history this province was also independent of France. Dauphiné or Dauphiny was one of the successor-states of the break up of Charlemagne's empire (or a successor-state of the successor-states). In the twelfth century its rulers adopted the title of Dauphin of Viennois; and then when the childless Humbert II sold his principality to the King of France in 1349, he made a condition that the king's eldest son and heir should thenceforth be known as the Dauphin, just as the eldest son of the King of England had recently become known as Prince of Wales. To the north-east Savoy remained sovereign for much longer. The ruling house founded by another Humbert, 'aux blanches Mains', the white-handed, in the eleventh century, gradually extended its territories to cover much of what is now north-eastern Italy, the Valais and Vaud in Switzerland, Bugey and Bresse. In the thirteenth century the dynasty established an English connection when Henry III of England married Eleanor of Savoy and made his father-in-law, Count Pierre II, Earl of Richmond, whose brother became Archbishop of Canterbury. It was Pierre who built the Savoy Palace on the north bank of the Thames west of Blackfriars, where its name remains. If 'Burgundy' in English means a wine and a colour, 'Savoy' in London means the Savoy Chapel of slightly dodgy reputation ('What a squalid wedding!' Celia tells Charles of her own in *Brideshead Revisited*: 'the Savoy Chapel was the place where divorced couples got married in those days'), the Savoy Hotel with its much-networked Grill, and the Savoy Operas of Gilbert and Sullivan, first performed at the Savoy Theatre.

Like Burgundy, Savoy enjoyed a period of greatness in the late Middle Ages, under a series of rulers called Amadeus, one of whom, Amadeus VIII, was made Duke of Savoy and Piedmont by the Emperor in the early fifteenth century. Like Burgundy, Savoy came into conflict with France. Like Burgundy, Savoy might, if the tides of history had flowed differently, have remained an independent state. It still was one in the eighteenth century, when the great general Victor Amadeus II fought against the French in the war of the Austrian Succession, and then, in one of those shufflings of chips on the board in which the *ancien régime* delighted, his house picked up Sicily, swapped it for Sardinia, regained their lands after the Revolutionary and Napoleonic period, but became almost without noticing it Italian princes. Victor Emanuel I of Sardinia was the future king of Italy anointed by the Risorgimento (hence the pre-unification slogan 'Viva Verdi', addressing the great national composer of the Risorgimento, could also subversively intend 'Viva *V*ittorio *E*mmanuele *Re d'I*talia'). On his way to the top in 1860 he struck a secret deal with Napoleon III in the treaty of Plombières, finally severing his family's ancient connection with Savoy when he ceded it to France. And there Savoy has remained, although that didn't stop Mussolini including 'Savoia', along with Nizza and Corsica, in his irredentist demands on France, not without historical reason.

The capital of the Dauphiny is Grenoble, once a pleasant small town, now a flourishing city whose population has quadrupled since 1945, with a famous university and high-tech industries including a very prominent 'Synchrotron' particle accelerator. Alas for Grenoble, its most famous son hated the place, its society, and his own complacent lawyer father, who was – said Henri Beyle, otherwise Stendhal – 'the least elegant, the most cunning, the shrewdest, in a word the most Dauphinois of men'. In what was one of the first manifestations of that not uniquely but peculiarly French phenomenon, bourgeois self-hatred, he said that 'Everything that is mean and vulgar in the bourgeois way reminds me of Grenoble, everything that reminds me of Grenoble fills me with horror, no horror is too noble a word, with nausea . . .'

Few who have followed the Tour on any of the thirty-seven occasions it has visited Grenoble are likely to share Stendhal's neurotic rage. They are more likely to look in at the fine museums, including the old church of St-Laurent, and then maybe lunch at the Chaumière at Voiron not far to the north-west, or due south at the Chalet in Gresses-en-Vercors. Not that all memories of the Vercors, that massif often crossed by the riders, are pleasant. Grenoble was occupied by the Italians after the fall of France but became a great centre of the Resistance, as was the Vercors. In the summer of 1944 one of the largest risings of the Resistance seized much of the up-country on the plateau, strengthened by paratroops dropped in, but ferociously crushed: at Vassieux-en-Vercors is a memorial to the many résistants who were captured, often wounded, and massacred there by the Germans before liberation came just too late to save them.

A few other literary echoes are heard in Savoy. There are two pretty lakes, the Lac d'Annecy, with the town of Annecy at its head, visited a couple of times by the Tour, and the Lac de Bourget with the spa town of Aix-les-Bains, twenty-two times a *ville-étape*, on its west bank, and Chambéry to the south, in a house outside which the regrettable Jean-Jacques Rousseau wrote his *Confessions*. Lamartine was sent to Aix for his health and fell in love with a married woman who died soon after, a doomed romance that inspired his poem 'Le Lac'.

Higher up in Savoy there are fewer writers' memories, which isn't surprising given how inaccessible and poor it was until recently. Equally the Savoy has a somewhat limited cuisine of its own, apart from the indigenous raclette and the not-so-indigenous fondue, both direly indigestible and neither anything like as good as the simple cold meats and mountain cheeses found in any village shop. The village of Cordon, lying below the ski resorts of Megève and Cluses and the Col des Aravis – all on the seventeenth stage in 2002 – does have not only a couple of grand hotels but, what is rarer in these parts, a comfortable simple hotel, the Cordonant, with very good and modestly priced food. But for *cuisine savante*, you need to return towards Grenoble. A few minutes to its south-east is the superb Grand Hotel at Uriage-les-Bains, as good a place as could be to fortify oneself before setting off on a long circuit over those famous Tour passes, the Col du Glandon, Col de la Croix de Fer, then south to the Col du Galibier, Col du Lauteret, Col d'Izoard, Col de Vars, with the Col d'Allos further south, each of them with its own distinctive characteristic and allure.

Merely driving over these – in winter if they aren't closed by snow as they often are, or in summer, before or after the Tour is run – is taxing enough to make anyone hungry and thirsty, and Embrun beckons. 'The Nice of the Alps' is a slightly hyperbolic tag, and an unnecessary one, since it is a really delightful town on its own terms, sitting on the high reaches of the Durance, with a fine twelfth-century cathedral and the neighbouring Tour Brune. In mid-winter the place Mairie is turned into a skating rink, and there are street fairs selling Christmas presents. Pictures of the Tour hang in cafés round the square, on one side of which is the Hotel Mairie with its admirable restaurant. I shall be there when the ninth stage of the centennial Tour de France passes through Embrun from Bourg d'Oissan to Gap on the *quatorze juillet* 2003, before watching the riders once again cross those great passes.

They may have their own fascination and majesty, but the peloton never faces any of them without some sense of dread. Seeing the field climb several thousand metres in an icy wind after covering 150 kilometres in baking heat, you might wonder in seriousness whether the human frame was possibly intended for this ordeal, and what it does to the riders. When the Tour de France began life a hundred years ago, the men who rode in it weren't such unusual physical specimens, but average artisans of their day, though plainly a good deal fitter and stronger than most. Nor has cycling ever been a sport for freaks, or oddities, in the way that some have. No one can play in the scrum for an international rugby team today who weighs much under 16 stone or 100 kilos, or play as a linebacker for an NFL team who weighs much less than 280 pounds, or play basketball in an NBA team who is much shorter than 7 foot. Soccer is happily still a game which men of normal build can play at the highest level. With a Giggs or a Zidane, lack of stature is more than made up for by agility and skill, not to say sheer courage, though even on the football field goalies seem to be growing bigger all the time.

Although the tiny cyclists seen on earlier Tours mightn't flourish now, some are still quite short, and many are slight. The physique of a shot-putter or sumo wrestler would obviously not be ideal on a bike, or even that of some track sprinters, and the frame for a cyclist tends to be wiry and compact. Standing amid the riders before the start, or watching them working on rollers, you see nothing very startling in appearance, apart from the rather kinky shaved arms and legs (so that grazes and gashes with dirt and gravel can be quickly cleaned and dressed without hair getting in the way), and the fearsome muscles, too often rippled by varicose veins.

What now distinguishes the bodies of great cycling champions is invisible to the eye: they are likely not to be conspicuous from the outside, but to have almost freakish internal organs. Lance Armstrong's heart is a third larger than those of most men of his height and weight. And Miguel Induráin's lungs are wholly abnormal, so huge that at full stretch they displace much of his stomach. In his prime he could inhale eight litres (almost two gallons) of air in a breath, against a normal man's four. And with that, his resting pulse of twenty-eight beats a minute was half the rate of a fit amateur racing cyclist, let alone a man watching the Tour in a bar.

But if the physique, strength and stamina of Tour riders is extraordinary, what racing takes out of them is alarming. It is impossible (though it would be interesting) to ascertain the dates of birth and death of every one of the men, now approaching 4500 in number, who have ridden in the Tour. It is possible (though it might be statistically misleading) to give an average life expectancy for Tour winners. What's for sure is that many have died before their time, and the more so as the twentieth century went by, when life expectancy was of course steadily increasing in France and throughout the West. Winners in the first quarter-century include one man who died by his own hand, three killed in action, and one who was murdered. Others lived to ripe old ages, beginning with Maurice Garin, winner of the 1903 Tour, who died at eighty-five. His immediate successors Henri Cornet and Louis Trousselier died at fifty-six and fifty-seven; after those deaths from non-natural causes of Pottier, Petit-Breton, Faber and Lapize, the last winners before the Great War, Gustave Garrigou, Odile Defraye and Philippe Thys, all lived to more than seventy-five, well over the average for their generation, as did the post-war winners Firmin Lambot and Léon Scieur.

Then comes a sudden premonition with Henri Pélissier, who died at only forty-six. Sylvère Maes died at fifty-seven, Lucien Buysse and Nicolas Frantz lived to their eighties, André Leducq, Antonin Magne and Georges Speicher to their seventies, and Romain Maes to sixty-nine. Of other prewar winners, Roger Lapébie and Gino Bartali both died at eighty-five, and of post-war winners as I write, Ferdi Kubler is eighty-three, Roger Walkowiak, Charly Gaul and Federico Bahamontes are all in their seventies.

Against them is a more striking necrology. Among riders who won the Tour after the Second World War, Jean Robic died at fifty-nine, Fausto Coppi at forty, Hugo Koblet at thirty-nine, Louison Bobet at fifty-eight, Jacques Anquetil at fifty-three, Gastone Nencini at forty-nine, Luis Ocaña at forty-eight and, only in February 2004, Marco Pantani, aged thirty-four. That is, six out of the ten riders who won the Tour between 1947 and 1960 died before they were sixty. As with the pre-1914 period, these included violent deaths:

'The pedlar of charm' Koblet died in a car crash in 1964, as did Robic in 1980, and Ocaña had been the second Tour winner to commit suicide. Nevertheless, the other five died of what are called natural causes, and at an average age just under fifty-two.

In several cases the primary cause was cancer, and the Tour was to have another still more famous 'cancer victim', but one who survived and conquered; we look at Armstrong's fantastic story in the next chapter. There doesn't appear to be any direct connection between riding and cancer, although doctors observe that cycling does have other specific dangers: a man riding a bicycle (as opposed to a horse or even motorbike) is much of the time holding the weight of his torso on the very base of the penis where blood and nerves enter, and this is likely to explain why, among the other sacrifices they make for their sport, cyclists have an unusually high rate of both sterility and impotence (in their correct respective senses of inability to procreate and inability to copulate). And one must wonder whether there is a connection between the racing cyclists' rate of mortality and their way of life.

When the great cols are climbed in sunshine but between snow-banks, as sometimes happens, it might be designed by a perverse medical scientist to cause bronchitis and pneumonia, but in any case riding a bike up the Galibier is not a normal activity. The development of those organs isn't normal either: heart and lungs are remarkably elastic, and although Induráin and Armstrong are plainly physical prodigies, their careers have made their bodies more prodigious still. With men not quite so tough in the first place, the strain put on the heart by cycling may tax it beyond the limit.

And that's without artificial stimulants. 'I get no kick from cocaine,/Mere alcohol doesn't thrill me at all . . .': even in the first half of the century, many riders could not have convincingly sung 'I Get a Kick Out of You', as they consumed heroic quan-tities of both, even before the vogue for amphetamines. All of those are mood-altering as much as performance-enhancing drugs. They make you feel good, they keep you going, they tell you you're riding better, but they don't do the body much good. All of those deceased champions rode before the new generation of drugs that swept through sport in the last decades of the twentieth century, different in kind rather than degree from cocaine, or *la bomba*. Growth hormones and EPO (erythropoietin) don't quell tiredness or lift the spirits, they actually alter the metabolism. Cancer doctors deal with a very wide range of drugs for different purposes; in England they not long ago used quite legally to prescribe moderate doses of cocaine and heroin as effective painkillers for those in extreme suffering, and EPO, like many drugs forbidden to, but used by, athletes is no more than an artificially or synthetically manufactured version of a hormone produced naturally by the human body: one of the complications of Armstrong's story, and the accusations against him, was that he had indeed been prescribed EPO as part of his cancer treatment. Hormones produce dramatic and unnatural growth, as could be seen with plenty of East European shot-putters and weightlifters, not to mention the alarming effects that they can have on someone's gender balance. EPO raises the red-corpuscle count in the bloodstream, which sends more oxygen to the muscles and makes them tougher and more endurant. Julian Barnes may be exaggerating slightly when he says that, of two riders of equal ability, 'the one taking EPO will always beat the one who remains clean; it is as simple as that', but not exaggerating much, and it was no wonder that this miracle drug became so popular.

With the same will to win outweighing sense and safety, few riders bothered to learn that this wonder drug could be literally lethal, thickening the blood and leading to clotting. A number of otherwise inexplicable heart attacks in the middle of the night must be put down to this cause. Or maybe riders did know, just as they knew Simpson's principle: 'If it takes ten to kill you, I'll have nine,' and were even prepared to dice with ten. Whatever the exact medical explanations, the great race consumed all too many victims.

15

L'affaire Festina

1995–1998

After nine years without a victory, the mood of French cycling was nervy and a little sour, and possibly the mood of France also. In 1995 Mitterand's long and ultimately sordid presidency ended, and he was succeeded by the conservative Jacques Chirac, not yet as assertive and self-confident as he had become by early 2003, but already consciously shouldering the mantle of de Gaulle. Sporting expressions of Gaullism weren't so easy to come by. France was the best of the northern-hemisphere countries in this year's rugby World Cup but still third behind South Africa and New Zealand, and although the French football team won a record 10–0 victory, this might have been more impressive if the opponents hadn't been Azerbaijan. There were some French achievements in cycling, with Jeannie Longo returning to her best to win two gold medals in the World Championships. And this was 'l'année Jalabert', with the hugely popular 'Ja Ja' heading the UCI classification after he had won Paris–Nice, Milan–San Remo and the Vuelta, as well as taking the green jersey in the Tour, in which he wore the yellow jersey early on and led his ONCE team to victory in the team classification. All the same, when the yellow jersey really mattered, on the last day, he could come no higher than fourth. The new president of the Tour's parent company was the great skier Jean-Claude Killy, but even that only seemed to emphasize that French success was nowadays more likely on the piste than the *parcours*.

After a Prologue in St-Brieuc won by Jacky Durand, the race had left Brittany for Normandy and crossed the new Pont de Normandie over the Seine estuary on the way from Alençon to Le Havre. The lead passed from Durand to Jalabert to Gotti to Riis to Bruyneel, who won the Charleroi–Liège stage in his native Belgium, before Induráin flexed his muscles in the Ardennes. On the Huy–Seraing time trial he struck. They were riding in a heat-wave, with the temperature touching 34°C (93°F), but a scorching pace was set by the Danish rider Bjarne Riis, fortified by wearing the yellow jersey the day before. With only five kilo-metres to go to the line, Induráin learned that he was five seconds behind Riis. Pumping his incredible lungs, he went into overdrive as no other rider could have done, not only to close the gap but to finish twelve seconds ahead. A crestfallen Riis said, 'I didn't know I was that close. I just lacked the guts to finish it off.'

He was being hard on himself: nobody could have matched Induráin that day, as he hit an average speed of 50.4 k.p.h. for the 54 kilometres, to win the stage and take the GC lead, which he now held for two weeks more through the Alps and the Pyrenees and round back to Paris, winning the remaining time trial at Lac de Vassivière on the penultimate day to be on the safe side. In this way Induráin rode what had become the standard winning Tour of recent times: choose an advantageous point to take the lead, take it, and then hold it. It's held carefully rather than dashingly, which means by methodical teamwork, the *domestiques* riding in hard and disciplined fashion to protect their leader, and their leader's lead. Induráin himself said that 'My plan was to build a gap between me and my main rivals, including the best climbers.'

He also emphasized the importance of working with the team, insisting that there is no point in being aggressive or abusive: 'I never shout or scream at my team-mates. You achieve more by having several good friends around you,' as indeed he did. It may have taken some of the suspense and the glamour out of the Tour, but it worked.

There were sadder stories in the course of this race, and one tragedy. The decent and admirable Chris Boardman crashed badly in the rain and abandoned on the Prologue: 'It was dark and I couldn't see where the slippery patches were on the road. I was pushing it a bit too hard, doing about 80 k.p.h. downhill, when the back wheel slipped away,' whereupon he slid into the barriers and was then hit by a team car. But his woes were trivial compared with what happened eighteen days later in the Pyrenees on the St-Girons–Cauterets stage. Fabio Casartelli was an outstanding roadman, who had won the gold medal at the 1992 Barcelona Olympics. He hadn't completed his first Tour in 1994, but was riding well in his second when he crested the Col de Portet d'Aspet. Descending at full speed he crashed violently, flew off his bike, and went headfirst into a rock, splitting his skull open.

His monument at the place he died, the Stèle Casartelli, is more elegant than Simpson's on Mont Ventoux, a modestly modernistic, well designed and carefully polished stone which lists his achievements and mourns his passing. The next day, despite some riders who thought it an improper precedent, his Motorola team-mates were allowed to take the lead as the field approached Pau, where his room-mate Andrea Peron rode across the line first in tribute to the third rider to pay the ultimate price riding in the Tour de France.

Apart from Induráin there were several heroes this year. Pantani took two stages in the Alps and ended as best young rider, Virenque won the climber's jersey alongside Jalabert's green. In 1989, his first year as a pro, Jalabert had ridden in the

Kellogg's Tour of Britain as a more than competent *domestique*, returning the next year to ride in the race and lead for a couple of days. He had ridden in, and completed, the Tour in 1991 and 1992, abandoned in 1993, and then been knocked out of the 1994 race by the horrific pile-up at Armentières at the end of the first stage. In 1995 he bounced back to ride the best of many good races in the Tour before he retired in 2002 amid a great wave of emotion that swept round the country. He was by then at the peak of his form, and a most unusual all-rounder, sprinter, climber and time-triallist. On that Huy–Seraing stage he was caught by Induráin, a still greater time-triallist, but where most riders would have accepted defeat, Jalabert thought, 'Why not try and hang on?' and did so for many miles before Induráin finally dropped him.

Then on the climb to l'Alpe d'Huez, riding in the green sprinter's jersey as he had been for days past, Jalabert was passed by Pantani, who went on to win the stage, and by Virenque, who was wearing the mountain-man's red-peas jersey. Again, instead of gracefully conceding, Jalabert fought back to catch and drop Virenque. As an awestruck *Cycling Weekly* said, 'Riders in the green jersey are not supposed to do this to polka-dots on l'Alpe d'Huez!' And then again, on the *quatorze juillet*, Jalabert not only won the road stage from St-Étienne to Mende, with the help of his ONCE team (whose Alberto Leanizbarrutia once said that 'Ja Ja' was the cleverest of all strategists), he left Induráin, helpless for once, six minutes down on the day. There was one more portent in 1995: by winning the antepenultimate stage to Limoges, a second stage win to follow his first in 1993, Lance Armstrong announced that he was in the Tour to stay.

By contrast 1996 was very much not Jalabert's year, nor Induráin's either. After a Prologue in 's-Hertogenbosch (where Hieronymus came from) won by Zülle, the lead was taken by Frédéric Moncassin, a French stalwart of the peloton, and then by the French champion Stéphane Heulot, who was still wearing the yellow jersey when he abandoned on the seventh, Chambéry–Les Arcs stage won by Leblanc. There in the Alps two riders began to emerge from the field. Berzin won the Bourg-St-Maurice–Val-d'Isère stage and Riis, third the previous year, the next stage to Sestrières (which was much abbreviated from 189.5 to 46 kilometres after snow had closed the Iseran and Galibier) and took the lead. Others fell by the wayside. Jalabert was taken ill and also abandoned, while Induráin was showing unheard-of signs of flagging.

By the Pyrenees it was more than that. In his very own country, the stage to Pamplona, he slumped, and showed real courage to finish the race at all, let alone make it to eleventh place. The previous day Riis had decisively won the stage to Hautacam and now had the Tour in his grasp. He kept it there until the finish, when he became the first Danish rider to win. He was a good journeyman, whose seventh Tour this was, having abandoned twice while in the first five, in 1993 and 1995; not an unworthy winner, but maybe a lucky rather than a great one, as he suggested when coming seventh and eleventh in the next two years. One real champion had emerged. Erik Zabel of Germany won the green jersey, which he would make his private property, winning it for the next five years. There were two formidable team performances, by Telekom, for whom Riis rode, and by Festina who won the team prize. And the King of the Mountains for the third successive year was Richard Virenque. Within two years, the names of Virenque and Festina would have entered the annals of the Tour for very different reasons.

In Rouen on 5 July the 1997 Tour began very happily with a Prologue win for Boardman, before Mario Cipollini won the next two stages and took the lead. As the race headed south-west by way of Vire and Plumelec, Cédric Vasseur took over the yellow jersey at Le Châtre in Berry, dead south of Paris, after a 147-kilometre solo escape, and held it for five days. The race was now developing into a team duel, again between Festina and Telekom. Riis was Telekom's leader, but if anything his team-mate Jan Ullrich was looking better. By the Pyrenees he was also feeling better, but also felt bound by the code of loyalty. On the Luchon–Andorra stage there were five climbs. On the fourth Ullrich was itching to attack, but first dropped back to ask his team manager Walter Godefroot what he should do. Godefroot didn't hesitate, and told him to go for it; Riis would understand.

Riding like a man inspired, Ullrich escaped at the foot of the fifth and last climb to Arcalis. Only Virenque, destined to finish with his fifth consecutive red-peas jersey, could live with him as the others were dropped, before Ullrich dropped him too, reaching the line a minute clear of him and Pantani. Whether or not Riis really did understand may well be wondered: he was fifth for the stage, and seventh when they reached Paris nearly two weeks later. For Ullrich to win on only his second Tour was a feat, and it was a tribute to training methods in his native country. He was now a citizen of the Federal German Republic, but by birth and upbringing he was an 'Osti' or East German, and had benefited from the way in which that unlovely country had hand-picked promising athletes in all fields, treated them and their victories, notably at the Olympics, as a matter of national prestige, and given them every possible advantage, not least copious quantities of steroids when needed.

Whether or not that was true of Ullrich, he certainly didn't always confine himself to legal stimulants, as events would show. *Ein guter Kerl*, a good bloke, to the adoring German public, Ullrich had the reputation in the peloton of being a big baby, not to say a greedy baby in more ways than one. He was both a fine fierce climber and a dashing time-triallist, with a flair for winning big races, at least sometimes. But he suffered from constant problems with his weight, often putting on very many kilos in the off-season, which seemed to testify less to any special metabolic difficulty than plain lack of self-discipline. His intermittent will to win was matched by a lack of real mental fortitude, so that his career was punctuated with tantrums and feuds. And his appetite for money, as well as food, drink and at least recreational drugs, would have made him an unloved team-mate even when managers wanted him.

Maybe he should have retired after he stepped down from the podium on 27 July 1997. Maybe Virenque and Pantani, the second and third, should have done. Maybe every rider in the Tour should have done. Maybe the Tour de France should have ended there and then. If Ullrich knew his country's greatest writer, he might later have thought of his glorious day in the Champs-Élysées as that moment Goethe speaks of which, once lost, eternity will never give back.

After his third place, it was Pantani's turn to win in 1998. In another highly elastic definition of 'France', the Tour began in Dublin. I was in Ireland to watch the race in its second, rather tepid stage across Leinster and Munster from Enniscorthy to Cork won by Jan Svoroda (who was, more than usually confusingly, even in this time of the shaking of nations, a citizen of Czechoslovakia, then of Slovakia, then of the Czech Republic). There weren't many serious French contenders, but then the attention of sporting France was otherwise engaged. In the spring the French rugby team had won a back-to-back Grand Slam, which included (how are the mighty fallen!) a 51–0 trouncing of Wales, and in July the country was gripped by the World Cup, staged in France, and won by the home team when Brazil were beaten 3–0 in the final, to give France her first ever victory in the Cup and confirm the magnificent Zinédine Zidane as one of the country's greatest ever heroes.

An ironical Providence decided that the Prologue this year of all years would be won once more by Boardman, one of the purest spirits in sport, who never touched any illicit substance. He might have been thought a prig by some of his colleagues; he himself simply said that 'My own reasons for not taking drugs are ultimately more practical than moral. Why should I risk it?' He didn't want to damage his health, not for any victories, and the medical record of cycling, with the low life expectancy of cyclists, suggests that he was right. Too many others, maybe more driven than Boardman, maybe greedier, maybe with a greater will to win (if all those can be separated), were prepared to take any risk in the pursuit of success, even the ultimate risk that this might shorten their lives. Then Boardman had another fall on the second stage and had to abandon, for good as it turned out. Not long afterwards he left cycling to undergo treatment requiring medication at the hands of his doctors, prompting the memorable *Guardian* headline, 'Chris Boardman retires to take drugs'.

The yellow jersey subsequently passed to Zabel, Bo Hamburger of Denmark, Stuart O'Grady of Australia, Laurent Desbiens of France, and Ullrich, as the race, having crossed to Roscoff after its Irish sojourn, ran through Brittany and the west. There were two convenient detours. On the fifth stage from Cholet to Châteauroux the field rode through the village of Neuilly-les-Abiers, birthplace of the director-general of the Tour, Jean-Marie Leblanc, and two days later it finished in Corrèze, where Monsieur and Madame Jacques Chirac, the president of the republic and his wife, were happily present.

In the Alps there was a gallant last stand from Ullrich when he rode brilliantly over the Col de la Madeleine, to win the Vizille–Abertville stage. But the race had been decided the day before when Pantani took the stage from Grenoble to Les Deux Alpes to seize the lead. He then held it for the next week to win in Paris from Ullrich and the American Bobby Julich. Zabel took the green jersey, of course, two Frenchmen picked up prizes, Christophe Rinero the Mountains and Durand for *combativité*, and Ullrich was still best young rider.

This is how the eighty-fourth Tour de France was decided as a bike race; and to relate all of that is reminiscent of the lame joke, 'But how did you enjoy the play, Mrs Lincoln?' Everything else about the 1998 Tour had been overshadowed by what happened three days before it began and then the repercussions. Festina was a Spanish watchmaking company, registered in Andorra, which had gone into the Tour with a splash, collecting a talented and thus pricey team to sponsor, among them the French pin-up Virenque, with Bruno Roussel as *directeur sportif* and Willy Voet, a Belgian, as team *soigneur*. Although press people, as well as fans, drive their own cars when they follow the Tour, all the officials with teams as well as with the race itself drive logo-festooned cars laid on by sponsors, Fiat for some years.

On 7 July the Festina Fiat was picked up in Paris by Voet. He was meant to go to Calais, cross the Channel and then drive across England to catch another ferry to Ireland and the start of the race, but he first set off for Belgium, and was returning thence from Dronkaert, to Neuville-en-Ferrain in France on 8 July. On a country road, where traffic was very rarely stopped, he expected to go straight through. Maybe because its gaudy sponsors' devices caught their eye, maybe for no particular reason, the frontier guards flagged him down and asked to look inside. What they found changed cycling history. The Festina car was an enormous mobile pharmacy, containing just about every possible illicit performance-enhancing drug, from faintly démodé growth hormones to the *tout ce qu'il y à de chic* EPO, that formidable if dangerous blood-strengthening potion erythropoietin. The news of this discovery wasn't released until two days later, when there followed an epic of denial and evasion. Just before the race began, Roussel tried to disown Voet: 'We know nothing about this. End of statement.' The director of the Tour was scarcely more impressive. It had happened hundreds of kilometres away, Leblanc said with heroic disingenuousness. 'If it's a doping case, it's not directly connected to a rider and not directly connected to this race.' He would be eating those words before long, and so would Voet, who had, in his case with sublime chutzpah, initially insisted that all these medicaments were for his own personal use only.

By the third day of the race in Cholet, with the French police throwing their weight around and also leaking like sieves, it was public knowledge that Voet had admitted the drugs were for his riders. A shocked, utterly shocked Miguel Rodriguez, boss of Festina, said that if anything was proved his company would immediately cancel its sponsorship, while Roger Legeay, who was both coach of the GAN team and head of the French professional cyclists' league, said a little obviously that the Tour couldn't have the affair 'hanging over us. This must be resolved quickly.' Resolved it was, but not quickly. Roussel was arrested, as was the Festina team doctor, Eric Ryckaert, another Belgian, while everyone else shuddered with embarrassment and confusion. Bernard Thévenet, now a television commentator, may have taken the prize for meiosis when he said that 'It's a very delicate matter,' while Johnny Weltz, *directeur sportif* of US Postal, made his own contribution to the blindingly obvious: 'It's hard to figure out what's the real story.'

Before the Tour was a week old, enough of the real story was known for the whole Festina team to be expelled, Virenque, Zülle and all. They threatened a kind of anti-strike – they would ride anyway – until Leblanc told them not to be silly, and Virenque departed with a defiant 'Vive le Tour de France 1998!' Rodolfo Massi went more quietly when he was ejected from the race at Luchon after he had actually just won the stage and was wearing the red-peas jersey. Many other riders were angry, not at what Festina had done but at what was being done to them, and there was talk of a protest in solidarity as there had been with Delgado ten years before. But the riders mercifully thought better of it.

At least they did until the seventeenth stage, when the field stopped twice, the riders tore off their numbers to make it impossible for the stage to be officially controlled, and six teams withdrew: all of this not so much in solidarity as in protest at what they called the intolerably heavy-handed conduct of the police. There was even a kindling of sympathy outside the peloton after the TVM team had been rounded up in a sudden night raid on their hotel and taken to hospital for blood, urine and hair tests. 'They treated us like criminals, like animals,' Jeroen Blijlevens said, complaining that his roommate Bart Voskamp had been hauled out of the shower. After that, the flics were persuaded to conduct their inquiries with a gentler hand, and the riders were persuaded not to call off the Tour in mid-race for the first time in its history, as had looked for a moment on the cards. It may have been just as well that the riders and teams keenest on the most drastic forms of protest, such as Jalabert and ONCE, had already quit. US Postal by contrast took the opportunity to burnish its self-created straight-arrow reputation by saying that they must remain 'for the glory of the sport'.

There was no very satisfactory conclusion to *l'affaire Festina*, and little light was shed when the two prime suspects later published books with conflicting versions. Voet's wonderfully bumptious and evasive *Breaking the Chain: Drugs and Cycling – The True Story* with its implausible sub-title had been preceded by Virenque's *Ma Verité*, likewise one of the most ill-named books of the age, unless the title were intended ironically: What is truth? asked jesting Virenque, and did not stay for an answer. After a long period of denial, in both the legal and psychological senses, Virenque cracked under cross-examination in a courtroom and came clean, or at least a little cleaner. What both men finally said in effect was that they had done it, and that everyone was at it: drugs were rife throughout the game. And it had to be admitted that, whatever else Voet said, when he blithely recounted Virenque's preparation for a time trial in the 1997 Tour – 'Given his regular treatments of EPO and especially growth hormones, he was as ready as he would ever be. All he needed was a well-timed injection of caffeine, plus Solucamphre' – it had a ring of truth.

All of which only served to cast a cloud of suspicion over the whole race, which has yet to lift. Quite how many riders out of the 189 who had set off that year had been illicitly fuelled will never be known. 'Say it ain't so, Joe,' the heart-broken little boy called out to 'Shoeless' Joe Jackson, accused of throwing the 1919 World Series for the Chicago White Sox. No one said that now to the Tour riders; there was no innocence left to lose; everyone knew it was so.

16

The American Enemy

1999-2002

In the wake of the worst year in the history of the Tour something, or someone, was needed to rescue the race from the mire and mud of the Festina scandal. Sure enough, a great new champion came forward, who won four consecutive Tours to surpass Thys, Bobet and LeMond, and, as the Tour reached its centenary, stood every chance of equalling Anquetil, Merckx, Hinault and Induráin, the men who had won five times each, or even setting a new record of six victories. What's more, Lance Armstrong achieved his victories in peculiarly heroic personal circumstances. He should have been the white knight coming to the rescue of the Tour and erasing the stain. Alas, it didn't work out quite like that. For all Armstrong's heroism, he has achieved his victories amid a continual miasma of allegation and suspicion. Not only starry-eyed optimists wanted to see the Tour cleaned up; not only cynical pessimists believed that day was very far off.

A Texan hailing from Austin, the handsome and pleasant state capital, and seat of the great university of Texas, Armstrong came from what in American terms was a distinctly modest background, born when his mother was seventeen and brought up in no lap of luxury. He was a precociously and poly-mathically gifted athlete, a champion swimmer at twelve, then a triathlete before concentrating on cycling. In 1993, aged twenty, he was road World Champion, the second American to win the championship in the footsteps of LeMond, and then in his very first Tour in 1993 he announced his arrival by winning a stage, from Châlons-sur-Marne to Verdun. He didn't complete that year or the next but was thirty-sixth in 1995 after winning the antepenultimate stage to Limoges. A year later, although he again failed to complete the race, he felt he was finally coming into his prime, taking second place in the Liège–Bastogne–Liège race, and winning the Flèche-Wallonne – its first American winner – and the Tour du Pont in Carolina.

In that hour of triumph something was wrong, although it was the fans who noticed what he hadn't noticed himself: 'Usually, when I won a race, I pumped my fists like pistons as I crossed the finish line. But on that day, I was too exhausted to cel-ebrate on the bike. My eyes were bloodshot and my face was flushed.' All the same he was in high spirits when he held his twenty-fifth birthday party in September. He was stepping out with 'a beautiful co-ed', he had signed a $2.5 million contract with Cofidis, the leading French team. 'I'm the happiest man in the world,' he told his mother. In his elation, he didn't immedi-ately pay full attention to the fact that he really wasn't feeling well. 'When my right testicle became slightly swollen that winter, I told myself to live with it, because I assumed it was something I had done to myself on the bike, or that my system was com-pensating for some physiological male thing.'

As the world knows, it was neither of those. In October Armstrong was diagnosed with fourth-stage testicular cancer. That was grave enough, but the really bad news came soon after-wards when lesions began to appear on his brain, and his doctors gave him a 40 per cent chance of survival; as a bookmaker would say, 6–4 against. As the world also knows, he won his bet with destiny. For several months he underwent advanced medical intervention, both chemotherapy and surgery. What he went through can scarcely be imagined. The very photographs from this time are harrowing enough: Armstrong emaciated by chemo treatment, Armstrong with his skull shaved and marked by a dozen blobs for surgical entry. But there is also one very touching snap. Armstrong was visited in hospital in Austin by his friend Eddy Merckx, the greatest Tour winner of all, at least until Lance himself, a man often depicted as the cold and heartless Cannibal, but a gladiator, a hugely brave fighter, a hero who recognized another, and saluted him.

When that 6–4 shot came up and the treatment worked, Armstrong was discharged in 1997. He was desperate to get back on his bike, but plenty of people understandably wondered whether he could ever ride races again. Cofidis told him as politely as they could that they didn't think he could be re-employed; he waited for offers from other teams; the offers didn't come. Finally he began to ride seriously again and signed with a new – not immediately promising, and quaintly named – team, United States Postal Service. Lee Dembart of the *International Herald Tribune* isn't the only one to have wondered 'How come the US Postal Service [that is, the Post Office] sponsors a pro bicycle racing team?', a question we can glance at again in the Epilogue. At any rate, and whatever the organization may be like at delivering mail, the 'Posties' brought Armstrong good fortune, in the long run. Admittedly, 'At first, the 1999 season was a total failure.' He crashed and almost broke his shoulder in the Tour de Valencia, he finished in mid-pack after grim struggles in the Paris–Nice and Milan–San Remo, crashing again. Undaunted, he concentrated on his return to the Tour de France, staking everything on the great race.

To cut this unimaginably extraordinary story short, Armstrong won the Puy de Fou Prologue on 3 July by seven seconds from

Zülle, lost the yellow jersey to the Estonian Jaan Kirksipuu in St-Nazaire two days later, then won it back after six days in the Metz time trial, this time fifty-eight seconds ahead of Zülle, whom he beat yet again two days later, after a transfer rest day, in the first Alpine stage from Le Grand Bonnard to Sestrières, and held the lead to the end, through Alps, Midi, Pyrenees, and on to Paris, where he was an easy 7'37" ahead of Zülle. Mario Cipollini won four consecutive stages between Laval and Thionville, Tom Steels of Belgium won three, David Extabarria of Spain won two, Erik Zabel of Germany won the green jersey for the fourth year running, although he would have been impressed by a young rival, the Australian sprinter Robbie McEwan, who won the last stage.

But there was only one conquering hero – and there was nothing in the least lucky or doubtful about Armstrong's crushing victory. He had won four stages, he was the first rider since Induráin to win all three time trials – except that he made up much more time in them – and he had ridden a quite amazing race in every possible way. Any cyclist who had done this would have been dazzling; for a man in remission from metastasized cancer it seemed impossible to believe. It should have been a time of rejoicing, not to say, in the phrases of the day, a time for healing and a time to move on.

Instead of which, dark clouds still hung over the Tour. In truth the race had begun in very unhappy circumstances. Desperate to restore the Tour's reputation, Leblanc had tried to exclude Virenque because of his part in the Festina scandal. But the French public warmed to Virenque. It was a display of characteristic national perversity, or what can sometimes be an appealing tendency to side with the underdog, or at least with anyone kicking over the traces of authority. Ever since then, Virenque's name has been painted on the road during the Tour more than anyone else's. And so the UCI, with pusillanimous double standards no less striking for being predictable, yielded to pressure and insisted that he be allowed to ride. Back in the race, he climbed so well that he ended with the red-peas jersey, salving the pride, if that's the word, of France, whose riders hadn't won a stage and whose best finisher was, of all people, Virenque himself in eighth, a national hero even if a dubious and tainted one.

And Armstrong? It might have been supposed that a man in his situation would have been afforded universal and untempered admiration, but this was far from the case. Even before the race began, a harsh spotlight had been trained on him by the French press. One rider was later quoted as saying that if he had to choose 'the "cleanest" Tour winner, my money would go on Armstrong', but ill-wishers placed their bet otherwise. It should be stressed that Lance Armstrong has not only always insisted that he has never in his life taken any performance-enhancing drug, he has never once failed a test in a sport that is more and more rigorously controlled.

Even then, nothing he can say or do has been able to shake off the suspicions. The *Monde* always regards itself as, and sometimes actually looks like, one of the world's great newspapers, and is with the *Figaro* the nearest thing France has to a national paper, for all its quaint method of publication, a Paris evening paper bearing the date of the following day when it will be available in Bordeaux, Brest and Briançon (hence the Parisian quip, 'Le journal de demain avec les nouvelles d'hier'). It has never devoted much space to cycling as such, or indeed any other sport, and it may be wondered how many *Monde* editors could tell a *dérailleur* from a *domestique*. But the paper is very interested indeed in *dopage*, and claimed that on that first victorious Tour Armstrong was taking corticoids.

So he was, he replied: in a skin cream called Cematyl prescribed to him for allergies. The amount of corticoid in the cream, Armstrong said, 'was so minute that it was there one day and not the next, the traces are so small it has absolutely nothing to do with performance'. The UCI, which was supposed to abide by a rigid code of confidentiality, broke silence to confirm that he had furnished a medical certificate for using the cream. As we have seen, Armstrong had also taken the acutely sensitive EPO, but as part of his chemotherapy for cancer. Even that didn't quieten the paper, which persisted with what proved to be unsubstantiated allegations that Armstrong had tested positive. On 12 September 2001, in the shadow of a great horror in New York, the *Monde* was to proclaim that 'Nous sommes tous des Americains,' but the paper has sometimes had a funny way of showing its Americanism.

Not surprisingly, Armstrong was bitter about what he called 'vulture journalism'. It had blighted his victory, but he proposed to ignore it: 'It's been hard, I've suffered more from the stress on the bike, and some journalists wanted me to crack, but I wasn't going to crack for them.' At all events this combination of triumph and suspicion set the tone for the following years. First of all, in 2000, Armstrong completed his double. Jean-Claude Killy had been succeeded by Patrice Clerc, and there were a few gimmicky innovations. Apart from a couple of new *étapes*, at Loudun in Poitou (where Aldous Huxley's devils came from) and Draguinan, the race reached Troyes on the penultimate day and then transferred to Paris by the Orient Express, before the final stage of 138 kilometres spun round the streets of Paris, which had been decorated with a *concentration cyclotouristique* to mark the millennium.

Several riders were in fine fettle. Armstrong's team-mate Tyler Hamilton had announced US Postal's strength in depth by winning the Dauphiné Libéré, Zabel displayed the prowess that would win him the green jersey again by winning his third Milan–San Remo in four years, and young David Millar – no kin of Robert, but like him in international competitions a Scot, albeit from the Highlands of Buckinghamshire – showed that he was now a force to be reckoned with by winning the Prologue at

Futuroscope from Armstrong by two seconds. The lead was then taken by Jalabert, followed by the Italian Alberto Elli, as the race ran from Brittany to the south-west.

But they were all waiting for Armstrong to move. He duly did so on the first Pyrenean stage from Lourdes to Hautacam. This was won by Javier Otxoa, one of several good young Spanish riders with the Kelme team who blossomed during this Tour, Roberto Heras another. Armstrong looked all over the winner across the south, not faltering on Mont Ventoux with a successful defensive ride – even though he never liked the great peak – before riding calmly in the Alps. Botero and Pantani won stages in the mountains, and so, to the glee of the unruly French, did Virenque. But Armstrong was waiting for his moment, a stage where he could flatten the field, and it came in the Fribourg-im-Breisgau–Mulhouse time trial. All unlike Wotan's fearful 'Nicht durch den Rhein!', Armstrong hadn't a care in the world as he crossed the Rhine in a pulverizing display, which ensured that he would reach the finish in Paris more than six minutes ahead of Ullrich.

For Virenque luck was running out. His culpability in the scandal now became so clear that the wavering authorities were obliged to suspend him for a season. Although he showed at the end of this *saison blanche* that he was still, among other things, a very fine rider by winning the Paris–Tours, he missed the 2001 Tour. That race began with a Prologue at Dunkirk won by Christophe Moreau before pottering through the Channel ports and then heading clockwise to Verdun, Strasbourg and the Alps. The lead passed from Marc Wauters, to the Australian Stuart O'Grady, who wore the yellow jersey from Seraing to Colmar and then again from Pontarlier to l'Alpe d'Huez after his Crédit Agricole colleague Jens Voigt had worn it for a day. François Simon then took the lead from the Alps to the Pyrenees, but the real event of the Alpine stages had been Armstrong's two wins, from Aix-les-Bains up to the summit at l'Alp d'Huez and then the next day in the Grenoble–Chamrousse time trial. It was only a matter of time before he pounced to take the yellow jersey, which he did from Foix to St-Lary-Soulan. On that stage Jalabert made a long and successful escape that ensured that he would pinch the red-peas jersey from Laurent Roux, and Zabel pinched the green jersey from O'Grady. But the Tour was once again Armstrong's, once again from Ullrich.

In 2002 the Tour began in Luxembourg, a part of Europe little frequented except by Eurocrats and the Luxembourgers themselves, but a most charming town of castles and valleys fit for a fairy prince. The reigning champion starts the Prologue last and, in the shadow of the US Postal team bus parked in the departure village, I stood for some time transfixed, a few feet away from Armstrong as he rode his bike on rollers, as intent as a man at prayer, while his mechanic tuned the gears. He had had a perfect preparation for the race, winning both the Midi Libre and the Dauphiné Libéré. And as if his form weren't good enough, his rivals fell away. Gilberto Simoni was busted for using cocaine during the Giro and suspended, and Ullrich withdrew with a damaged knee, although he also had another little difficulty when he was arrested off duty for using good old-fashioned recreational drugs in a nightclub.

No one pretended that this was an open race in which there would be many surprises. The Tour director Jean-Marie Leblanc admitted that it was less likely to offer cliffhanging suspense than an opportunity to watch a very great athlete at his peak, while that athlete himself said that 'It's up to us, the riders, to make the race exciting.' After the Prologue Rubens Bertogliati took the yellow jersey on the second day. On the Wednesday US Postal looked as if they might be thwarted by ONCE in the team time trial from Epernay to Château-Thierry, but a puncture for ONCE's Mikel Pradera gave the 'Posties' an uncovenanted advantage, which they seized to finish only sixteen seconds behind. I watched them cruise into town not long after I had stopped a policewoman to find the way to the finish. She asked whether I was driving, I said I had left my car on a boulevard on the edge of town, she said 'Sage décision,' before showing me the best way to get there on foot, and I thought what a wonderful country it was where a lady *agent de police* could make such a reply.

Although Igor Gonzalez de Galdeano of ONCE had taken the yellow jersey, Armstrong was now an ominous third in the GC. On the road to Rouen there was a gruesome pile-up, and a luckless Steels abandoned. The second Sunday of the race began at St-Martin-de-Landelles, birthplace of the great Daniel Mangeas. Had they chosen the village because of him, Leblanc was asked, and replied with pleasing candour, 'Of course,' just as he had explained why the race had begun in Luxembourg: 'Because they asked us.' The following day Armstrong dropped to eighth overall, but Gonzalez had no illusions. When reminded that he had beaten Armstrong in a time trial in the Midi Libre, he said, 'One can't compare such things. When he comes to the Tour, Armstrong is a superman, a different rider. He is very difficult to beat.'

True enough, though as it happened Armstrong had a rare lapse in a time trial the following day which he was expected to win, coming eleven seconds behind Botero and allowing Gonzalez to keep his lead. But there were to be no real shocks now, except one that blighted this Tour for all of us who covered it. On the tenth stage, from Bazaas to Pau on 17 July, the publicity caravan was passing through the village of Retgon throwing out sweets and knick-knacks when a seven-year-old boy saw his grandparents on the other side of the road. As he ran to join them, he was knocked down by a publicity Land Rover belonging to one of those sweet companies and killed instantly.

It wasn't the first such accident in Tour history: a child had been killed in Ireland in 1998 and another on the Avignon–Draguinan stage on Bastille Day in 2000, and as I have said, to watch the Tour, not least the caravan, is sometimes to wonder why there are not more accidents. The Tour authorities are conscious of this and, following the 2000 accident, they had made some efforts to improve at least the standards of driving. On this very 2002 Tour more than 300 speed controls had been carried out on vehicles, and several drivers had been stripped of their right to drive on the *parcours* with the coveted stickers on their cars. For Daniel Baal, deputy chairman of the Société du Tour de France, dismay was matched by despair: 'We have put special security measures in place, speed limits, regulations, warnings, and we divert as many people as possible off the *parcours* every day, but this still happens. Every day we see children crossing the road when the race is coming and it really scares me.' It scares everyone, all the more after the name of young Melvin Pimple was engraved for ever in the sad annals of the Tour.

A little over halfway through the race Armstrong won the first mountain stage in the Pyrenees, with more than a little help from his friends. The 'Posties' slogged it out over the big climbs, while Armstrong tracked his colleague Heras, before making off in the last five kilometres to catch and pass Boleti and take the yellow jersey. He characteristically said that 'I've never celebrated any victory before the final day in Paris and I won't now,' but the race was now as good as over. David Millar cheered British fans with a stage win to Béziers, before Armstrong was beaten up Mont Ventoux by Virenque. 'I rode as good as I could and as strong as I could, and Richard was stronger,' he said, but his good nature was not reciprocated by the French fans, who continue to hound Armstrong.

'If I had a dollar for every time somebody yelled "Dopé, dopé," I'd be a rich man,' he said. 'The people are not very sportsmanlike.' But he took the best form of revenge. After Botero won one Alpine stage, the 'Posties' rode superbly together on the stage up to La Plagne. The Dutchman Michael Boogerd won the stage and, as US Postal reached the line, Armstrong in seigneurial tradition allowed Carlos Sastre to go ahead and finish second, since he knew that, barring accidents, the race was now won, with Armstrong more than five minutes ahead of Joseba Beloki, a lead he kept until the end.

On the last day, riding through Brie towards Paris and the finish, the 'Posties' cheerfully or even insolently clinked champagne glasses from bike to bike, before they reached the Champs-Élysées. There Armstrong stood on the podium next to Beloki, who had ended 7′12″ behind him, and the Lithuanian Raimondas Rumsas in third. It was less than a year after the horror that will always be associated with the date '11 September', and emotions were higher than ever as the Stars and Stripes unfurled over the Champs-Élysées and 'The Star-Spangled Banner' was played. The French cheered, as it were, through gritted teeth. This was also the year that Philip Roger published *L'Ennemi Américain: Genealogy de l'antiamericainisme français*, one of several analyses of that phenomenon. Armstrong's relationship with the land of the Tour de France might have made more than a footnote for students of the subject.

At least it had seemed a clean and scandal-free Tour. That was until those festivities in Paris, when another car was stopped a long way away containing a mobile pharmacy. This time the driver wasn't a *soigneur* but a spouse. Edita Rumsas, wife of the third, was arrested at Chamonix on the very day the Tour ended, on her way to Italy, and her car was found to be stuffed with 'medications that could be considered as doping products'. The rooms of her husband's Lampre team were searched inconclusively, while Rumsas himself disappeared. He sent word, apparently true, that he had tested negative, added a note of music-hall burlesque by saying that these manifold medicaments had been intended for his mother-in-law, before finally agreeing to meet the police for questioning if Edita was released and allowed to rejoin their three children. Compared with four years earlier, it was a trivial and almost risible affair, except to remind everyone that *dopage* simply wasn't going to go away.

17

A Big Injustice

2003-2006

As the centennial Tour de France approached, there was an intense mood of expectancy, tinged with apprehension. Might the great event be marred by another scandal? Would it, could it, live up to its historic importance? In the event, the ninetieth running of the race, which began in the shadow of the Eiffel Tower and returned three weeks later to the Champs-Élysées across the Seine, was worthy of the occasion, one of the very best Tours for years. For all of us who covered the race it was a privilege as well as a pleasure to have been there; or so it seemed at the time.

After his rather tame victory in 2002, there was quite enough drama in Armstrong's life in the early months of 2003. He announced his prospective retirement, although not until after two more seasons; he separated from his wife; and he publicly opposed the war against Iraq waged by his friend and fellow-Texan President George W. Bush. The timing of his intended departure from racing in late 2004 meant that he hoped to ride in two more Tours, which meant in turn that he might become the first man to win the race six times; and his new season began as usual with only one serious goal in mind. In March, Armstrong was in Spain riding in the five-day Tour of Murcia, with no intention of winning: 'I need to see where I am in relation to others,' he said, in his gnomic way.

He saw a little more, and the hard way, when he crashed in the Dauphiné Libéré, but if anything his training clock was running fast. Some riders take a winter holiday in the sun, others take a long break on the ski slopes as a means of both unwinding and tuning up again. Skiing uses much the same muscles as cycling and it can also, the *mauvaises langues* do say, act as a useful way of sweating illicit substances out of the system. Armstrong spent the late winter in Spain and by March he could say that 'my fitness, weight and body fat are about a month ahead of last year', all of them checked by his trainers. One of these had played a crucial part in Armstrong's career. Johan Bruyneel of Belgium rode in six Tours, with no little success, winning the Evreux– Amiens stage in 1993 and Charleroi–Liège in 1995, when he also wore the yellow jersey. But if he was a good rider, he has been a brilliant manager since taking up as *directeur sportif* of US Postal and supervising his great star's victories.

Early in the year, Bruyneel was as happy as ever about the Posties' prospects, and about Armstrong's progress, insisting that his team leader wouldn't be distracted by the trial separation from his wife Kristen, whom he had married in 1998 shortly after his treatment. They were soon back together again but not for long, and not many weeks after the 2003 Tour had ended, Armstrong announced sadly that his marriage had ended as well: he and Kristen were devoted to each other, but couldn't live together, and were hoping for a *divorce à l'amiable*.

Nor for that matter would he be distracted – or any more than anyone else – by the war, although Armstrong's attitude must have surprised some of those fans who had held up 'Don't mess with Texas' banners on Mont Ventoux. 'I'm no fan of war,' he said. He was no fan of Saddam Hussein or terrorism either, 'but it's wrong to go to the front without the support of Europe or the United Nations'. This was not the spirit of Desgrange in 1914, nor indeed of Texas and Washington in the spring of 2003, and Armstrong's words were a reminder if any were needed of the atmosphere in which the centennial Tour was being run.

The war was opposed by President Jacques Chirac, the French government, and an overwhelming majority of the French people. Franco-American relations were at their lowest ebb for decades, with a wave of anti-American sentiment in France matched by contemptuous rage across the Atlantic, where "French fries" were childishly removed from menus. But while Bush and his cabal might have consoled themselves with the Duke of Wellington's words, 'We always have been, we are, and I hope that we always shall be detested in France,' Armstrong could scarcely say that before the Champs-Élysées: come the summer and he would again be much the most prominent American in a France where Americans were less loved than ever. It would be unfair to suggest that he was hedging his bets or covering his back, but his position was certainly delicate.

An appropriately nostalgic and even respectful parcours was mapped out for the centennial Tour. It included all the *villes-étapes* of 1903, Paris, Lyons, Marseilles, Toulouse, Bordeaux, Nantes, and back to Paris; but of course the changes in a hundred years were as striking, with seven mountain stages taking the riders over the great cols of the Télégraphe, Izoard, and Peyresourde. Against that, the road stages were much less intimidating. A total of 3350 kilometres compared with the 2428 kilometres of the first Tour, but also with 5745 kilometres in 1926. In 1903 the shortest stage was 268 kilometres and the longest 471, in 2003 (time trials apart) those distances are 160 and 230 kilometres. One curiosity unnoticed by most was the return of Marseilles as a *ville-étape*. It was of course one of the towns visited in 1903, and thirty-one times in all up to the centenary, but never between 1971 and 1989. That was because of an untoward incident when the timing went wrong, the riders arrived earlier than expected and Gaston Defferre, imperious mayor of the great city, was made to look silly; he vowed that the race would never return there under his aegis.

After a huge crowd watched the riders leave the Eiffel Tower on 6 July, thrills and spills came from the beginning. Armstrong could have won the Prologue, and Millar should have won it, but by uncharacteristic oversight Armstrong didn't properly reconnoitre the tricky course round the streets of Paris beforehand, and it showed when he finished seventh, while Millar's chain-ring slipped at a sharp corner and he lost crucial time, for which he compensated afterwards by way of a violent row with his team officials and mechanics. A first week from Paris across eastern France to Lyons and the Alps saw a series of bunch sprint finishes dominated by Petacchi, who won four stages in all beginning on the first Sunday into Meaux.

But the action that day was immediately behind him: a horrendous pile-up near the line brought down scores of riders and badly hurt several. Armstrong escaped bruised but intact; not so Tyler Hamilton. He had fractured his collarbone, but far from abandoning the race, the next morning he was still in the field, and the morning after, and after that. Hamilton might be thought a glutton for punishment – he had ridden the previous year's Giro with a broken shoulder, and had to be told to quit the Tour of the Netherlands a month after this 2003 Tour when he broke his hip – but he managed to continue riding in acute pain, strapped up, with the pressure in his tyres reduced to make the roads less unbearable. We were in for something quite out of the ordinary.

After McGee took the yellow jersey on the first stage, it passed to Jean-Pierre Nazon. The third road stage was marked by one incident which reminded us of something which would become much more important later, the Tour's unwritten code of etiquette. An unknown rider called Anthony Geslin, a 23-year-old

Frenchman with Brioches–La Boulangère, achieved fifteen minutes of fame when he 'grilled the *ravito*': that is to say, he attacked and left the peloton while the musettes was being collected at the *zone de ravitaillement*, the feeding station. The peloton made its feelings known to the wretched Geslin, who nevertheless hung on in and finished the Tour in 114th place. David Millar complained that 'there is less and less respect in the bunch' and that younger riders would do anything to escape, even if it meant ignoring custom and practice. We were told also of Armstrong slowing down for Ullrich after his crash two years before; if anyone thought such traditions had been forgotten, they were soon to be proved wrong.

The next day the Colombian Victor Hugo Peña of US Postal took over the yellow jersey when the Posties won what Armstrong called a 'highly technical' team time trial. Before the race, the Posties' form had seemed a little shaky, but they silenced the doubters as they crushed ONCE, to move Armstrong handily up the GC. There had been an interminable will-he-won't-he duet between the organisers and Cipollini: would he and his Domina Vacanze team be invited as a wild card? Almost until the beginning of the race it looked as though he might be in the field, but at the last moment he was outvited, as the Germans say, and his sponsors took him off to a beach at Sharm el Sheikh. Whatever ostensible reasons given, the Tour does not, for all his popularity, regard him as an *homme sérieux*, and resents the way he turns up at races, strikes attitudes, wins the odd stage, and then goes home. The organisers must have felt justified by Cipollini's behaviour a couple of months later when he played around before the Vuelta, was finally invited, then gave an ignominious display, riding so feebly on the first day that his team-mates had to push him, before he abandoned and flew home the next morning. It was Virenque who got stuck in when the climbing began and was soon in the red peas jersey, which he held until the end of the race, winning the Mountains Prize very easily.

On the second Sunday it looked as if the piece might be played according to the script: up into L'Alpe d'Huez, Iban Mayo won the stage from the very promising young Russian Alexander Vinokourov, with Armstrong behind them in fourth taking the yellow jersey for the first time. But the plot had gone awry. The real story of that afternoon as we watched it unfold from the mountain top was Armstrong's failure to seize the lead with the complete authority he had shown on equivalent stages in previous years. As he said himself, 'I couldn't chase them.' He was only 40″ ahead of Joseba Beloki in the GC, with Vinokourov and Ullrich panting hard behind. A technical hitch had been unnoticed by Armstrong, let alone by spectators: his rear brake was dragging slightly against the rim, not bringing him to a halt but quite enough to make his task harder and his time slower. But even allowing for that, Armstrong conceded that he was in far from his best form: 'I had to face the fact that I wasn't riding well and could lose the race.'

One man riding very well indeed was Beloki, who could perhaps have won the race. The next day he was chasing down an escape by Vinokourov with Armstrong pedalling hard to stay on his wheel. But when Armstrong likes to say 'I'd rather be lucky than right', he knows what he's talking about. He followed Beloki on to a seemingly inoffensive stretch of road between harvested cornfields. The heat had been mounting as the race was run and was now intense; a couple of weeks later the Tour would have been practically impossible, when France was swept by the most extreme heatwave for decades, in which many thousands of elderly people died. Beloki's fate was less grim, but bad enough. He hit a patch of road which had actually melted in the heat, the tarmac turned to treacle. His front tyre was ripped off and his bike threw him ferociously forward. Just in time to avoid colliding, Armstrong behind him tried to brake but felt his wheel locking up and chose the alternative of swerving into the field. Despite bouncing over furrows and stubble, he emerged unscathed, unlike Beloki who broke several bones.

With one rival removed, Armstrong was still not out of the woods. There were few changes in the order before the first individual time trial near Toulouse on the second Friday, but there Ullrich struck devastatingly. With more unaccountable carelessness, Armstrong didn't take enough liquid beforehand, even though 'I already felt sapped and thirsty as I waited in the starting gate'. Before the end of the 47 kilometres he was so badly dehydrated that he lost fifteen pounds, while Ullrich rode one of his finest stages to be 96″ behind the leader. Armstrong was terribly disheartened, and when his team-mate and fellow-countryman George Hincapie came up to him the next morning he thought he would hear some words of sarcastic consolation. But he was wrong. 'What you did yesterday was the most impressive thing I've seen you do,' Hincapie said. 'Because I could see you were suffering and you hung in there.' His words were prophetic as well as generous.

In the first two stages over the Pyrenees, Ullrich was riding a storm, and by the last Monday morning he was only 15″ behind Armstrong, closer than anyone except perhaps Armstrong himself had ever foreseen before the race. But no one could possibly have foreseen that the stage that day from Bagnères-de-Bigorre to Luz-Ardiden would be one of the greatest in the history of the Tour.

There was a tough battle over the Col d'Aspin, before the Tourmalet where Ullrich dropped Armstrong but was then caught by him before Armstrong passed Mayo on the last climb up to the finish. Armstrong was riding at his best when he crashed. It was an absurd incident. The over-enthusiastic Basque crowd were rabbling Armstrong but he managed to avoid them, until he caught his handlebars in a little bag carried by a spectator and came down. For a moment it looked as though it was all over for him, but although Armstrong was winded, he was soon up and riding again, now behind Ullrich and Hamilton. There was to be some dispute as to how soon Ullrich slowed – 'In replays he seems to me to be riding in race tempo,' Armstrong later said – and it was, of all people, Hamilton, still there, still in pain, still near the lead after two weeks, who waved to the others to follow tradition and wait for the yellow jersey who had been in trouble, and so they did.

Rarely has a sporting episode caught the imagination of so many millions, and it brought plaudits for Ullrich's chivalry, but he might well have gnashed his teeth at that unspoken rule. Within minutes, Armstrong had caught the leaders and then, scarcely believably, he passed them, 'fuelled by residual fright and rage from the crash,' he said. 'And by pent-up resentment from weeks of crashes and ordeals, and doubts.' He crossed the line 67″ ahead in the GC, which 'after two weeks of suffering and self-doubt' felt like hours. When the rest of the Posties finished they were taken away in the team bus, but Armstrong wanted to see them and jumped into Bruyneel's car, which the boss drove as fast as he could to catch up. The bus pulled over, Armstrong jumped aboard, stood in the aisle, and roared at his comrades, 'How do you like me now? *How do you fucking like me now?*' There was ten minutes of pandemonium, as grown men shouted, hugged and wept.

After a rest day, a last Pyrenean stage went from Pau to Bayonne. As if we hadn't seen enough heroics, who should win it but Hamilton, visibly in tears of pain on the climbs. 'Today's made up for everything,' he said, and he dedicated the win to his CSC team-mates, not just from sentiment, since they had rescued him early in the day when he fell back from the leaders. Still in the yellow jersey, Armstrong applauded as he crossed the line and embraced his old colleague, the incredible Tyler.

On pancake-flat stages from Dax to Bordeaux to Saint-Maixent-l'Ecole it became clear that the sprinting teams had slumped. In the case of Fassa Bortolo it wasn't so much a case of slump as disintegration: by the second week, only four out of nine riders were still in the race. This meant that those teams could no longer control the peloton, curb unruly escapes, and set up sprint finishes, as was shown by the way outsiders won the stages with long breakaways. The Dutchman Servais Knaven of Quick-Step won into Bordeaux, the Spaniard Pablo Lastras of iBanesto won into Saint-Maixent at the head of a sixteen-strong *echapée-fleuve* well ahead of the peloton led by McEwen, who was still in the green jersey. The times were very fast – Lastras was more than half an hour faster than the quickest time estimated by the Tour in its 'Livre de Route' and averaged an astonishing 50.185 kph – just as they had been in some previous stages, which caused a few tongues and fingers to wag, and even led to a little ill-conditioned speculation in the French press about just what might lie behind these startling improvements.

But at Saint-Maixent-l'Ecole, no one was much concerned with the stage winner; all thoughts were on the following day's time trial. Armstrong and Ullrich had finished together and there was now just 65″ separating them, a feasible target for Ullrich in the light of his devastating ride in the previous time trial. It might have been desperately close at the very end, but Armstrong was still favoured by *la chance* as well as *l'addresse*. This time he made no mistake as he surveyed the 49-kilometre course, and it was Ullrich who didn't take enough care.

On a fine day that might not have mattered, but in foul drizzle and on a road that might as well have been covered in washing-up liquid, he took one bend fractionally too fast, and crashed. That was it. The time Ullrich lost ended his chances. Armstrong's earpiece brought him the news, and there was now no pressure on him to push his pedals: he could ride the course carefully, with no unnecessary risks. Indeed he rode with such restraint that he allowed Millar to take the stage, a compensation, albeit slightly bloodless, for the Prologue. The following day saw the coronation in Paris: Armstrong won by 61″ from Ullrich, with Vinokourov in third and, most miraculous of all, Hamilton in fourth, at only 6′17″. Baden Cooke took the Green Jersey prize, which had been contested till near the end, and Denis Menchov was best youngest. It was Armstrong's fifth Tour victory, far from his easiest, maybe his greatest.

And it might have been better if it had been his last – or even the final Tour of all. The next three runnings of the race brought Armstrong two more victories, to set a record that may never be matched; it saw him succeeded on the winner's podium by another American; and it saw bike racing, the Tour most of all, engulfed by wave after wave of scandal which almost threatened to submerge the great race for ever.

A sardonic Providence could not have made the point more cruelly as 2004 began. In February, Marco Pantani was found dead in his flat in Rimini. The winner of the 1998 'Tour de Farce' had been discounted at the time, overshadowed as his victory was by the Festina scandal. His moment of muted glory, the Giro–Tour double that year, proved to be a peak from which it was then down-hill all the way. He was easily leading in the 1999 Giro, with only one mountain stage left, when he showed up with an excessive haemocrit count – for red cells and thus EPO – and was ejected.

He raced no more that year but took part in the 2000 Tour, winning two stages while spitting nails at Armstrong (who didn't help by calling him 'Elefantino', the nickname inspired by his large ears). He only raced a little in 2001 and 2002, and by June 2003 he was in a drug clinic suffering from depression. As his death showed, any treatment hadn't worked: the autopsy found acute cocaine poisoning. While 20,000 mourners gathered at his funeral, Pantani's mother accused the sporting authorities of abandoning her son, and Cipollini said that the death was 'a tragedy of enormous proportions for everyone involved in cycling,' which may have been truer than he knew.

Even Armstrong had a cloud darkening over him, with the imminent publication of *L.A. Confidentiel: Les secrets de Lance Armstrong*, an exposé by his long-standing foe David Walsh and a French colleague. Armstrong seemed out of sorts in the Dauphiné Libéré, failing to win up Mont Ventoux – yet again, and for the last time – and finishing the prep race behind Mayo and Hamilton. But it made no difference once the Tour began. Jaan Kirsippu won the Prologue in Liège before the race made its way through north-eastern France and Belgium, past the sombre names of Namur and Waterloo, before turning west. Hushovd took over the yellow jersey, then Nazon and then McEwen before the team trial in which another formidable performance by Armstrong's team put him in yellow. As the race headed inland to the Massif Central there were a few happy days for French cycling, which hadn't had much to cheer about for years past. On the fifth stage to Chartres, the GC lead was taken and held for days by Thomas Voekler – 'Tit-blan' to friends and fans, from the dialect for 'little white boy' in Martinique, where he had grown up. While Virenque again moved into a commanding position for the Mountains Prize, Voeckler kept the yellow jersey for a remarkable nine days, the longest any Frenchman had worn it for many years.

His streak lasted only until the Pyrenees. By La Mongie Armstrong had moved into second, and on the next stage to Plateau de Beille he and his team showed that they were as ferocious as ever, Armstrong taking victory from Basso at the finish. The parcours looked as if it might have been designed to offer a personal challenge to him, and it was certainly intended to make a closely competitive race, with two individual time trials both scheduled in the last week, one of them a fierce climb up L'Alpe d'Huez.

But there was no challenge and not much competition. This 15.5-kilometre time trial up the twenty-one hairpin bends of L'Alpe d'Huez was dedicated to Pantani. The only problem for

Armstrong, and for the other riders, was the crowds lining the road, who were unruly and in some cases hostile. Armstrong passed Basso on the road before he won by an insulting 61″ from Ullrich, with Kloden in third. As if he needed to, Armstrong then thrashed his rivals in the final time trial in Besancon, co-incidentally again finishing 61″ ahead of Ullrich in second. And so to the foregone triumph in Paris.

And yet the most riveting moment of the race wasn't any time trial or climb, it was an incident on the eighteenth stage, an otherwise uneventful ramble from Annemasse to Le Grand-Bornand to Lons-le-Saunier, with Armstrong unassailably in the lead. After about 32 kilometres Filippo Simeoni of Domina Vacanze took off from the peloton, trying to join a six-man breakaway. Suddenly another rider was alongside him, chasing him down and instructing him to fall back with some frank but well-chosen words: none other than Armstrong himself.

When a minor rider – and poor 'Pippo' Simeoni was distinctly minor, at the time in 144th place, 2 hours 42′55″ off the lead – from a minor team makes an escape he is usually ignored; if a breakaway does have to be chased down, this is always the work of *domestiques* from the big teams – never, ever the yellow jersey himself. The explanation was painfully simple: in the course of all the to-and-fro over doping, many accusations and recriminations, Simeoni had given evidence against Dr Michele Ferrari, whose services he had once used. Armstrong had called him a liar, and in return Simeoni was now suing the champion for defamation.

'I was the victim of a big injustice today,' Simeoni said. 'It wasn't possible for Armstrong to let a little rider like me have a chance for a little glory in the Tour de France. That's a sin.' Bruyneel agreed that 'it was something to do with what happened in the past,' while Armstrong claimed that he was merely 'protecting the interests of the peloton'. 'He isn't a rider that the peloton wants to be up front,' he went on, 'because all he does is attack the peloton and say bad things about the other riders. All he wants to do is destroy cycling and the sport that pays him. To me, that's not correct.'

This was a striking display of Armstrong's character, a man who would not be crossed, but also of his obtuseness. It wasn't only what could be construed as schoolboy bullying – and Armstrong wonders why fans didn't love him – it was the defiant way he responded to all accusations, sometimes in a way that served only to remind us about them all over again.

If Armstrong thought that his righteous anger would quieten all suspicions about him and the sport, he was soon disabused. The month following the 2004 Tour, Tyler Hamilton, so heroic in the centennial Tour, won a gold medal at the Athens Olympics. And the month after that, he was accused of blood doping at the Games, transfusing his or someone else's blood, on the strength of his A sample. There was an absurd confusion when the lab managed to spoil his B sample, and he protested his innocence, but at the end of a long story he was suspended for two years, one more great name sullied.

Throughout the following winter Armstrong played hard to get, hinting that he might not ride again, while devoting a good deal of energy to litigation and to arranging a possible new team. The United States Post Office had finally returned to its business of attempting to deliver mail and had been replaced as sponsor by the Discovery Channel, but not until February did Armstrong confirm that he would take part in one last Tour.

The race began with not a Prologue but a short time trial of 19 kilometres on the coast of the Vendée, crossing a long causeway to Noirmoutier en l'Ile, past salt flats and oyster beds. On Friday, the last training day, Ullrich and his team were riding the course when the team car stopped dead and Ullrich ran into the back of the car, hurtling through the back window. He claimed to have suffered no ill effects, but it didn't seem like that when the action began.

A very fast time – the fastest, as it proved – was set early by David Zabriskie, an American rider with CSC. But the drama came at the end of the afternoon. Ullrich left second last, followed by Armstrong. Despite a mishap coming down the ramp, when his shoe came out of the pedal, Armstrong was soon at his terrifying best, closing on Ullrich, passing him and then dropping him to finish at 2″ from Zabriskie but 66″ ahead of the German. 'L'Impitoyable,' read the headline in the *Equipe* the next day, and it was true enough: Armstrong was still the pitiless one.

Although Zabriskie kept the lead for three days, he lost it dramatically in the Tuesday team time trial, from Tours to the lovely city of Blois. The previous day had offered a little comic relief when Robbie McEwen head-butted Stuart O'Grady close to the line in some quaint Australian duel. Although McEwen crossed the line third, the judges knocked him to the back of the main pack, dealing quite a blow to his hopes of a fourth green jersey. In the team time trial CSC began the day as leading team and were in good form, faster than Discovery as the stages were timed one by one. Armstrong led from the front, taking longer and longer pulls, but CSC might still have won if Zabriskie hadn't crashed nastily on the streets of Blois only 1500 metres from the line. He remounted and crossed the line in a yellow jersey spattered with blood, but because the point of the crash wasn't past the *flamme rouge* he couldn't take the same time as the rest of his team. With unwonted chivalry Armstrong didn't wear the yellow jersey the next day, until the organisers asked him to.

A flat run to Montargis was won in a sprint finish by McEwen, his first win of the Tour by a wheel over Tom Boonen, but still only putting him in fourth for the green jersey due to his being relegated to 186th in the third stage. As the race made its way eastward there was an equally poignant moment as they rode to Nancy, where Christophe Mengin hails from. He led a breakaway after 24 kilometres and was joined by several other riders, including Kirsipuu. Around 10 kilometres from the finish Kirsipuu attacked, but Mengin stuck with him and then dropped him. Although two other riders caught up with him, it looked as though Mengin would win the stage into his home town until he cornered fractionally too fast only 700 metres from the finish and crashed. It was small consolation that much of the peloton also came down when they reached the same point.

On the next stage, from Lunéville to Karlsruhe in Germany, Fabian Wegmann tried to make it a patriotic victory and entered his country in the lead, but was reeled back, leaving McEwen to win in a well-timed sprint. Then the serious climbing began, after a bizarre interlude at Courchevel when the start was held up for forty minutes by protesting farmers. In France, farmers usually have something to protest about, but not often as esoteric as a plan by ecologically over-eager enthusiasts to reintroduce wolves to the Alps. Lone wolf as ever, Armstrong was still so strong that his team couldn't keep up with him when he attacked on the first passes and was in turn attacked by Rasmussen. Armstrong tried to win the stage with a late sprint but was pipped by Valverde just at the end, but the times put Armstrong back in the GC lead. The next day started badly. Dario Figo, an Italian who had won the 2001 Paris–Nice, was slung out when EPO was found in his wife's car. Yevgeni Petrov had already been disqualified for failing a test. And the day after that was the Quatorze Juillet, when Moncoutié enjoyed a French victory, but he pooped his own party. Referring darkly to the startlingly fast times being recorded in the race, he said, 'You can draw your own conclusions.'

After the Alps the Tour crossed the Midi clockwise before entering the Pyrenees. And there, instead of wolves, the slogans plastering the roads read 'Mort aux ours,' death to the bears, which another group of crazed environmentalists were bringing back to the mountains. A stage to Pau was won by Iscar Peiror, while Cadel Evans showed Aussie grit crossing the Col d'Aubisque four years after he had fallen and broken his collar-bone on the same great climb.

But it was Armstrong who now had the race in his own bear hug, and finished the day 2'46" ahead of Basso. Having marked the first mountain climb ever ridden in the race by crossing the Ballon d'Alsace once more, this Tour more sadly commemorated the death of Casartelli as the riders passed the Col du Portet d'Aspet exactly ten years after his fatal crash.

So it went north-east to Albi, Issoire, Le-Puy-en-Veley (where the press were given as many of the town's famous green lentils as they could carry away) and a final time trial at Saint-Étienne. As that day began Rasmussen was lying second to Armstrong, but the American, showing a kind of uncanny psychic as well as physical dominance over the race, predicted that Rasmussen would fare badly and, as if the warlock had cast a spell, everything duly went wrong for the Dane. He slipped and fell after 4 kilometres, was given a new bike, but seemed to panic, and on a tricky descent he ended in a ditch, and finished bedraggled after changing his bike and his wheels twice. A disastrous time saw him plummet in the GC, while Armstrong won the day with Ullrich at 23" and Vinokourov at 1'17". In Paris the next day the jury invoked the 'rain rule' so that Armstrong won the Tour the first time he passed the finish line, rather than on the eighth time round, taking the race by 4'40" from Basso and 6'21" from Ullrich. 'Time is not on my side,' Armstrong had said before the race, but nor did it seem to be on anyone else's, and he now retired for good on a completely triumphant note.

With his seventh consecutive victory, Armstrong had broken all records, exhausted all superlatives, but not quite won all hearts, and there were plenty of ill-wishers who hoped for bad news. Less than four weeks after his last appearance on the winner's podium they got worse than bad news. An astonishing story broke in the *Equipe*. Samples taken from Armstrong during the very first of those victorious Tours, in 1999, had been frozen in a lab. At the time they were taken, there was no reliable test for EPO, but one had since been developed and had been belatedly used on the samples, which had apparently tested positive.

'The witch-hunt continues,' Armstrong said, and for once that much overused word might have been apt. After such an interval, he could not be held accountable juridically or stripped of the victory, and he couldn't be suspended, since he had just retired; he could only be smeared with a charge which, as indeed in a witchcraft trial, he could not refute. And there was something fishy as well as distasteful about the way the story was leaked.

Still and all, as his countrymen say, cycling had it coming, and there was disgrace enough with leaked six-year-old evidence. In September, Roberto Heras set a record of his own by winning the Vuelta for a fourth time, including a crushing and frankly surprising victory in the last time trial. Weeks later came the news that, on that very day, he had tested positive for EPO. While he inevitably protested his innocence and vowed to clear his name, he was stripped of his title, an unprecedented shame for the sport which didn't think it could take much more scandal or disgrace. But more was exactly what was coming.

When 2006 began it was thus a new year in every sense: the first Tour without Armstrong for so long, and also, as optimists thought, a time when a new start might be made, while pessimists reckoned that after recent events things could not become any more wretched. They had forgotten the chilling lines from *King Lear*: 'The worst is not, / So long as we can say, "This is the worst."' After Basso won the Giro in May he was favourite for the Tour, while some thought that Ullrich could have a last chance, and other riders had put down markers. The Paris–Nice 'Race to the Sun' in March had become something of an American benefit, won the year before by Bobby Julich of CSC and in 2006 by Floyd Landis of Phonak.

In the event this running of the Tour saw some good bike racing, not to say a thrilling last week, but it will no more be remembered for what happened on the road than was the 1998 Tour. After a Prologue in Strasbourg, the parcours ran anti-clockwise north and then west, through Normandy towards Rennes on the coast of Brittany before skipping down to Bordeaux and into the Pyrenees, crossing the Midi through Carcassonne and Montelimar and then the Alps, with an uphill finish in L'Alpe d'Huez, another climb to Morzine and a second individual time trial (the team time trial once again having been dropped).

All was set, with the teams and press gathering in Strasbourg, when the news exploded. A police investigation in Madrid called Operación Puerto (Operation Gate or Mountain Pass) had raided the offices of Dr Eufemiano Fuentes, a 'sports doctor', and found it a Dracula's trove of bottled blood as well as drugs. His files suggested that he had been serving a large number of sports-men including many Spanish footballers, but also cyclists. The Tour authorities decided that in the name of rough justice – which is better than no justice – they had no choice but to eject anyone whose names had been mentioned in connection with this raid, and those included none other than Basso and Ullrich, the two favourites. Vinokourov wasn't implicated, but his team was, and he was left stranded with no one to ride for.

And so the race began on this absurdly melodramatic note and with a gravely depleted field. The Prologue, back to 7.1 kilometres, was won by the sometime world champion Thor Hushovd, a Norwegian with Credit Agricole, although George Hincapie, the American with Discovery, shared his time. The first week then saw a sprinters' ding-dong, with the yellow jersey passing from Hushovd to Hincapie, back again, then to Boonen, riding for Quick-Step, who held the lead through St Quentin, Caen and Vitré. A first time trial in Rennes was won by the Ukrainian Serge Honchar of T-Mobile by 61″ from Landis, who was now stepping right into the picture. When they reached the Pyrenees, Menchov won over the passes to Pla-de-Beret, but Landis took the GC lead, only to lose it to the Spaniard Oscar Pereiro of Caisse d'Epargne after two days.

Then came an unforgettable last week. On the Tuesday, Frank Schleck and Damiano Cunego fought a thrilling duel in the climb up to L'Alpe d'Huez, while Landis finished fourth and reclaimed the yellow jersey from Pereiro. After triumph came disaster. On the Wednesday they rode from Le Bourg d'Oisans to La Toussuire over four gruelling climbs, including the Galibier. Until the last 15 kilometres, up a category-one climb, Landis appeared still to be in command. But when Schleck's CSC team-mate Carlos Sastre attacked, Landis cracked. In fact he almost fell apart, finishing the stage 24th, a disastrous 10′4″ behind the winner, ceding the yellow jersey again to Pereiro, and seeming to have lost all hope in the race.

And then there was the Thursday. In the morning, nobody covering the race gave Landis any chance of regaining the lead, which would require an unprecedented feat over five more big climbs. On the first, Landis attacked, helped by his Phonak team, dropping one after another of the contenders. He did it again on the Col de la Colombière, putting so much time into his rivals that suddenly and almost incredulously we realised that he had for the moment reclaimed the GC lead.

On and on he rode in this breathtaking performance, leaving everyone in his wake, to win the stage by 5′4″ from Sastre. Pereiro finished well enough to cling on to the yellow jersey, but the Tour was now Landis's for the taking, as he duly took it: in the time trial on the penultimate day, he was third behind Honchar and Klöden but decisively put enough time into his rivals, regaining the yellow jersey and triumphantly raising his arms in the Champs-Élysées, where the Stars and Stripes were raised for the eighth successive year.

In some ways he was an unlikely champion. There have been many obvious rascals riding in the Tour over the years, and few winners have been men of entirely saintly character. Landis was the straightest of straight arrows, brought up in Pennsylvania in a Mennonite community, strict puritanical protestants. Since his family eschewed television, movies and most other aspects of modern life, it was a curious childhood, not least when his father tried to keep him from the useless pastime of riding a bike.

He began competing on mountain bikes, switching to road racing in 1999. Armstrong spotted him and hired him for the Posties. He rode with them for three of Armstrong's victories, from 2002 to 2004, before accepting an offer from Phonak. In 2005, he finished ninth in the Tour GC and was a plausible contender the next year, although nobody knows what Basso or Ullrich might have done.

We thought it was all over, and that there could be no more horrible tidings. Four days after the Tour ended came the news that, on that sublime Thursday, Landis had tested positive for abnormal levels of testosterone. He immediately, and then repeatedly, protested his innocence (and still does), but the first analysis was confirmed by his B sample. He was not formally stripped of his title as yet, but fell into a legal limbo, with the Tour authorities saying that they did not recognise him as the winner.

His devout Mennonite parents said they refused to believe a word of the charges, but a pall of shame fell. His father-in-law committed suicide, although family friends said that the doping charges were unlikely to have been the main cause. Into the new year Landis continued to claim that mistakes had been made by technicians who handled his two urine samples. And the rest of us were left stunned and bewildered.

Epilogue

London, 2007

One way and another 2006 finished as whatSamuel Abt in the *International Herald Tribune* called 'a bad year, an extremely bad year' for cycling, but as that year began there had been good news for at least one man. In late January, after the usual endless process of lobbying and bidding and negotiating, Ken Livingstone, the Mayor of London gleefully announced that the following year's Tour would start in the capital, a third English visit after the 1974 and 1994 Tours. After a Prologue round Buckingham Palace and Trafalgar Square on Saturday 7 July 2007, the first stage on Sunday follows Chaucer's pilgrims to Canterbury, before the Tour crosses the Channel.

For most of his life Livingstone has been a controversial figure. As a young extreme leftist, he took control of the old Greater London Council in a putsch. Years later, after the GLC had been abolished by the Thatcher government and then an elective post of Mayor of London had been created by the Blair government, he was the first mayor to be elected, as a Labour renegade. In a wonderful display of double-dealing and backtracking Tony

Blair was desperate to stop Red Ken at all costs, but then bowed to the inevitable and welcomed, or at least accepted, him back into the Labour fold when a second term became inevitable.

Since then Livingstone had made his mark with various innovations such as a charge for cars entering central London, and he had shared Blair's exultation when London won the right to host the 2012 Olympics, although neither man is going to be around to deal with the cost – already four times the original estimate – or the other woes the games will mean for Londoners. By comparison, bike racing is cheap if not always cheerful, and David Brailsford, manager of Team GB, thinks moreover that the 'Tour de Londres' will encourage people to take up cycling: 'It's fantastic for our best British riders to perform in the biggest race in the world on home soil, particularly Bradley Wiggins and Dave Millar,' he said, and what's more, 'in light of the 2012 Olympics it's great to be able to show we're capable of hosting one of the biggest events in the world'.

After that weekend in south-east England, the 2007 Tour picks up from where the British army left sixty-seven years earlier though in the opposite direction, leaving Dunkirk on the Monday for Ghent in Belgium and then on to a clockwise *grand boucle*, south through Champagne and Chablis to Autun and Bourg-en-Bresse. Three days in the Alps go over the cols, Cornet de Roslend, d'Iseran, Galibier, from Tignes through Val d'Isère to Briançon, and then on to Marseilles and the Midi. Once again there is no team time trial, but there are two individual time trials, the first of 54 kilometres in the great cathedral city of Albi on the penultimate Saturday. Then come three days in the Pyrenees, the last finishing with a fierce climb up the Col d'Aubisque on the final Wednesday. Two stages to Cahors and then Angoulême precede the final time trial, 55 kilometres from Cognac back to Angoulême, before the Tour flies off for the Sunday procession into Paris, to complete a race of 3457 kilometres.

We may all hope for a good Tour, but whether it will lay the ghosts at the feast is another question. Cycle sport has come close, in Abt's words, to acquiring 'all the credibility of professional wrestling', and it is more with hope than expectation to suppose that 2007 will be an improvement. Until the Tour begins, or even then, it is also more than usually idle to speculate as to the likely winner, since we don't know who will be eligible to ride, and we scarcely like to think of any fresh bad news that may break.

After his ejection from the Tour Ullrich was dropped by T-Mobile and, after many months fruitlessly searching for a new team, at last announced his retirement in February. He will stay in the sport as a media consultant for the Volksbank team, a minor outfit based in Austria, and will also work with its young riders, a case of the blind leading those who should still be able to see. 'I couldn't live without cycling,' Ullrich said. 'It's my passion and my life,' which is fine for him, but what is his real legacy to this 'passion'? As to Basso, after likewise being dropped by CSC, he has been signed by Discovery Channel, to the considerable ire of the UCI. Discovery's behaviour is certainly unimpressive in view of the fact that, while protesting his innocence, Basso has refused to give a DNA sample which might have cleared him.

The UCI is angry enough in any case. A bitter rift has opened between UCI and ProTour on the one hand and the organisations which own and run the three grand tours, Giro, Tour and Vuelta. Rather like the Premier clubs breaking away from the Football League in England, the big three, ambitious or greedy according to taste, want to operate their own syndicate and skim the cream off the milk of everyday bike racing. It would be tedious to relate the details of this scission or adjudicate its rights and wrongs, if any, but anyone who loves the game can surely see that it needs a united front today more than ever before, and that this squabble is damaging as well as sordid. The UCI has been more generally angered by the snail's pace of the 'Puerto' investigation in Spain, which began so explosively but showed few signs of coming to a conclusion.

In March 2007 the season began with victories in the Paris–Nice for the Spaniard Alberto Contador of Discovery Channel, who also took the best young rider prize, and for the German Andreas Klöden of Astana in the Tirreno–Adriatico. But yet again mere cycling was overshadowed. Just as the 2006 Tour was about to begin the news of the Puerto investigation had broken; just as the 2007 Paris–Nice was about to begin an almost more extraordinary story broke from Madrid. The entire Puerto investigation had collapsed, with Antonio Serrano, the judge who had been leading it, announcing that there was no evidence that any crimes had been committed under Spanish law: 'There was no law that penalised doping practice under Spanish legislation at the time the case begun.' This produced understandable consternation, and everything about it was baffling at best and sinister at worst. Was there really no such law, and why not, in the country where, after all, Heras had been stripped of his victory in the 2005 Vuelta for failing a test? Why had the investigation been so absurdly dilatory, a question which applied to Jaime Lissavetzky, the Spanish sports minister as well as to the judge? For Vincent Lavenu, the directeur sportif of the AG2R team, the decision was scandalous. 'There are people who have cheated and now they won't be punished. If the cheaters won't be punished, it will only encourage them.' Christian Prudhomme, the recently appointed director of the Tour, said that 'these people were caught red-handed,' and that 'cycling would be the first victim' of the abortive investigation. And Pat McQuaid said that for the UCI, whose president he is, 'the investigation is still ongoing'.

Not that cycling is unique.

One sport after another has been beset by the problem of doping. In the summer of 2006, baseball fans who watched Barry Bonds on his dubious progress toward Babe Ruth's record of 714 home runs, held up placards reading '715*' (the asterisk meaning that his record would always be in a special and dubious category of its own) and 'Ruth did it on hot dogs and beer', after the unfolding story of Balco, the Californian pharmaceutical company which had been supplying steroids to Bonds among others, with results visible to the naked eye: his performance with a bat improved dramatically after he emerged at the beginning of one season looking, in one writer's words, as though someone had stuck a bicycle pump in him and blown him up.

Meantime the runner Marion Jones, who won five medals at the 2000 Olympics in Sydney, has been accused of using steroids by her ex-husband; and her former boyfriend, the sprinter Tim Montgomery, was barred from competition for two years because of his connection with Balco. Nor was the remarkable robustness of the famous Italian football club Juventus at one time (if players with English teams are to be believed) attributable merely to quantities of *cannelloni al forno*. And discerning tennis critics lament that what was once a game of skill and intelligence graced by players like Rod Laver and Ilie Nastase has become, thanks to chemical bodybuilding, just another endurance sport.

What makes it so much worse is the accumulating evidence of how dangerous the latest performance-enhancing drugs are, more than anything that killed poor Simpson. Bonds' sometime lady-friend says that his back was covered with acne and that he was often impotent, but those classic symptoms of steroid use are trivial compared with the effects of EPO. It does actually increase energy, but it also makes the blood harder to circulate, and we can look back and date its arrival as a sporting drug with horrible accuracy: between 1987 and 1992, seven young Swedish orienteering enthusiasts, and as many as twenty Belgian and Dutch cyclists, died mysteriously from nocturnal heart attacks, a death toll that continues – in that centennial year of 2003, three more cyclists died suddenly.

Not only are steroids and EPO far more pharmacologically advanced and far more dangerous; methods of disguising their use have also become more sophisticated. In an endless to and fro, offence and defence, the dopers find new performance-enhancing substances, the testers find new ways of detecting them, and the dopers find more effective ways of disguising their use. Both learned experts and moderately cynical laymen assume that it's the dope-maskers who have been ahead of the game for some years.

After all, the eighty-fifth Tour will always be remembered as the most scandalous of all, with *l'affaire* Festina followed by Virenque's and Voet's confessions; and as David Walsh drily points out, 'There were 108 drug tests at the 1998 Tour de France, all of them negative.' Walsh is an Irish sports journalist who has covered the doping question more thoroughly than most. He has never concealed his view that doping remans rife in sport and especially cycling, and he has had a long legal duel with Armstrong: *L.A. Confidentiel*, the denunciation of the champion which Walsh co-wrote, remains to this day unpublished in English.

Without cycling as within, masking is now the crucial issue. The Australian Shane Warne, the greatest leg-spinner in history, was sent home in disgrace from the 2003 cricket World Cup in South Africa after he tested positive for a diuretic which, he art-lessly said, his mother had given him to lose weight, but which is also, as it happens, an effective agent for disguising steroids. Other sportsmen make a parade of their virtue, in more or less convincing manner. One other baseball player over whom a cloud hangs is Sammy Sosa of the Chicago Cubs. When he was interviewed for *Sports Illustrated* by Rick Reilly, Sosa boasted that he had a gym in his house where 'I work out every day, seven days a week. Sometimes at two or three in the morning.' He was angry with the media. 'They think everybody is guilty. They judge me, but they don't know me.' Sosa had previously said that, if baseball began testing for steroids, he wanted to be the first in line. 'Well, why wait?', Reilly said, giving him the name and number of a nearby lab where he could have an immediate test and set an example to the young, at which Sosa exploded, 'This interview is over. Over, motherfucker!' That might have been the watchword of many sportsmen, cyclists included, to nagging media men.

If doping was the gravest problem for the Tour it was not the only one. Professional cycling faces a financial crisis, and the team system is creaking under acute strain. Sponsorship has made its way into almost every sport, and left an unattractive trail. The cricket World Cup was preceded by a grotesque row between the moneybags who thought they had acquired the rights and individual players who had sponsorship deals of their own. More ludicrous still was the sight of spectators in South Africa having Coca-Cola removed from them by ground officials, at the behest of Pepsi, the sponsors, who didn't want their investment in any way diluted by a mere televisual glimpse of a curvaceous bottle or overly red can.

With all these indignities, many sports are mired in trouble, for reasons it doesn't take a financial genius to understand. Like individual people, organisations can cherish false hopes, they can make over-optimistic investments, and they can live beyond their means. 'Annual income twenty pounds, annual expenditure nineteen six, result happiness. Annual income twenty pounds, annual expenditure twenty pounds ought and six, result misery' remains a wise principle, and one sporting body after another found that great expectations, when unfulfilled, lead to hard times. A wildly exaggerated estimate of the popularity of First Division football in England almost ruined one television company, not to say that league itself, while another ill-judged bet has left international cricket dangling by a financial thread.

And so with cycling. A dozen leading teams all have annual budgets between four and six million euros, little enough by the standards of many other sports, and all are feeling the pinch, while sponsors find that bike racing ever more resembles sexual intercourse in Lord Chesterfield's definition, the posture ridiculous, the pleasure transitory, and the expense exorbitant. There was the sombre warning of Festina, who had paid a great deal of money for their name to be bathed in a new lustre, only to find it covered in slime. Scandal indirectly affected all sponsors, more and more of whom became increasingly chary – iBanesto.com, which was meant to have been the great new hope of Spain, pulled out after 2003.

For all that, the riders still undergo what is by comparison with almost any other sport an awe-inspiring physical ordeal, and quite literally risk life and limb. We were grimly reminded of that four months before the centennial Tour. Riding in the La Clayette–Saint-Etienne stage of the Paris–Nice race for his new Cofidis team, Kivilev fell and fractured his skull. He was in a coma when he reached hospital in Saint-Etienne, where he died. He had not been wearing a helmet: although helmets are now compulsory for amateur competitive cyclists, they had not yet become so in pro cycling. Since Robic was teased by his colleagues for wearing a helmet fifty years ago, more and more cyclists have worn a variety of protective headgear. The two characteristic patterns at present are the sci-fi-looking aero-dynamic helmet with a long point at the back, like a fibreglass snood, worn in time trials, and the slotted helmet, like a large colander, worn widely on road stages. Many Tour riders still prefer to wear their traditional cotton casquettes much of the time, and Armstrong usually looked happier in his little blue cap than in anything heavier. But Kivilev's death not surprisingly led to a demand that all riders should wear helmets at all times, as they now do.

And what of the France around which the Tour runs? It looks much the same on a map as a hundred years ago, except for the increase, as everywhere, in built-up areas. The borders of the country are little changed, except for the re-annexation of Alsace-Lorraine after the Great War and a few adjustments during the next war which were then readjusted, but it is in reality a very different country, two great wars, an occupation, and three republics and hundreds of governments later. The population has grown, though not so very much, from around thirty-nine million when Desgrange began his race to some fifty-seven million today. During the Third Republic, the low birth rate in France and the country's inability to keep pace in population with its neighbours and rivals was a constant anxiety. 'Demography is destiny,' Auguste Comte said, and the belief that France's destiny was bleak in this respect led even the anticlerical Third Republic to outlaw birth control. By the twenty-first century, the population of France – as of most of Europe – was not merely stable but actually declining, with the birth rate below the necessary figure for equilibrium.

But the character of this French populace has changed radically. When the first Tour was run, France was still a predominantly rural country, yet to experience the industrial revolution and urbanisation which had transformed England and Belgium. In the course of the twentieth century, France at last became an industrial country, and urban, or, like so many other places, more accurately suburban. It is enormously more prosperous, with one of the highest per capita incomes of any country.

Not only Desgrange, with his tinge of racism, but Ali Neffati of Tunisia when he rode in the 1913 Tour or Abbes Abdel-Kader when he was the first Algerian rider in 1936, would be astonished at the way the population has changed. The Muslim population of France, mostly from the former empire in North Africa, is now five million strong, and very visible in – or more often on the outskirts of, in those *banlieues* for which 'suburbs' is a misleadingly genteel translation – most of the cities through which the Tour passes. In those bleak municipal estates, rapidly becoming slums, the impoverished and embittered residents are a cause for anxiety in an age of Islamic radicalism and terrorism. Even before the horrors of 11 September 2001, resentment against these incomers was welling up, and the fascistic National Front under Jean-Marie Le Pen won an alarming series of electoral victories, taking control of Orange (a *ville-étape* in 1974) and making large gains in Marseilles.

In the 2002 French presidential election, the world was startled when Le Pen came second to Jacques Chirac on the first round of voting and humiliatingly eliminated the socialist prime minister Lionel Jospin. This enabled Chirac to win a second term triumphantly, and doubtless strengthened his resolve a year later when he embarked on a course of opposition to the American war with Iraq, which made him the most popular leader France had known for many years. But then in 2005, in the autumn after Armstrong's last victory, there was an explosion in Paris and other cities, which were swept by riots. The rioters were youths of Arab and African origin, excluded, embittered, hopeless. Nicolas Sarkozy, the remarkably ambitious interior minister aspiring to succeed his patron-turned-rival Chirac as president, denounced the rioters as *racaille*, which the British and American papers rendered as 'scum', although 'rabble' would be nearer. He then turned nice cop to his own tough cop and said that we should try to understand these youths, and treat them more kindly; in particular policemen should not call any of these young men '*tu*', the insulting rather than intimate use of the second person singular.

One man the rioters revered was Zidane, son of Algerian immigrants who had become a French national hero, but even his career illustrated fading national *gloire*. The national football team he adorned had followed its victory in the 1998 World Cup by winning the 2000 European nations' competition, but his last World Cup in 2006 turned sour when France lost the final and 'Zizou' himself was sent off for head-butting an Italian who had goaded him. The other *bleus*, the rugby team, were more successful, following back-to-back grand slams in 1997–98 with two more in 2002 and 2004. However that might be, one thing that had been quite certain about the centennial Tour de France was that it would not be won by a rider born inside the *hexagone*, and nor will any Tour in the foreseeable future.

With or without a French champion, the Tour remains one of

France's greatest gifts to the world, and that is with all its faults; one could almost borrow Pascal's saying about mankind itself, and call the Tour the shame and the glory of creation. Those 'unconscious and hardy sowers of energy' whom Desgrange apostrophised a hundred years ago have often shown human weakness and even baseness, but they are heroes all the same, from the realms of legend and myth. When I first read Roland Barthes on 'Le Tour de France comme Epopée', I thought him a little high-flown or far-fetched; as I have watched successive Tours unfold, I realised that Barthes was right. What Armstrong did, or Hamilton in 2003 or Landis on the last Thursday in 2006, was heroic by any standards.

At the centennial Tour, Patrice Clerc and Jean-Marie Leblanc, president of the AOS parent company and director-general of the Tour, had saluted the memory of the forefathers, Géo Lefevre, Henri Desgrange, and Jacques Goddet. To their names one should add those of every great rider from Garin to Armstrong; the immortal champions Bottecchia, Magne, Bartali, Coppi, Anquetil, Merckx, Hinault and Induráin; the men who gave their lives, whether on the battlefield, like Faber, Petit-Breton and Lapize, or on the parcours itself, like Cepada, Simpson and Casartelli; and those who could not live with their victories, Pottier, Ocana and now Pantani. Not for nothing does the Tour de France end in 'the Elysian Fields': as the winners reach the Champs-Élysées, they are greeted by the shades of Achilles and Aeneas.

And yet too many are heroes in the Shakespearean sense, brave men undone by their folly and ambition. It is possible to admire the courage of the cyclists over the years while saying that there can be no more excuses, and that the Tour de France cannot survive many more years like 1998 or 2006. A new generation of cyclists must learn that, while bike racing is a wonderful sport and the Tour a great race, they are worth living for, but not worth dying for.

Some Tour Words

For all of George Orwell's violent condemnation of foreign phrases, English is a magpie language which has always borrowed from others, not least in specialized pursuits. Music borrows from Italian, philosophy from German, cookery from French. And so with sport: in a linguistic two-way street, most other languages have borrowed the name 'football' from English, just as English borrows 'yacht', 'ski' and 'deuce'. Thanks largely to the Tour, English fans who otherwise may not speak French know what *peloton* and *palmarès* mean. In listing several of the terms below again I may risk either stating the obvious or repeating myself. But then the obvious sometimes needs stating, and the late Lord Dacre of Glanton (Hugh Trevor-Roper) told us in his 'Ten Commandments of literary style' that 'Thou shalt not fear to repeat thyself, if clarity require it, nor to state facts which thou thinkest as well known to others as to thyself; for it is better to remind the learned than to leave the unlearned in perplexity.' So, let us start with a simple preposition:

à, *at* or @ – when finishing times are given for a stage or a race, the winner's time is followed by the second, third etc. 'at' so many hours, minutes and seconds behind him (as 'Hinault at 10'32" ')

abandon – a rider abandons when he leaves the race and is stripped of his dossard and the number on his bike *affaissement* – *défaillance* or collapse

arrivée – finish of a stage or the race

arrivée en altitude – a stage finishing uphill, as to a ski resort, in the deleterious recent fashion

attack – a rider attacks when he begins to ride hard, to stretch rivals, and perhaps to break away from the field

balai – broom: the *car balai* or broom car (more likely a van or small truck), formerly decorated with a witch's broomstick, which follows the field and sweeps up riders who have broken down

bidon – plastic, formerly tin, flask for water or other fluid, clipped on frame of bike, or on handlebars for consumption on the move

bonification – bonus of time deducted for first finishers and other meritorious riders, improving their GC position

bonk – English riders' word (before it acquired another colloquial meaning) for *défaillance* or collapse; utter prostration when blood sugar is exhausted

breakaway, break – see *escape*

car balai – see *balai*

caravane publicitaire – publicity parade which precedes the field daily, touting wares and throwing out trinkets

casquette – small cotton cap worn and much liked by riders, now doomed in the name of safety

classement général (CG) – see *GC*

clm – contre la montre, against the watch, i.e. time trial

clm par équipes – team time trial

commissaire – race official: umpire or referee

contre la montre – 'against the watch': see *time trial*

crever – puncture

critérium – a one-day race, usually following a circuit round a town

défaillance – 'failure or extinction'; breakdown or collapse, physical or mental, of a rider

dégringoleur – 'downhill tumbler': an expert descender

départ – start of race or stage

Derny-paced – kind of race paced behind a small motorbike

directeur sportif – manager of a bike team, generally used in English as well as French

domestique – 'servant', a lesser member of a team who serves his leader

dossard – panel on back of a rider's jersey with his race number

drop – a rider is or riders are dropped when falling behind another or others attacking

échappée – escape

échappée fleuve – 'river escape', group breakaway of several riders

échappée bidon – fruitless escape (not as in flask but in the sense *c'est du bidon*, 'that's codswallop' : the *dossier bidon* in 2002 was the Blair government's 'dodgy dossier'), ending without success; a forlorn hope

équipe – team

équipe de marque – commercially sponsored team

escape – sometimes *breakaway*, when a rider or riders breaks or break free of the field *étape* – stage: a day's section of a three-week or any multi-day race; a stage can be divided into *demi-étapes*

fugue – escape

fugue solitaire – individual escape

GC – general classification (*classification général*); the cumulative ranking after each stage which decides who holds overall lead

flamme rouge – red light marking last kilometre of a stage

Grand Prix de la Montagne – Mountains prize

green jersey – awarded daily and at end of Tour on 'points' decided in hot spots, at finishes etc., favouring sprinters

griller le ravito – 'grill the feeding station' by stealing a march on other riders as they feed; much frowned upon

grimpeur – 'climber'; not as in alpinism or social ambition, but a rider who specializes in or excels at uphill cycling

hot spot – section marked on a road stage where riders can race a measured sprint

lanterne rouge – red lamp: last rider to finish a stage, sometimes thereby eliminated – or the last rider to finish the race

maillot – jersey

maillot blanc – white jersey

maillot blanc à pois rouges – 'white jersey with red peas' or polka-dot jersey: see *red peas jersey*

maillot jaune – yellow jersey

maillot vert – green jersey

meilleur grimpeur – best climber: see next

Mountains prize, King of the Mountains – Grand Prix de la Montagne: prize awarded since 1933, based on points over climbs

musette – cotton feeding bag picked up at a *ravitaillement* station, discarded when rider has transferred food to his jersey pockets

neutralisation – period before start when riders are pedalling but not racing; a passage of the race can also be neutralized for technical reasons

palmarès – 'prize-list or honours list': generally used in English as well as French for a rider's c.v. of wins, places, stages won etc.

parcours – the circuit or itinerary of the Tour

peloton – 'group or cluster'; the bunched field on a road stage; by extension the Tour riders; the lads

pénalité – time added on for any infringement

pistard – track rider

point chaud – hot spot

points jersey – green jersey

polka-dot jersey – see *red peas jersey*

primes – special prizes awarded daily, for climbs, first to reach a village etc.

pursuit – kind of track racing with riders starting from opposite sides of circuit; for 'Australian pursuit' and 'Italian pursuit', see *The Oxford Companion to Sports and Games*

ravitaillement – 'revictualling or provisioning', taken from military usage: riders pass through a *contrôle de ravitaillement* or feeding zone to pick up their *musettes*

red peas jersey – '*maillot blanc à pois rouges*': polka-dot jersey awarded from 1975 to the Mountains winner

révélation – as it sounds: much used by journalists for a young rider who has emerged in a Tour

routier – road-racer

routier-sprinter – road racer specializing in sprinting and points prizes

soigneur – 'carer': a team's masseur cum physio (cum just occasionally dealer), who treats riders at each day's end for tired muscles and all known ailments

succeur de roues – wheel-sucker: one of sundry terms of abuse for a parasitic rider who hides in the slipstream behind others to pounce opportunistically

team time trial – see pp.214–15

tifoso – cycling fan, a word which has spread beyond Italy

time trial – a stage in which riders or teams set off at intervals and are timed over the distance

UCI – International Cycling Union, governing body always known from the initials of its French name, Union Cycliste Internationale

voiture balai – see *car balai*

white jersey – awarded to the best young rider in Tour

yellow jersey – worn on all stages by GC leader, and at finish by winner of the Tour de France

Some Tour Books

Although this book scarcely pretends to be a work of scholarship, writing it has presented some interesting problems which, *si parva componere magnis*, echo those of more serious students. As I suggested in the Preface, the sources for the history of the Tour de France are exiguous, inaccessible, and largely corrupt. Plenty of popular books on the subject are riddled with error; and when three different, officially sanctioned reference works, the *Tour Encyclopédie*, the press office's *Histoire*, and the Tour's website, can't agree on the number of entrants in the field one year, or on the spelling of a rider's name, then it's tempting to echo Sir Francis Hinsley in *The Loved One* – 'I was always the most defatigable of hacks' – and give up. Having nevertheless persevered, I wanted to suggest some idea of the books I had found most useful, with some suggestions for further reading. The place of publication is London unless otherwise specified.

Of reference books, the *Tour Encyclopédie* (6 vols, Ghent 1997–2002) is much the most detailed, giving the entrants each year listed by teams, the complete result of each stage run in each Tour, and the final times for all finishers. Another essential work – the bible of the Tour, as it impiously if understandably calls itself – is Jean Nelissen's *De bijbl van de Tour de France* (Amsterdam/Antwerp 1999). When Lord Rees-Mogg was Chairman of the Broadcasting Standards Council and custodian of national morals, he ruefully admitted that it might not be possible to prevent obscene films being transmitted from Holland to England, 'but at least they'll be in Dutch'. Also ruefully, I compared this volume with inferior books which were at least in English, but it isn't so difficult to make sense of elementary terms (*gele trui* is 'yellow jersey' and *Tourwinnaar* is 'Tour winner'). The official Tour website www.letour.com is useful for checking the palmarès of individual riders, although like so many websites it isn't impeccable. *L'histoire, les archives*, handed out each year as part of the Tour's press pack, is also occasionally peccant, but well worth having. *Tour de France 100 ans*, ed. Gerard Enjès et al (3 vols, Paris 2002) is a magnificent production drawing on the incomparable resources, photographic and reportorial, of the *Auto* and then the *Equipe*, and I much regret that it wasn't available until my own book was nearly finished. A single volume selection has been published in English, *The Official Tour de France Centennial* (2003). One other reference book which is very helpful s.v. 'Cycling', as well as in general, is the excellent *Oxford Companion to Sports and Games*.

As to general narratives, I enjoyed *Le Tour: Histoire Complète* by P. Portier (Paris 1950) covering the first half-century, for all that it's written in a ripe vein of old-fashioned journalese, with its own sins of commission and omission (another defatigable hack, Portier will give a list of names, and add 'd'autres encore que j'oublie'). The story is continued in *Ici, 60 ans de Tour de France* by Georges Briquet (Paris 1962) and more seriously in *Le Tour de France et le vélo: histoire sociale d'une épopée contemporaine* by Philippe Gaboriau (Paris 1995). *The Tour de France* by Peter Clifford (1965) is helpful if uninspired, and *The Tour de France* by R. C. Howard (1985) has some value. Then there is *The Tour de France and its Heroes: a Celebration of the Greatest Race in the World* by Graham Watson (1990), while both *Le Tour: the Rise and Rise of the Tour de France* by Geoffrey Nicholson (1991) and *Inside the Tour de France* by David Walsh (1994) are still more illuminating, as are *Le Tour de France* by Jacques Billardière (Paris 1994) and *Le Mythe des géants de la route* by Jacques Calvet (Grenoble). Several books worth having came out in the centennial year of 2003: *Golden Stages of the Tour de France*, eds. Richard Allchin and Adrian Bell; *A Century of Cycling: The Classic Races and Legendary Champions* by William Fotheringham; *Le Tour: A Century of the Tour de France* by Jeremy Whittle; *The Yellow Jersey Companion to the Tour de France*, ed. Les Woodland; and *The Escape Artist* by Matt Seaton. One other book is a classic, *Tours de France: chroniques intégrales de 'L'Equipe' 1954–1982* by Antoine Blondin (Paris 2001), a wonderful collection from the greatest of Tour writers.

From a large if not always nourishing field of biographies and – usually ghostwritten – autobiographies, a selection may here be mentioned: *Fausto Coppi: the True Story* by Jean-Paul Ollivier, who is one of the best-known of French television commentators (trans. Richard Yates nd), *Master Jacques: The Enigma of Jacques Anquetil* by Richard Yates (2001), and *Gloire sans le maillot jaune* by Raymond Poulidor (Paris 1977). *Put Me Back on My Bike: In Search of Tom Simpson* by William Fotheringham (2002) is an admirable biography, and is supplemented by the excellent essay on Simpson and the Tour, originally published in the *New Yorker*, in *Something to Declare* by Julian Barnes (2002). There is much information in *Eddy Merckx: the Greatest Cyclist of the 20th Century* by Rik Vanwalleghem (trans. Steve Hawkins 2000), and *Induráin: a Tempered Passion* by Javier Garcia Sanchez (trans. Jeremy Munday 2002) as well as in *Champion: Bicycle Racing in the Age of Induráin* by Samuel Abt (1993). *It's Not About the Bike: My Journey Back to Life* by Lance Armstrong with Sally Jenkins (2001) is in a class of its own among memoirs, and is complemented by *Lance Armstrong's Comeback from Cancer: a Scrapbook of the Tour de France Winner's Dramatic Career* by Samuel Abt (San Francisco 2000).

Of books about individual Tours, *The Great Bike Race* by Geoffrey Nicholson (1976) is a classic which illuminates much more than the one race it covers. Another good 'one year' book is *1988 Tour de France* by Phil Liggett (1988). For the most notorious of all Tours, ten years later, *In Pursuit of the Yellow Jersey: Bicycle*

Racing in the Year of the Tortured Tour by Samuel Abt and James Startt (San Francisco 1999) is a collection of dispatches. One of the most experienced of Tour reporters, Abt has also published *Tour de France: Three Weeks to Glory* (1991). His 1998 book is notably more detached than *Breaking the Chain: Drugs and Cycling: the True Story* by Willy Voet (trans. William Fotheringham 2001) or *Ma verité* by Richard Virenque (Paris), both more interesting for what they don't say as for what they do. A more specialized study about the political background of the 1948 Tour is *Un grande trionfo al Tour de France e un attentato politico: due storie intrecciate nella storia d'Italia: Bartali and Togliatti* by Paolo Facchinetti (Rome 1981). Two books by Graeme Fife, *Tour de France: the History, the Legend, the Riders* (1999) and *Inside the Peloton* (2001), enjoy the perspective of someone who has intrepidly climbed most of the cols on his own bike, and *The Unknown Tour de France: the Many Faces of the World's Biggest Bicycle Race* by Les Woodland (2000) is an agreeable pot-pourri. I was unable to consult *Wide-eyed and Legless: Inside the Tour de France* by Jeff Connor (1988), but I like the title.

My 'Repos' draw on Jules Michelet's *History of France*, in the enjoyably fruity translation by G. H. Smith (1844–6). It's striking that some much-praised histories of France in the twentieth century barely mention sport or the Tour, but two books I have particularly admired are by Eugen Weber, *Peasants into Frenchmen: The Modernisation of Rural France 1870–1914* (1997) and *The Hollow Years: France in the 1930s* (1995). I also profited by two remarkable essays, 'Le Tour de France comme épopée' by Roland Barthes in his *Mythologies* (Paris 1957, and not alas included in the English selection of the same title), and 'Le Tour de France' by Georges Vigarello in *Les France* (Paris 1992), volume III of the brilliant symposium *Les Lieux de Mémoire*, ed. Pierre Nora. John Ardagh's *Writer's France* (1989) is an engaging and handsome literary gazetteer by someone who knows and loves the country, while there are two most entertaining anthologies, *A Bicyclette*, ed. Edward Nye (Paris 2000), and *Cycling*, ed. Jeanne Mackenzie (Oxford 1981).

Several films mentioned in the course of my story are worth listing again. *Le Roi de la Pédale* (1925) starred the popular actor Biscot; *Pour le Maillot Jaune* was made during the 1939 Tour starring Albert Préjean and Meg Lemonnier; *La Cours en Tête* (1974) is centred around Eddy Merckx; there are also *For a Yellow Jersey* written and directed by Claude Lelouch (1986) and most recently the witty cartoon *Belleville Rendezvous* (2003). And finally, a delicious CD of Tour songs, *Le Vélo en Chansons 1927–1950*.

Some Tour Facts

1903

Start: Montgeron–Villeneuve-St-Georges, route de Corbeil, 1 July – *Finish*: Ville-d'Avray, restaurant du Père Auto, 19 July
2428 km – 6 stages – *longest*: Paris–Lyons (467 km); *shortest*: Toulouse–Bordeaux (268 km)
60 riders – 21 finishers – *prize money*: 20,000 Frs; *first prize*: 3,000 Frs
Winner: Garin in 94h33'14″ *2nd*: Pothier at 2h49'45″; *3rd*: Augereau at 4h29'38″
Lanterne rouge: Millocheau at 64h47'22″

1904

Start: Montgeron–Villeneuve-St-Georges, 2 July – *Finish*: Ville-d'Avray, restaurant du Père Auto, 24 July
2428 km – 6 stages – *longest*: Paris–Lyons (467 km); *shortest*: Toulouse–Bordeaux (268 km)
88 riders – 27 finishers – *prize money*: 21,000 Frs; *first prize*: 5,000 Frs
Winner: Cornet in 96h05'55″; *2nd*: Dortignacq at 2h16'14″; *3rd*: Catteau at 9h01'25″
Lanterne rouge: Deflotrière at 101h36'

1905

Start: Noisy-le-Grande, 9 July – *Finish*: Auberge de la Maison Blanche, 30 July
2994 km – 11 stages – *longest*: Paris–Nancy (340 km) and Grenoble–Toulon (342 km); *shortest*: Rennes–Caen (171 km)
60 riders – 24 finishers – *prize money*: 25,000 Frs; *first prize*: 4,000 Frs
Winner: Trousselier; *2nd*: Aucouturier; *3rd*: Dortignacq (no times – race decided on points until 1913)
Lanterne rouge: Lacroix

1906

Start: Vélodrome Buffalo de Neuilly, 4 July – *Finish*: Parc des Princes, 29 July
4637 km – 13 stages – *longest*: Marseilles–Toulouse (421 km); *shortest*: Caen–Paris (259 km)
82 riders – 14 finishers – *prize money*: 25,000 Frs; *first prize*: 5,000 Frs
Winner: Pottier; *2nd*: Passerieu; *3rd*: Trousselier
Lanterne rouge: Bronchard

1907

Start: Pont Bineau, 8 July – *Finish*: Parc des Princes, 4 August
4488 km – 14 stages – *longest*: Brest–Caen (415 km); *shortest*: Caen–Paris (254 km)
93 riders – 33 finishers – *prize money*: 25,000 Frs; *first prize*: 4,000 Frs
Winner: Petit-Breton; *2nd*: Garrigou; *3rd*: E. Georget
Lanterne rouge: Chartier

1908

Start: Pont Bineau, 13 July – *Finish*: Parc des Princes, 9 August
4488 km – 14 stages – *longest*: Brest–Caen (415 km); *shortest*:

Caen–Paris (254 km)
112 riders – 36 finishers – *prize money*: 30,000 Frs; *first prize*: 4,000 Frs
Winner: Petit-Breton; *2nd*: Faber; *3rd*: Passerieu
Lanterne rouge: Antoine

1909

Start: Pont de la Jatte, 5 July – *Finish*: Parc des Princes, 1 August
4497 km – 14 stages – *longest*: Brest–Caen (424 km); *shortest*:
Caen–Paris (254 km)
150 riders – 55 finishers – *prize money*: 25,000 Frs; *first prize*: 5,000 Frs
Winner: Faber; *2nd*: Garrigou; *3rd*: J. Alavoine
Lanterne rouge: Devilly

1910

Start: Ponte de la Jatte, 3 July – *Finish*: Parc des Princes, 31 July
4734 km – 15 stages – *longest*: Brest–Caen (424 km); *shortest*:
Nîmes–Perpignan (216 km)
110 riders – 41 finishers – *prize money*: 25,000 Frs; *first prize*: 5,000 Frs
Winner: Lapize; *2nd*: Faber; *3rd*: Garrigou
Lanterne rouge: Collet

1911

Start: Pont de la Jatte, 2 July – *Finish*: Parc des Princes, 30 July
5343 km – 15 stages – *longest*: La Rochelle–Brest (470 km); *shortest*:
Perpignan–Luchon (289 km)
84 riders – 28 finishers – *prize money*: 30,000 Frs; *first prize*: 5,000 Frs
Winner: Garrigou; *2nd*: Duboc; *3rd*: E. Georget
Lanterne rouge: Roquebert

1912

Start: Luna-Park, Porte Maillot, 30 June – *Finish*: Parc des Princes, 28 July
5289 km – 15 stages – *longest*: La Rochelle–Brest (470 km); *shortest*: Perpignan–Luchon (289 km)
131 riders – 41 finishers – *prize money*: 32,500 Frs; *first prize*: 5,000 Frs
Winner: Defraye; *2nd*: Christophe; *3rd*: Garrigou
Lanterne rouge: Lartigue

1913

Start: Boulogne-Billancourt, 29 June – *Finish*: Parc des Princes, 27 July
5287 km – 15 stages – *longest*: Brest–La Rochelle (470 km); *shortest*: Perpignan–Aix-en-Provence (321 km)
140 riders – 25 finishers – *prize money*: 39,900 Frs; *first prize*: 5,000 Frs
Winner: Thys in 197h54′00″; *2nd*: Garrigou at 8′37″; *3rd*: M. Buysse at 30′55″
Lanterne rouge: H. Alavoine at 63h12′17″

1914

Start: Saint-Cloud, 28 June – *Finish*: Parc des Princes, 26 July
5380 km – 15 stages – *longest*: Brest–La Rochelle (470 km); *shortest*: Luchon–Perpignan (323 km)
145 riders – 54 finishers – *prize money*: 45,000 Frs; *first prize*: 5,000 Frs
Winner: Thys in 200h28′48″; *2nd*: H. Pélissier at 1′40″; *3rd*: J. Alavoine at 36′53″
Lanterne rouge: Leclerc at 99h04′45″

1919

Start: Parc de Princes, 29 June – *Finish*: Parc des Princes, 27 July
5560 km – 15 stages – *longest*: Les Sables d'Olonne–Bayonne (482

km); *shortest*: Strasbourg–Metz (315 km)

69 riders – 11 finishers – *prize money*: 50,000 Frs; *first prize*: 5,000 Frs

Winner: Lambot in 231h07'15"; *2nd*: J. Alavoine at 1h32'54"; *3rd*: Christophe at 2h16'31"

Lanterne rouge: Nempon at 21h24'12"

1920

Start: Argenteuil, 27 June – *Finish*: Parc des Princes, 25 July

5503 km – 15 stages – *longest*: Les Sables–Bayonne (482 km); *shortest*: Strasbourg–Metz (300 km)

113 riders – 22 finishers – *prize money*: 80,765 Frs; *first prize*: 15,000 Frs

Winner: Thys in 228h36'13"; *2nd*: H. Heusghem at 57h21"; *3rd*: Lambot at 1h39'35"

Lanterne rouge: Raboisson at 69h05"

1921

Start: Argenteuil, 26 June – *Finish*: Parc des Princes, 24 July

5485 km – 15 stages – *longest*: Les Sables–Bayonne (482 km); *shortest*: Toulon–Nice (272 km)

123 riders – 38 finishers – *prize money*: 80,000 Frs; *first prize*: 15,000 Frs

Winner: Scieur in 221h50'26"; *2nd*: H. Heusghem at 18'36"; *3rd*: H. Barthélémy at 2h01'

Lanterne rouge: Catelan at 63h19'57"

1922

Start: Luna Park, Porte Maillot, 25 June – *Finish*: Parc des Princes, 23 July

5375 km – 15 stages – *longest*: Les Sables–Bayonne (482 km); *shortest*: Briançon–Geneva (260 km)

120 riders – 38 finishers – *prize money*: 80,000 Frs; *first prize*: 10,000 Frs

Winner: Lambot in 222h08'06"; *2nd*: J. Alavoine at 41'15"; *3rd*:

Sellier at 43′02″
Lanterne rouge: D. Masson at 65h53′41″

1923

Start: Luna Park, Porte Maillot, 24 June – *Finish*: Parc des Princes, 22 July
5386 km – 15 stages – *longest*: Les Sables–Bayonne (482 km); *shortest*: Briançon–Geneva (260 km)
139 riders – 48 finishers – *prize money*: 100,000 Frs; *first prize*: 10,000 Frs
Winner: H. Pélissier in 221h15′30″; *2nd*: Bottecchia at 30′41″; *3rd*: R. Bellenger at 1h04′43″
Lanterne rouge: D. Masson at 48h31′07″

1924

Start: Luna Park, Porte Maillot, 22 June – *Finish*: Parc des Princes, 20 July
5425 km – 15 stages – *longest*: Les Sables–Bayonne (482 km); *shortest*: Nice–Briançon (275 km)
157 riders – 60 finishers – *prize money*: 100,000 Frs; *first prize*: 10,000 Frs
Winner: Bottecchia in 226h18′21″; *2nd*: Frantz at 35′36″; *3rd*: L. Buysse at 1h32′13″
Lanterne rouge: Lafosse at 45h12′05″

1925

Start: Le Vésinet, 21 June – *Finish*: Parc des Princes, 19 July
5440 km – 18 stages – *longest*: Metz–Dunkirk (433 km); *shortest*: Bordeaux–Bayonne (189 km)
130 riders – 49 finishers – *prize money*: 99,000 Frs; *first prize*: 15,000 Frs
Winner: Bottecchia in 219h10′18″; *2nd*: L. Buysse at 54′20″; *3rd*:

Aimo at 56'17"
Lanterne rouge: Besnier at 36h10'50"

1926

Start: Evian, 20 June – *Finish*: Parc des Princes, 18 July
5745 km – 17 stages – *longest*: Metz–Dunkirk (433 km); *shortest*:
Bordeaux–Bayonne (189 km)
126 riders – 41 finishers – *prize money*: 109,000 Frs; *first prize*: 15,000 Frs
Winner: L. Buysse in 238h44'25"; *2nd*: Frantz at 1h22'25"; *3rd*: Aimo
at 1h23'51"
Lanterne rouge: Drobecq at 26h05'03"

1927

Start: Les Vésinet, 19 June – *Finish*: Parc des Princes, 17 July
5398 km – 24 stages – *longest*: Perpignan–Marseilles (360 km); *shortest*: Dieppe–Le Havre (103 km)
142 riders – 39 finishers – *prize money*: 100,000 Frs; *first prize*: 12,000 Frs
Winner: Frantz in 198h16'42"; *2nd*: Dewaele at 1h48'21"; *3rd*: J.
Vervaecke at 2h25'06"
Lanterne rouge: Pfister at 31h03'51"

1928

Start: Le Vésinet, 17 June – *Finish*: Parc des Princes, 15 July
5476 km – 22 stages – *longest*: Hendaye–Luchon (387 km); *shortest*:
Pontarlier–Belfort (120 km)
162 riders – 41 finishers – *prize money*: 100,000 Frs; *first prize*: 12,000 Frs
Winner: Frantz in 192h48'58"; *2nd*: Leducq at 50'07"; *3rd*: Dewaele
at 56'16"
Lanterne rouge: Persin at 26h56'19"

1929

Start: Le Vésinet, 30 June – *Finish*: Parc des Princes, 28 July
5286 km – 22 stages – *longest*: Perpignan–Marseilles (366 km); *shortest*: Cannes–Nice (133 km)
155 riders – 60 finishers – *prize money*: 150,000 Frs; *first prize*: 10,000 Frs
Winner: Dewaele in 186h39'15"; *2nd*: Pancera at 44'23"; *3rd*: Demuysère at 57'10"
Lanterne rouge: Léger at 31h37'54"

1930

Start: Le Vésinet, 2 July – *Finish*: Parc des Princes, 27 July
4822 km – 21 stages – *longest*: Nice–Grenoble (333 km); *shortest*: Cannes–Nice (132 km)
100 riders – 59 finishers – *prize money*: 606,000 Frs; *first prize*: 12,000 Frs
Winner: Leducq in 172h12'16"; *2nd*: Guerra at 14'13"; *3rd*: A. Magne at 16'03"
International Challenge: France – *Lanterne rouge*: Ilpide at 15h10'18"

1931

Start: Le Vésinet, 30 June – *Finish*: Parc des Princes, 26 July
5091 km – 24 stages – *longest*: Les Sables–Bordeaux (338 km); *shortest*: Gap–Grenoble (102 km)
81 riders – 35 finishers – *prize money*: 650,000 Frs; *first prize*: 25,000 Frs
Winner: A. Magne in 177h10'03"; *2nd*: Demuysère at 12'56"; *3rd*: Pesenti at 22'52"
International Challenge: Belgium – *Lanterne rouge*: Lamb at 5h29'05"

1932

Start: Les Vésinet, 6 July – *Finish*: Parc des Princes, 31 July

4479 km – 21 stages – *longest*: Nantes–Bordeaux (382 km); *shortest*: Gap–Grenoble (99 km)

80 riders – 57 finishers – *prize money*: 700,000 Frs; *first prize*: 30,000 Frs

Winner: Leducq in 154h11'49"; *2nd*: Stoepel at 24'01"; *3rd*: Camusso at 26'11"

International Challenge: Italy – *Lanterne rouge*: Risch at 5h05'14"

1933

Start: Le Vésinet, 27 June – *Finish*: Parc des Princes, 23 July

4395 km – 23 stages – *longest*: Belfort–Evian (293 km); *shortest*: Luchon–Tarbes (91 km)

80 riders – 40 finishers – *prize money*: 749,000 Frs; *first prize*: 30,000 Frs

Winner: Speicher in 147h51'37"; *2nd*: Guerra at 4'01"; *3rd*: Martano at 5'01"

International Challenge: France – *Mountains prize*: Trueba – *Lanterne rouge*: Neuhard at 3h57'44"

1934

Start: Le Vésinet, 3 July – *Finish*: Parc des Princes, 29 July

4470 km – 23 stages – *longest*: Belfort–Evian (293 km); *shortest*: La Rochelle–La Roche-sur-Yon (81 km)

60 riders – 39 finishers – *prize money*: 737,610 Frs; *first prize*: 30,000 Frs

Winner: A. Magne in 147h13'58"; *2nd*: Martano at 27'31"; *3rd*: R. Lapébie at 52'15"

International Challenge: France – *Mountains prize*: René Vietto – *Lanterne rouge*: Folco at 7h15'36"

1935

Start: Le Vésinet, 4 July– *Finish*: Parc des Princes, 28 July

4338 km – 21 stages – *longest*: Perpignan–Luchon (325 km); *shortest*: La Rochelle–La Roche-sur-Yon (81 km)

93 riders – 46 finishers – *prize money*: 1,092,050 Frs; *first prize*: not known

Winner: R. Maes in 141h32'00"; *2nd*: Morelli at 17'52"; *3rd*: F. Vervaecke in 24'06"

International Challenge: Belgium – *Mountains prize*: F. Vervaecke – *Lanterne rouge*: Kutschbach at 7h40'39"

1936

Start: Les Vésinet, 7 July – *Finish*: Parc des Princes, 2 August

4442 km – 21 stages – *longest*: Perpignan–Luchon (325 km); *shortest*: Cholet–Angers (67 km)

90 riders – 43 finishers – *prize money*: 1,000,000 Frs; *first prize*: 100,000 Frs

Winner: S. Maes in 142h47'32"; *2nd*: A. Magne in 26'55"; *3rd*: F. Vervaecke in 24'06"

International Challenge: Belgium – *Mountains prize*: Berrendero – *Lanterne rouge*: Bertocco at 4h49'07"

1937

Start: Le Vésinet, 30 June – *Finish*: Parc des Princes, 25 July

4415 km – 20 stages – *longest*: Paris–Lille (263 km); *shortest*: Royan–Saintes (37 km)

98 riders – 46 finishers – *prize money*: 800,000 Frs; *first prize*: 200,000 Frs

Winner: R. Lapébie in 138h55'31"; *2nd*: Vicini at 7'17"; *3rd*: Amberg at 26'23"

International Challenge: France – *Mountains prize*: F. Vervaecke – *Lanterne rouge*: Klensch at 6h39'25"

1938

Start: Le Vésinet, *5 July* – *Finish*: Parc des Princes, 31 July
4694 km – 21 stages – *longest*: Briançon–Aix-les-Bains (311 km); *shortest*: Rheims–Laon (48 km)
96 riders – 55 finishers – *prize money*: 900,000 Frs; *first prize*: 100,000 Frs
Winner: Bartali in 148h29′12″; *2nd*: F. Vervaecke at 18′27″; *3rd*: Cosson at 29′26″
International Challenge: Belgium – *Mountains prize*: Bartali – *Lanterne rouge*: Hellemons at 5h20′34″

1939

Start: Le Vésinet, 10 July – *Finish*: Parc des Princes, 30 July
4224 km – 18 stages – *longest*: Pau–Toulouse (311 km); *shortest*: Béziers–Montpellier (70 km)
79 riders – 49 finishers – *prize money*: 900,000 Frs; *first prize*: 100,000 Frs
Winner: S. Maes in 132h03′17″; *2nd*: Vietto at 30′38″; *3rd*: Vlamynck at 32′08″
International Challenge: Belgium – *Mountains prize*: S. Maes – *Lanterne rouge*: Le Moal at 4h26′39″

1947

Start: Paris–Pierrefitte, 25 June – *Finish*: Parc des Princes, 20 July
4642 km – 21 stages – *longest*: Brussels–Luxembourg (314 km); *shortest*: Marseilles–Montpellier (165 km)
100 riders – 53 finishers – *prize money*: 4,580,000 Frs; *first prize*: 500,000 Frs
Winner: Robic in 148h11′25″; *2nd*: Fachleitner at 3′58″; *3rd*: Brambilla at 10′07″
International Challenge: Italy – *Mountains prize*: Brambilla – *Lanterne rouge*: Tarchine at 7h28′29″

1948

Start: Paris–St Cloud, 30 June – *Finish*: Parc des Princes, 25 July
4992 km – 21 stages – *longest*: Roubaix–Paris (286 km); *shortest*:
Nantes–La Rochelle (166 km)
120 riders – 44 finishers – *prize money*: 7,000,000 Frs; *first prize*:
600,000 Frs
Winner: Bartali in 147h10'36"; *2nd*: Schotte at 26'16"; *3rd*: G.
Lapébie at 28'48"
International Challenge: Belgium – *Mountains prize*: Bartali – *Lanterne
rouge*: Seghezzi at 4h26'43"

1949

Start: Paris–Livry-Gargan, 30 June – *Finish*: Parc des Princes, 24 July
4808 km – 21 stages – *longest*: Nancy–Paris (340 km); *shortest*:
Luchon–Toulouse (134 km)
120 riders – 55 finishers – *prize money*: 12,000,000 Frs; *first prize*:
1,000,000 Frs
Winner: Coppi in 149h40'49"; *2nd*: Bartali at 10'55"; *3rd*: Marinelli
at 25'13"
International Challenge: Italy – *Mountains prize*: Coppi – *Lanterne rouge*:
De Santi at 6h07'21"

1950

Start: Paris–Nogent-sur-Marne, 13 July – *Finish*: Parc des Princes, 7
August
4773 km – 21 stages – *longest*: Dijon–Paris (314 km); *shortest*:
Menton–Nice (96 km)
116 riders – 51 finishers – *prize money*: 14,000,000 Frs; *first prize*:
1,000,000 Frs
Winner: Kubler in 145h38'56"; *2nd*: Ockers at 9'30"; *3rd*: Bobet at
22'19"

International Challenge: Belgium – *Mountains prize*: Bobet – *Lanterne rouge*: Zbinden at 4h06'47"

1951

Start: Metz, 4 July – *Finish*: Parc des Princes, 29 July
4690 km – 24 stages – *longest*: Dijon–Paris (322 km); *shortest*: Tarbes–Luchon (142 km)
123 riders – 66 finishers – *prize money*: 18,278,000 Frs; *first prize*: 1,000,000 Frs
Winner: Koblet in 142h20'14"; *2nd*: Geminiani at 22'; *3rd*: L. Lazaridès at 24'16"
International Challenge: France – *Mountains prize*: Geminiani – *Lanterne rouge*: Zaaf at 4h58'18"

1952

Start: Brest, 25 June – *Finish*: Parc des Princes, 19 July
4898 km – 23 stages – *longest*: Vichy–Paris (354 km); *shortest*: Bagnères-de-Bigorre–Pau (149 km)
122 riders – 78 finishers – *prize money*: 28,000,000 Frs; *first prize*: 1,000,000 Frs
Winner: Coppi in 151h27'20"; *2nd*: Ockers at 28'17"; *3rd*: Ruiz at 34'38"
International Challenge: Italy – *Mountains prize*: Coppi – *Lanterne rouge*: Paret at 7h15'06"

1953

Start: Strasbourg, 3 July – *Finish*: Parc des Princes, 26 July
4476 km – 22 stages – *longest*: Nantes–Bordeaux (345 km); *shortest*: Pau–Cauterets (103 km)
119 riders – 76 finishers – *prize money*: 35,000,000 Frs; *first prize*: 2,000,000 Frs

Winner: Bobet in 129h23'25"; *2nd*: Mallejac at 14'18"; *3rd*: Astrua at 15'01"

International Challenge: Pays-Bas – *Mountains prize*: Lorono – *Green Jersey*: Schaer – *Lanterne rouge*: Rouer at 4h09'10"

1954

Start: Amsterdam, 8 July – *Finish*: Parc des Princes, 1 August

4656 km – 23 stages – *longest*: Angers–Bordeaux (343 km); *shortest*: Rouen–Caen (131 km)

110 riders – 69 finishers – *prize money*: 38,445,000 Frs; *first prize*: 2,000,000 Frs

Winner: Bobet in 146h06'05"; *2nd*: Kubler at 15'49"; *3rd*: Schaer at 21'46"

International Challenge: Switzerland – *Mountains prize*: Bahamontes – *Green Jersey*: Kubler – *Lanterne rouge*: Dierkens at 6h07'29"

1955

Start: Le Havre, 7 July – *Finish*: Parc des Princes, 30 July

4495 km – 22 stages – *longest*: Briançon–Monaco (275 km); *shortest*: Le Havre–Dieppe (102 km)

130 riders – 69 finishers – *prize money*: 36,685,000 Frs; *first prize*: 2,000,000 Frs

Winner: Bobet in 130h29'26"; *2nd*: Brankart at 4'53"; *3rd*: Gaul at 11'30"

International Challenge: France – *Mountains prize*: Gaul – *Green Jersey*: Ockers –*Lanterne rouge*: Hoar at 6h06'

1956

Start: Rheims, 5 July – *Finish*: Parc des Princes, 28 July

4498 km – 22 stages – *longest*: Montluçon–Paris (331 km); *shortest*: Rouen–Caen (125 km)

120 riders – 88 finishers – *prize money*: 38,000,000 Frs; *first prize*: 2,000,000 Frs

Winner: Walkowiak in 124h01'16"; *2nd*: Bauvin at 1'25"; *3rd*: Adriaenssens at 3'44"

International Challenge: Belgium – *Mountains prize*: Gaul – *Green Jersey*: Ockers – *Lanterne rouge*: Chaussabel at 4h10'18"

1957

Start: Nantes, 27 June – *Finish*: Parc des Princes, 20 July

4669 km – 22 stages – *longest*: Libourne–Tours (317 km); *shortest*: Caen–Rouen (134 km)

120 riders – 56 finishers – *prize money*: 40,000,000 Frs; *first prize*: 2,000,000 Frs

Winner: Anquetil in 135h44'42"; *2nd*: Janssens at 14'56"; *3rd*: Christian at 17'26"

International Challenge: France – *Mountains prize*: Nencini – *Green Jersey*: Forestier – *Lanterne rouge*: Million at 4h41'11"

1958

Start: Brussels (Exposition), 26 June – *Finish*: Parc des Princes, 19 July

4319 km – 24 stages – *longest*: Dijon–Paris (320 km); *shortest*: Pau–Luchon (129 km)

120 riders – 78 finishers – *prize money*: 40,000,000 Frs; *first prize*: 2,000,000 Frs

Winner: Gaul in 116h59'05"; *2nd*: Favero at 3'10"; *3rd*: Geminiani at 3'41"

International Challenge: Belgium – *Mountains prize*: Bahamontes – *Green Jersey*: Graczyk – *Lanterne rouge*: Favre at 3h49'28"

1959

Start: Mulhouse, 25 June – *Finish*: Parc des Princes, 18 July
4358 km – 22 stages – *longest*: Dijon–Paris (331 km); *shortest*:
Bagnères-de-Bigorre–Saint-Gàudens (119 km)
120 riders – 65 finishers – *prize money*: 41,710,000 Frs; *first prize*:
2,000,000 Frs
Winner: Bahamontes in 123h46'45"; *2nd*: Anglade at 4'01"; *3rd*:
Anquetil at 5'05"
International Challenge: Belgium – *Mountains prize*: Bahamontes – *Green
Jersey*: Darrigade – *Lanterne rouge*: Bisilliat at 3h12'35"

1960

Start: Lille, 26 June – *Finish*: Parc des Princes, 17 July
4173 km – 22 stages – *longest*: Angers–Limoges (248 km); *shortest*:
Lille–Bruxelles (108 km)
128 riders – 81 finishers – *prize money*: 400,000 Frs; *first prize*: 20,000 Frs
Winner: Nencini in 112h08'42"; *2nd*: Battistini at 5'02"; *3rd*:
Adriaenssens at 10'24"
International Challenge: France – *Mountains prize*: Massignan – *Green
Jersey*: Graczyk – *Lanterne rouge*: Berrendero at 4h58'59"

1961

Start: Rouen, 25 June – *Finish*: Parc des Princes, 16 July
4397 km – 21 stages – *longest*: Perigord–Tours (309 km); *shortest*:
Rouen–Versailles (136 km)
132 riders – 72 finishers – *prize money*: 500,000 Frs; *first prize*: 20,000
Frs
Winner: Anquetil in 122h01'33"; *2nd*: Carlesi at 12'14"; *3rd*: Gaul at
12'16"
International Challenge: France – *Mountains prize*: Massignan – *Green
Jersey*: Darrigade – *Lanterne rouge*: Geneste at 4h13'56"

1962

Start: Nancy, 24 June – *Finish*: Parc des Princes, 15 July
4274 km – 22 stages – *longest*: Nevers–Paris (271 km); *shortest*:
Spa–Herenthals (147 km)
149 riders – 94 finishers – *prize money*: 583,425 Frs; *first prize*: 20,000
Frs
Winner: Anquetil in 114h31'54"; *2nd*: J. Planckaert at 4'59"; *3rd*:
Poulidor at 10'24"
Team prize: Helyett-Saint-Raphaël – *Mountains prize*: Bahamontes –
Green Jersey: R. Altig – *Lanterne rouge*: Marcaletti at 4h29'23"

1963

Start: Paris–Nogent, 23 June – *Finish*: Parc des Princes, 14 July
4138 km – 21 stages – *longest*: Rouen–Rennes (285 km); *shortest*:
Rennes–Angers (118 km)
130 riders – 76 finishers – *prize money*: 550,000 Frs; *first prize*: 20,000
Frs
Winner: Anquetil in 113h30'05"; *2nd*: Bahamontes at 3'35"; *3rd*:
Perez-Frances at 10'14"
Team prize: Gitane-Saint-Raphaël – *Mountains prize*: Bahamontes –
Green Jersey: Van Looy – *Lanterne rouge*: Derboven at 2h45'10"

1964

Start: Rennes, 22 June – *Finish*: Parc des Princes, 14 July
4504 km – 22 stages – *longest*: Clermont-Ferrand–Orléans (311 km);
shortest: Orléans–Versailles (118 km)
132 riders – 81 finishers – *prize money*: 543,200 Frs; *first prize*: 20,000 Frs
Winner: Anquetil in 127h09'44"; *2nd*: Poulidor at 55"; *3rd*:
Bahamontes at 4'44"
Team prize: Pelforth-Sauvage-Lejeune – *Mountains prize*: Bahamontes –
Green Jersey: Janssen – *Lanterne rouge*: Novak at 3h19'02"

1965

Start: Cologne, 22 June – *Finish*: Parc des Princes, 14 July

4188 km – 22 stages – *longest*: Lyons–Auxerre (299 km); *shortest*: Saint-Brieuc–Châteaulin (147 km)

130 riders – 96 finishers – *prize money*: 414,275 Frs; *first prize*: 20,000 Frs

Winner: Gimondi in 116h42'06"; *2nd*: Poulidor at 2'40"; *3rd*: Motta at 9'18"

Team prize: KAS – *Mountains prize*: Jimenez – *Green Jersey*: Janssen – *Lanterne rouge*: J. Groussard at 2h37'39"

1966

Start: Nancy, 21 June – *Finish*: Parc des Princes, 14 July

4329 km – 22 stages – *longest*: Chamonix–Saint-Etienne (265 km); *shortest*: Orléans–Rambouillet (111 km)

130 riders – 82 finishers – *prize money*: 424,700 Frs; *first prize*: 20,000 Frs

Winner: Aimar in 117h34'21"; *2nd*: Janssen at 1'07"; *3rd*: Poulidor at 2'02"

Team prize: KAS – *Mountains prize*: Jimenez – *Green Jersey*: Willy Planckaert – *Lanterne rouge*: Manucci at 2h05'26"

1967

Start: Angers, 29 June – *Finish*: Parc des Princes, 23 July

4779 km – 22 stages – *longest*: Clermont-Ferrand–Fontainebleau (359 km); *shortest*: Fontainebleau–Versailles (104 km)

130 riders – 88 finishers – *prize money*: 541,300 Frs; *first prize*: 20,000 Frs

Winner: Pingeon in 136h53'50"; *2nd*: J. Jimenez at 3'40"; *3rd*: Balmamion at 7'23"

International Challenge: France – *Mountains prize*: Jiminez – *Green Jersey*: Janssen – *Lanterne rouge*: Genet at 2h21'

1968

Start: Vittel, 27 June – *Finish*: Piste Municipale de Vincennes, 21 July
4492 km – 22 stages – *longest*: Sallanches–Besançon (243 km); *shortest*: Forest–Roubaix (112 km)
110 riders – 63 finishers – *prize money*: 574,850 Frs; *first prize*: 20,000 Frs
Winner: Janssen in 133h49'42"; *2nd*: Van Springel at 38"; *3rd*: Bracke at 3'03"
International Challenge: Spain – *Mountains prize*: Gonzales – *Green Jersey*: Bitossi – *Lanterne rouge*: Clarey at 2h43'28"

1969

Start: Roubaix, 28 June – *Finish*: Vincennes, 20 July
4117 km – 22 stages – *longest*: Clermont-Ferrand–Montargis (329 km); *shortest*: Thonon-les-Bains–Chamonix (111 km)
130 riders – 86 finishers – *prize money*: 600,000 Frs; *first prize*: 20,000 Frs
Winner: Merckx in 116h16'20"; *2nd*: Pingeon at 17'54"; *3rd*: Poulidor at 22'13"
Team prize: Faema – *Mountains prize*: Merckx – *Green Jersey*: Merckx – *Lanterne rouge*: Wilhem at 3h51'53"

1970

Start: Limoges, 27 June – *Finish*: Vincennes, 19 July
4254 km – 23 stages – *longest*: Sarrelouis–Mulhouse (270 km); *shortest*: Lisieux–Rouen (95 km)
150 riders – 100 finishers – *prize money*: 605,525 Frs; *first prize*: 20,000 Frs
Winner: Merckx in 119h31'49"; *2nd*: Zoetemelk at 12'41"; *3rd*: G. Pettersson at 15'54"
Team prize: Salvarani – *Mountains prize*: Merckx – *Green Jersey*: Godefroot – *Lanterne rouge*: Hoogerhelde at 3h52'12"

1971

Start: Mulhouse, 26 June – *Finish*: Vincennes, 18 July
3608 km – 20 stages – *longest*: Rungis–Nevers (257 km); *shortest*:
Luchon–Superbagnères (19.6 km)
130 riders – 94 finishers – *prize money*: 470,600 Frs; *first prize*: 20,000
Frs
Winner: Merckx in 96h45'14"; *2nd*: Zoetemelk at 9'51"; *3rd*: Van
Impe at 11'06"
Team prize: Bic – *Mountains prize*: Van Impe – *Green Jersey*: Merckx –
Lanterne rouge: Chappe at 3h04'54"

1972

Start: Angers, 1 July – *Finish*: Vincennes, 23 July
3846 km – 20 stages – *longest*: Vesoul–Auxerre (257 km); *shortest*:
Aix-les-Bains–Mont Revard (28 km)
132 riders – 88 finishers – *prize money*: 552,000 Frs; *first prize*: 20,000 Frs
Winner: Merckx in 108h17'18"; *2nd*: Gimondi at 10'41"; *3rd*:
Poulidor at 11'34"
Team prize: Gan-Mercier – *Mountains prize*: Van Impe – *Green Jersey*:
Merckx – *Lanterne rouge*: Bellouis at 4h03'33"

1973

Start: The Hague, 30 June – *Finish*: Vincennes, 22 July
4090 km – 20 stages – *longest*: Sainte-Foy-la-Grande–Brive (248 km);
shortest: Thuir–Pyrénées 2000 (76 km)
132 riders – 87 finishers – *prize money*: 660,000 Frs; *first prize*: 20,000
Frs
Winner: Ocaña in 122h25'34"; *2nd*: Thévenet at 15'51"; *3rd*: Fuente
at 17'15"
Team prize: Bic – *Mountains prize*: P. Torrès – *Green Jersey*: Van
Springel – *Lanterne rouge*: Hochart at 4h51'09"

1974

Start: Brest, 27 June – *Finish*: Vincennes, 21 July
4098 km – 22 stages – *longest*: Lodève–Colomiers (249 km); *shortest*: Vouvray–Orléans (112 km)
130 riders – 105 finishers – *prize money*: 802,650 Frs; *first prize*: 30,000 Frs
Winner: Merckx in 116h16'58"; *2nd*: Poulidor at 8'04"; *3rd*: Lopez-Carril at 8'09"
Team prize: KAS – *Mountains prize*: Perurena – *Green Jersey*: P. Sercu – *Lanterne rouge*: Alaimo at 3h55'46"

1975

Start: Charleroi, 26 June – *Finish*: Champs-Elysées, 20 July
4000 km – 22 stages – *longest*: Albi–Super-Lioran (260 km); *shortest*: Charleroi–Molenbeek (94 km)
140 riders – 86 finishers – *prize money*: 842,695 Frs; *first prize*: 30,000 Frs
Winner: Thévenet in 114h35'31"; *2nd*: Merckx at 2'47"; *3rd*: Van Impe at 5'01"
Team prize: GAN-Mercier – *Mountains prize*: Van Impe – *Green Jersey*: Van Linden – *White Jersey*: F. Moser – *Lanterne rouge*: Boulas at 3h31'21"

1976

Start: Saint-Jean-de-Monts–Merlin Plage, 24 June – *Finish*: Champs-Elysées, 18 July
4017 km – 22 stages – *longest*: Le Touquet–Divonne-les-Bains–l'Alpe-d'Huez (258 km); *shortest*: Lacanau–Bordeaux (71 km)
130 riders – 87 finishers – *prize money*: 1,004,500 Frs; *first prize*: apartment in Merlin-Plage to the value of 100,000 Frs
Winner: Van Impe in 116h22'23"; *2nd*: Zoetemelk at 4'14"; *3rd*: Poulidor at 12'08"
Team prize: KAS – *Mountains prize*: Bellini – *Green Jersey*: F. Maertens –

White Jersey: E. Martinez-Heredia – *Lanterne rouge*: Van der Hoek at 3h12'54"

1977

Start: Fleurance, 30 June – *Finish*: Champs-Elysées, 24 July
4096 km – 22 stages – *longest*: Vitoria–Seignosse-le-Penon (258 km); *shortest*: circuit of Fribourg-en-Brisgau (70 km)
100 riders – 53 finishers – *prize money*: 1,168,490 Frs; *first prize*: apartment in Merlin-Plage to the value of 100,000 Frs
Winner: Thévenet in 115h38'30"; *2nd*: Kuiper at 48"; *3rd*: Van Impe at 3'32"
Team prize: Ti-Raleigh – *Mountains prize*: Van Impe – *Green Jersey*: Esclassan – *White Jersey*: Thurau – *Lanterne rouge*: Loysch at 2h24'08"

1978

Start: Leiden, 29 June – *Finish*: Champs-Elysées, 23 July
3908 km – 22 stages – *longest*: Caen–Mazé-Château de Montgeoffroy (244 km); *shortest*: Valence d'Agen–Toulouse (96 km)
110 riders – 78 finishers – *prize money*: 1,227,545 Frs; *first prize*: apartment in Merlin-Plage to the value of 100,000 Frs
Winner: Hinault in 108h18'; *2nd*: Zoetemelk at 3'56"; *3rd*: Agostinho at 6'54"
Team prize: Miko-Mercier – *Mountains prize*: M. Martinez – *Green Jersey*: F. Maertens – *White Jersey*: Lubberding – *Lanterne rouge*: Tesnière at 3h52'26"

1979

Start: Fleurance, 27 June – *Finish*: Champs-Elysées, 22 July
3765 km – 24 stages – *longest*: Belfort–Evian (248 km); *shortest*: circuit of l'Alpe-d'Huez (120 km)

150 riders – 90 finishers – *prize money*: 1,338,120 Frs; *first prize*: apartment in Merlin-Plage to the value of 100,000 Frs
Winner: Hinault in 103h06'50"; *2nd*: Zoetemelk at 6'50"; *3rd*: Agostinho at 26'53"
Team prize: Renault-Gitane – *Mountains prize*: Battaglin – *Green Jersey*: Hinault – *White Jersey*: Bernaudeau – *Lanterne rouge*: Schombacher at 4h19'21"

1980

Start: Frankfurt, 26 June – *Finish*: Champs-Elysées, 21 July
3842 km – 22 stages – *longest*: Frankfurt–Metz (276 km); *shortest*: Beauvais–Rouen (92 km)
130 riders – 85 finishers – *prize money*: 1,487,930 Frs; *first prize*: apartment in Merlin-Plage to the value of 100,000 Frs
Winner: Zoetemelk in 109h19'14"; *2nd*: Kuiper at 6'55"; *3rd*: R. Martin at 7'56"
Team prize: Miko-Mercier – *Mountains prize*: R. Martin – *Green Jersey*: Pevenage – *White Jersey*: Van der Velde – *Lanterne rouge*: Schombacher at 2h10'52"

1981

Start: Nice, 25 June – *Finish*: Champs-Elysées, 19 July
3753 km – 24 stages – *longest*: Le Mans–Aulnay-sous-Bois (259 km); *shortest*: circuit of Nice (97 km)
150 riders – 121 finishers – *prize money*: 2,324,000 Frs; *first prize*: apartment in Merlin-Plage to the value of 100,000 Frs plus 30,000 Frs
Winner: Hinault in 91h34'14"; *2nd*: Van Impe at 14'34"; *3rd*: Alban at 17'04"
Team prize: Peugeot – *Mountains prize*: Van Impe – *Green Jersey*: F. Maertens – *White Jersey*: Winnen – *Lanterne rouge*: Cuelli at 4h29'54"

1982

Start: Basle, 2 July – *Finish*: Champs-Elysées, 25 July

3507 km – 21 stages – *longest*: Basle–Nancy (246 km); *shortest*: Pau–Saint-Lary-Soulan (122 km)

169 riders – 125 finishers – *prize money*: 2,207,220 Frs; *first prize*: apartment in Merlin-Plage to the value of 120,000 Frs plus 30,000 Frs

Winner: Hinault in 92h08'46"; *2nd*: Zoetemelk at 6'21"; *3rd*: Van der Velde at 8'59"

Team prize: Coop-Mercier – *Mountains prize*: B. Vallet – *Green Jersey*: Kelly – *White Jersey*: Anderson – *Lanterne rouge*: Devos at 3h04'44"

1983

Start: Fontenay-sous-Bois, 1 July – *Finish*: Champs-Elysées, 24 July

2809 km – 22 stages – *longest*: Roubaix–Le Havre (299 km); *shortest*: Issoire–Saint-Etienne (145 km)

140 riders – 88 finishers – *prize money*: 2,304,260 Frs; *first prize*: apartment in Merlin-Plage to the value of 120,000 Frs plus 40,000 Frs

Winner: Fignon in 105h07'52"; *2nd*: Arroyo at 4'04"; *3rd*: Winnen at 4'09"

Team prize: Ti-Raleigh – *Mountains prize*: Van Impe – *Green Jersey*: Kelly – *White Jersey*: Fignon – *Lanterne rouge*: Laurens at 4h02'46"

1984

Start: Montreuil-sous-Bois, 29 June – *Finish*: Champs-Elysées, 22 July

4021 km – 23 stages – *longest*: Nantes–Bordeaux (338 km); *shortest*: Valenciennnes–Béthune (83 km)

170 riders – 124 finishers – *prize money*: 2,561,450 Frs; *first prize*: apartment in Merlin-Plage to the value of 120,000 Frs plus 40,000 Frs

Winner: Fignon in 112h03'40"; *2nd*: Hinault at 10'32"; *3rd*: LeMond at 11'46"

Team prize: Renault – *Mountains prize*: Millar – *Green Jersey*: Hoste – *White Jersey*: LeMond – *Lanterne rouge*: Glaus at 4h01'17"

1985

Start: Plumelec, 28 June– *Finish*: Champs-Elysées, 21 July

4109 km – 22 stages – *longest*: Vannes–Lanester (256 km); *shortest*: Luz-Saint-Sauveur–Col d'Aubisque (52 km)

180 riders – 144 finishers – *prize money*: 3,003,050 Frs; *first prize*: apartment in Merlin-Plage to the value of 120,000 Frs plus bonus gifts

Winner: Hinault in 113h24'23"; *2nd*: LeMond at 1'42"; *3rd*: Roche at 4'29"

Team prize: La Vie Claire – *Mountains prize*: Herrera – *Green Jersey*: Kelly – *White Jersey*: Parra – *Competitive prize*: Madiot – *Super-competitive prize*: Ducrot – *Lanterne rouge*: Ronchiato at 4h13'48"

1986

Start: Boulogne-Billancourt, 4 July – *Finish*: Champs-Elysées, 27 July

4094 km – 23 stages – *longest*: Poitiers–Bordeaux (258 km); *shortest*: Nanterre–Sceaux (85 km)

210 riders – 132 finishers – *prize money*: 4,500,680 Frs; *first prize*: apartment in Merlin-Plage to the value of 120,000 Frs plus 180,000 Frs

Winner: LeMond in 110h35'19" *2nd*: Hinault at 3'10"; *3rd*: Zimmermann at 10'54"

Team prize: La Vie Claire – *Mountains prize*: B. Hinault – *Green Jersey*: Vanderaerden – *White Jersey*: Hampsten – *Competitive prize*: Caritoux – *Super competitive prize*: Hinault – *Lanterne rouge*: Salvador at 2h55'51"

1987

Start: West Berlin, 1 July – *Finish*: Champs-Elysées, 26 July
4231 km – 25 stages – *longest*: Orléans–Renazé (260 km); *shortest*:
Stuttgart–Pforzheim (79 km)
207 riders – 135 finishers – *prize money*: 6,284,700 Frs; *first prize*:
apartment in Merlin-Plage to the value of 120,000 Frs plus 180,000
Frs
Winner: Roche in 115h27'42"; *2nd*: Delgado at 40"; *3rd*: J. F. Bernard
at 2'30"
Team prize: Système U – *Mountains prize*: Herrera – *Green Jersey*: Van
Poppel – *White Jersey*: Alcala – *Competitive prize*: Clère – *Lanterne rouge*:
Hermans at 4h23'30"

1988

Start: La Baule, 4 July – *Finish*: Champs-Elysées, 24 July
3286 km – 22 stages – *longest*: Besançon–Morzine (232 km); *shortest*:
Tarbes–Pau (38 km)
198 riders – 151 finishers – *prize money*: 7,567,250 Frs; *first prize*:
value 1,300,000 Frs comprising a Peugeot 405 (value 118,000), a
studio in Merlin (value 190,000 Frs), prize from Crédit-Lyonnais
(500,000 Frs) and an art object.
Winner: Delgado in 84h27'53"; *2nd*: Rooks at 7'13"; *3rd*: Parra at
9'58"
Team prize: PDM – *Mountains prize*: Rooks – *Green Jersey*: E.
Planckaert – *White Jersey*: Breukink – *Competitive prize*: J. Simon –
Lanterne rouge: Wayenberg at 3h28'41"

1989

Start: Luxembourg, 1 July – *Finish*: Champs-Elysées, 23 July
3285 km – 21 stages – *longest*: Poitiers–Bordeaux (258.5 km); *shortest*:
Bourg-d'Oisans–Villard-de-Lans (91.5 km)

198 riders – 138 finishers – *prize money*: 8,104,215 Frs; *first prize*: 1,500,000 Frs

Winner: LeMond in 87h38'35"; *2nd*: Fignon at 8"; *3rd*: Delgado at 3'34"

Team prize: PDM – *Mountains prize*: Theunisse – *Green Jersey*: Kelly – *Best Youngest*: Philippot – *Competitive prize*: Fignon – *Lanterne rouge*: Hermans at 3h04'01"

1990

Start: Futuroscope, 30 June – *Finish*: Champs-Elysées, 22 July

3504 km – 21 stages – *longest*: Avranches–Rouen (301 km); *shortest*: Geneva–Saint-Gervais Mont-Blanc (118.5 km)

198 riders – 156 finishers – *prize money*: 10,073,450 Frs; *first prize*: 2,000,000 Frs

Winner: LeMond in 90h43'20"; *2nd*: Chiappucci at 2'16"; *3rd*: Breukink at 2'29"

Team prize: Z – *Mountains prize*: Claveyrolat – *Green Jersey*: Ludwig – *Best Youngest*: Delion – *Competitive prize*: Chozas – *Lanterne rouge*: Massi at 3h16'26"

1991

Start: Lyons, 6 July – *Finish*: Champs-Elysées, 28 July

3914 km – 22 stages – *longest*: Dijon–Rheims (286 km); *shortest*: circuit of Lyons (114.5 km)

198 riders – 158 finishers – *prize money*: 9,017,850 Frs; *first prize*: 2,000,000 Frs

Winner: Induráin in 101h43'20"; *2nd*: Bugno at 3'36"; *3rd*: Chiappucci at 5'56"

Team prize: Banesto – *Mountains prize*: Chiappucci – *Green Jersey*: Abdoujaparov – *Best Youngest*: Mejia – *Competitive prize*: Chiappucci – *Lanterne rouge*: Harmeling at 3h25'51"

1992

Start: Saint-Sébastien, 4 July – *Finish*: Champs-Elysées, 26 July
3983 km – 21 stages – *longest*: Dôle–Saint-Gervais Mont Blanc
(267.5 km); *shortest*: La Défense 92–Champs-Elysées (141 km)
198 riders – 130 finishers – *prize money*: 10,162,950 Frs; *first prize*:
2,000,000 Frs
Winner: Induráin in 100h49'30"; *2nd*: Chiappucci at 4'35"; *3rd*:
Bugno at 10'49"
Team prize: Carrera – *Mountains prize*: Chiappucci – *Green Jersey*:
Jalabert – *Best Youngest*: Bouwmans – *Fair Play trophy*: Roche –
Competitive prize: Chiappucci – *Lanterne rouge*: Quevado at 4h12'11"

1993

Start: Le Puy-du-Fou, 3 July – *Finish*: Champs-Elysées, 25 July
3714 km – 20 stages – *longest*: Isola 2000–Marseilles (285 km); *shortest*: Evreux–Amiens (158 km)
180 riders – 136 finishers – *prize money*: 11,000,000 Frs; *first prize*:
2,000,000 Frs
Winner: Induráin in 95h57'09"; *2nd*: Rominger at 4'59"; *3rd*: Jaskula
at 5'48"
Team prize: Carrera – *Mountains prize*: Rominger – *Green Jersey*:
Abdoujaparov – *Best Youngest*: A. Martin – *Fair Play trophy*: Bugno –
Competitive prize: Ghirotto – *Lanterne rouge*: Van Hooydonck at
3h30'01"

1994

Start: Lille, 2 July – *Finish*: Champs-Elysées, 24 July
3978 km – 21 stages – *longest*: Cherbourg–Rennes (270.5 km); *shortest*: Bourg-d'Oisans–Val-Thorens (149 km)
189 riders – 117 finishers – *prize money*: 11,597,450 Frs; *first prize*:
2,200,000 Frs

Winner: Induráin in 103h38'38"; *2nd*: Ugrumov at 5'39"; *3rd*: Pantani at 7'19"

Team prize: Festina-Andorra – *Mountains prize*: Virenque – *Green Jersey*: Abdoujaparov – *Best Youngest*: Pantani – *Competitive prize*: Poli – *Lanterne rouge*: Talen at 3h39'03"

1995

Start: Saint Brieuc, 1 July – *Finish*: Champs-Elysées, 23 July

2635 km – 20 stages – *longest*: Fécamp–Dunkirk (261 km); *shortest*: Sainte-Geneviève-des-Bois–Paris (155 km)

189 riders – 115 finishers – *prize money*: 12,091,250 Frs; *first prize*: 2,200,000 Frs

Winner: Induráin in 92h44'59"; *2nd*: Zulle at 4'35"; *3rd*: Riis at 6'47"

Team prize: Once – *Mountains prize*: Virenque – *Green Jersey*: Jalabert – *Best Youngest*: Pantani – *Competitive prize*: Buenahora – *Lanterne rouge*: Cornillet at 3h36'26"

1996

Start: 's-Hertogenbosch, 29 June – *Finish*: Champs-Elysées, 21 July

3907 km, distance reduced to 3765 km – 21 stages – *longest*: Argelès-Gazost–Pamplona (262 km); *shortest*: Monestier-les-Bains–Sestrières (46 km)

198 riders – 129 finishers – *prize money*: 12,002,250 Frs; *first prize*: 2,200,000 Frs

Winner: Riis in 95h57'16"; *2nd*: Ullrich at 1'41"; *3rd*: Virenque at 4'37"

Team prize: Festina – *Mountains prize*: Virenque – *Green Jersey*: Zabel – *Best Youngest*: Ullrich – *Competitive prize*: Virenque – *Lanterne rouge*: Masdupuy at 3h49'52"

1997

Start: Rouen, 5 July – *Finish*: Champs-Elysées, 27 July
3950 km – 21 stages – *longest*: Saint-Valéry-en-Caux–Vire (262 km); *shortest*: Bourg-d'Oisans–Courchevel (148 km)
198 riders – 139 finishers – *prize money*: 11,972,150 Frs; *first prize*: 2,200,000 Frs
Winner: Ullrich in 100h30'35"; *2nd*: Virenque at 9'09"; *3rd*: Pantani at 14'03"
Team prize: Telekom – *Mountains prize*: Virenque – *Green Jersey*: Zabel – *Best Youngest*: Ullrich – *Competitive prize*: Virenque – *Lanterne rouge*: Gaumont at 4h26'09"

1998

Start: Dublin, 11 July – *Finish*: Champs-Elysées, 2 August
3875 km – 21 stages – *longest*: Plouay–Cholet (248 km); *shortest*: Melun–Paris Champs Elysées (147 km)
189 riders – 96 finishers – *prize money*: 12,019,650 Frs; *first prize*: 2,200,000 Frs
Winner: Pantani in 92h49'46"; *2nd*: Ullrich at 3'32"; *3rd*: Julich at 4'08"
Team prize: Cofidis – *Mountains prize*: Rinero – *Green Jersey*: Zabel – *Best Youngest*: Ullrich – *Competitive prize*: Durand – *Lanterne rouge*: Nazon at 3h12'15"

1999

Start: Le Puy du Fou, 3 July – *Finish*: Champs-Elysées, 25 July
3870 km – 20 stages – *longest*: Saint-Flour–Albi (236.5 km); *shortest*: Arpajon–Paris (143.5 km)
180 riders – 141 finishers – *prize money*: 14,964,950 Frs; *first prize*: 2,200,000 Frs
Winner: Armstrong in 91h32'16"; *2nd*: Zülle at 7'37"; *3rd*: Escartin at 10'26"

Team prize: Banesto – *Mountains prize*: Virenque – *Green Jersey*: Zabel – *Best Youngest*: Salmon – *Competitive prize*: Durand – *Lanterne rouge*: Durand at 3h19'09"

2000

Start: Futuroscope, 1 July – *Finish*: Champs-Elysées, 23 July
3662 km – 21 stages – *longest*: Belfort–Troyes (254.5 km); *shortest*: Paris–Tour Eiffel–Champs Elysées (138 km)
177 riders – 128 finishers – *prize money*: 15,500,500 Frs; *first prize*: 2,200,000 Frs
Winner: Armstrong in 92h33'08"; *2nd*: Ullrich at 6'02"; *3rd*: Beloki at 10'26"
Team prize: Kelme-Costa Blanca – *Mountains prize*: Botero – *Green Jersey*: Zabel – *Best Youngest*: Mancebo – *Competitive prize*: Dekker – *Lanterne rouge*: Perraudeau at 3h46'37"

2001

Start: Dunkirk–Côte d'Opale, 7 July – *Finish*: Champs-Elysées, 29 July
3458 km – 20 stages – *longest*: Pau–Lavaur (232.5 km); *shortest*: Tarbes–Luz-Ardiden (144.5 km)
189 riders – 144 finishers – *prize money*: 16,470,750 Frs; *first prize*: 2,200,000 Frs
Winner: Armstrong in 86h17'28"; *2nd*: Ullrich at 6'44"; *3rd*: Beloki at 9'05"
Team prize: Kelme-Costa Blanca – *Mountains prize*: Jalabert – *Green Jersey*: Zabel – *Best Youngest*: Sevilla – *Competitive prize*: Jalabert – *Lanterne rouge*: Casper at 3h52'17"

2002

Start: Luxembourg, 6 July – *Finish*: Champs-Elysées, 28 July

3277km – 20 stages – *longest*: Vaison-la-Romaine–Les Deux Alpes (226.5km); *shortest*: Règniè-Duvette–Mâcon (50 km)

198 riders – 153 finishers – *prize money*: 2,700,000 euros; *first prize*: 350,000 euros

Winner: Armstrong in 82h05′12″; *2nd*: Beloki at 7′17″; *3rd*: Rumsas at 8′17″

Team prize: Once-Eroski – *Mountains prize*: Jalabert – *Green Jersey*: McEwen – *Best Youngest*: Bassó – *Competitive prize*: Jalabert – *Lanterne rouge*: Flores at 3h35′52″

2003

Start: Paris, Eiffel Tower, 5 July – *Finish*: Champs-Elysées, 27 July

3350 km – 20 stages – *longest*: Lyons–Morzine (226.5 km); *shortest*: Gaillac–Cap'Découverte (48.5 km)

198 riders – 147 finishers – *prize money*: 2,700,000 euros; first prize: 350,000 euros

Winner: Armstrong in 83h41′12″; 2nd: Ullrich at 1′01″; 3rd: Vinokourov at 4′14″

Team prize: Team CSC – *Mountains prize*: Virenque – Green Jersey: Cooke – *Best Youngest*: Menchov – *Competitive prize*: Vinokourov – *Lanterne Rouge*: de Clercq at 4h48′35″

2004

Start: Liège, 3 July – *Finish*: Champs-Elysées, 25 July

3391 km – 20 stages – *longest*: Limoges–St-Flour (237 km); *shortest*: Bourg d'Oisans–Alpe d'Huez (15.5 km)

189 riders – 147 finishers – *prize money*: 3,000,000 euros; *first prize*: 400,000 euros

Winner: Armstrong in 86h15′02″; *2nd*: Klöden at 6′19″; *3rd*: Basso at 6′40″

Team prize: T-Mobile – *Mountains prize*: Virenque – *Green Jersey*: McEwen – *Best Youngest*: Karpets – *Competitive prize* – Virenque – *Lanterne rouge*: Casper at 3h55'49"

2005

Start: Fromentine, 2 July – *Finish*: Champs-Elysées, 24 July

3391 km – 20 stages – *longest*: Pau-Revel (239.5 km); *shortest*: Fromentine–Noirmoutier en l'Ile (19 km)

189 riders – 155 finishers – *prize money*: 2,877,705 euros; *first prize*: 400,000 euros

Winner: Armstrong in 83h36'02"; *2nd*: Basso at 4'40"; *3rd*: Ullrich at 6'21"

Team prize: T-Mobile – *Mountains prize*: Rasmussen – *Green Jersey*: Hushovd – *Best Youngest*: Popovych – *Competitive prize*: Pereiro – *Lanterne rouge*: Flores at 4h20'24"

2006

Start: Strasbourg, 1 July – *Finish*: Champs-Elysées, 23 July

3657 km – 20 stages – *longest*: Béziers–Montélimar (230 km); *shortest*: Saint-Grégoire–Rennes (52 km)

189 riders – 139 finishers – *prize money*: 2,033,500 euros; *first prize*: 1,005,000 euros

Winner: Landis in 89h39'30"; *2nd*: Pereiro at 0'57"; *3rd*: Klöden at 1'29"

Team prize: T-Mobile – *Mountains prize*: Rasmussen – *Green Jersey*: McEwen – *Best youngest*: Cunego – *Competitive prize* – De La Fuente – *Lanterne rouge*: Vansevenant at 4h02'01"

Index

Abdel-Kader, Abbes, 337
Abdoujaparov, Djamolidine, 270
Abran, Georges, 18, 43
Abt, Samuel, 329, 331
Adriaenssens, Jan, 184, 185
advertising logos, 171
Aerts, Jean, 108, 109, 112
Agostinho, Joaquim, 221, 222
Aimar, Lucien, 197, 198
Aimo, Bartolomeo, 77, 78
Aix-les-Bains, 280
Alavoine, Henri, 33
Alavoine, Jean, 33, 42, 47, 49, 66,
    67, 69, 70, 72, 81
Alcala, Raul, 269
Alcyon, 31–2, 33, 37, 42, 43, 81,
    82, 84, 86, 89, 101
Alcyon-Dunlop, 81
Allos, Col d', 42
Alps, 34, 201, 276–7
Amaury, Phillipe, 260
Amberg, Leo, 126
Amont, Marcel, 176
Anderson, Kim, 252, 255
Anderson, Phil, 250, 251
Anglade, Henry, 182, 184, 190
Anquetil, Jacques, 112, 154, 159,
    168, 180, 182, 184, 197, 208,
    338; background and military
    service, 168–9; character, 169;
    death, 262, 283; ill-health, 190;
    personal life, 194; retirement
    from the Tour, 198; specialism of
    the time trial, 189; wins 1957
    Tour, 169–70; wins 1961 Tour,
    185–6; wins 1962 Tour, 188;
    wins 1963 Tour, 189–90, 191;
    wins 1964 Tour, 192–3

Archambaud, Maurice, 108, 109,
    110, 111, 113, 117, 120, 122,
    124, 130–1
Ardagh, John, 93
Armstrong, Lance, 53, 79, 114,
    159, 272, 282, 289, 298–301,
    309–25, 328, 333, 336–8;
    background, 298–9; and cancer,
    284, 285, 299–300; personal life,
    309, 310–11; suspicions over
    taking drugs, 302–3, 307, 324;
    and 2003 season, 309–10; wins
    1999 Tour, 20, 300–1, 303; wins
    2000 Tour, 303, 304; wins 2001
    Tour, 304–5; wins 2002 tour, 305,
    306, 307–8; wins 2003 tour, 318;
    wins 2004 tour, 321; wins 2005
    tour, 324–5
Aucouturier, Hippolyte, 18–20, 21,
    22, 23, 24, 25–6, 28
Auto, 12, 13, 16, 22, 30, 37, 38, 63,
    72, 74, 89, 104–5, 137
Automobile Club de France, 12
Automoto, 37
Automoto-Hutchinson, 81
Auxerre, 174–5

Baal, Daniel, 307
Babe Ruth, 76
Baden-Powell, Robert, 58
Bahamontes, Federico, 115, 163,
    167, 181, 190, 191, 192, 283;
    wins 1959 Tour, 182–3
Balco, 332
Ballon d'Alsace, 28, 48
Bannister, Roger, 80–1
Barnes, Julian, 285
Barone, Nicolas, 170

Barrès, Maurice, 52–3
Barrichello, Rubens, 79
Bartali, Gino, 124–5, 126, 127, 148, 149, 151, 159, 283, 338; rivalry with Coppi, 129, 137, great heroism 139, 149, 158; wins 1938 tour, 128–9; wins 1948 Tour, 145–7
Barthélémy, Honoré, 64, 67, 68, 69
Barthes, Roland, 177, 178, 179, 199, 338
Basso, Ivan, 319–20, 324–6, 328, 331
Battistini, Graziano, 185
Bauer, Steve, 264, 265, 268
Baugé, Alphonse, 68
Bauvin, Gilbert, 163, 167
Bayard, Col, 24, 25
Bedwell, David, 164
Belgium, 35; cycling in, 42–3, 116; dominance of Tour, 41, 42, 66
Bellenger, Romain, 67, 68, 77
Bellini, Giancarlo, 233
Belloni, Gaetano, 33
Beloki, Joseba, 308, 314–5
Benoit, Adelin, 77, 78, 86
Benoit-Faure, 106, 108, 110, 118
Berlin Olympics (1936), 119
Bernard, Jean-François 262
Bernard, Tristan, 10
Bernaudeau, Jean-René, 259
Berrendero, Julian, 120
Bertin, Yvon, 236
Bertogliati, Rubens, 305
Berzin, Evgeny, 273, 290
Beuffeuil, Pierre, 185, 198
Biagoni, Serafino, 153, 154
Biarritz, 93
bicycle industry: and the Tour, 37, 245
bicycles: dangers of riding looked into, 8–9; gears, 37–8, 123, 154; origins and history, 1–4, 6–7; technological and design changes, 109, 111, 123, 224, 228
Bidot, Marcel, 103, 161, 186–7, 213

Big-Mat-Aber, 319
Binda, Alfredo, 104, 147, 149
Binggeli, René, 199
Bitossi, Franco, 213
Blair, Tony, 329–30
Blériot, Louis, 33
Blijlevens, Jeroen, 296
Blondin (stuntman), 3
Blondin, Antoine, 179, 224, 242
Blum, Léon, 119, 126
Boardman, Chris, 132, 273, 288, 290, 292–3
Bobet, Jean, 35
Bobet, Louison, 115, 146, 147, 152, 153, 154, 159, 164, 165–6, 168, 177–8, 181, 283; death, 166, 252; last Tour (1959), 182; personality and behaviour, 162, 163; wins 1953 Tour, 160, 161, 162; wins 1954 Tour, 163; wins 1955 Tour, 165
Boleti, 307, 308
Bonduel, Frans, 104, 108
Bonds, Barry, 332–3
Bontempi, Guido, 264
Boogerd, Michael, 307
Boonen, Tom, 322, 326
Bordeaux, 91–2, 96
Borgarello, Vincenzo, 47
Bortolo, Fassa, 317
Botero, Santiago, 304
Bottecchia, Ottavio, 71–2, 78, 86, 159, 338; murder of, 83–4; opponent of Mussolini, 75; wins 1924 Tour, 73, 74–5; wins 1925 Tour, 77
Boulon, Albert, 32
Bouvatier, 265
Braeckeveldt, Adolf, 125
Brailsford, David, 330
Bramard, André, 129
Brambilla, 144
Brange, Eugène, 19
Brankart, Jean, 165, 171
Brasher, Chris, 206

Brest, 238
Breyer, Victor, 22, 33
Brioches–La Boulangère, 313
Britain, 5; attitude towards sport, 56–7; competing in Tour, 122, 164, 262, 273; cycling, 54–5
Brittany, 238–41
Brocco, Maurice, 28, 37, 38, 39, 41, 44, 47
Brotherton, Peter, 164
Bruyère, Joseph, 227
Bruyneel, Johan 273, 287, 310, 316, 320
Buchonnet, Roger, 154
Bugno, Gianni, 270, 272
Burgundy, 172–5
Burl, Bill, 122
Bush, George W., 309, 311
Buysse, Jules, 78
Buysse, Lucien, 47, 48, 283; wins 1926 Tour, 78, 79, 82
Buysse, Marcel, 42, 44, 45, 47, 48

Cadolle, Georges, 60
Caen, 138
Caillaux, Madame, 46
Caisse d'Epargne, 327
Calais, 96
Callens, Norbert, 151
Calmette, Gaston, 46
Calvade, M., 23
Calvet, Jean, 176
Calvez, Léon le, 109
Camusso, 106, 109, 118, 125
Canes, Georges de, 157
caravane publicitaire, 101–2
Carensio, Jean-Pierre, 266
Carlesi, Guido, 186
Carpentier, Georges, 40, 100
Carrère, Maurice, 25
Casartelli, Fabio, 117, 288, 324, 339
Caviller, Georges, 149
Cazalis, Lucien, 43
Cepeda, Francesco, 117

Chany, Pierre, 149
Charron, Frederic, 10
Chaussabel, Roger, 167
Chiappucci, Claudio, 268–9, 270, 271
Chicago Cubs, 334
Chirac, Jacques, 286, 311, 337
Christophe, Eugène, 32–3, 41, 42, 43, 44–5, 47, 64, 65, 66, 67, 69, 70, 161–2
Cipollini, Mario, 290, 301, 313, 318
Clarion Cycling Club, 55
Clemens, Mathis, 128
Clerc, Patrice, 303, 338
CLM par équipes, 214–15
Cloarec, Pierre, 130
clothing: of riders, 171
Club Vélocipédeque de Bordeaux, 9
Cobb, Richard, 66, 140–1
Cofidis, 335
Cohen, Jack, 76
Colas, Paul, 41
Colinelli, Angelo, 153
Combes, President, 16
Comte, Auguste, 336
Congress of the French Association for the Advancement of Science, 8–9
Connolly, Cyril, 91
Cooke, Baden, 318
Coppi, Fausto, 47, 145, 147–9, 152, 153, 154, 161, 183–4, 207, 338; background and cycling career, 148–9; death, 183, 283; personal life, 183; rivalry with Bartali, 129, 137, 149, 158; wins 1949 Tour, 150–1; wins 1952 Tour, 157–9
Cordon, 280–1
Cornet, Henri, 22, 23, 24, 81, 283
Cosson, Victor, 128
Courcol, Jean-Pierre, 264
Cours en tête, Le (film) 227
Coventry Gentleman's Bicycle, 6

Credit Agricole, 326
Crupelandt, Charles, 35, 41, 44
CSC, 316, 322, 325, 327
Cunego, Damiano, 327
cycling clubs, 9
Cyclistes Girondins, 9

Daily Mail, 11
Danguillaume, Jean-Pierre, 227
Darrigade, André, 162, 166, 168, 170, 180, 186
de Gaulle, Charles, 133, 139, 162, 181–2, 185, 211
Decoin, Henri, 72
défaillance, 28
Defferre, Gaston, 312
Defraye, Odile, 41, 42, 44, 47, 283; wins 1912 Tour, 42, 43
Deledda, Adolphe, 181
Delgado, Pedro, 259, 261, 262, 264, 267; wins 1988 Tour, 265
Delisle, Raymond, 229, 231, 232
Deloor, Gustaaf, 125
Dembart, Lee, 300
Demuysère, Jef, 89, 106, 107, 109
Derrigade, André, 215
Desgrange, Henri, 18, 22, 33, 39, 42, 44, 128, 336, 338; and *Auto*, 12, 37, 47–8; background, 12–13; and bicycle industry, 37; cedes some of his authority over race, 40–1; death, 136; establishment of Tour, 16–17; and First World War, 59; on Henri Pélissier, 71; homage to by Goddet, 141; starting up Tour after War, 62–3; and teams, 81, 101; and time trials, 87, 88, 89; and Tour innovations and rules, 19, 20–1, 43, 68–9, 82–3, 101; and yellow jersey idea, 64–5
Dewaele, 81, 86; wins (1929) Tour, 89
Di Paco, Raffaele, 105, 106, 107, 108, 109, 110, 117, 118

Diederich, Jean, 144, 152, 157
Dijon, 175
Diot, Maurice, 144
Discovery Channel, 321–2, 326, 331
Dojwa, Philippe, 273, 274
domestiques, 39–40, 82, 256
Domina Vacanze, 313, 320
Dortignacq, Jean-Baptiste, 22, 23, 24, 26, 28
Drais, Baron Karl von, 2
Dreyfus, Captain Alfred; Dreyfus Affair, 11–12, 16, 28, 30, 162
Driessens, Guillaume, 219; attitude towards doping by Tour, 265; doping tests, 196, 211–12, 235; and EPO, 285, 294, 303; and Festina scandal (1998), 204, 210, 294–7; taking of by riders, 74, 196–7, 207–8; and 2002 Tour, 308
Duboc, Paul, 33, 39–40, 44
Ducazeaux, Sauveur, 121, 166
Dumas, Dr Pierre, 211
Dunlop, John Boyd, 7
Durand, Jacky, 166, 273–4, 287, 293
Dussault, Marcel, 151
Dutt, Palme, 76

échappée, 32
Echávarri, José Miguel, 270–1
Echave, Federico, 261
Egg, Oscar, 47, 48
Egli, Paul, 120
Elli, Alberto, 304
Elliott, Shay, 190, 191
Embrun, 281
Engel, Emile, 60
English Mechanic, 4
EPO, 285, 294, 303
Équipe, 139, 141, 263
Errandonea, José-Maria, 198
Evans, Cadel, 323
Extabarria, David, 301
Ezquerra, Federico, 113, 120

Faber, Ernest Paul, 33
Faber, François, 26, 27, 28, 29, 35,
  36, 36–7, 38, 45, 47, 283, 338;
  killed during First World War,
  59–60; wins 1909 Tour, 31, 32, 33
Fachleitner, Edouard, 144
Faema, 215, 247
Fallon, Keith, 80
Fantinato, Bruno, 195
Faure, Alfred, 21
Ferguson, James, 2
Ferrari, Dr Michele, 320
Festina, 333, 335; scandal (1998),
  294, 295, 298
Figaro, 46
Fignon, Laurent, 252–3, 261, 267,
  268–9; wins 1983 Tour, 252;
  wins 1984 Tour, 253
Figo, Dario, 323
Filliat, Paul, 81
First World War, 49, 50–1, 52,
  59–60, 61–2, 99
Fischer, Josef, 18
Fontan, Victor, 87, 88, 90
Fontenay, Jean, 130
football, 4–5, 10
Forestier, Jean, 168, 170
Française, La, 37, 42, 81
Frantz, Nicolas, 73, 75, 79, 81,
  159, 283; wins 1927 Tour, 82,
  85, 86; wins 1928 Tour, 86, 87–8
Fréchaut, Jean, 127
Fuentes, Dr Eufemiano, 326,
  332
Fuerte, Anselmo, 261

Gachon, Pierre, 122
Gaelic Athletic Association, 93–4
Galibier, Col du, 39, 68, 110
Garin, César, 22
Garin, Maurice, 21, 81, 161, 170,
  283, 338; disqualified from 1904
  Tour, 22; wins 1903 Tour, 17,
  18, 19–20
Garrigou, Gustave, 28, 29, 32,
  35–6, 36, 37, 38, 40, 44, 47,
  283; wins 1911 Tour, 40
Gastone, Cols, 307–8
Gauban, Henry, 25
Gaul, Charly, 162, 164, 165, 167,
  186, 283; wins 1958 Tour, 181
Gauthier, Bernard, 144
Gauthier, Jean-Louis, 252
Gayant, Martial, 261
gears, bicycle, 37–8; derailleur,
  123, 154
Geldermans, Ab, 213
Geminiani, Raphael, 115, 153,
  157, 158, 161, 171, 181
Georget, Emile, 25, 26–7, 28, 36,
  38–9, 40, 41, 44, 47
Georget, Léon, 18, 19
Geslin, Anthony, 313
Giffard, Pierre, 12, 22
Gimondi, Felice, 199, 212, 223,
  229; wins 1965 Tour, 194–5
Girardengo, Constante, 47, 48
Giro, 145, 148, 149, 180, 184, 196
Globe, Le, 31, 37
Goasmat, Jean-Pierre, 128
Goddet, Jacques, 99, 136, 141,
  167, 184, 221, 250, 260, 338
Godefroot, Walter, 218, 291
Godivier, Marcel, 38, 40
Goethals, 68, 69
golf, 102
Gonzalez, Aurelio, 213
Gonzalez de Galdeano, Igor, 306
Gordini, Michele, 85
Graffigney, H. de, 7
Grand Prix du Midi Libre, 150
Granier, Honoré, 118
green jersey, 107, 160, 247
Grenoble, 279–80
Grèves, René le, 109
Groussard, Georges, 192
Guerra, Learco, 103, 109, 111
Guily, Jean Le, 158
Guimard, Cyrille, 222, 223, 231,
  232, 252

Hamburger, Bo, 293
Hamilton, Tyler, 303, 312, 316, 318, 319, 321, 338
Hampsten, Andrew, 272
Hanegraaf, Jacques, 253
Hassenforder, Roger, 160, 162
Haussmann, Georges, 97
Hawthorn, Mike, 207
Hélière, Adolphe, 35
helmets, 160
Heras, Roberto, 304, 307, 324
Hérault, Jean-Claude, 264
Herrera, Luis, 259
Heulot, Stéphane, 289–90
Heusghem, Hector, 67, 68, 69, 70
Hinault, Bernard, 17, 253, 254–5, 256, 258–60, 338; abandoning of 1980 race due to bad knee, 236; wins 1978 Tour, 234–5; wins 1979 Tour, 235–6; wins 1981 Tour, 250; wins 1982 Tour, 251; wins 1985 Tour, 256
Hincapie, George, 315, 326
Hoar, Tony, 164
Hoban, Barry, 215
Hobbs, Jack, 76
Holland, Charley, 122
Honchar, Serge, 326–7
horse racing, 79–80
Huret, Constant, 17
Hushovd, Thor, 319, 326
Hutton, Len, 143, 150
Huyse, Omer, 78
Huysmans, Joseph, 197, 221

Ibanesto.com, 317, 335
Impanis, Raymond, 143
Induráin, Miguel, 159, 255, 287, 290, 338; background and cycling career, 270–1; and lungs, 282; wins 1991 Tour, 269, 270; wins 1992 Tour, 271, 272; wins 1993 Tour, 272–3; wins 1994 Tour, 273, 274; wins 1995 Tour, 287–8, 289

International Cycling Union, 243
International Herald Tribune, 329
Ireland, 260
Italy, 128, 144
Izoard, Col d', 70

Jacquelin, Edmond, 12, 17
Jacquinot, Robert, 64, 69, 71, 72
Jalabert, Laurent, 204, 246, 272, 274, 286, 287, 288–9, 290, 304, 305
Janssen, Jan, 192, 198, 200, 216; wins 1968 Tour, 213
Janssens, Edward, 229
Jaskula, Zenon, 273
Jaurès, Jean, 49
jerseys 64–6 *see also* individual colours
Jimenez, Julio, 192, 195, 197, 199–200, 245–6
Jones, Marion, 332
Jones, Stan, 164
Jospin, Lionel, 337
Julich, Bobby, 293, 325
Juventus, 332

Karstens, Gerben, 227
Kawamuro, Kisso, 78
Keith-Falconer, Mr, 5
Keller, Hans, 231, 232
Kelly, Sean, 251, 252, 254, 256, 262, 264
Killy, Jean-Claude, 287, 303
King of the Mountains prize, 110, 113, 115, 163, 182, 197, 228, 233, 246, 273
Kint, Marcel, 124, 131
Kipling, Rudyard, 57, 58, 230–1
Kirkham, Donald, 47
Kirsipuu, Jaan, 301, 319, 323
Kivilev, Andrei, 335, 336
Kloden, Andreas, 320, 327
Knaven, Servais, 317
Knetemann, Gerrie, 235–6, 250

Koblet, Hugo, 152, 163, 283, 284; wins 1951 Tour, 153–4
Koechli, Paul, 255
Konishev, Dmitri, 269, 270
Krebs, Fred, 164
Kubler, Ferdi, 160, 163, 283; wins 1950 Tour, 152

Laffrey, Col de, 24, 25
Lafourcade, 36
Lambot, Firmin, 47, 48, 67, 283; wins 1919 Tour, 66; wins 1922 Tour, 70
Lambrecht, Roger, 151
Landis, Floyd, 325–8, 338
Laon, 53
Lapébie, Roger, 109, 113, 114, 118, 122, 147, 283; wins 1937 Tour, 125–6
Lapize, Octave, 33, 38, 41, 42, 44, 47, 48, 283; killed in First World War, 60; wins 1910 Tour, 35, 36, 37
Lastras, Pablo, 317
Laurent, Michel, 252
Lauridi, 178
Laver, Rod, 332
Lazaridès, Jean (Apo'), 139, 143
Lazaridès, Lucien, 165
Le Bert, Raymond, 163
Le Drogo, Ferdinand, 84
Le Pen, Jean-Marie, 337
Leblanc, Jean-Marie, 267, 294, 301, 305, 338
Leblanc, Luc, 270, 274
Leducq, André, 81, 85, 86, 88, 106, 113, 114, 117, 126, 127, 128, 283; death, 237; wins 1930 Tour, 103, 104; wins 1933 Tour, 108, 109
Lefèvre, Géo, 16, 338
Left News, 55
Legeay, Roger, 295
Lemaire, Georges, 111
LeMond, Greg, 253, 254, 255–6, 258, 269, 270 in shooting

accident, 266; wins 1986 Tour, 259–60; wins 1989 Tour, 266, 267–8; wins 1990 Tour, 268
Level, Léon, 122
Lévitan, Félix, 245, 250, 260
Lino, Pascal, 271, 273
Livingstone, Ken, 329–30
Londres, Albert, 74
Longo, Jeannie, 286
Lopez-Carril, 227
Lorient, 238
Louviot, Raymond, 113
Loy, Xavier, 172
Lubberding, Henk, 252, 265
Lucotti, Luigi, 64, 68
Luduq, 87
Luxembourg, 35
Lyons, 95

McEwan, Robbie, 301, 326
Macmillan, Kirkpatrick, 3
Madoit, Marc, 252–3
Maechler, Erich, 261
Maertens, Freddy, 104, 231, 232, 250
Maes, Romain, 73, 86, 120, 252, 283; wins 1935 tour, 116–17, 118, 119
Maes, Sylvère, 115, 116, 118, 125, 127, 283; wins 1936 Tour, 120–1, 122; wins 1939 Tour, 130, 131, 213
Maeterlinck, Maurice, 1, 11
Magne, Antonin, 85, 86, 87, 103, 106, 108, 109, 110, 111, 117, 120, 121, 126, 127, 193, 283, 338; death, 252; wins 1931 Tour, 105, 106–7; wins 1934 Tour, 114
Magne, Paul, 87
Magni, Fiorenzino, 151
Mahé, François 161
Maitland, Bob, 164
Maitron, Julien, 24
Majerus, 124, 126
Malaparte, Curzio, 149

Mallejac, Jean, 161, 162
Mangeas, Daniel, 233
Marcillou, Sylvain, 127
Mariano, Luis, 176
Marie, Thierry, 258, 268, 269
Marinelli, Jacques, 151, 154
Marseilles, 95
Martano, 113, 114, 117
Martin, Hector, 84
Martin, Raymond, 236–7
Martinet, Charles, 86
Martinez, Mariano, 227
Martinez-Heredia, Enrique, 233, 234
Martinez-Oliver, Juan, 265
Masselis, Jules, 43
Massi, Rodolfo, 295
Masson, Emile, 64, 67
Mauriac, François, 92, 138
Maye, Paul, 127
Mayo, Iban, 314, 315, 319
Mazeaud, Pierre, 228
McEwan, Robbie, 317, 319, 322–3
McGee, Brad, 312
Ménager, Constant, 33
Menchov, Denis, 318, 326
Mengin, Christophe, 322–3
Mente, Col de, 196
Merckx, Eddy, 47, 79, 92, 116, 194, 213, 225, 227, 234, 245, 247, 259, 275, 338; and 1975 Tour, 227–30; and Armstrong, 300; background and cycling career, 216; character, 216; and Driessens, 219–20; film made about, 227; made Chevalier of the Legion d'Honneur, 228; retirement, 234; seriously injured in crash, 217; and team system, 248; tested positive for drugs (1969), 213–14; unpopularity of, 218; wins 1969 Tour, 215, 216, 217; wins 1970 Tour, 104, 217–18; wins 1971 Tour, 218, 219, 220–2; wins 1972 Tour, 223; wins 1974 Tour, 227

Mersch, Arsène, 120, 121
Merviel, Jules, 118
Metz, 52
Michaux, Pierre, 3
Michelet, Jacques, 51, 65, 92, 95, 277
Michelin Guide, 10
Michelin, André and Edouard, 7
Michiels, Guillaume, 219
Middelkamp, Theo, 120
Milk-for-Stamina Tour of Britain, 242
Millar, David, 303–4, 307, 312, 313, 317, 330
Millar, Robert, 252, 265, 267
Millocheau, 20
Mitterand, François, 249, 286
Moineau, Julien, 118
Molteni, 218, 245
Moncassin, Frédéric, 289
Moncoutié, David, 323
Monde, Le, 139, 302
Montgomery, Tim, 332
Moore, James, 5
Moreau, Christophe, 304
Mortensen, Leif, 220
Moser, Francesco, 228, 233, 234, 253
Motta, Gianni, 196
Mottet, Charly, 261, 262, 267
Mottiat, Louis, 42, 48, 68
Mountains prize see King of the Mountains prize
Muller, Edouard, 144
Munro, Ivor, 47
Murphy, Charles M., 6
Muynck, Johan de, 216

Nancy, 52
Nantes, 96, 239
Nantes Medical Society, 8
Naquet-Radiguet, Jean-François 260
Nastase, Ilie, 332
Nazon, Jean-Pierre, 312, 319
Neffati, Ali, 43–4, 336–7

Nempon, Jules, 64
Nencini, Gastone, 170, 184, 237, 283; wins 1960 Tour, 184, 185
Netherlands, 35
Nicholson, Geoffrey, 42, 242–3, 245–6; *The Great Bike Race*, 241
Nijdam, Jelle, 265
Normandy, 133–5
Nozal, Isidro, 328

Obree, Graham, 273
Ocaña, Luis, 219, 220–2, 225, 245, 247; commits suicide, 274–5, 283, 284; wins 1973 Tour, 223, 224
Ockers, Stan, 67, 158, 159, 160, 171
O'Grady, Stuart, 293, 304, 305, 322
ONCE, 287, 289, 296, 305, 306
Opperman, Hubert, 86–7
Orléans, 132
Otxoa, Javier, 304

pacing, 82
Pagie, Emile, 18
Pantani, Marco, 288, 289, 304, 318; wins 1998 Tour, 292, 293; death of, 283
Paris, 15, 140, 140–1
Paris–Brest race (1891), 10, 13
Paris–Clermont race (1892), 10–11
Parisien Libéré, 141
Parmentier, Léon, 78
Pasquier, Dominique, 266
Passerieu, Georges, 25, 26, 28
Paul, Ernest, 37
Pauwels, Eddy, 190
Payan, Ferdinand, 21
Peeters, Ludo, 251
Peiror, Iscar, 323
Pelier, Joel, 256
Pélissier, Charles, 78, 89, 103, 104, 105, 106–7, 109, 110, 113, 118
Pélissier, Francis, 64, 69, 72, 77, 78, 84, 168

Pélissier, Henri, 43, 47, 48, 49, 64, 66, 67, 68, 69, 77, 78, 109, 168, 283; departure from 1924 Tour, 73–4; use of stimulants, 74; wins 1923 Tour, 71, 72
Pena, Victor Hugo, 313
Pensec, Ronan, 268
Pepsi, 334
Pereiro, Oscar, 327
Peron, Andrea, 288
Persin, Henri, 157
Pesenti, Antonio, 106, 108
Petacchi, Alessandro, 312
Petit tour (1946), 139
Petit-Breton, Lucien, 23, 31, 35, 43, 45, 47, 48, 60, 159, 283, 338; background, 27; crash in 1911 Tour, 37; retires from 1912 Tour, 41; wins 1907 Tour, 27–8; wins 1908 race, 28–9
Petrov, Yevgeni, 323
Petterson, Gosta, 218
Peugeot, 32, 33, 81, 163
Pevenage, Rudy, 236
Philipot, Fabrice, 266
Phonak, 325, 327, 328
Piasecki, Lech, 260
Picardy, 51–2
Pickwick Bicycling Club, 5
Pimple, Melvin, 307
Pingeon, Roger, 212, 215; wins 1967 Tour, 198–200
Planckaert, Eddy, 265
Poblet, Miguel, 165
points system, 23, 24–5, 43, 71, 107, 110, 160
Pascal, Blaise, 338
Poli, Eros, 274
politics: and sport, 93–4, 112–13, 119, 132, 146
Pollentier, Michel, 235
Porte, Col de, 26
Portier, 70, 104
Pothier, Louis, 17, 19, 20, 22
Pottier, André, 26

Pottier, René, 23, 24, 28, 275, 283; commits suicide, 26; wins 1906 Tour 25, 26

Poulidor, Raymond, 17, 186–7, 198, 199, 200, 212, 213, 215, 218, 222, 224, 227; and 1966 Tour, 195–6, 197, 198; and 1975 Tour, 231; admiration for, 195; background, 187; duels with Anquetil, 186–7, 188, 192–3, 193–4; last Tour (1976), 232; made Chevalier of the Order of Leopold, 228

Pour le Maillot Jaune (film), 99

Pradera, Mikel, 305

Privat, René, 170

prize money, 17, 29, 44, 145, 157, 184, 246–7

Pro Tour, 331

Prologue, 198, 264

Provence, 201–4

Pusey, Bernard, 164

Puy de Dôme, 157, 192, 201

Pyrenees, 33–4, 92, 201

Quick-Step, 317, 326

Quilfen, Bernard, 234

radio: and sport, 99–100

Rasmussen, Michael, 323–4

Ravat-Wonder, 86

Raymond, Christian, 218

Rebry, Gaston, 107, 109

red-peas jersey, 228, 246

regulations, 20–1, 23, 41, 48–9, 63, 73, 126, 145, 243

Reilly, Rick, 334

Rennes, 238–9

Reybroeck, Guido 212, 259

Rheims, 53

Ribeiro, Mauro, 269

Richard, Pascal, 267

Riis, Bjarne, 287, 291; wins 1996 Tour, 290

Rinero, Christophe, 293

Ritter, Ole, 230

Rivière, Roger, 168, 180, 182, 184

Roi de la Pédale, Le (film), 99

Robic, Jean, 36, 139, 151, 157–8, 159, 160–1, 163, 182, 237, 283, 320, 335; wins 1947 Tour, 144

Robinson, Brian, 164

Roche, Stephen, 254, 256, 264, 272; wins 1987 Tour, 260, 261–3

Rodriguez, Miguel, 295

Rolland, Antonin, 165

Rominger, Tony, 272–3, 274

Roncini, 143, 144

Rooks, Steven, 265

Rossi, Giovanni, 152

Rossi, Jules, 125

Rossius, Jean, 47, 48, 49, 67

Rouen, 132

Roussel, Bruno, 294, 295

Roux, Laurent, 305

Rover Safety bicycle, 6–7

Rozet, Georges, 172

rugby, 58, 105

Ruinart, Paul, 10

Ruiz, Vittorio, 154, 158, 159

Rumsas, Edita, 308

Rumsas, Raimondas, 308

Russia, 273

Ruth, Babe, 332

Ryckaert, Eric, 295

Sánchez, Javier García, 270

Santoni, Joel, 227

Santy, Alain, 227

Sappey, Col du, 26

Sarkozy, Nicolas, 337

Sastre, Carlos, 307, 327

Saunier, Baudry de, 8

Savoy, 277–81

Sawyer, William, 3

Schaer, Fritz, 160

Schepers, Alfons, 106

Schleck, Frank, 327

Schoenmaecker, Jos de, 229

Schotte, Briek, 144, 146, 147

Scieur, Léon, 67, 70, 283; wins 1921 Tour, 68, 69
scoring system 73, 152 see also points system
Second World War, 133, 136–7, 138–9, 142
Sercu, Patrick, 227
Sheil, Norman, 164
Simeoni, Filippo, 320
Simon, François 304
Simon, Pascal, 252
Simoni, Gilberto, 305
Simpson, Tom, 118, 188, 197, 198, 199, 205–7, 208, 210, 332, 339
Sobers, Sir Gary, 209
Société d'Exploitation du Tour de France, 223, 236, 264
Soerensen, 269
Sosa, Sammy, 334
Speicher, Georges, 105, 108, 109, 118, 124, 127, 283; wins 1933 Tour, 111–12
sponsorship, 186, 190, 245
sport: collaboration in, 79–81; and equipment, 102; and politics, 93–4, 112–13, 119, 132, 146; and radio, 99–100
Sport et Vie, 35
Sporting Times, 63
Sportive, La, 68
Sports Illustrated, 334
St-Malo, 240
St-Raphael, 186
Stablinski, Jean, 180
Starley, James, 6
Starley, John Kemp, 6
Stavisky, Alexander, 112
Steel, Ian, 164
Steels, Tom, 301
Steenbergen, Jan, 157
Steinès, Alphonses, 34, 38
Stevens, Julien, 215
Stieda, Alex, 258
Stoepel, Kurt, 105, 108

Svoroda, Jan, 292

T-Mobile, 326, 331
Tailleu, 78
Tapie, Bernard, 253
Tassin, Eloi, 130
Taylor, Major, 12–13, 137
Tchmil, Andrei, 273
Team GB, 330
Teisseire, Lucien, 144
Télégraphe, Col de, 39
television: and the Tour 147, 157, 256–7
Thévenet, Bernard, 218, 223, 224, 228, 231, 266, 295; wins 1975 Tour, 229, 230; wins 1977 Tour, 233, 234
Thiberghien, 47
Thurau, Dietrich, 233, 234
Thys, Philippe, 45, 67, 70, 77, 159, 283; wins 1913 Tour, 44, 45; wins 1914 Tour, 47, 48, 49; wins 1920 Tour, 67, 105
time bonuses, 73, 107, 113, 152
time trials, 82, 84, 87, 88, 89, 113, 189, 198
Timmis, Adrian, 262
Tour de France: (1903), 16–20; (1904), 20–2; (1905), 22–4, 25; (1906), 25–6; (1907), 26–8; (1908), 28–9; (1909), 31–3; (1910), 33–4, 35–7; (1911), 37–40; (1912), 41–2, 43; (1913), 43–5; (1914), 46–9; (1919), 63–6; (1920), 66, 67, 105; (1921), 67–9; (1922), 69–70; (1923), 71–2; (1924), 73–5; (1925), 77; (1926), 77–9, 82; (1927), 82, 83, 84–6; (1928), 73, 86–8; (1929), 88–9; (1930), 101, 103–4; (1931), 105, 106–7; (1932), 107–9; (1933), 105–6, 109–12; (1934), 20, 113–15; (1935), 73, 116–19; (1936), 119–22; (1937), 122–3, 124–6;

(1938), 126–8; (1939), 129–31; (1947), 142–4; (1948), 145–7; (1949), 132, 150–1; (1950), 151, 151–2; (1951), 152–4; (1952), 156–9; (1953), 160–2; (1954), 162–3; (1955), 164–5; (1956), 20, 166, 167; (1957), 169–70; (1958), 180–1; (1959), 182–3; (1960), 183, 184–5; (1961), 186; (1962), 186–8, 205; (1963), 189–92; (1964), 192–3; (1965), 194–5; (1966), 195–8;(1967), 117, 198–200; (1968), 211–13; (1969), 214–16, 217; (1970), 217–18; (1971), 218–22; (1972), 222–3; (1973), 223–4; (1974), 225–7; (1975), 227–31; (1976), 231–2, 246; (1977), 233–4; (1978), 234–5; (1979), 235–6; (1980), 236–7; (1981), 250; (1982), 251; (1983), 251–3; (1984), 253–4; (1985), 254–6; (1986), 257–60; (1987), 260–2; (1988), 264–5; (1989), 266–7; (1990), 268–9; (1991), 269–70; (1992), 271–2; (1993), 53, 272–3; (1994), 273–4; (1995), 117, 287–9; (1996), 289–90; (1997), 290–2; (1998), 292–7; (1999), 20, 300–3; (2000), 303–4; (2001), 304–5; (2002), 50, 204, 209, 212, 305–8; (2003), 25; (2004), accidents involving spectators, 306–7; area covered, 43, 91, 95–6, 142, 145, 152, 156; budget, 245; cancelling of during Second World War, 136; changing in character of, 104; collaboration amongst riders, 79, 81–2; commercialization of, 244–5; crossing of Channel, 225–6; death of cyclists during First World War, 59–60; deaths of riders during, 117, 288; distance covered, 17, 25, 37, 64, 78, 108, 243–4; establishment of, 13, 16–16; humanization of, 105; improvement in standard of riders, 105–6; life expectancy of riders, 283–4; as myth and epic, 176–9; patriotic overtones, 94; physique of riders, 281–2; songs about, 175–6; spectators, 244; speeds, 20, 24, 75, 123; team sponsors, 186; teams, 11, 81–2, 86, 88, 126, 233–4, 247–8; use of 'anonymous' bikes, 101, 102

Tour de France par Deux Enfants, 13

Trousselier, Louis, 26, 27, 28, 36, 47, 283; wins 1905 Tour, 23, 24, 25

Trueba, 108, 110, 111

Tuvache, Gaston, 25

tyres, 6–7, 29

UCI, 286, 301–2, 303, 331–2

Ugrumov, Letton, 274

Ullrich, Jan, 204, 291–2, 304, 305, 313–8, 320–2, 324–6, 328, 331; wins 1997 Tour, 291

Union Cyclistes des Postes et Télégraphes, 9

United States, 8; beginning of competitive cycling, 5–6

US Postal, 296, 300, 303, 305, 307, 310, 313, 316, 321, 328

Vallet, Bernard, 251

Valverde, Alejandro, 323

Van de Casteele, Camille, 87

Van Der Poel, Adri, 253

Van Est, Wim, 153, 165

Van Houwaert, Cyrie, 32, 36

Van Impe, Lucien, 221, 223, 228, 233, 234, 250, 251; wins 1976 Tour, 231, 232

Van Slembroeck, Gustaaf, 78

Van Springel, Herman, 213, 220

Van Vliet, Teun, 265

Vanderaerden, Eric, 252, 253, 255

Vasseur, Cédric, 290
Vélo, 12, 22
Ventoux, Mont, 154, 201, 203–4
Verdun, 53
Verhaegen, 86
Verstraeten, Aloi's, 64
Vervaecke, Félicien, 115, 118, 127, 128
Vervaecke, Julien, 85, 106
Vichy, 133
Vicini, 126, 128
Viejo, José-Luis, 231
Vietto, René, 113–14, 115, 117, 118, 120, 127, 130, 131, 139, 143, 144
Vigarello, Georges, 172, 175, 179
Village-Départ, 264
Ville, Maurice, 73
Vinokourov, Alexander, 314, 318, 324, 326
Virenque, Richard, 115, 204, 209–10, 246, 271, 274, 288, 289, 290, 291, 301–2, 307, 313, 319, 333; and Festina scandal, 294, 295, 296, 301, 304
Virot, Alex, 170
Voekler, Thomas, 319
Voet, Willy, 294, 295, 296, 333
Voigt, Jens, 304
Volksbank team, 331

Wabst, Fernand, 217
Wagner, René, 170

Wagtmans, Marinus, 219, 220, 221
Wagtmans, Wout, 163, 165
Walkowiak, Roger, 20, 283; wins 1956 Tour, 166, 167
Walsh, David, 313, 319, 333
Warne, Shane, 333
Wauters, Marc, 304
Weber, Eugen, 94, 100
Wegmann, Fabian, 323
Weltz, Johnny, 295
white jersey, 233, 266
Wiggins, Bradley, 330
Wilhelm II, Kaiser, 30
Williams, Ted, 116, 143
Winterberg, Guido, 259
Wolber, 29
Wolf, Alfons de, 254–5
Wood, Bev, 164

Yates, 273
yellow jersey, 64–5, 66, 141, 247

Zaaf, Abdel-Kader 153
Zabel, Erik, 290, 293, 301, 303, 305
Zabriskie, David, 322
Zidane, Zinedine, 338
Zilloli, Italo, 217
Zimmermann, Urs, 269
Zoetemelk, Joop, 217, 219, 220, 222, 223, 225, 235, 236; wins 1980 Tour, 237
Zülle, Alex, 271, 289, 295, 301